Dictionary of Painting and Decorating

Other Griffin books of interest

Painting and decorating   A. E. HURST
Outlines of paint technology   W. M. MORGANS
Structural surveying   H. E. DESCH
The storage and handling of petroleum liquids:
    practice and law   J. R. HUGHES
Science data   J. N. FRIEND

Dictionary of
Painting and Decorating

Covers also allied industrial finishes

> **A detailed reference work for craftsman, student, and teacher**

J. H. GOODIER

Holder of the City and Guilds Insignia
   Award in Technology
Fellow of the Royal Society of Arts
Fellow of the Incorporated Institute of
   British Decorators and Interior Designers
Liaison Officer, City of Stoke-on-Trent
   College of Building and Commerce

Justice of the Peace

GRIFFIN LONDON

CHARLES GRIFFIN & COMPANY LIMITED
42 DRURY LANE, LONDON WC2B 5RX

Copyright © J. H. GOODIER, 1974
All rights reserved

First edition   1961
Reprinted with supplement 1966
Second edition   1974

698.1
(03)

Metric Demy Octavo, viii + 308 pages
ISBN 0 85264 224 5

Set by E. W. C. Wilkins Ltd, London N12 0EH
Printed in Great Britain by Compton Printing Limited
London and Aylesbury

PREFACE

When I was first asked to undertake a work which had not previously been attempted, namely the writing of a complete dictionary of painting and decorating terms, I approached the task with great reluctance, being very doubtful of the response such a work would evoke. But the doubts were quickly dispelled, for wherever I travelled I found people eager to talk about the dictionary, which first appeared in serial form in the Painting and Decorating Journal.

For various reasons it became desirable that the dictionary should be published in book form. Even to the decorator possessing a library of technical books there was an obvious advantage in being able to find information on both industrial and decorative processes in a single volume, and there were also a great many people employed in paint distribution who had not had the advantage of a craft education and who required a convenient book of reference. Perhaps the strongest reason, however, was the need for a book in non-technical language about the constantly widening range of highly complex modern paint materials.

Since the book was first published many changes have occurred. Clearly, new materials and processes have been developed. This has sometimes led to the neglect of processes that were commonplace a few years ago, with the result that when a particular type of treatment is required for some specific purpose there is a shortage of people with the necessary knowledge to carry it out. The painter himself has now a much shorter time in which to master the complexities of his craft, as the period of apprenticeship has been considerably reduced and the basic training is now limited to the simplest elements of the work. Under these conditions the original aims of the book are still valid and indeed more important than ever before, namely to present information on as many aspects of the work as possible in the simplest clearest language without at any time sacrificing accuracy.

In trying to satisfy this need I have noticed that many of the terms in common use have changed their meaning – sometimes quite drastically – in recent years, and that other terms are so vague and imprecise as to be capable of many different interpretations so that their use may easily lead to confusion. It seemed to me that merely to supply a definition of a term was not sufficient and that to leave an enquiring person uncertain as to where to find further information would be shirking the issue; as far as possible I have tried to give a reasonable summary of all the salient points relating to each of the terms included.

This new edition has been completely revised and reset, and amongst the many changes is the introduction of SI units.

Since the previous publisher was unable to continue production of this book, my personal thanks are due to Charles Griffin and Company Ltd. for undertaking the new publication; indeed everyone connected with painting and decorating has cause to be grateful to this firm for ensuring that the continued demand for an established work is not left unsatisfied. No work of this kind could be produced without the help and cooperation of other people, and in particular I wish to thank my wife for her loyalty and her active help over a very long period; without her continual encouragement I could never have carried the work through.

Stoke-on-Trent   J.H. Goodier
October, 1973

CONVERSION FACTORS

To convert	Multiply by
Inches into millimetres	25.4
Millimetres into inches	0.039
Feet into metres	0.305
Metres into feet	3.281
Yards into metres	0.914
Metres into yards	1.094
Miles into kilometres	1.609
Kilometres into miles	0.621
Square inches into square feet	0.007
Square feet into square inches	144
Square inches into square centimetres	6.452
Square centimetres into square inches	0.155
Square feet into square metres	0.093
Square metres into square feet	10.764
Square yards into square metres	0.836
Square metres into square yards	1.196
Cubic inches into cubic feet	0.0006
Cubic feet into cubic inches	1728
Cubic inches into cubic centimetres	16.387
Cubic centimetres into cubic inches	0.061
Cubic yards into cubic metres	0.765
Cubic metres into cubic yards	1.308
Cubic feet into gallons	6.235
Gallons into cubic feet	0.160
Cubic inches into gallons	0.004
Gallons into cubic inches	277
Cubic feet into litres	28.32
Litres into cubic feet	0.035
Cubic centimetres into pints	0.0018
Pints into cubic centimetres	567.936
Pints into litres	0.568
Litres into pints	1.760
Gallons into litres	4.544
Litres into gallons	0.220
Ounces into grammes	28.349
Grammes into ounces	0.035
Pounds into kilogrammes	0.454
Kilogrammes into pounds	2.205
Tons into kilogrammes	1016
Kilogrammes into tons	0.00098
Tons into tonnes (i.e. metric tons)	1.016
Tonnes into tons	0.984
Pounds per square inch into bars	0.069
Bars into pounds per square inch	14.504

Feet and inches into metres, centimetres, millimetres, and vice versa
For centimetres move point two to right
For millimetres move point three to right

inches												
feet	**0**	**1**	**2**	**3**	**4**	**5**	**6**	**7**	**8**	**9**	**10**	**11**
						metres						
0	—	0.025	0.051	0.076	0.102	0.127	0.152	0.178	0.203	0.229	0.254	0.279
1	0.305	0.330	0.356	0.381	0.406	0.432	0.457	0.483	0.508	0.533	0.559	0.584
2	0.610	0.635	0.660	0.686	0.711	0.737	0.762	0.787	0.813	0.838	0.864	0.889
3	0.914	0.940	0.965	0.991	1.016	1.041	1.067	1.092	1.118	1.143	1.169	1.194
4	1.219	1.245	1.270	1.295	1.321	1.346	1.372	1.397	1.422	1.448	1.473	1.499
5	1.524	1.549	1.575	1.600	1.626	1.651	1.676	1.702	1.727	1.753	1.778	1.803
6	1.829	1.854	1.880	1.905	1.930	1.956	1.981	2.007	2.032	2.057	2.083	2.108
7	2.134	2.159	2.184	2.210	2.235	2.261	2.286	2.311	2.337	2.362	2.388	2.413
8	2.438	2.464	2.489	2.515	2.540	2.565	2.591	2.616	2.642	2.667	2.692	2.718
9	2.743	2.769	2.794	2.819	2.845	2.870	2.896	2.921	2.946	2.972	2.997	3.023
10	3.048	3.073	3.099	3.124	3.150	3.175	3.200	3.226	3.251	3.277	3.302	3.327
11	3.353	3.378	3.404	3.429	3.454	3.480	3.505	3.531	3.556	3.581	3.607	3.632
12	3.658	3.683	3.708	3.734	3.759	3.785	3.810	3.835	3.861	3.886	3.912	3.937
13	3.962	3.988	4.013	4.039	4.064	4.089	4.115	4.140	4.166	4.191	4.216	4.242
14	4.267	4.293	4.318	4.343	4.369	4.394	4.420	4.445	4.470	4.496	4.521	4.547
15	4.572	4.597	4.623	4.648	4.674	4.699	4.724	4.750	4.775	4.801	4.826	4.851
16	4.877	4.902	4.928	4.953	4.978	5.004	5.029	5.055	5.080	5.105	5.131	5.156
17	5.182	5.207	5.232	5.258	5.283	5.309	5.334	5.359	5.385	5.410	5.436	5.461
18	5.486	5.512	5.537	5.563	5.588	5.613	5.639	5.664	5.690	5.715	5.740	5.766
19	5.791	5.817	5.842	5.867	5.893	5.918	5.944	5.969	5.994	6.020	6.045	6.071
20	6.096	6.121	6.147	6.172	6.198	6.223	6.248	6.274	6.299	6.325	6.350	6.375
21	6.401	6.426	6.452	6.477	6.502	6.528	6.553	6.579	6.604	6.629	6.655	6.680
22	6.706	6.731	6.756	6.782	6.807	6.833	6.858	6.883	6.909	6.934	6.960	6.985
23	7.010	7.036	7.061	7.087	7.112	7.137	7.163	7.188	7.214	7.239	7.264	7.290
24	7.315	7.341	7.366	7.391	7.417	7.442	7.468	7.493	7.518	7.544	7.569	7.595

ABRASIVE   Any material which, by a process of rubbing or grinding down, tends to make a surface become smooth. Such materials are very important to the decorator in the work of preparation; correct and adequate preparation is essential if a good finish is to be produced, and is all too often neglected. The abrasives used by the painter include pumice in its various forms, cuttlefish bone, numerous abrasive papers, steel wool, etc., each kind having its own particular purpose.

ABRASIVE PAPERS   Sharp abrasive materials such as sand, flint, garnet, etc., attached to a stout paper backing for convenience of handling, and including glasspaper, sandpaper and waterproof sandpaper. The two former are used for the dry rubbing down of such surfaces as new woodwork, of leadless paint films and such materials as water filler and watermixed plastic paints. Waterproof sandpaper is used for rubbing down paint films containing lead and for flatting down gloss coats in place of the old fashioned "felting down" methods.

ABSORBENCY   The extent to which a surface will absorb or "suck in" a liquid. The absorbency of a surface has a great bearing on the quality of the painter's work, and the object of many of the priming coats and pre-paratory processes he employs is to reduce or equalize the absorbency. For example, the priming of soft woods and certain forms of plaster is directly intended to reduce their absorbency, because if undercoatings were applied to a highly absorbent surface the thinner and binding medium would be sucked into the surface making it impossible to level the paint out quickly enough and therefore leading to "ropiness". In the same way a gloss finish applied to an absorbent surface would lose some of its binding medium and the gloss would be reduced. The absorbency of plaster surfaces is often patchy and variable and one object of applying glue size before papering is to help to equalize the absorbency. The painter often speaks of highly absorbent surfaces as "hot", and he experiences difficulty in applying paint or distemper to them.

ABSTRACT DESIGN   Anything which is abstract is separated from any particular thing—an idea which exists only in the mind— and abstract design is the formation of pattern which relies for its effect on the inter-play of masses, shapes or colours rather than on naturalistic or conven-tional shapes. It may, of course, be *based* on some natural object or form, but the treatment is such that the basis is often hidden in the interrelation of the shapes.

ACCELERATED WEATHERING   Anything which speeds up or hastens the natural process of decomposition. The paint manufacturers make great use of what are termed "accelerated weathering tests" in which paints which are under review are applied to small panels and placed in a revolving drum where they are subjected alternately to ultra-violet light rays and to soaking with a spray of cold water in constant succession. This imposes a great strain on the paint and the effect of several months' normal outdoor ex-posure can be reproduced in a few days. Paints do not necessarily behave under such tests exactly as they will under normal conditions, but any paint which

1

gives a good performance under test is shown to have possibilities which are worth further consideration and experiment.

ACCELERATORS IN PLASTER The anhydrous plasters (i.e., anhydrous gypsum plaster, Keene's and Parian, and anhydrite) have accelerators such as alum or zinc sulphate added during manufacture to speed up their setting, because they do not combine with water very quickly and there is a danger of the water used to mix with them evaporating before the setting action is complete. This leads to a fault known as "dry-out", which may have serious consequences for the decorator. The actual fault may not be observed but if water is introduced during the decoration the plaster may absorb some of it and resume the setting action which was not completed, causing the skimming coat to buckle and flake off. A form of dry-out sometimes caused by impatience on the part of the painter or his customer is dealt with under the letter "D".

ACETATE A compound which may be considered as derived from treating a substance with acetic acid. Those of interest to the decorator are lead acetate (sugar of lead) used as a drying agent in oil paint, and a group of slow-evaporating solvents used in the preparation of nitro-cellulose lacquers, which include ethyl acetate, propyl acetate, butyl acetate and amyl acetate.

ACETONE A strong solvent, water-white in colour, which has several applications to the painting trade. It is the chief ingredient in many paint removers and is also used in the preparation of cellulose ester lacquer. The use of acetone to scrub the surface of "greasy" woods such as cedar and teak before they are painted is often recommended.

ACETYLENE BLOW-TORCH A piece of burning-off equipment comprising a cylinder of compressed acetylene gas, a flexible rubber hose and a lightweight metal handpiece with burner attachment and regulator for adjusting the proportions of gas and air. The flame can be adjusted from a broad fan to a narrow pencil, to cope with large areas or narrow window bars or any width between the two. The running costs are higher than those of operating a blow-lamp but there are many advantages which largely outweigh this factor—the ease of operation and lightness of weight which materially reduce fatigue, the instantaneous lighting which avoids the time wasted in waiting for a lamp to warm up, the absence of time spent in refilling, and the ability to burn off in cold windy weather without any loss of pressure.

ACHROMATIC Free from colour; transmitting light without decomposing it into its three primary colours. To the painter and decorator the term might be used to apply to white and neutral greys.

ACICULAR A term used to denote the crystalline form of a pigment, indicating that the particles are needle shaped. The term is applied in particular to zinc oxide, the acicular form of which is considered to give increased durability and better tint retention.

ACID (a) Acids are substances that neutralize, and are neutralized by, alkalis; they are compounded of hydrogen and another element or other elements; they are generally sour to the taste and corrosive, and they turn vegetable blues to reds.

(b) Some knowledge of the action of acids is important to the painter in the following connections:

(i) In industrial areas the pollution of the atmosphere is such that a deposit of soot and grime accumulates on the surfaces the painter is called upon to treat; these deposits are of an acid nature and are activated by rainwater which is also polluted and mildly acid. They bite into the paintwork and if not removed before repainting will attack the new paint film from beneath.

(ii) The interior treatment of industrial premises is often complicated by the presence of acids. The problem occurs not only in chemical laboratories and chemical producing plant, where such conditions can be expected, but in such places as rayon factories, etc., where the chemicals used in the manufacturing processes combine with the humidity of the air to produce in what appears to be normal condensation of moisture a mild acid which is destructive to a paint film.

(iii) Certain pigments are affected by acids; for example, both white lead and zinc oxide "feed" when mixed with acid media (the resins chosen to form media for these pigments being selected for their low acid content) and zinc chrome and ultramarine blue are decomposed by contact with acid.

(iv) Acid, as shown under another heading, can be used in certain decorative treatments.

ACID ETCHING A process used in a specialized branch of signwriting whereby glass is etched or partially eaten away by the action of hydrofluoric acid. Parts of the glass are protected by means of an acid resist and other parts exposed to the action of the acid, producing a contrast between the polished surface and the texture created by the etching process. Acid etching is used to produce decorative effects on windows and mirrors, and the contrast of textures is frequently enhanced by gilding and other treatments.

ACID-REFINED LINSEED OIL This is linseed oil which has been refined by mixing with strong sulphuric acid to char out the mucilage and other "break" materials. The process produces an oil of good wetting properties and very pale colour, which is especially suitable for the manufacture of paste paints. It is also esteemed in the process of lead pugging, when purified white lead is removed from the filter press containing about 25% of water. When this is mixed with acid-refined oil the water is displaced and the oil preferentially wets the white lead, thus avoiding the expense of drying the press cake lead before mixing it with oil, besides being more hygienic.

ACID RESIST A term used for the protective coating applied to those parts of the glass which are not intended to be etched in the acid etching process just described. The resist used is generally Brunswick black.

ACID RESISTING PAINTS Paints designed for use in buildings and on surfaces where the acid concentration would render oil paints unsuitable and consisting of selected pigments ground in synthetic resin media. Under certain conditions use is made of chlorinated rubber paints which have high resistance to acids, high resistance to moisture penetration and great flexibility, and of certain bituminous preparations some of which are applied in a thick plastic coating by a special process carried out by specialists employed by the manufacturers of the product. Advice should be sought from reputable manufacturers as to the most suitable form of acid resisting paint for any particular conditions which give rise to difficulty.

ACID VALUE A measure of the free acidity of a substance, such as, for instance, an oil or varnish medium expressed as the number of milligrammes of potassium hydroxide required to neutralize the acidity of one gramme of the substance.

ACOUSTIC MATERIALS It frequently happens that public halls, both large and small, are ideally suited for such purposes as presenting plays, holding meetings and the performance of musical concerts except in one most important particular—that due to some defect in the design or construction of the hall the sounds are so blurred that it is a penance for anyone to have to sit and listen and an impossibility for any speaker however gifted to make himself heard clearly. It has been found that very often the drawback to some extent can be overcome if the smooth hard wall and ceiling surfaces are covered with panels of sound deadening materials which are known somewhat loosely as "acoustic materials".

As their effectiveness can be marred by the wrong painting treatment the decorator should know how to deal with them, and how to advise his customers if he is asked to treat them wrongly. Some of these acoustic materials consist of thick wallboards, vegetable fibre boards, etc., of a highly absorbent nature, or sprayed asbestos, asbestos blanket, etc.; they rely for their effect on being absorbent, and if the surface is sealed with oil paint or a continuous water paint film of normal consistency they are spoiled for sound deadening purposes. Decoration should be in the nature of very thin water paint or distemper applied by spray, the spray gun being held at some distance from the work so as to deposit the material in the form of spray dust. Another form of acoustic material is faced with wallboard or thin plaster and perforated with a large number of regularly spaced holes; this may be painted with either oil paint of water paint provided the perforations are not filled; a thin coat applied by spray may generally be considered the most suitable.

Very often these acoustic materials are put up without any imagination by builders who have no feeling at all for the appearance of a room. Instead of being used with restraint and fitted to conform to the contours of the room they are erected so crudely as to throw the whole room out of balance. In this form they present a depressing task for the decorator, who very often, it is to be feared, takes the easiest way out and uses white water paint with no thought for the colour scheme as a whole. It seems worth stressing that from a decorator's point of view it is all wrong to cure the acoustic drawbacks of a hall at the expense of condemning it to sheer

4

ugliness, and the more imaginative use of colour is urged when such structural makeshifts are to be painted.

A third form of acoustic material, which is applied by the decorator himself, and is therefore not subject to this stricture, is supplied by The Wall Paper Manufacturers Ltd. in separate panels. It acts by breaking up the smooth surface into fairly heavy relief, and can be painted or water painted in any way that is desired.

ACRYLIC RESINS   The name given to a large group of resins prepared from numerous derivatives of acrylic or methacrylic acid. These resins have been used for quite a long time in the manufacture of well-known plastics such as perspex and in the leather and textile industries, and are becoming increasingly popular in the formulation of paints and particularly in emulsion coatings. The properties given to a paint coating by acrylic resins include rapid drying, excellent durability, good colour retention and freedom from yellowing, good adhesion and ease of application. Emulsion coatings based upon them are recoatable in less than half-an-hour and are almost odourless, an important feature in hospital or restaurant work. They are readily applied by brush, spray or roller.

In recent years acrylic resin has been increasingly used in the formulation of water-thinned paints for general use. The fact that such paints allow moisture vapour to escape from a surface but resist the entry of water indicates that they may have useful properties in the protection of timber, with the added advantage that acrylic-based primers are able to seal knots without the prior application of shellac knotting. Their main drawback lies in the difficulty which is experienced in eliminating brushmarks.

Acrylic resin is also used to produce stoving paints, with particular reference to the motor car industry. Such paints are more durable and possess a greater degree of flexibility and colour retention than cellulose paints.

ACTINIC LIGHT   The actinic rays or ultra-voilet rays, those components of the sun's light which exert a very destructive effect upon a paint film. To some extent they are filtered by the smoke pall which blankets industrial areas so that their influence is greater in coastal districts.

ACTIVATOR   A substance which, when added to some mixture or material, sets in motion a chemical or physical process which could not hitherto take place. The term is used specifically in painting and decorating with reference to certain modern products such as some types of epoxy resin paints, wood finishes, etc., which are supplied as two-pack materials and which cannot develop their distinctive properties until the two packs are mixed together, i.e., until the activator is added.

ADHESION   This, to a painter, means the extent to which a material will stick to a given surface. It is a subject of great concern to him, since many failures of decoration such as blistering of paintwork, flaking of water paint and springing and peeling of wallpaper are failures of adhesion that he might have been able to foresee and prevent.

ADJUSTABLE BASE PLATE   A base plate, for use with tubular scaffolding, which incorporates a screw jack which enables it to be adjusted to suit varying levels.

ADULTERANT   Something which is added to a substance or a mixture in order to cheapen it or degrade it.

Almost anything could be adulterated if the person handling it felt so inclined; linseed oil might be adulterated with fish oil, knotting with rosin, a bristle brush by the inclusion of cheaper hair, and so on. But, of course, no reputable manufacturer would contemplate such practices; we get what we pay for and if we trade with reputable firms and pay a fair price for their products we can rely on receiving fair value. This point is mentioned because a tendency has been noticed recently to use the term adulterant without due regard to its meaning. There are many substances used in paint which, when employed in their correct proportions, perform a useful function, but which used in excess would be classed as adulterants. For example, on the manufacturing side, the addition of a small quantity of barytes to other pigments can improve their efficiency, whereas added in a wholesale or excessive manner it would be adulteration. In the same way, in trade practice the painter thins down a paint to a consistency which enables him to spread it evenly on the surface; used properly the thinning of paint is not only legitimate but necessary to prevent the paint being applied too thickly and to assist its penetration. If an excess of thinners were added with the object of cheapening the paint by spreading it far beyond its proper coverage this would constitute adulteration, but no painter with regard for his reputation would be guilty of this. But it is by no means unknown for people in charge of painting contracts to condemn any form of paint thinning out of hand as adulteration. Painters have been seen struggling to use priming paint in far too round a condition because they were instructed that to thin it down at all was adulteration, and honest master painters have been accused of dishonesty when trying to convince some clerk of works of the necessity of thinning.

ADVANCING COLOURS   Colours generally on the yellow to red range, which when used on a particular surface tend to make that surface appear more prominent so that it "advances" or asserts itself.

AEROSOL SPRAYING   A method of spray application for the refinishing of small articles and for touch-up work on motor vehicles, intended chiefly for the amateur and house operator. The aerosol pack, which is supplied complete and ready for use, contains a mixture of fluid paint and a liquid propellent gas, the free space above the fluid being saturated with the vapour of the gas which is sufficient to eject a stream of fluid from the spray aperture when the valve is released. The liquid gas acts as a thinner to the paint and vaporizes rapidly when it emerges into the atmosphere, thereby atomizing the paint.

Spraying with an aerosol pack must be carried out intermittently to allow some of the gas inside the container to vaporize and fill the space vacated by the paint; continuous spraying results in momentary loss of pressure. If the pack is held too close to the work, runs and sags will form in the paint film and the film will be unduly wet, since the gas will not have had time to vaporize completely before reaching the surface. The pack must be shaken well before use to disperse any pigment which has settled in storage; pigment settling is more likely to occur than in a conventional paint container because of the low viscosity of the paint/gas mixture. Care should be taken to ensure that the empty containers are not thrown away in any place where they are liable to become overheated or they may explode.

Aerosol packs are expensive, but against this must be set the fact that they can be used without any expenditure on spray plant, and also the fact that there will be no time to be spent in cleaning out containers and equipment after use.

AFTER-IMAGE The phenomenon which is experienced when a person concentrates his gaze for a length of time upon one figure or object and then transfers his gaze to a blank surface; for a little while afterwards the shape of the figure or object appears to be still present before his eyes, though in a completely different colour. Gradually, of course, the after-image fades away. Usually the colour of the after-image is complementary to the colour of the original object. Thus, a person staring at a blue-green shape for any length of time tends to see the same shape in red when he transfers his attention elsewhere, especially if the surface to which he transfers his gaze is achromatic, i.e., white or neutral grey. The appearance of the after-image is due to the fact that part of the eye's mechanism, the receptors which respond to certain colours in light, become fatigued under the influence of continual stimulation; when the gaze is transferred else-where they tend to rest for a time while the receptors which respond to the complementary colours come into play.

AFTER-TACK A term used to describe a condition of a film, which dries normally up to a point but which permanently retains a slight degree of tack. It is a defect associated with long-oil compositions, especially those in which a soft drying oil predominates; the painter may encounter the condition if he uses a long-oil outdoor quality varnish for indoor work.

AGEING The term is sometimes loosely used by the painter to mean the natural process whereby an exposed film grows older and undergoes the gradual changes associated with growing older; the term is actually one used by the paint manufacturer to mean the storage of a material (e.g., a varnish) in order to mature it and allow it to stabilize itself before it is offered to a customer.

AGITATOR Used in two connections.
(a) In one sense it is applied to a mechanical device for the rapid shaking of tins of paint, whereby paint kept in stock can be periodically shaken up to prevent the contents from settling.
(b) The term is also applied to a device fitted to the pressure tank of spray painting plant whereby the material is kept constantly stirred while in use. On some plant the agitator may be operated by hand when required; on other types of equipment the agitator is mechanically driven.

AIR BRUSH A very small spray gun, not much larger than a fountain pen, designed for use as an artist's tool. Its application to the decorating trade is mainly in the preparation of perspective drawings.

AIR CAP The front part of a spray gun which directs the air into the paint stream to "atomize" it—that is, to split it up into fine particles—and to form it into a suitable spray pattern, The usual type of air cap has three holes, but multiple jet caps can be used for the more viscous materials.

AIR COMPRESSOR That part of a high pressure spray plant which takes in air, compresses it to a given maximum pressure, and delivers the compressed air to force out the paint as and when required.

AIR DRYING The drying of a paint due to exposure to the air at a normal temperature, as opposed to forced drying and stoving.

AIR FLOTATION Sometimes called "dry levigation". A term used to describe a method of preparing certain pigments; it consists briefly of feeding dry ground pigment into a current of air in order to separate the finer particles from the coarse.

AIR HOSE The tubing which conveys the air from the compressor to the pressure tank and to the spray gun or (when the paint is being fed to the gun from the feed cup) direct from the plant to the gun. To avoid confusion, the air hose is coloured red or orange whereas the hose which conveys paint is coloured black.

AIR LEAKAGE Air leaking from the front of the spray gun before the trigger is pulled and caused by defective assembly of the gun, broken or worn gun parts or the presence of dirt on the valve or seating of the gun.

AIR PRESSURE The pressure, measured in lb/in^2 (British) or kg/cm^2 (metric) or bars (SI)*, of the air delivered by the spray plant. In general, the higher the pressure the more finely the paint will be atomized. In the air-volume method of spraying comparatively low pressures are employed, dependent on the size and speed of the fan which blows the current of air along. In a high pressure unit the air is compressed to a higher pressure and pumped into a cylinder from which it is drawn as required, and regulators are fitted so that the pressure actually fed to the gun may be considerably lower. If a pressure tank or a regulator-type paint cup is being employed, further regulators are included in the system, so that one pressure is used to force the paint along the hose and a different pressure is used to atomize the paint. The pressure on the paint is not very high unless a heavy-bodied material like spray plastic is being used, but needs to be stepped up if the work is at some height above the plant; the pressure on the air line varies according to the viscosity of the material, the length of the hose in use and the effect desired.

---

* $1 \text{ bar} = 10^5 \text{ N/m}^2 = 10^5 \text{ pascals} = 1 \cdot 02 \text{ kg/cm}^2 = 14\frac{1}{2} \text{ lb/in}^2$

AIR REGULATOR A pressure reducing valve which allows the operator to reduce the air pressure delivered by the compressor to one suitable to the type of paint in use.

AIR STORAGE TANK OR AIR RECEIVER The cylinder in which compressed air is stored. When maximum pressure is reached in this tank, the motor driving the compressor cuts out and runs idle. As air is drawn off from the tank, when a certain level is reached the motor cuts in again. The purpose of the tank is to provide a steady supply of air whenever required, with the utmost economy in the running of the plant.

AIR TRANSFORMER A device incorporated in spray plant in order to condense air, oil and moisture, strain the air, indicate the pressure and provide outlet for guns and air tools.

AIR VALVE A valve in the body of a spray gun, which is opened and closed by the action of a trigger and which controls the supply of air.

AIR VOLUME SYSTEM A type of spray painting equipment which, unlike the high pressure systems, does not require a compressor. It is operated by pump or blower, which propels a stream of air along the air line at a moderate pressure and flows continuously through the gun; when the trigger is pressed, paint is released into the stream of air and is split up and directed on to the wall surface. Because the pressure is not so high, the paint is not so finely split up as in the high pressure system; on the other hand, there is considerably less rebound and spray-fog. It is quiet and simple in operation and very useful for decorative spraying and general domestic work.

AIRLESS SPRAYING Airless spraying has developed so rapidly that although it was only introduced a few years ago it is already being widely used in building and maintenance painting as well as in other branches of industry, and plant is now available which brings the advantages of this process within the reach of normal painting and decorating operations.
    The principle of airless spraying is quite unlike that of the conventional spraying systems. Conventional spray plant operates by the process of feeding a trickle of fluid paint into a flowing stream of compressed air, which results in the fluid being atomized or broken up into small particles, the particles being conveyed by the forced air stream to the wall surface where they reunite to form a coherent film. Airless spraying consists of subjecting the fluid paint to an extremely high pressure and then forcing it through a tiny aperture with the result that the release of the paint causes it to explode into a cloud of very fine particles. Atomization of the paint is therefore due to pressurizing of the fluid and not to any action of compressed air; there is no compressed air used in the spray gun, and no stream of forced air travelling and conveying the particles to the wall; in airless spraying the exploding cloud of paint particles is slowed down by air resistance in its progress to the wall, and it reaches the wall with so little impact that it has none of the tendency to bounce off again that is associated with conventional spray systems. This means that there is a

complete absence of spray fog, that the paint will penetrate into a corner or an angle or a small crevice quite freely because there is no pocket of compressed air to deflect it, and that the paint does not lose its volatile solvent content by evaporation while travelling to the wall and is therefore able to form a wet paint coating on arrival at the wall surface and is able to flow freely as if it had been brush applied.

These are not, however, the only advantages offered by the airless spray system. Probably the most spectacular feature is the very high speed of operation on broad areas, which is the direct result of the very wide spray pattern produced by the gun; in some circumstances the only limiting factor to the speed of coverage is the inability of the operator to move his arm any faster. Another advantage is the very considerable reduction in paint wastage.

Almost all the normal range of paint products can be sprayed by this method, and because it is not necessary to thin them down before spraying they are applied with a higher proportion of solid content which can be used to produce an extra-heavy film or a thicker-than-normal coating where required, such as, for example, on structural steel; an additional factor is the elimination of waste by loss of solvent.

The high pressurization of the paint is achieved by means of a pump unit with an air to fluid ratio of 1 to 30, so that an input of air at $100\,lb/in^2$ is converted to a fluid pressure of $3000\,lb/in^2$; pressures of this order are only required for the heaviest type of material, and normal average working pressures are $80\,lb/in^2$ [$5\cdot6\,kg/cm^2$ (metric), $5\cdot5$ bars (SI)] air input, $2400\,lb/in^2$ [$169\,kg/cm^2$ (metric), 172 bars (SI)] fluid pressure. The paint is fed to the gun along a single fluid line of stainless steel flexible hose with a plastic solvent-resistant lining capable of withstanding the pressures employed. The paint is forced through an extremely fine orifice in the spray cap, and when it emerges from the orifice it instantly expands; there is an angled slot in the cap in front of the orifice which channels the atomized paint into a set fan pattern. A wide range of spray caps is available to cope with varying weights and viscosities of material and to provide a choice of pattern widths and flow rates suitable for the particular type of work in hand. The spray tips are of tungsten carbide to withstand the erosive abrasive action of paint particles under extreme pressure. The pump unit is fitted with a valve to relieve pressures in the system when the spray cap needs to be changed.

Fully automatic airless spray units are employed in heavy industry, and these are very often coupled to shotblasting units and conveyor systems. The type of unit of most interest to the painter and decorator is the small portable plant of 20- or 25-litre fluid capacity which weighs about 9 kg when empty and which is suitable for all except the heaviest materials. There are also heavy-duty units of 50 litre fluid capacity which are mounted on pneumatic tyred trolleys and which have take-off points for two operators to work simultaneously; this type of plant will handle all materials, even including solventless epoxies and coal tar paints. There are, however, certain materials of a highly corrosive or gritty nature which are not suitable for application by airless spray because of the damage they

---

1 bar $=\ 10^5\,N/m^2\ =\ 10^5$ pascals $=\ 1\cdot02\,kg/cm^2\ =\ 14\frac{1}{2}\,lb/in^2$

would cause to the plant; the decorator, for example, would be well advised not to attempt to spray cement paints by this method.

Airless spraying demands a different spraying technique on the part of the operator. The gun should be held at right angles to the surface throughout the stroke at a distance of 300 mm. The strokes should be overlapped by 50% to produce an all-over level coating. The trigger must be pressed firmly and completely at the beginning of each stroke and released abruptly and completely at the end, with no attempt at feathering. The hand should commence to move before the trigger is operated and should continue to move after the trigger is released. The speed of the stroke must be considerably greater than that used with conventional spray equipment. On no account must the gun be aimed at the body.

It is essential that the equipment be cleaned every day with the solvent appropriate to the material in use; paint must never be allowed to dry in the pump, hose or gun. The gun must not be immersed in solvent during cleaning as this causes an accumulation of deposits to build up in the fluid passages. If the spray cap becomes choked it should be freed by blowing with compressed air from the front; blowing from the back causes particles to become more firmly wedged in the orifice. Sparking may occur between the gun and the wall surface due to the generation of static electricity by the pressures in the paint; equipment supplied by the reputable manufacturers is earthed to prevent this.

ALCOHOL   The name given to a large and important group of solvents; the most important from a practical viewpoint is ethyl alcohol, so much so that when the word "alcohol" is used without being qualified it is generally assumed that it refers to this.

ALKALI   (a) A compound of hydrogen and oxygen with sodium, potassium, calcium or other bodies, which is soluble in water and which produces caustic and corrosive solutions capable of neutralizing acids and changing the colour of vegetable substances.
(b) A knowledge of the action of alkalis is of the utmost importance to the painter for the following reasons:
(i) Many of the vegetable oils used in paints are badly affected by contact with alkaline materials; they react with the alkali to form a soap, and the effect seen by the painter is that the dry paint film softens up, becoming sticky, soft and soapy.
(ii) Several of the materials used in building (for example, lime plaster, Portland cement, asbestos cement sheeting, etc.) are of an alkaline nature, so that when painting such surfaces the risk of alkaline attack on the paint must be considered and countered.
(iii) The paint may be attacked on the face by contact with an alkaline solution, a danger often met with in the painting of factories, workshops, and other industrial premises. Faulty procedure in washing down a paint film with mildly alkaline materials can also lead to the film being attacked.
(iv) Certain of the pigments used in paint are subject to alkaline attack.

ALKALI-RESISTING PAINTS   Finishing materials intended to withstand the attack of chemical concentrations and dust in the atmosphere, caustic soda spray, etc., i.e., alkaline attack on the face of the paint. Among the materials which are more resistant to such attack than normal oil paint films are certain of the phenolformaldehyde resins, chlorinated rubber and bituminous paints; the actual choice of a finish for any particular surface would be dictated by local conditions and requirements.

ALKALI-RESISTING PRIMER This is intended to prevent damage to the paint film from alkaline materials present in the actual surface which is to be painted, i.e., attack on the paint film from behind (in a previous paragraph lime plaster, asbestos cement, etc., were instanced as such materials.). The primer is usually based on tung oil reinforced with coumarone resins, tung oil being more resistant to alkaline attack than linseed oil. It should be noted that while such a primer is less likely to be softened by alkali than a linseed oil primer it is *not* completely proof against attack; it is a common fallacy to regard alkali-resisting primers as being sealers which completely insulate the paint from the chemically active surface.

ALKYD RESINS The name given to an important group of synthetic resins widely used in the making of both decorative and industrial paints, and based on a chemical combination of phthalic anhydride and glycerine, modified with drying oils, semi-drying oils and other resins. They possess many useful features, including paleness of colour, good colour retention, great flexibility combined with hardness of finish, and great durability.

ALLIGATORING A clumsy term to denote the extensive cracking of paint in which the surface resembles alligator hide.

ALLOY A mixture of metals. Alloys are of interest to the painter and decorator in two connections: (a) the metallic paints produced by mixing aluminium and bronze powders or, in the case of gold bronze paints, by mixing copper, zinc and aluminium, and (b) the various substitutes for gold leaf, such as Dutch metal, which is an alloy of copper and zinc. These substitutes are generally thicker and more brittle than real gold leaf, and they tend to tarnish if not protected with lacquer.

ALPHABET (a) A series of symbols by which the form of a spoken language can be set down by one person and interpreted, or read, by another. In the case of a picture alphabet, each symbol represents an object, but what we use in our Western civilization is a "phonetic" alphabet, in which each symbol represents a sound. It will be seen that a phonetic alphabet such as ours, with only 26 symbols, is far less cumbersome and is easier to learn and read than a picture alphabet composed of several thousand characters. When we consider what a vast influence the written and printed word exerts upon the spread of every kind of knowledge and learning, it does not seem an exaggeration to describe the invention of a system of writing as probably the most important and far-reaching invention of all time.
(b) The term "alphabet" is often used to refer to a particular style in which the shapes of the letters of the alphabet are painted or depicted; for example, we speak of a "Roman" alphabet, meaning that the characters are slender

and elegant with strokes of varying thickness, and of a "block" alphabet, in which the characters are in a bolder and heavier style. Examples of various styles are described under the appropriate headings.

The painter when called upon to reproduce the letters of the alphabet in the medium of paint should be concerned to make them convey their meaning as readily as possible, in as pleasing a form as possible; this involves a careful study of the various kinds of alphabets, the ability to select those best suited to the work in hand and harmonizing best with the surroundings, and a sound knowledge of colour and design.

ALUM A double sulphate of aluminium and potassium.

A small piece of alum is often added to a mixing of non-washable distemper to harden it and render it less soluble in water, and to ease the work of distempering a "hot" surface; it is useful in helping to cover surface stains but it makes the subsequent removal of the distemper difficult.

Some paperhangers make a practice of adding a lump of alum to their paste, but this is unnecessary and undesirable, as it may affect the colours of the paper.

ALUMINA The oxide of aluminium, forming the basis of alum and a constituent of all clays. It is a soft fluffy white powder which becomes transparent when mixed with oil; it is used as a suspending agent with heavy pigments to prevent their settling.

ALUMINIUM A white ductile metal. Combined as silicate it is very abundant; as a metal it is extracted principally from the ore bauxite but also to some extent from nepheline, felspar, corundum and leucite. In various forms it has numerous applications to the painting and decorating craft.

ALUMINIUM FOIL A material which is being increasingly used in the thermal insulation of buildings, because it combines the properties of high reflectivity of radiant heat and low emissivity of transmitted heat with lightness of weight and resistance to fire, and is also vermin proof. It may be obtained both as plain and corrugated sheets and is often supplied in rolls of 533 mm width. Although it does not normally come into his province the decorator is sometimes called upon to apply the foil; when this is the case it should be remembered that aluminium is affected by contact with alkalis, wet brickwork, plaster, cement, etc., and should there be any doubt as to the conditions to which the foil is to be exposed it should, before application, be coated with a special thin transparent lacquer which protects it without seriously reducing its reflective properties. The fixative may be a bitumen compound or a fairly slow gold size. The insulating value of the foil is increased by using two layers with an air gap between, but this involves a method of fixing which is outside the decorator's normal practice. A recently developed form of aluminium foil for use by the decorator on damp surfaces consists of sheets 3 metres long by 762 mm wide which are coated on the back with a synthetic rubber adhesive; the sheets are applied direct to the plaster with a hot domestic iron.

ALUMINIUM LEAF A thin foil of the metal, used for decorative purposes, is sold in books in similar form to gold leaf. Each book contains 25 leaves, the size of the leaf varying from 82 mm to 152 mm square. It is much thicker than gold leaf and is therefore less delicate to handle. The fixative used is Japan gold size.

ALUMINIUM PAINT—NON-LEAFING There are certain finishes in which the leafing characteristics are not required, and if the particles are non-leafing they remain in the body of the paint film as it sets instead of rising to the surface; the result is that the flakes, being set at random, catch the light at varying angles, producing a satin or silky effect.

ALUMINIUM PAINTS These are made from aluminium paste or powder mixed with a suitable medium, and fall into three main categories:
(i) Decorator's finishing quality.
(ii) Decorator's priming paints.
(iii) Industrial or pyroxylin type.
   The most widely used medium for (i) and (ii) is varnish, which can be made from a variety of resins including phenolin, paracoumarone and alkyd resins, ester gums, resins made from crepe rubber, chlorinated rubber, etc. Cellulose and synthetic gums can be combined to form binders for the pyroxylin type.

ALUMINIUM PAINTS—PROPERTIES OF Apart from the characteristic "leafing" referred to elsewhere the features of aluminium paint may be classed as follows:
(a) *Mechanical strength*. The aluminium flakes within the dried film act as a reinforcing pigment, strengthening the film.
(b) *Opacity*. Being actual metal particles, the flakes are themselves opaque, and as the paint film is composed of numerous overlapping flakes it will generally hide the underlying surface perfectly in one coat.
   A further point that follows on the fact of the flakes being opaque is that they do not transmit light or other forms of radiant energy (including the damaging ultra-violet rays of the sun) so that the flakes in the upper layers of a paint film tend to protect the underlying layers of medium.
(c) *Moisture resistance*. The individual aluminium flakes, although very thin, do not permit the passage of liquids nor even of gases; in a paint film composed of such flakes moisture can only penetrate by the devious means of finding a path across and around the edge of each flake it encounters. Since the length and width of a flake are generally several hundred times its thickness it follows that such penetration is slow and difficult, giving the film great resistance to water.
(d) *"Sealing" properties*. The thin foil of metal which results from the overlapping of the flakes when set in a suitable medium is of value in sealing materials which have a tendency to "bleed". Aluminium powder added to shellac knotting will check the penetration of creosote, bitumen, bleeding reds, soot, etc., and when very resinous timber is to be treated aluminium paint is often found to have enough mechanical strength to hold back the resin where a lead primer would soon be blistered and lifted off the surface.

14

(e) *Reflectivity*. This is almost as great as that of the metal itself, which reflects up to 75% of the radiant energy which strikes it. This is an important factor in lowering temperatures inside various kinds of structure—for example, the painting of storage tanks with aluminium to prevent losses by evaporation.

(f) *Emissivity*. Very low, since emissivity is the opposite of reflectivity; the radiation of heat from hot sources can be reduced by painting them with aluminium. This factor is made use of when it is required to conserve heat, but is often overlooked when radiators are being painted; coating radiators with aluminium paint for decorative purposes seriously reduces their efficiency.

(g) *Spreading capacity and ease of application*. Very good, the average being usually in the order of 18 to 22 square metres per litre.

ALUMINIUM PASTE The finest aluminium powders are usually mixed with sufficient liquid to form a paste, since in this form they are easier to handle and use, and quicker to mix.

ALUMINIUM POWDER There are two main classes of aluminium powder; flake and granulated. The length and breadth of a flake particle are much greater than its thickness (often several hundred times greater), whereas the length, breadth and thickness of a granulated particle are all roughly the same; it follows that flake particles are essentially flat whereas granulated particles are spherical or ovoid.

Granulated powder is produced by "atomization"; the aluminium is melted and blown into a stream of cold air which breaks it up into minute solid particles. Flake powders for use in paint are made by feeding granulated powder into a ball mill with a suitable lubricant; here the particles are flattened into flakes. (Flake powder can be produced by a stamping process, but this is only used in the chemical and explosive industries.) The type of powder and its method of manufacture have a great bearing on its use, e.g., it is essential that the flakes of the powders used in primers should have "leafing" properties, whereas non-leafing flakes of various grades are needed to produce satin finishes, polychromatic paints, and hammered, crackle or wrinkle finishes.

Aluminium powders are often polished during manufacture to give extra brilliance.

ALUMINIUM POWDERS—"LEAFING" PROPERTIES The minute metal flakes of the powders used in most aluminium paints are polished and coated during manufacture so that the surface is not readily "wetted" by normal paint media. This produces a high degree of interfacial tension between the flakes and the liquid medium, with the result that the flakes, although heavier than the liquid, tend to float to the surface and arrange themselves parallel with the surface, overlapping each other. This phenomenon, which resembles the way in which fallen leaves overlap one another in flat layers on the ground, is known as "leafing". The paint film therefore consists of innumerable layers of overlapping metal flakes with layers of medium between them. The extent of the leafing has a great bearing both on the appearance and the characteristic properties of the film.

ALUMINIUM STEARATE A complex salt of aluminium and stearic acid, incorporated in several preparations used by the painter. It is chiefly used as a flatting agent, but is also used as an anti settling agent to keep pigments in suspension, as a water repellent for use on porous structural surfaces, and as an ingredient in transparent glazes for use in broken colour work.

ALUMINIUM UNITS—THE PAINTING OF The metal aluminium seems to have a great affinity for grease, and absorbs a fair amount of grease during the process of rolling or fabrication. Before it is painted a thorough de-greasing is essential either with one of the proprietary materials or with petrol or white spirit; it is advisable also to etch the surface with steel wool or fine abrasive paper. The use of alkaline detergents should be avoided because the metal is dissolved by contact with caustic solutions. After de-greasing, zinc chromate primer should be used.

AMBER A yellow translucent fossil resin, found chiefly on the southern shores of the Baltic, and the hardest resin known.

AMBER VARNISH A very pale varnish. The name refers to the colour and quality of the varnish and not to the type of resin used in its manufacture; amber would be too expensive to be used for this purpose.

AMERICAN CLOTH A glazed cotton fabric of the oil-cloth type, often used as a wall hanging in kitchens and similar rooms where a strong waterproof hygienic surface is required.

AMERICAN TURPS A volatile solvent distilled from the oleo-resin which is obtained from certain species of pine and fir trees. It has many qualities which make it practically the ideal paint solvent, but it is no longer in such general use due to its cost. It used to be commonly held that American turps was of higher quality than that produced elsewhere, but this opinion was largely due to prejudice and seems to have no valid basis in fact.

AMMONIA A colourless gas with pungent smell and strong alkaline reaction. A little liquid ammonia is often added to water for washing down and preparing old paintwork in preference to sugar soap; it is milder in action but not so effective in removing grease. Ammonia is also used as a chemical stain for wood, as, for example, in the process of fuming oak.

AMORPHOUS PIGMENTS Pigments whose particles are of shapeless structure and lack definite form, as opposed to crystalline pigments.

ANAGLYPTA An embossed paper made from good quality rags in both high and low relief designs to give the appearance of modelled plaster, plastic paint and other effects. The high relief is supplied in hollow backed panels, the low relief in rolls of normal width. Normally it is coated with flat oil paint, water paint or emulsion paint after hanging, but it can also be supplied in ready decorated form.

ANALOGOUS COLOURS Colours which lie close to one another on the colour circle.

ANATASE   One of the crystalline forms of titanium dioxide.

ANGLE ROLLER   A paperhanger's roller, usually 25 mm in width, the drum of which is supported on one side only to enable it to be used close in to an angle.

ANHYDRITE   Sulphate of lime, an anhydrous form of gypsum; that is to say, a form of gypsum with no water in its composition which occurs naturally as a mineral.

ANHYDRITE PLASTER   A plaster made by grinding the natural mineral anhydrite and adding an accelerator. It behaves like the moderately burnt anhydrous plasters when setting and gives an extremely hard but fairly porous finish.

ANHYDROUS GYPSUM PLASTER   A group of plasters and cements made by heating the rock gypsum to a temperature of 400° Celsius* in order to drive off the whole of the water of crystallization. When water is added by the plasterer it combines with them to replace the water of crystallization which was expelled. The group includes the plasters known by the trade names of Sirapite, Glastone, Statite, Victorite and Xelite; it also includes Keene's or Parian cement and those varieties of Keene's sold under the proprietary names of Astoplax, Pixie Keene's and Superite; and in addition it includes anhydrite which, as mentioned in a previous paragraph, is not made from gypsum but from a naturally occurring mineral form of anhydrous calcium sulphate.

None of these materials combines readily with water, and an accelerator is added during manufacture; otherwise they would take too long to set and harden. The various types of plaster in the group differ from one another in detail, but it may be said, as a general characteristic of the group, that their set is slow and continuous; this is an important point for the decorator, because should they for any reason dry before they are completely hydrated (i.e., before the water of crystallization has been completely replaced) defects such as "dry-out" and "delayed expansion" may occur. Another consequence of their slow setting which is of importance to the decorator is that the plasterer, having plenty of time to trowel them, often brings them to a smooth glassy finish which presents very little "key" to paint or distemper.

The anhydrous gypsum plasters, when used as they are sold, rarely have any chemical action on paint, but, if they are gauged with even a small quantity of lime, caustic alkali is formed which will give rise to saponification. They should be tested for alkalinity before painting.

ANODE   The positive plate in electrolysis.

ANODIZING   The covering of an aluminium surface with a layer of aluminium oxide by the process of electrolysis. The layer protects the metal, and can be dyed in various colours.

---

* The word "Centigrade", for the unit of temperature, has been changed to "Celsius" to avoid confusion with Continental practice. The units remain the same, as does the abbreviation, °C.

ANTHEMION A term given to honeysuckle or palmette ornament in classical architecture.

ANTI-BACTERIA PAINTS Paints to which poisonous metallic salts (e.g. salts of sodium, mercury, zinc or magnesium) have been added to check the growth of bacteria and fungus. See also Fungicidal paints.

ANTI-CLIMB PAINTS Paints which instead of drying after application remain wet and slippery. They have been developed for the specific purpose of combating crime and vandalism and are used in such situations as the painting of downspouts (to deter cat-burglars) and the painting of marker buoys and posts to prevent removal and theft. Their properties are due to the use of a medium based upon non-oxidizing castor oil. They are applied in heavy coatings, by brush, and have a very low spreading capacity.

ANTI-CONDENSATION PAINTS Materials made to minimize the condensation of moisture on cold surfaces such as metal or plaster. Several proprietary brands are on the market, consisting of an absorbent material suspended in a suitable emulsion; these are applied in a thick coating of about 4·5 to 5·5 square metres/litre, and are often stippled as a finish. To increase the thickness two coats are often preferable to one. Applied in this way their effectiveness is due to three factors: the provision of a thick buffer layer which insulates the surface; the absorption of some of the moisture; and the fact that air tends to stagnate in the pockets or cavities formed by the stippling, providing further insulation. Another form of anti-condensation paint, which however is purely functional and does not present so pleasing an appearance, is formed by painting the surface with a strongly adhesive material on to which, when it has become tacky. granulated cork is blown.

ANTI-FOULING PAINTS Materials devised to minimize the loss of speed caused by the accumulation of barnacles etc., on the hulls of ships. They consist of highly poisonous substances such as copper salts or arsenic, bound in a very tenacious non-drying medium. Their effectiveness is due to the salts leaching out into the water to poison any marine growth. There are three types in general use:- (a) a dark red/brown paint supplied in ready mixed form which is more expensive than normal industrial paints, (b) a bright metallic copper material which is more expensive than (a) and in which the bronze powder is mixed in the medium immediately before use, and (c) a white paint which is twice as expensive as (a) and which is supplied in ready-mixed form. All these materials can be applied by brush, roller or spray. Care is needed in their use because of their toxic properties.

ANTIMONY Antimony white, an oxide of antimony, is produced by roasting the black mineral called stibnite (sulphide of antimony) in the presence of air, the fumes being condensed to form an amorphous white pigment. It is fine textured and very opaque, has a tendency to discolour in the presence of sulphur, and has a retarding effect on the drying of linseed oil but is improved by combination with zinc oxide. When combined in this way, it is used to reduce the chalking of titanium oxide; it is also considered to offer good protection against sea air.

Antimony orange and antimony vermilion are sulphides of antimony, rather unstable as pigments and nowadays rarely used in paint.

ANTISEPTIC WASHES Chemical solutions, of which several proprietary makes are on the market, used to eradicate mould growth, etc., from a surface prior to decoration.

ANTWERP BLUE Used principally as an artists' colour. It consists chemically of zinc ferrocyanide; its properties are very similar to those of Prussian blue, but it is a lot paler in colour and of a more greenish blue.

APPLIQUÉ MOTIFS Strictly speaking, this means any ornamental work which is laid on to some other material. In painting and decorating the term normally applies to paperhanging—to the various decorative devices which are superimposed on to the finished papering, their placing being at the discretion of the decorator. The name embraces such devices as perforated corner pieces, nursery and bathroom cut-outs, high relief motifs, etc.

APSE A semi-circular or multangular (many-angled) recess, generally at the east end of the chancel in a church.

ARABESQUE Surface decoration of a rhythmic linear character composed of scroll work and foliage.

ARCHITECTURAL DRAWING Precise and accurate drawing of rooms, the exteriors of buildings, or architectural features, usually relying for its effect upon good line work and neat draughtsmanship.

ARCHITRAVE The moulded frame around doors or windows.

ARCHROME RANGE A range of colours specially recommended for use in schools, and introduced in the Ministry of Education Bulletin No. 9 ("Colour in Schools") published in 1953. The range was incorporated in the B.S. 2660 range of colours but B.S. 2660 was withdrawn in 1973. See also *Paint Colours for Building Purposes*.

ARGENT The heraldic term for silver, which is very often depicted in heraldic painting by white.

ARMENIAN BOLE A red earth powder dusted on to the thin tissue pages which separate the leaves of gold in a book of gold leaf; its purpose is to prevent the gold from sticking to the tissue.

ARRIS A sharp external edge formed when two faces of a structural member meet; the external angle on wood, stone, plaster or steelwork. Paint tends to recede from a sharp angle, leaving a thinner coating on the arris which thereby becomes a weakness in the film.

ASBESTOS A fibrous crystalline material, a form of the mineral hornblende, which possesses the property of resisting fire very strongly and is often woven into fireproof fabrics.

ASBESTOS CEMENT   Asbestos, when mixed into a slurry with cement, is pressed into sheets of various sizes and shapes or moulded into the form of spoutings, etc., which, when dry, compose prefabricated units of great importance to the building trade. Their many advantages include ease of assembly and resistance to fire; one of their drawbacks is their brittle nature. The factor of greatest importance to the painter is the alkaline nature of the material; it is perhaps not generally realized that cement forms 85% of the content of asbestos cement sheeting. The alkalinity decreases as the material becomes weathered, but under present conditions the demand for asbestos cement units is so heavy that they are often incorporated into buildings when quite new and raw, and alkali resisting treatment is needed to prevent the saponification of applied paint coatings.

ASBESTOS WOOD   This material is supplied in sheets and is used in the making of fire-resisting walls and ceilings. Its composition is 50% asbestos fibre and 50% cement (by weight). It is less brittle than asbestos cement sheeting, and is more adaptable in the sense that asbestos cement units , are used as fabricated whereas asbestos wood sheets can be sawn to shape with a hand saw, can have circular holes cut in with a pad saw, and may be nailed or screwed into position. It is much more absorbent than asbestos cement, and some authorities recommend soaking the surface in boiled oil to stop the suction prior to painting. The manufacturers of the product recommend a proprietary brand of primer without this pre-treatment.

ASH   A hard wood which is not used greatly in building but because of its resilience is widely used in coachwork. In colour and grain markings it is very similar to light oak, and in fact the two are very often confused. Its colour is a little lighter than oak, and the heartwood markings are more smoothly rounded, but it requires a practised eye to distinguish between the two.

ASHLAR   Masonry or squared stones in regular courses.

ASHLAR EFFECTS   The imitation of ashlar in decorative materials; for example, with stone paints or plastic paint, the ashlar joints being scored out with a small screwdriver or shaped piece of wood while the paint is wet, or by setting out the joints with narrow masking tape before applying the paint and removing these before it is set. The effect can be enhanced by emphasizing the joints with white or any colour desired.

ASPHALTUM   Mineral pitch, a dark brown or black form of bitumen, the purest varieties being used in the manufacture of black Japan, and various grades and qualities being used in the production of bituminous paints.

ASSERTIVE COLOURS   See *Advancing Colours*.

ASTRAGAL A small semi-circular moulding, often ornamented with a bead or reel.

ATOMIZED PAINT A term used in paint spraying to describe the breaking up of the paint into tiny globules when it encounters the forced air stream in the spray gun.

ATRIUM The outer or entrance court to a building, open in the centre; the open space before the entrance to a building.

AUTOMATIC SPRAYING A system of spraying used in industrial coating when a large number of identical or similarly shaped objects is to be painted and where high speed production is required. The spray guns are mounted either on a fixed bar or on a movable carriage, and are controlled mechanically, a device being fitted which prevents them from spraying unless some object is within range. The carriage and mountings can be adjusted to cope with changes of contour such as are found, for instance, on a car body. The object to be treated can be made to rotate while being sprayed so that the whole area is painted.

AXONOMETRIC PROJECTION A projection is a method of linking together the plan and elevations of a room, building or other object, so as to present a three-dimensional picture. An axonometric projection is produced by drawing the plan to scale (and, in the case of a room, all the furniture, etc., is also drawn in on the plan). The plan is set at an angle, usually 30, 45 or 60 degrees, from the horizontal. Vertical lines are drawn from each corner (and through the corner of each object in the case of a room) to the same scale as the plan. The drawing of rooms is stressed because the principal value of this projection to a decorator is to show the interior of rooms. It gives a good idea of the solid shape of the room and its contents, and also, because the plan is indicated and everything on the plan and elevation is to the same scale, it can be referred to as an accurate working drawing.

AZURE The heraldic term for blue.

B

BACK PRIMING This refers to coating up, for protective purposes, those parts of a structure and those materials which will be out of sight when the building is completed. Door frames and window frames, for instance, should be primed before fixing, because their back edges, when fixed in position, are in direct contact with the brickwork and therefore liable to absorb a great deal of water from this source; the water thus absorbed might very well seek to escape through the outer face of the woodwork after the painting has been completed, leading to blistering and peeling of the paintwork. An aluminium primer, being almost completely impervious to moisture, is eminently suitable for the back priming of such frames, and two coats are to be recommended in preference to one.

The term back priming also refers to the very sound practice of painting the backs of such materials as asbestos sheeting before they are fixed; the alkaline content of such materials (which may be dormant when the paint is first applied) can be re-activated by the re-introduction of moisture at a later date, and back priming with, say, bituminous paint is a wise safeguard to prevent this occurring.

BACK PUTTY Otherwise known as bedding putty; the putty which is run into a window frame and into which the pane of glass is bedded.

BACKGROUND STENCIL Otherwise known as a negative stencil, one in which the background is cut out and the design itself forms the ties. Background stencilling is very important to the decorator; for such things as the running bands which are often applied around large halls, churches, etc., a negative pattern is more satisfying than a positive pattern, in which the design is cut out, largely because it avoids the spotty effect which a positive pattern produces when repeated several times.

BACKING UP A term used in glass gilding. It is impossible to apply loose leaf gold exactly to the size and shape of the lettering or ornament that is required; it is laid in such a way as to extend beyond the bounds of the shape that is actually required and then, when it is dry, the shape is painted on to the gold with backing up paint applied with a writing pencil. When the backing up is dry the surplus gold is removed. Paint for backing up may be made by mixing black Japan and red lead, or one of the proprietary materials sold by the gold beating firms may be used.

The term is also sometimes applied to a coat of paint given to the whole of a glass window after it has been lettered; the object of this coat is to make the lettering more prominent and the window opaque.

BADGER HAIR A very soft hair, derived, as its name implies, from the badger. The peculiar feature of badger hair is that it tapers both at the root and the tip and is broadest in the centre; for this reason, when a group of hairs is bunched together and secured at the roots it forms a compact and sturdy mass for most of its length but the tips are more widely separated. This principle is followed in the making of softening brushes for graining, which are very soft and light at the tips.

BADGER SOFTENER A brush with a filling of badger hair and having a long slender handle; it is used for softening the markings in water colour graining, but is too delicate to be used for oil colour.

BALL FLOWER The characteristic ornament of the decorated period of Gothic architecture.

BALL MILL A revolving drum, containing steel balls or pebbles of varying sizes, which is used in the preparation of pigments and paints. As the drum rotates, the continual tumbling action of the balls subjects the pigment to extremely fine and uniform grinding and blends it very thoroughly with the medium.

BALSAM Oleo-resinous matter obtained from coniferous trees, consisting of resin, essential oils and other compounds. See *Oleo-resin.*

BALUSTER A column or pillar supporting a handrail or coping; a series of these forms a balustrade.

BANDSTAND A colloquial term for a splithead. See *Splitheads.*

BARGE BOARD A broad board extending along the edge of a gable to cover the ends of the rafters.

BARRELLING A method of paint application used in industrial finishing; It is otherwise known as tumbling (q.v.).

BARRIER COAT A coating intended to prevent a new paint system from being affected by some harmful substance in the surface to which it is applied. Examples of barrier coats would be an alkali resisting primer preventing new cement from saponifying the paint applied to it and stop-tar knotting preventing creosote from bleeding through a new film.

BARRIER CREAM A smooth paste applied to the skin to form a protection against toxic or irritant materials. There is a wide variety of these creams, affording protection against many types of chemical; they are used in several industrial processes in factories, the operatives spreading the creams on their hands before commencing work. They could, with advantage, be used more freely in the painting trade for the less pleasant operations (such as those involving the use of caustic materials) where rubber gloves would be a hindrance but some form of protection is desirable.

BARYTES A crystalline substance, its chemical composition being a normal sulphate of barium, which occurs naturally in the form of a mineral called heavy spar. It is of no value as a pigment on its own because of its poor opacity and rough texture, but is very widely used as an extender in the manufacture of paint; provided it is not used in excess it imparts extra durability when mixed with other pigments.

BASE PLATE A square flat metal plate with 150 mm sides (22,500 mm^2 area) used in tubular scaffolding to distribute the load from a standard or raker; it has a central shank over which the tube fits loosely. There are two small holes in the plate through which spikes can be driven to secure the fitting to a sole plate.

BASTARD FLAT A painters' term for a semi-flat paint as opposed to a completely matt finish.

BATH ENAMELS Enamels designed for brush application and used in the renovation of the old-fashioned type of bath; they are hard drying enamels with high waterproofing qualities and resistant to alkaline attack to enable them to withstand the action of hot soapy water for a reasonable period. They are supplied in small tins containing sufficient for the painting of one bath and are applied over an undercoating system of white lead and gold size.

BATTER A term applied to a wall with an inclined face.

BAYS Compartments into which the roof of a building is divided; the spaces between columns; projecting windows.

BEAD A small cylindrical moulding, frequently carved with an ornament resembling a string of beads.

BEADING A length of bead moulding.

BEAK HEAD A moulding enrichment of the Norman period.

BED A painters' term for a flat recessed surface, such as the bed of a ceiling as distinct from the cornice or frieze.

BEDDING PUTTY The putty into which a pane of glass is bedded; see *Back Putty*.

BEER Stale beer is often used as a binder for water graining colour. It should not be used too strong; otherwise a crop of small blisters may occur. Generally it is used in the approximate proportions of one part of beer to two parts of water.

BEESWAX A material secreted by bees and used in the construction of the honeycomb; it has various applications to the painting trade and is obtained by extracting and melting down the combs. Normally, it is deep yellow in colour, but it can be refined to make a bleached wax or "white wax". It has been used from very early times as a painting medium, and even today an emulsion of saponified beeswax is sometimes used in washable distempers. Occasionally a small proportion is incorporated in flat varnish and flat oil paints, but it is principally used in wax polishes and stains.

BENCH An essential item of workshop equipment. For the greatest convenience in colour mixing and matching, it should be placed beside a North light window; it should for preference be zinc covered to facilitate cleaning.

BENZENE One of a number of volatile solvents obtained from coal tar.

BENZOL A similar material, not so pure as benzene (actually benezene is obtained from benzol by treating it with sulphuric acid followed by distillation). It is used as a thinner for cellulose ester materials, as a solvent for oil-soluble dyes in wood stains (because of its high penetrative power), as an ingredient in paint removers, and occasionally in small quantities to increase the solvent power of turpentine substitutes.

BILLET   A Norman moulding, consisting of small cylinders or cubes at regular intervals.

BINDER   An adhesive material which binds together the particles of pigment in any type of paint, holding them in suspension while the paint is wet and then drying to form a skin which keeps the particles together and holds them firmly to the surface. The binder in soft distempers is glue size, water paints have a binder of emulsion of oil, and oil paints are bound with vegetable drying oils, varnishes, etc.

BINDING DOWN   The process of applying a viscous binding material over the top of a loosely bound film in order to fix it. Its two main applications to the trade are:
(a) When graining with water colour medium. The graining colour is loosely bound, either with a weak solution of beer (as described in a previous paragraph) or with some similar composition such as vinegar and water, skimmed milk and water, etc. The pigment is bound sufficiently to remain in place and resist mild rubbing, but is not bound firmly enough for more graining colour to be applied and further operations to take place without "rubbing up" and consequent blurring or loss of the grain markings already applied. To fix the graining colour before the next stage is begun, it is "bound down" with a half and half mixture of varnish and turps, which, when applied quickly, binds it securely to the surface and makes it proof against further disturbance.
(b) When applying coatings, particularly of emulsion or water paint, over loosely bound or powdery surfaces. A plastered surface, for example, which has previously been decorated with a soft glue-bound distemper and is now to be finished in water paint, may be scrubbed and washed to remove the old distemper, but the most thorough washing cannot be guaranteed to remove all traces of whiting, which always tends to leave a light powdering on the surface when dry. A thin coat of proprietary primer as supplied by the manufacturers of the water paint, or a sharp coat of white lead, will "bind down" the particles of loose distemper and, by fastening them firmly to the surface will prevent them from affecting the adhesion of the new material.

BIRDCAGE SCAFFOLD   An interior scaffold used in the decoration of churches, public halls and similar structures with large ceiling areas; it consists of a close-boarded platform supported by a framework based upon rows of standards which are spaced at approximately equal distances apart both lengthways and breadthways. Those parts of the scaffold adjacent to the wall may be adapted to support working platforms from which the walls can be painted.

BIRD'S EYE MAPLE   A light coloured wood with considerable possibilities for the decorator. Its characteristic features are a softly mottled background, small clusters of "birds' eyes" (i.e., small horseshoe-shaped markings of darker colour), and curly irregular grain markings of soft colouring. It can be imitated in oil colour, but grainers generally prefer to work with water colour on a white or cream ground colour; the mottling can be imitated with a washleather or mottler, the birds' eyes inserted with a small brush called a "dotter", shaped for the purpose, and the curly markings run in with Conté rayon. Because the two later stages do not disturb the mottling, binding down between coats is unnecessary and a satisfactory imitation of this wood can therefore be achieved quite economically.

BITTINESS A defect in painting whereby bits of grit, fluff and other foreign bodies contained in the paint mar the appearance of the finished film. Although there are times when it occurs in spite of the utmost care, in the majority of cases it is caused by carelessness. Bittiness can often be traced to the use of dirty brushes; to brushes which, through careless storage, have become caked with hard paint in the stocks and which have then been "cleaned" with a scraper or wire brush; to dirt and grit being picked up during painting; to failure to remove grit from the surface after rubbing down; to the use of dirty pieces of wood for stirring paint; to the inclusion of broken skins in the paint during stirring; to the failure to strain paint on which skin has formed; to the use of badly cleansed spray equipment; and so on. Occasionally the paint in an unopened tin may become bitty during long storage, but in this case careful straining will remove the trouble.

BITUMEN EMULSION PAINTS These are prepared from bituminous materials, emulsified with an agent such as soap so that they can be thinned with water, and pigmented with lime-resisting pigments and dyes. Useful for exterior painting on cement stucco, concrete, etc., they give reasonable resistance to weathering. They offer certain advantages in the treatment of damp surfaces, since they do not trap moisture but allow it to escape and dry out along with the moisture contained in the emulsion. The range of colours in which they can be obtained is somewhat limited, and, since bitumen is a dark brown material, all the available colours tend to be of a sombre cast. Subsequent decoration should be carried out with similar materials, as these emulsions have a marked tendency to bleed.

BITUMENS Plastic substances mainly composed of hydrocarbons, generall of dark colour and considerable chemical stability.

Various varieties are known somewhat loosely by the names *asphalt, asphaltum* and *pitch*; in general the terms *asphalt* and *asphaltum* may be taken to refer to the natural bitumen, associated with mineral matter, which is found in many parts of the world of which Trinidad is perhaps the best known, while *pitch* refers to artificial bitumen obtained by distilling coal tars, woods, oil, resins, etc.

BITUMINOUS PAINTS These range in quality from the highest grade black Japans to the cheaper black varnishes, Brunswick blacks and tar blacks. Black Japan, a non-bleeding material, is dealt with in a separate paragraph; the term "bituminous paint", as used in the trade generally, implies a material widely used in industrial painting for the protection of steelwork and for anti-corrosive purposes. It is made from pitch, asphaltum or coumarone resin in combination with heat treated oils and suitable solvents. Its properties include good tenacity, resistance to moisture, a high measure of resistance to chemical and atmospheric conditions, flexibility, and durability. After application it tends to remain soft and plastic, for which reason many authorities claim that it is the most satisfactory finish for iron and steel. The available range of colours is limited, principally to black, dull reds, browns, sombre greens and aluminium, although other shades can be obtained on request. To some extent it is disintegrated by light, a defect which can be overcome by adding aluminium powder to the bitumen. It should not be used under ordinary oil paints because it will bleed through, and for the same reason subsequent painting of bitumen-coated surfaces should be carried out with the same materials. Nor should it be used on top of ordinary oil paint, as the thinners used in the bituminous paint—often solvent naphtha— may well dissolve the previous paint film. (In the case of bituminous paint applied over a red-lead primer, sufficient time—three or four weeks—must elapse for the primer to become thoroughly hard before the next coat is put on.)

Bituminous paints are in considerable use for the painting of bridges, cranes, steel and chemical works installations, dock installations, gas holders and gas works, sewage plant, colliery head gear, etc.

BITUMINOUS PAINTS FOR SPECIAL PURPOSES The firms which specialize in the production of bituminous paints supply a range of special materials for use where normal conditions do not apply. One example is a tasteless, odourless, non-contaminating bitumen solution of great anti-corrosive power, supplied in the form of an enamel, for the internal treatment of water pipes, tanks, reservoirs, pressure filters, brewery vats and food containers. This product is marketed in two forms, in one it can be applied by brush or spray, in the other it is applied hot by a process carried out by specialist operatives employed by the manufacturers of the product. Another example is heat-resisting bituminous paint supplied for the painting of smokestacks, boiler fronts, ducts and pipe systems, which will withstand heat up to a temperature of $260°C$ ($500°F$). A "super-service" bitumen paint is also available for use in extreme corrosive conditions.

BLACK AND GOLD MARBLE Also known as "Porter". A marble which was very popular at one time for the decoration of string-courses, chimney pieces, etc. It is worked from a black ground with a palette of raw and burnt sienna, black and white. The characteristic feature of the marble is that the veins follow a chain-like formation, which can be imitated by using a writing pencil with a rolling, dragging motion.

BLACK ASH A strongly alkaline material sometimes used as a constituent of caustic paint remover.

BLACK JAPAN A bituminous black made from the finest grade of asphaltum cooked with oil and blended with a good copal varnish, thinned with turpentine. The best black Japans for coachwork dry slowly to a thoroughly hard but elastic film, and are non-bleeding; they can be varnished without any greenish discolouration occurring.

Black Japan is heat resisting and is often used as a stoving enamel; even when it is not made for stoving it will withstand heat sufficiently well to make a good radiator paint. It has several other applications, such as when mixed with turpentine to produce a rich walnut floor stain, etc.

BLACK VARNISH This is a very cheap bituminous black made by neutralizing tar and thinning it down with naphtha or similar solvent. Such things as rainwater spouting, when made from iron or asbestos-cement, are often dipped in black varnish before leaving the works, which leads to a good deal of trouble from bleeding, etc., when paint is subsequently applied.

BLACKBOARD PAINT Slightly thixotropic lead-based paint containing a high proportion of slate powder, which dries to a matt finish to produce a non-slip surface for chalk. When the paint is properly compounded it is possible to remove the chalk with ease and without polishing the surface. Although known as blackboard paint, it is available in various colours as well as black, and in fact a dull green is often used as being less tiring to the eyes.

BLANC FIXE An artificially produced form of barytes; chemically it is the same as barytes but differs in its physical structure, which is amorphous instead of crystalline. It is produced by precipitating solutions of barium salts by means of sulphuric acid. It is bulkier, finer in texture and more opaque than the natural pigment and, although more costly, is much superior. Like barytes it loses its opacity when mixed with oil, but it is used considerably in water paint and also as a base for the precipitation of lake pigments and as a constituent of lithopone and titanium white.

BLEACHING Not to be confused with fading. The whitening of a substance due to exposure to light or to chemical agent. Certain colours are bleached by chemical action: Prussian blue, and any mixture of colours containing Prussian blue, are bleached by alkaline attack; ultramarine is bleached by exposure to acid fumes, etc.

BLEACHING OF WOOD Lightening the colour of wood when stains caused by exposure to the weather have to be removed or when variations in the natural colouring of the wood have to be corrected. It is very often carried out with an oxalic acid solution, used hot, applied liberally with an old brush or with a cloth. After application it is allowed to stand for half an hour and then rinsed off. The usual strength is 100 grammes of oxalic acid crystals to one litre of water. Other solutions which are sometimes used consist of hydrogen peroxide, sodium perborate or sodium bisulphite. There are now a number of proprietary wood bleaches on sale which are more effective, more certain and more consistent in their action than home-mixed solutions.

BLEEDER TYPE GUN A spray gun designed for use with low pressure (air-volume) spraying equipment in which a current of air is flowing all the while the plant is in operation. The gun is so called because it allows the air to "bleed" or flow through constantly; pressure on the trigger releases paint into the air stream, whereas in the non-bleeder type of gun air does not flow until the trigger is operated.

BLEEDING The action of any material in penetrating and discolouring coatings applied on top of it. There are many substances which will bleed and stain new coatings in this way. Red pigments used to be notorious in this respect and, although with modern materials the danger is not nearly as common, certain red lakes and dyestuffs still give trouble, particularly when the old paint containing them has been rubbed down and the new coatings applied before the abraded surface has had time to harden off again. Water soluble red dyes in distemper and wallpaper can give rise to trouble, and when these materials are being washed off care is needed to prevent their penetrating the surrounding paintwork.

Bituminous products can cause a great deal of trouble; if oil paint is applied over them it rapidly develops brown stains and its drying is impeded. Anything derived from tar can be expected to bleed; old tar and creosote coatings on exterior work may become weathered to the point where oil paint can be applied without damage, but there is no means of knowing or guaranteeing when the safe point has been reached.

Other materials which will bleed through new coatings are the resinous content of knots, certain kinds of timber heavily impregnated with resin which exudes freely all over the surface, soot penetrating through cracks in the vicinity of chimney breasts, nicotine deposits on the ceilings of public halls and hotel rooms, and copying ink pencil markings. Vandyke brown when ground in oil also shows a tendency to bleed.

The main difficulty with bleeding is that it is usually impossible to remove the offending coating completely, and the only remedy is to apply a buffer coat between the old and new systems. But while such materials as shellac, stop-tar knotting, etc., will often seal the bleeding material quite effectively, they will, if applied over elastic films such as bitumen paint, very soon develop cracks.

BLENDER A short square-ended brush, generally made of sable or ox hair, for blending light and dark colours in shaded effects in signwriting.

BLENDING The operation of producing a gradation of colour from light to dark or from one colour to another. Blending on small scale work can be achieved with a spray, and decorative spraying consists largely of using masks and templates to produce an alternation between hard distinct outlines and soft edges where the spray colour blends into the ground. But on large scale working, when it is required to blend colour either in water paint, oil paint or glaze, the best method is to apply the colours by brush, make the preliminary blending with the brush and complete the blending with hair stipplers.

BLISTERING A defect in painting in which the paint film rises away from the surface in bubbles due to lack of adhesion. Among the factors which give rise to blistering are the following:

(a) Moisture contained within the surface such as when new plasterwork, etc., is painted before it has had time to dry out, when unseasoned wood is painted, or when timber has been fixed in a new building with inadequate priming or without back priming so that moisture is absorbed into the timber from the brickwork.

(b) Moisture introduced into a surface, such as when a surface is painted during wet or foggy weather, or when work which has been washed down is painted before it has had time to dry.

(c) Water introduced into the paint, by means of paint brushes which have been stored in water overnight and put into use before all the water has been removed from them, by means of the careless use of paint strainers lifted straight from a bucket of water, or by the use of paste pigments and paste driers which have been stored under a layer of water.

(d) Resin exuding from knots.

(e) Resinous matter becoming gaseous when heated, such as when timber with a very high resin content is painted and, under the influence of sunlight, develops numerous small blisters which are found to contain no moisture when opened.

(f) The use of soft oily undercoats and old fatty colour.

(g) Surfaces which offer little adhesion to paint being painted without the correct pre-treatment, as in the case of galvanized iron and other zinc coated surfaces.

It has been noticed that dark colours are more prone to blistering than light ones because they absorb more heat.

BLOOMING A milky white cloudiness which sometimes occurs on, or in, work finished in gloss materials; varnish, enamel and hard gloss paints are all liable to be affected.

The term "blooming" covers two distinct types of defects. One, called "crater blooming", takes the form of small pits and depressions in the dried gloss film which cause the light which falls on the surface to be scattered instead of being reflected evenly, giving a hazy appearance. The other type, called "crystalline blooming", is much more common; this consists of a crystalline layer—generally of ammonium sulphate crystals — on the surface of the gloss film. Crystalline bloom can often be removed from the surface by rubbing, but when a surface is pitted by crater bloom its lustre cannot as a rule be restored without recourse to felting down and refinishing.

Considerable research has gone into the subject of blooming, and the exact causes have not yet been fully established. It seems likely that crater blooming is caused by condensation of moisture or dew deposition on the surface before the gloss film is completely dry. Crystalline blooming is known to originate from the presence of sulphur dioxide and ammonia in the atmosphere, but the bloom only occurs when certain atmospheric conditions prevail, and it seems that the conditions leading to condensation of moisture are a factor in this type of bloom also.

The gloss film is most susceptible to these various influences during its drying period, when it is tacky but not fully set. To some extent the formation of bloom can be avoided if attention is paid to this fact. It is good sound trade practice to refrain from applying gloss finishes out of doors late in the day, when a rapid drop in temperature would cause sudden chilling of the partially dried film. In this connection it should be remembered that a rapid fall of temperature can occur just as easily in the summer as in the winter months, and the temptation to proceed with glossing late in the afternoon should be resisted. On indoor work, gloss finishes should not be exposed to draughts or chills during the drying period.

Blooming often occurs near to open gas jets; adequate ventilation is necessary to avoid this, but direct draughts should be avoided. It may also occur when moisture is introduced into the gloss material or on to the surface through carelessness.

Surfaces which have been flatted down must be allowed time to dry out thoroughly before they are varnished, with particular attention to the mouldings and quirks where moisture is liable to lodge. Water-colour graining and glazing must be completely dry before varnish is applied. And, of course, no attempt should be made to apply gloss materials during foggy or misty periods.

When blooming has occurred it may be possible to restore the lustre. A mild case may respond to sponging down with lukewarm water and a brisk rubbing over with a wash-leather. More obstinate cases may yield to treatment by polishing with a mixture of linseed oil and vinegar—some authorities advise linseed oil, vinegar and methylated spirits in equal parts. If these methods fail the only remedy is to felt the work down and refinish it in gloss under good dry conditions.

BLOWING A defect in plastered surfaces caused by the use of imperfectly slaked lime. It takes the form of small craters formed by the blowing of flakes of plaster due to the expansion which takes place when the particles of unslaked lime gradually combine with water after the main body of the plaster has set and hardened. Quite often the defect does not become apparent until the surface has been decorated, and the blowing may continue for a number of years. It is beyond the control of the decorator. The treatment is to cut out the craters and fill them with Keene's or a lime-free filler; if the trouble is too widespread for this, it may be necessary to line the surface.

BLOWLAMP A portable appliance which directs heat upon a given spot and is used to soften up old paintwork in the process known as "burning off". Some types are designed for use with petrol as fuel, others with paraffin, or methylated spirit.

BLOWLAMP PRICKER A small tool for clearing the nipple of a blowlamp when it becomes clogged with carbon.

BLOWN OILS Drying oils, such as linseed oil, castor oil, etc., which have been thickened by a process whereby a rapid stream of air is passed through heated oil without the addition of driers. The nature of the product depends on the operating temperature and the rate of blowing and varies from a lightly bodied oil, suitable for use in paint, to a solid gel suitable for linoleum manufacture.

BLUEING   The adding of a touch of blue to certain white pigments or paints in order to neutralize their yellowish cast and make them appear whiter, as, for example, when lime blue is added to a white distemper to improve its apparent whiteness.

BLUSHING   A milky white filming (the equivalent of "blooming" in varnish and enamel) which spoils the appearance of nitrocellulose lacquers, spirit varnishes and French polish, and is caused when these materials are applied in cold or humid weather. Moisture deposited on the surface reduces the solubility of the resins or the cellulose so that some are precipated out of the solution; the defect is generally confined to lacquers, etc., which dry solely by the evaporation of the solvents.

BOAT VARNISH   A varnish with outstanding properties of water resistance made for application to wood.

BODY   A term which is used freely and rather loosely, so as very often to lead to confusion.
(a) In one sense it is taken to mean the consistency or viscosity of a material, not as measured exactly against some standard, but judged according to the ease with which the material can be spread, the way in which it pours, or the "feel" of the material as it is being stirred. This is perhaps the most usual implication, hence the terms "full-bodied" and "heavy-bodied" as applied to various varnishes and paints.
(b) The term is sometimes used to describe the covering power or hiding power of a paint, although in this connection the word "opacity" would be a better term to use, being less ambiguous.
(c) The term can also be taken to mean the "build" or thickness of a dried paint film.

BODY COLOUR   (a) As applied to oil paint the term refers to a pigment of great opacity or obliterating power.
(b) When applied to artists' materials the term is used to denote an opaque poster colour, as opposed to ordinary water colour which relies for its effect upon its transparency.

BODYING-UP   A term used in French polishing to describe the building-up of a thickness of shellac before the final spiriting off. Bodying-up is carried out with a "rubber", a pad of cotton wool wrapped in linen.

BOILED LINSEED OIL   Linseed oil which has been heated to a fairly high temperature for a number of hours and to which a small proportion of driers has been added in order to increase its property of absorbing oxygen. Boiled oil has higher viscosity than raw oil, is more resistant to moisture, is darker in colour and tends to darken further on exposure to sunlight. It dries more rapidly than raw oil, for which reason a paint containing boiled oil requires less added drier; it produces a hard lustrous coat but the film is inclined to be brittle and liable to crack. Boiled linseed oil is used to produce an oil gloss finishing paint for exterior ironwork, woodwork or stucco where an enamel finish would be considered too expensive, and is also to be preferred to raw. oil as the medium for priming paints for steelwork, etc., on account of its greater viscosity.

BONDERIZING   A chemical treatment whereby small metal units used in building are rendered rust inhibitive and suitable for the reception of paint.

BONE BLACK   A black pigment produced by burning bones and other animal refuse in closed retorts; a good quality bone black is also known as drop black. It is of gold black colour and produces a bluish grey when mixed with white; it is not so strong for tinting purposes as coal tar black and, because it tends to retard the drying of oil, it is generally supplied ground in turps.

BOSUN'S CHAIR   A simple type of seat suspended by means of pulley blocks and operated by one man who is able to lower himself as required. It is used in the painting of small items in elevated positions where access from ladders is not possible and where the expense of erecting a scaffold or suspending a two-man operated cradle is not justified, such as, for example, isolated rainwater pipes or narrow metal strappings on lofty buildings; there are also some types of work where apart from any question of expense or convenience the chair provides the only reasonable form of access, which is often the case in the painting of either the inside or outside of metal smoke stacks. Flagpoles are another item sometimes painted from the bosun's chair.

BRACE   A tube inserted diagonally in a scaffold to give stability and to prevent the tendency for the framework to fold up.

BRACKET   Something which projects to support a weight, as for example the member supporting the cornice of a building, or a light construction supporting a shelf, etc.

BREAK   Vegetable oils are said to break if, when they are heated, a mucilage-like material separates; such a material once separated usually remains insoluble and cannot be re-dissolved with the oil. The term "break" is also applied to the actual mucilage or insoluble matter itself.

BREAKING IN   Generally used in connection with brushes. The process of making a new brush assume a certain shaping or certain characteristics, as when a new paint brush is used in such a way that a compact chisel edge is formed.

BRECHE VIOLET   A very decorative type of marble quarried in the Carrara Mountains; although the quarries are exhausted and the marble no longer produced, examples are often to be seen in public buildings and its colour and pattern make an appeal to decorators. Its basic colour is generally a clean creamy white clouded with delicate tones of blue-grey and it is broken into irregular angular shapes by a system of veining, the main veins being of blue-violet and the secondary veins being in a great variety of colours.

BRIDGING   A term used when a continuous film of paint is not in complete contact with the surface to which it is applied; it generally implies too thick a coating put on without sufficient attention to preparation or application. Common examples of bridging are (a) when paint is applied over unfilled cracks or small holes in plaster or woodwork in such a way as to conceal the gaps, and (b) when thick paint is applied over riveted or bolted portions of steelwork without being forced into the corners around the boltheads or rivets, so that the coating appears complete but is not actually in contact with the steel at these points. Bridging causes a weakness in the paint film which soon leads to the lifting and cracking of the dried film.

BRIDLE   A horizontal scaffold tube secured between two putlogs to give support to intermediate transoms across window openings.

BRIDLING   The process of binding a new paint brush with string in order to shorten the effective length of the bristles. Bridling is essential before a round brush of the old-fashioned type—sash tool, seconds tool or pound brush—is put into use, but such brushes have been very largely superseded by the flat paint brush with a metal ferrule, which cannot be properly bridled. A great advantage of the old-fashioned brush is that the bridling can be released a few turns at a time as the bristle wears down so that, when it is once broken in it retains its most efficient length for quite a long time and outlasts the flat brush by a wide margin.

BRING FORWARD   (a) A term used in the repainting and redecoration of old work when it is felt that certain local areas need an extra coat of paint to make them conform with the rest of the work before undercoating is commenced. For instance, some areas may be noticeably more absorbent than the main body of the work, various parts may have needed stripping and in some places new pieces of timber, etc., may have been inserted. When such areas are picked out and separately painted in order to bring them into line with the rest they are said to have been brought forward.
(b) In some districts the term is used more loosely to mean the general painting of any particular area. For example, in decorating the interior of a house it may be decided to bring one particular room a stage nearer to completion, in which case the painting of that room is referred to as "bringing the room forward"; again, it may be decided to concentrate on completing all the ceilings throughout the house before proceeding further with other parts of the work, in which case the ceilings are said to have been brought forward.

BRISTLE   A term which is used exclusively for the hairs of the hog, pig or boar, hairs which are of the utmost importance in the making of paint

34

brushes. The hairs are those obtained from the neck, shoulders and back of the animal. Bristle possesses certain unique features which make it an outstandingly suitable filling for most types of paint brush. These features are: (a) its resilience. (b) The fact that the filament tapers from root to tip, the root being the stiffest portion. (c) The surface is serrated or barbed, with the serrations pointing towards the tip; it is the barbed surface which has an affinity for paint and holds the paint, for bristle is not absorbent. (d) The tip is split forming what is called the "flag" and, as the bristle wears down, the flag is constantly renewed. (e) The hair is curved.

All these features combine to give a brush filling which is tough and springy and capable of standing up to hard wear, yet which has a fine soft tip enabling paint to be laid off without brush marks; the barbed surface holds the paint but the taper of the hair and the direction of the barbs force the paint to flow outwards towards the tip rather than inwards towards the handle, thereby assisting even distribution of the paint on the surface. The curve of the bristle is used by the brush manufacturers to produce a brush of good shape with a narrow chisel edge.

"Pure bristle" and "All bristle" are terms protected by law guaranteeing that the brushes so marked contain 100% hog bristles with no adulteration.

BROKEN COLOUR   A term describing any multi-coloured effect in which the patches of various colours are irregular in size, shape and distribution because their production is to some extent accidental. Such effects can be produced in a variety of ways, including the following:
(a) Blending of various wet opaque colours on a previously prepared ground colour.
(b) Use of transparent glazes, suitably tinted and applied over a solid ground colour and subsequently stippled with the hair stippler.
(c) Partial lifting of wet colour or wet glaze (in order to expose the ground colour in irregular patches) by means of manipulation with absorbent rags, wash-leathers, pieces of crumpled paper, steel combs, rubber stipplers of various patterns, sponges, etc.
(d) Distribution of spots of colour by means of sponge stippling, etc.

BROKEN WHITE   White paint—or other decorative material—which has been modified so as to avoid the somewhat harsh effect produced when a large area is treated in pure white and yet which is not tinted sufficiently to produce any definite colour. Generally (although not always) the pure white is broken by the addition of a very small quantity of a yellow pigment when broken white is required.

BRONZE POWDERS   Metallic powders made from alloys of copper and zinc or aluminium. Ready mixed bronze paints become dull and leaden when stored for any length of time; to achieve a good lustre it is better to mix the bronze powder with a suitable medium immediately before use. For display work, exhibition work and other types of work where durability is not an important consideration, bronze powders are now available ready mixed in quick-drying media in aerosol packs.

BRONZING A term with two connotations.
(a) The application of imitation gold or other metals either in powder form or in leaves.
(b) The characteristic metallic lustre displayed by certain highly coloured pigments, such as Prussian blue, when used in full strength.

BRONZING LACQUERS Transparent lacquers intended for application to bright metals in order to preserve their lustre and enrich their colour.

BRONZING MEDIUM OR LIQUID A medium specially formulated for use with aluminium or bronze powders.

BRUNSWICK BLACK A hard quick-drying bituminous black with a fair degree of heat resistance, used for painting stoves, etc.

BRUNSWICK BLUE A reduced quality of Prussian blue.

BRUNSWICK GREEN Brunswick blue combined with a pale chrome yellow.

BRUSH The traditional tool used for the spreading and distribution of paint, and consisting of either animal hair, vegetable fibre or synthetic filament secured to a suitable handle.

BRUSH FILLER A filling composition, used for producing a smooth level surface by filling up small indentations, thinned down to such a consistency that it can be applied with the brush.

BRUSH GRAINING The simplest form of wood effect obtained by drawing a clean duster brush or drag through newly applied graining colour.

BRUSH KEEPER A metal container, fitted with a hinged lid, in which paint brushes may be suspended in a suitable liquid while not in use; when the lid is closed dust is prevented from entering and the evaporation of the liquid is checked. As a general rule, far too little attention is paid to the care and maintenance of brushes, and brush keepers are not used as freely as they should be.

BRUSH MARKS Ridges left in a paint film by the brush.

BRUSH MARKS IN ENAMEL When this defect is seen it may be due to a fault in the enamel, which ought to flow out and eliminate all brush marks, but it is usually due to faulty application of the undercoat. Brush marks in the matt finish of an undercoat are not very noticeable, but become extremely prominent when a gloss coating is applied.

BUBBLING A defect caused by bubbles of air or bubbles of solvent vapour appearing in a paint film.

BUFFER COAT Any coating which serves to insulate one material from another. For example, if an oil scumble or a coat of clear varnish is to be applied over a metallic paint, a buffer coat consisting of a thin coating of clear lacquer is necessary between the two. In most metallic paints the metal floats to the surface of the medium, and unless a buffer coat is used the metal particles may "work up" in the scumble or varnish; moreover, the oil in the scumble or varnish would have an oxidizing effect upon the bronze. The buffer coat provides the insulation which prevents this.

BUFFING The polishing of a finishing material, usually a nitrocellulose finish, with abrasives and polishes.

BUFFING COMPOUNDS Materials for the buffing or polishing of a finishing coating, available in bar, paste or spray composition form. They are composed of various abrasives of very fine grit size, typical abrasives being powdered pumice, tripoli, rouge, lime, magnesium oxide, silica, silicon carbide and emery.

BUILD The thickness of a paint or varnish film.

BUILDING REGULATIONS The regulations which became operative in 1966 laying down standards governing the structural stability, fire resistance, thermal insulation and drainage of a building under the terms of the Public Health Act. Not to be confused with the Construction Regulations which relate to the safety, health and welfare of operatives.

BURLAP A course kind of canvas occasionally used as a wall hanging and sometimes subsequently painted. It can be supplied on a stout paper backing or in the unprepared and unbacked form. When backed it is trimmed with a knife and straightedge and is pasted and hung like wallpaper; when unbacked it is hung dry, the wall being pasted, and the pieces are allowed to overlap, a good joint being obtained by cutting through the overlap with a sharp knife.

BURNING OFF The softening of a paint film by the application of heat, and its removal by scrapers or shavehooks.

BURNISHING Polishing or improving the lustre of a material by means of friction. In the painting trade the term is generally used in connection with the polishing of gold leaf. Gold leaf which has been applied with a mordant of either Japan gold size or old oil gold size is burnished with a wad of cotton wool to give it as lustrous a finish as possible. Gold leaf used for glass gilding with a mordant of isinglass is burnished when dry with a small pad of warmed cotton wool before it is backed up with paint.

BURR WALNUT The burrs in walnut generally occur in a fairly old tree. Often they are caused by a growth which the tree puts out to surround an insect which is boring into it and causing irritation; sometimes they are the result of the trunk being bruised, or of a side shoot which has been struck off causing local damage to the trunk. The wood displaying these markings is found in the lower part of the trunk and is generally cut as a veneer. The graining of burr walnut is worked on a deep warm cream ground; water colour graining is employed, the palette consisting of Vandyke brown, burnt sienna and black.

BUTANE A flammable gas derived from petroleum; it provides one of the fuels that can be used to operate a blowtorch. See *LPG Containers.*

BUTT JOINTS A term used in paperhanging to indicate that the paper is hung with the edges lying side by side and not overlapping at all.

BUTTING TUBE A very short piece of tube used in tubular scaffolding to make it possible for a diagonal brace to be fastened to a standard with right-angled couplers instead of with swivel couplers, thus giving extra strength.

C

CADMIUM A bluish white metal resembling tin, and from whence various pigments are derived. Hence:

CADMIUM RED This is a compound of cadmium, sulphur and selenium; a brilliant red pigment, very opaque and with good staining power, stable, fast to light, unaffected by exposure to sulphur fumes, and with considerable resistance to heat. Used as an artists' colour and also in the making of vitreous enamels. Reduced qualities, lower in cost than the pure pigment, are used as a replacement for vermilion.

CADMIUM YELLOW A sulphide of the metal cadmium; a fine permanent pigment ranging from pale yellow to orange, more expensive than lead chrome but not affected by exposure to sulphur fumes as the lead chromes are, and used as an artists' colour and for high class decorative work. Although a derivative of sulphur it is quite inert and can be mixed with white lead or other lead pigments without reaction, but inferior grades may contain free sulphur which would react with pigments containing lead or copper and cause discolouration.

CADMOPONE YELLOW OR CADMIUM LITHOPONE A durable pale yellow lower in cost than pure cadmium yellow; by modifications in the manufacture a range of colours extending from yellow to deep crimson can be produced. Unlike the chromes, cadmium lithopone is heat-resisting, but if mixed with lead or copper pigments will cause discolouration.

CAKING The settling of the pigment particles of a paint into a hard mass which cannot readily be redispersed by stirring.

CALCINATION The process of roasting, involving the use of furnaces of various types, which among other things is employed in the preparation of certain pigments.

CALCIUM A chemical element; the basis of lime; a component of many chemical compounds. Hence:

CALCIUM CARBONATE A substance of great importance to the painter since it provides a material used in decorating and also a surface upon which decoration is applied. Calcium carbonate is derived from natural chalk or limestone and is the substance commonly known as whiting, which is the basis of soft distempers, cheap water paints and putty. Lime plaster, used as a skimming coat, is made by adding water to quicklime which in turn is obtained by calcining chalk or limestone, and when the skimming sets and hardens it does so by a process of "carbonation", whereby it reverts to the form of calcium carbonate.

CALCIUM HYDROXIDE Calcium hydroxide or slaked lime is formed by adding water to calcium oxide.

CALCIUM OXIDE Calcium oxide or quicklime is obtained by burning chalk or limestone.

CALCIUM PLUMBATE A metal primer in which the main pigment constituent is calcium plumbate prepared in a polymerized oil vehicle or, as is more usual, in a medium based on phenolic resin and tung oil, producing a paint film of outstanding weather resistance. It possesses properties that make it a very useful primer for galvanized iron, zinc sheeting, iron and steel. Its particular value for galvanized iron and zinc sheeting lies in the fact that it is the most convenient material for priming these metals on site work, since it can be used successfully direct upon the metal without the necessity for any prior etching or phosphating and without waiting for the surface to become weathered. On steelwork its protective and rust-inhibitive properties are due to both cathodic and anodic action, and it has much less tendency to blister than a red lead primer, it possesses good covering capacity and opacity, and its pale colour is more readily obscured by subsequent paint coatings than the strong colour of red lead. Calcium plumbate is sometimes mentioned as a suitable primer for woodwork, too, but there is little evidence to suggest that it offers any advantage in this connection which would lead to its replacing the conventional lead and aluminium primers. Some benefit might be gained by using it in situations where galvanized metal comes into contact with wood, such as, for instance, where a metal window frame abuts a wooden sill or casing, since the one primer would serve both surfaces without the necessity for cutting in, but this advantage has only a limited value.

CALCIUM SULPHATE The basis of a number of the plasters used in building, including the types referred to as plaster of Paris, retarded hemihydrate plasters, anhydrous gypsum plasters, Keene's and Parian cements and anhydrite. Such plasters are derived from the rock gypsum except in the case of anhydrite, which is obtained from naturally occurring anhydrite (or calcium sulphate with no water in its chemical composition).

CALOR GAS A trade name for butane (and propane). See *LPG Containers.*

CAMEL HAIR Animal hair used as a filling in certain types of brushes, but not, as its name would imply, obtained from the camel. It is actually *squirrel hair,* obtained from the tail of this animal, and its misleading name is said to be a corruption of "Keml's Hair" from the name of a Dutch artist who introduced it. It is very soft and when it is moistened has no springiness, so that for ordinary paint brushes, water colour brushes, or writers it is of no value at all; for glass work, however, its lack of spring may be an advantage and some signwriters prefer a camel hair pencil for this work because of the way it clings to the glass. For the same reason it is used for the mops and size brushes used in glass gilding, when its soft floppiness enables the isinglass to be flooded on to the glass very freely just where it is required. The softness of the hair also makes it ideal for the dabbers which are used to press gold leaf into moulded and carved work.

CANADA BALSAM Resinous matter, exuding from conifers, which solidifies when exposed to the air but which remains plastic and is used as a plasticiser in certain spirit varnishes. Fairly pure and transparent.

CANDLENUT OIL Similar in properties to tung oil; obtained from the fruit of the *Aleurites triloba* found in Fiji.

CANNONING A process in brush manufacture whereby the brush is given a bevel so that it is shaped ready for immediate use without having to be broken in.

CANTILEVER SCAFFOLD Also called a jib scaffold or trussed scaffold. A scaffold formed with tubes cantilevered out of a window or other opening so as not to obstruct the pavement on a busy throughfare.

CANVAS A coarse unbleached cloth made of hemp or flax, used in a variety of ways; for example (a) as a wall-hanging, which is often subsequently painted, (b) stretched over a wooden frame, as a surface upon which easel pictures are painted, and (c) stretched over a light framing to form screens, light roofing for caravans, etc.
   When canvas is to be painted it should first be given a coat of hot weak size in order to insulate the fabric from the paint; this is because the vegetable oils used in paint have a hardening effect upon the fibres and make them become brittle and easily torn. Strong coats of size should be avoided; the object is to impregnate the fabric, not to stop the suction.

CAPILLARITY The force of attraction between dissimilar substances. The phenomenon is seen when a fine tube is placed vertically in a liquid, the surface of the liquid inside the tube assuming a different level from the liquid outside the tube; if the liquid is water, it will be found that the level of the water inside the tube is higher than the level outside. The condition only occurs if the diameter of the tube is small, and the smaller the diameter the higher the water will rise; hence tubes which exhibit this property are called capillary or "hair-like" tubes. The condition also occurs between two flat plates of glass or similar material which are vertical and parallel. All substances with pores of sufficient size are capable of sucking up water by virtue of capillarity; hence the importance of the subject to the painter.

CAPITAL The crowning feature of a column or pilaster.

CARBOLIC ACID Otherwise phenol. Of considerable importance to the painting trade because, when treated with acqueous solutions of formalde- hyde, it forms the basis of certain synthetic resins from which paints and varnishes with good resistance to alkaline and corrosive conditions and to the effects of industrial atmospheres and sea air are obtained. Carbolic acid is also directly useful to the painter and decorator in another con- nection: glue size putrefies rapidly in hot weather, but a small quantity of carbolic acid (2%) added to the size will prevent this and act as a preservative.

CARBON BLACK OR GAS BLACK Practically pure carbon in an extremely fine state of division, produced by the incomplete combustion of natural marsh gas. An intense black of good staining strength but giving brownish-grey when reduced with white, light in weight and with high oil absorption. It is non-greasy, works well with water and fairly well with oil.

CARBONATION The process by which a substance combines with carbon or carbon compounds to become a carbonate. As mentioned in a previous paragraph, lime plasters undergo a process of carbonation; the drying and hardening of such plasters consists of the evaporation of their water con- tent and a slower and more gradual process of absorbing carbon dioxide from the atmosphere. This is of importance to the painter because if such plasters are painted too soon and are sealed with an impervious layer of oil paint they will be prevented from hardening properly and will always remain weak.

CARDIGLIO MARBLE A highly decorative type of marble, quarried in Sicily; a grey variety of the better known cipollino, with markings similar to the strong veins and bands of the latter but in grey instead of green.

CARMINE A brilliant deep fiery scarlet pigment prepared from cochineal; it works well in oil or water, and is used as an artists' colour and as a glaze colour, but fades badly.

CARPENTRY Structural woodwork, as opposed to joinery.

CARTOON A word that is frequently misunderstood and misused; it is a full-size working drawing, generally on strong detail paper. On important

41

mural work the design is fully worked out on the cartoon and then transferred to the wall. Very often cartoons are brought to a high degree of finish; the most famous cartoons in art history are the Raphael cartoons in the Victoria and Albert Museum, which should be seen and studied by every decorator.

CARTOUCHE   An ornamental scroll, usually providing space for a lettered inscription.

CARTRIDGE PAPER   A stout rough-surfaced paper, originally used for cartridge making and now used for drawing, stencil cutting, etc. It is available in numerous weights and grades.

CASEIN   The albuminoid or proteid in milk, extracted by treating skimmed milk with hydrochloric acid. It is of importance as a binding agent in soluble distempers supplied in powder form. Casein is insoluble in water but is freely soluble in alkaline solutions. The powdered casein is mixed with slaked lime and borax together with suitable pigments and stainers so that when water is added the casein, acted upon by the lime, becomes water soluble; when the distemper is exposed to the air the lime is carbonated and the casein reverts to its insoluble form. The distemper colour, therefore, when given sufficient time to harden presents a hard surface which can be sponged down without being softened.

CASEMENT WINDOW   A window casement which is hinged vertically to the frame, opening inward or outward.

CASING WHEEL   A circular cutter, mounted on a wooden handle, used in paperhanging. Its purpose is to cut and fit the paper rapidly and cleanly around architraves, door casings, etc., instead of the more laborious process of finishing with the scissors. See also *Corner Knife*.

CASTOR OIL   Derived from the castor plant which grows wild in nearly all tropical and sub-tropical countries, and which is cultivated chiefly in India, Brazil and East Africa. The oil remains liquid at low temperatures, it does not thin rapidly with a rise in temperature and it is notable for its high viscosity. Untreated castor oil is a non-drying oil and is used as a plasticiser; when polymerized and dehydrated it develops good drying properties; dehydrated castor oil has properties intermediate between linseed and tung oil. It produces a paint film which is flexible and durable, and when blended with synthetic resins gives good resistance to moisture and to chemical conditions.

CASTOR WHEELS   Wheels which enable a mobile tower to be formed from a tubular steel frame or a wooden scaffolding frame. Castor wheels can be fixed or swivelled, plain or fitted with tyres, and can incorporate a locking device.

CATALYST   A substance which, without undergoing a change itself, assists in producing a chemical change in other bodies or substances. The term is often seen in technical literature, as many of the chemical reactions used in the production of paint material require the presence or assistance of a catalyst. The painter and decorator is directly concerned with the use of a catalyst when he adds driers to paint, since some of the metallic oxides used as driers act in catalytic manner by absorbing oxygen from the atmosphere and passing it on to the oil in the paint, thereby speeding up its rate of oxidation. Many of the modern epoxy resin paints, wood finishes, etc., rely for their setting and for the development of their distinctive features upon the addition of a catalyst which is added by the painter and decorator immediately before the material is required for use.

CATALYST SPRAYING The process of spraying simultaneously a protective coating and a catalyst additive, where the two materials cannot be premixed because of incompatibility or where the materials have insufficient pot life to permit of application by conventional spraying equipment. A twin-headed spray gun is used so that the two materials are mixed in the spray pattern after they have left the gun and before they reach the surface. The gun has its head fitted with a standard atomizing and fluid nozzle but has another nozzle at the side of the head which feeds a controlled amount of catalyst into the atomized paint when the trigger is depressed. Two pressure feed tanks are used, one for the basic material and the other for the catalyst. The pressures are regulated separately, and because the proportion of catalyst to material is critical the catalyst tank has two regulators to compensate for any fluctuation in the main air line pressure. In addition there is a flow meter in the catalyst line so that once the correct rate of flow has been established it can be verified visually when required. The air cleaning and regulating gear used with the equipment is the standard pattern. The pressure feed tanks are similar to standard tanks except that corrosion-resistant metals and coatings are used for those parts which come in contact with the fluids.

CATHODE The negative plate in electrolysis.

CAUSTIC (Adjective) Burning, hot or corrosive.

CAUSTIC PAINT REMOVERS Strong caustic solutions, thickened to a paste by the addition of whiting, flour or starch to make them hold to a surface and to prevent them from splashing; they soften old paint films by saponifying them. They are rather crude materials and there are several drawbacks to their use.
(a) If used on porous surfaces, such as wood or plaster, the solution is absorbed into the surface and it is very difficult to remove it completely; any that remains is liable to discolour or saponify the new paint coating.
(b) A thorough wash down is necessary to try to remove all traces of the alkaline material and sometimes a wash with weak acid (such as vinegar) is used to try to neutralize the alkali; but this is very haphazard as there is no means of control or of knowing when the point of neutralization is reached.
(c) The plentiful use of water for washing down raises the grain of wood, so that extra time has to be spent in rubbing down and filling.

(d) These paint removers have a harmful effect upon the skin and are destructive to clothing and to bristle brushes.
(e) They have a solvent effect upon aluminium and zinc.

CAUSTIC PICKLE   A time-saving system, adopted by many firms, where a large cask containing a caustic soda solution is kept in the paint shop. Dirty paint cans returned from jobs are immersed in the cask so that the alkaline solution may soften the paint and clean them; thus the time that would otherwise be wasted in burning them out is saved. (Aluminium and zinc should not be placed in pickle because these metals are softened by alkali.)

CEDAR   A type of wood which sometimes presents difficulties to the painter; it has an oily nature which affects the drying and adhesion of paint. Generally the trouble can be overcome by scrubbing the wood with pure turps and a stiff brush to remove the oily residue; sometimes a wash with acetone is recommended. Following this treatment an aluminium primer should be used.

CEILINGS, DECORATION OF   Unless some special reason presents itself, it is correct when painting or papering ceilings to begin at the window and work away from it.

CELLULOSE   The principal carbohydrate constituent of many woody plants and vegetable fibres.

CELLULOSE COATINGS—PAINTS AND LACQUERS   These are based on chemically treated cellulose compounds with suitable solvents to keep them in solution, plasticisers to give flexibility, resins to give gloss and adhesion, and suitable pigments to provide colour. They are widely used in the motor car industry and in industrial finishing; their application to house painting and decorating is more limited.

The fundamental difference between cellulose materials and oil paint films is that cellulose paints dry entirely by the evaporation of the volatile solvent. They are more suitable to application with the spray than the brush (a) because their rate of drying is so rapid, and (b) because the dried film remains soluble in the cellulose solvents so that each coat softens the previous ones; this can be an advantage because each succeeding coat is welded into the previous ones, resulting in a completely homogeneous film. Special qualities are formulated for brush application, but their use on large surfaces is still limited. The speed of drying is an advantage owing to the saving of time which is effected, several coats being applied with only a short interval between. But, of course, the fact that spray application is generally necessary means that considerable masking up is required, so some of the time advantage is lost.

Cellulose paints produce hard films resistant to abrasion and general wear and tear, but although this hardness is often an advantage it can lead to cracking and flaking if the materials are used on soft woods or surfaces subject to much expansion and contraction. They have the advantage of being unaffected by alkalis and are immune to fungoid and mould growths.

There is a difficulty in applying cellulose paints over existing coatings as the cellulose solvents are so strong that they act as a stripper on oil paint films. Another disadvantage is their lack of "build", which necessitates a greater number of coats to achieve a satisfactory job. There are also statutory regulations to be observed about the storage and use of cellulose materials.

The use of cellulose paints in painting and decorating work is therefore bounded by several considerations, but a wide range of these products is available for various special purposes, such as the finishing of bar counters, the spraying of machinery, handrails, etc., and the production of metallic finishes. Cellulose is also used in various forms of spatter, decorative spray work and certain multi-coloured effects.

CELLULOSE PASTES A number of cellulose-based adhesives for use in paperhanging are now available; among the advantages they offer is the fact that even if not used for some time after mixing they will not deteriorate or putrefy. They are clear and colourless and it is claimed for them that they will not stain the most delicate paper even if the face of the paper is smeared; this claim, although correct up to a point, should be treated with reserve, as paste of any description when allowed on the face of a paper will loosen the colour so that a papering brush passed over the smear will dislodge some colour and leave a mark on the surface; it is just as important for the paperhanger to be skilful and scrupulously clean when using cellulose paste as when using any other fixative.

When cellulose paste is used, the same product, suitably thinned, should be used for sizing prior to papering; on no account should glue size be used for sizing if the use of a cellulose paste is intended. A heavy duty cellulose paste has now been produced for the purpose of hanging pvc fabrics and papers and various other kinds of wall hanging. It is supplied in powder form and contains a fungicidal agent; it is prepared for use by mixing with cold water.

CEMENT A term used to describe various adhesive substances which are applied as a paste and which harden to a stone-like consistency. To the painter and decorator these are the commonest applications of the term:—
(i) Portland cement. Calcinated lime and clay used as an external rendering to buildings in the form of cement stucco and also used in the floating coats for Keene's cement and other gypsum plasters, as well as being the essential ingredient in concrete, asbestos-cement sheeting, etc. It is made by burning limestone and clay together at a high temperature until a clinkered mass is formed, which is then ground to a powder; when water is added to the powder it replaces the water driven off in the burning and combines chemically with it to set into a hard mass. It is highly alkaline and is very destructive to oil paint; very often it remains very strongly alkaline for a considerable time.
(ii) Gypsum cement. A name often used to describe anhydrous gypsum plasters.
(iii) High alumina cements, often known as ciment fondu, and made by burning limestone and bauxite, the cooled mass being ground to a fine powder. They are very dark in colour and harden rapidly. Though not nearly so alkaline as Portland cement, it is wise to test them for alkalinity

before painting. Their moisture content, however, is as great as that of Portland cement, and if not given adequate time to dry out the pressure of moisture may be sufficient to force off an impervious coating. Before painting, they should be brushed down with a stiff fibre brush to remove any loose particles of efflorescence.

(iv) Hydraulic cements, or Roman cement, made by burning a naturally occurring cement rock and reducing it to a powder. They vary in colour from yellow to reddish brown. The exterior rendering of stucco fronts during the 19th century was of this type and some natural cements are still marketed under the name of "Roman" cement or "Natural Portland" cement. They should be tested for alkalinity before painting.

(v) Fixative cements of various kinds, such as, for example, those used for fixing lead foil, etc.

(vi) The cements used for securing the bristles into the binding of a brush, for which purpose vulcanized rubber or synthetic resins are generally used nowadays.

CEMENT PAINTS   These fall into two classes:
(i) The type which is composed basically of Portland cement with the addition of extenders, waterproofers and accelerating agents; this type of material is usually supplied in powder form and is mixed with water immediately before use. It is not too easy to spread with a brush and dries with a fairly rough finish. It provides a reasonably priced treatment for such surfaces as concrete, cement rendering, stucco, etc., because being similar in composition to these materials it suffers no adverse effects from their alkaline nature; it is also useful where the presence of steam or a constant condition of humidity would preclude the use of ordinary paints, and on damp surfaces both old and new where paints of other types would be unsuitable. However, it should not be used on new calcium sulphate plasters. The instructions provided by the manufacturers for mixing and applying cement paint should be strictly adhered to.

(ii) The type which consists of Portland cement used as the pigment or filler in a medium of linseed oil or oilvarnish. This material is used as a primer for steel, especially where the steel is exposed to concentrations of acid. It must be used within a few days of mixing as it deteriorates quickly when stored.

CEMENT PRIMER   This is one of those terms which is often used loosely and which may cause confusion. A cement primer is a priming paint composed of Portland cement in a suitable vehicle as mentioned in the last paragraph. Very often the term is used by painters, paint salesmen and others when they really mean a primer suitable for use on new cement—in other words, as a synonym for alkali resisting primer.

CENTRIFUGING   An industrial finishing process somewhat similar to barrelling or tumbling, except that the items to be painted are placed in a cylindrical basket and rotated at very high speed; at a certain point in the process a drain cock is opened and surplus paint allowed to run out. It is essentially a one-coat process.

CENTRING OF WALLPAPER This becomes necessary when a paper with a large prominent pattern is being hung; it means plotting beforehand where the various lengths of paper will lie so that the pattern appears nicely balanced in relation to the shape of the room. For example, in hanging a ceiling paper with big pattern, the exact centre of a pattern—or the edge of a pattern—is made to coincide with the centre of the ceiling, so that the number of repeats on either side of the centre is exactly balanced. Another example concerns the hanging of wallpaper; on a prominent feature of the room, such as the chimney breast, the paper is centred so that the repeats are balanced symmetrically. Again, when walls are panelled with a stiling border the pattern will be centred in each panel. A variation may occur when the mantelpiece is not placed centrally on the chimney breast; the paperhanger here must use his judgment and may decide that the mantel is a more important feature than the chimney breast itself and centre the pattern on the mantelpiece.

CERESINE WAX Used as a substitute for beeswax; a petroleum product obtained from Galician "earth wax", harder than paraffin wax and dazzling white in colour.

CESSING An alternative form of the term "cissing". For full details see *Cissing*.

CHALK Soft white limestone, carbonate of lime. A composition made from this is used in marking and setting out signs and decorative work. Coloured chalk is available as well as white chalk, but for setting out on paintwork the use of coloured chalk should be avoided wherever possible, as it contains dyestuffs which stain the paint and leave permanent marks upon it.

CHALK BOARD PAINT See *Blackboard Paint*.

CHALK LINE or SNAP LINE A length of thin string or twine which when rubbed with a block of chalk provides the means of setting out a straight line.

CHALKING The process whereby the surface of a paint film breaks down and becomes loose and powdery, due to the disintegration of the binding medium. Generally it is caused by the action of the weather; paint rarely chalks on interior work.

Chalking, unless it occurs prematurely, is not necessarily a drawback, firstly, because the paint retains some measure of its protective power and, secondly, because a chalking surface is easily prepared for repainting by means of a good rubbing down. But the early development of chalking is a serious fault due either to the quality of the paint, the use of an unsuitable paint or inadequate preparation.

Certain pigments such as white lead and titanium have a tendency to chalking, especially when exposed to sea air; where severe conditions are to be expected a paint should be selected which is so compounded as to

C

resist the tendency. The use of cheap paints may give rise to chalking if they contain an excess of barytes. Flat oil paint is unsuitable for outdoor use for two reasons; lithopone, which is generally used as the base pigment, has a strong tendency to chalk when used out of doors, and in any case the oil content of the paint is not sufficient to protect the pigment against outdoor conditions. Chalking will also occur if a paint is used on a surface absorbent enough to deprive it of some of its binding medium, so a cut price job which does not allow of the suction being adequately stopped is liable to this fault.

CHAMFER   The bevel which is formed by cutting off an arris diagonally, or by paring the arris. A hollow chamfer or concave chamfer, formed with the gouge, is a groove instead of a flat bevel. The word is derived from French roots which mean literally a "break-corner".

CHARCOAL   Wood which has been partially burnt. Sticks of willow charcoal, supplied by artists' colourmen, are excellent for the preparation of cartoons and the marking out of mural or decorative work on light coloured grounds.

CHARRING   The charring which occurs when woodwork is carelessly burnt off destroys the resinous nature of the wood and makes it greasy, so that the adhesion of the new paint film is affected.

CHECK ROLLER   A tool used in graining, to suggest the dark-coloured pores in oak. It consists of a number of serrated metal discs mounted on a wooden handle. One type of check roller is sold with a clip-on attachment of a mottler, which moistens the discs as they rotate. End finishers are a small type of check roller which permit the top and bottom angles of a panel to be completed without leaving a gap.

CHECKING   A form of cracking in which very fine cracks which do not penetrate the top coat of paint are distributed over the surface like a fine pattern.

CHEESY   A paint or varnish film is said to be cheesy when, although dry, it is rather soft.

CHEMICAL CHANGES   A chemical change is said to occur when a chemical combination takes place and the properties of the product or products are different from those of the consituents, or when a chemical action is accompanied by a change in the properties of the combining substances (the formation of new substances being due to the regrouping of atoms to form different molecular groups), and when the change is *permanent* in the sense that it is impossible to reverse the change by mechanical means. An example of a chemical change relevant to painting and decorating is the change which takes place when a vegetable drying oil, such as linseed oil, is exposed to the air, absorbing and combining with oxygen from the atmosphere in order to change from a liquid to a dry, tough, leathery substance called linoxyn.

CHEMICAL REACTION The chemical action of one substance upon another.

CHEMICAL SYMBOLS These are used as a convenient form of shorthand when describing chemical reactions, etc., and an understanding of their use is essential if the full benefit is to be derived from technical literature. The principle involved is that each element is given a distinctive letter of the alphabet, or a recognized combination of letters, e.g., O for oxygen, C for carbon, H for hydrogen, Pb for lead, and so on. As a simple illustration of their use, we might instance the symbol for water, H_2O, representing two atoms of hydrogen and one atom of oxygen combined to form a molecule of water.

CHEMICALLY RESISTANT PAINTS Paints formulated for use in situations where contact with chemicals (e.g., acids, alkalis, alcohols, mineral oils etc.) is to be expected.

CHEVRON A zig-zag moulding, commonly used in Norman architecture.

CHILLING Subjecting a material to the effects of a low temperature. Some materials are very susceptible to chilling during storage; varnish, for example, which has been exposed to severe cold will be found to contain innumerable small lumps of hard coagulated matter rendering it quite unfit for use, while water paint which has been exposed to frost will develop a crumbly consistency due to the breakdown of the emulsion; it is essential that such materials should be stored at a fair temperature and protected against the effects of cold.

Chilling can also have an adverse effect on materials after application. Varnishes, enamels and other gloss finishes are very sensitive to temperature changes during their drying period and if they become chilled at a certain stage they are very liable to bloom (see *Blooming*). Certain bituminous emulsions are liable to break down when exposed to severe frost, causing free water to be released, and for this reason it is safer when using these materials on steelwork to apply them over a red lead or similar protective primer rather than direct to the metal.

CHINA CLAY A fine white amorphous powder formed as a result of the decomposition of granite, and found extensively in many parts of the world, including Devon and Cornwall in this country. It is used to some extent as an extender in oil paints because of its low specific gravity, which helps to prevent heavy pigments from settling, but if used in excess it gives the paint a "soapy" working quality and weakens the dried film. It is also used as a flatting agent in flat oil paints and undercoats, as a base for the preparation of lake pigments, and in the production of ultramarine blue.

CHINA WOOD OIL or TUNG OIL A binding medium which is of the utmost importance in modern paint; it is obtained from the seed pods of several varieties of the aleurites or tung tree, found extensively in the region of the Yang Tse Kiang river but now being cultivated in parts of the

British Commonwealth as well as in America and Russia. It is pale amber in colour, dull in appearance and has an unpleasant taste and smell; it has a high specific gravity and a very high refractive index. It dries rapidly, polymerizing readily on heating. It cannot be used by the painter in its raw state because of the very careful heat treatment needed to render it suitable for use as a paint or varnish medium; unless properly heat treated it webs or frosts upon drying. The heat treated oil is quicker drying than linseed oil and has much greater resistance to water; it is also considerably more resistant to alkaline attack. It is extensively used in conjunction with natural and synthetic resins in a wide variety of paints and finishes, and its significance in modern paint manufacture cannot be over-estimated; it plays an essential part also in many alkali resisting primers, marine paints and boat varnishes.

CHINESE BLUE   A refined form of Prussian blue with good colour and a fine bronze lustre.

CHINESE INSECT WHITE   The deposit of an insect, a parasite on Asiatic trees. Used in the East like a beeswax, and sometimes exported from there.

CHINESE LACQUER   Obtained from the sap of a tree which is native to China; it is in the form of a thick, milky emulsion. When purified, this is applied thinly to a surface and hardens to a tough dark film which is very durable and takes a good polish. The famous Chinese lacquer ware relies for its effect on the application of numerous thin coats of this material.

CHINESE RED   Also known as American vermilion, chrome red, Derby red and Persian red; it is a chromate of lead.

CHINESE WHITE   The name under which zinc oxide was first introduced. Chinese white is now the recognized term for zinc oxide used in water as an artists' colour.

CHIPPING   A term with two meanings:
(i) A fault which takes the form of a dried paint film flaking off to expose the previous coatings, generally as the result of accidental damage or severe wear and tear. For instance, chipping is likely to occur on skirting boards, the bottom rails of doors or on stair treads and risers as a result of these surfaces being kicked, particularly after redecoration has taken place without the old paint coatings having been stripped. The possibility of chipping taking place is increased if at the time of redecoration the old paint work is not thoroughly prepared to give "key" to the new paint coating. Where a drastic change of colour is intended, from a light coloured finish to a dark one, or vice versa, it is safer to strip those parts of the work which are liable to be knocked or chipped; otherwise, the chipping which is almost bound to occur will be most unsightly. Floor finishes are very liable to chipping because of the constant pounding they receive from the passage of feet; paints and varnishes intended for application to cement or concrete floors or to lino should be sufficiently tough to withstand the abrasion, and the cement must be bone dry before painting. Stained floors need

thorough preparation before fresh coatings are applied and the use of cheap brittle stains should be avoided because of the danger of chipping.

(ii) Chipping, to the industrial painter, means the removal of paint, rust or mill scale from steel or ironwork by means of striking the surface rapidly and repeatedly with chipping hammers or pneumatic tools. Chipping followed by wire brushing is easily the most widely used method of cleaning steelwork for painting; it is tedious work and rarely effects a complete and efficient removal of the scale, but very often it is the only practical method that can be employed on an existing structure.

CHIPPING HAMMER or SCALING HAMMER   A hammer sold for the purpose of scaling steelwork by hand, consisting of a boat-shaped or wedge-shaped head with a sharp nose, set on a wooden handle.

CHLORINATED RUBBER   Chlorinated rubber paints are of considerable value as protective films on surfaces exposed to severe chemical and corrosive conditions, or where heavy condensation is present. They are derived from rubber treated with chlorine or carbon tetrachloride, many types, of widely differing composition, being available. They offer great resistance to acid and alkalis, high resistance to moisture penetration and great flexibility, but there are certain problems attendant on their use.

Very powerful solvents are needed to bring them to a working consistency, with the result that when they are applied by brush they tend to lift or "work up" the previous coatings, and when modified to correct this tendency their chemical resistance is lowered; the strength of the solvents used in chlorinated rubber paints makes the choice of a suitable primer rather difficult, and the advice of the manufacturer of any particular brand as to the correct primer for his product should always be followed; the adhesion of chlorinated rubber when applied to bare metal is rather poor; the paint film is rather soft and has a tendency to further softening at temperatures above 71°C (160°F).

Colours used. Chlorinated rubber paints are usually supplied in creams, greys and browns; they can be supplied in any desired colour but it must be remembered that if they include in their composition any coloured pigment which might be affected by chemical attack (e.g., lead chromes affected by acid, Prussian blue affected by alkali, etc.) they will no longer withstand the action of that chemical.

Chemical resistance. Besides their great resistance to water, chlorinated rubber paints withstand the attack of numerous corrosive agents including sulphuric, nitric, hydrochloric and phosphoric acids, chlorine, caustic soda, caustic potash, sulphur dioxide, sulphate of ammonia, ozone, alcohol, iodine, white spirit, methylated spirit, lubricating oils, brine and sea water. They are also resistant to mould growth.

Typical uses. In dye and bleach works, factories devoted to chemical manufacture and mineral water manufacture, fertilizer works, dairies, bottling or bottle washing establishments, laboratories, various sections of gas works, etc. These paints will withstand conditions where only bitumen can be used as an alternative and where sometimes heat precludes the use of bitumen.

Thixotropic types of chlorinated rubber paint have recently been developed which are easier to apply by brush and which produce a thicker paint film.

CHROMA The Greek word for colour. In American publications on colour theory the term "chroma" is used to denote the purity of a colour, that is its strength, intensity or saturation. In the Munsell system the chroma of any colour is specified by a number placed under the value number of the colour.

CHROMATED RED OXIDE A primer suitable for both aluminium and steel, consisting of a mixture of zinc chromate and red oxide in an appropriate medium. Provided it contains a substantial proportion of chromate it possesses good corrosion-inhibiting properties.

CHROMATED RED OXIDE PRIMER A good corrosion-inhibiting primer for iron, steel and aluminium, quick drying and non-toxic, composed of zinc chromate and red oxide.

CHROMATIC SCALE The whole range of colour generally arranged in a series of graduated wedges in a colour circle, passing from yellow through green, blue, violet, purple, red and orange and back to yellow.

CHROMATING The treatment of light alloys with chemical solutions containing chromic acid and/or chromates in a suitable acid medium in order to give increased protection against corrosion and to provide a good base for subsequent paint treatment.

CHROME GREEN A composite pigment made by combining a small proportion of Prussian blue with a pale yellow chrome by precipitating them together. By varying the proportion of blue a range of greens can be produced, extending from a light yellow-green to a deep blue-green; normally the pigment is sold as pale, medium or deep chrome green.
 Chrome greens are opaque and possess good staining power; they are fairly permanent, but paints made from them tend to turn blue when exposed to the weather, owing to the chrome fading more quickly than the blue. They are discoloured by contact with sulphur and alkali (sulphur reacting with the yellow chrome and alkali with the Prussian blue) and for this reason are quite unsuitable for use in water paints and distempers, and when mixed in oil are unsuitable for use on new plaster, cement and other alkaline surfaces unless alkali resisting primer has been used. Their colour is liable to deepen as the paint dries, making it difficult successfully to match a colour with them.

CHROME RED See *Chinese Red.*

CHROMES The chromates of lead, zinc, barium and strontium are generally classed under this head.

CHROMIUM OXIDE A very opaque green pigment with a rather yellowish or sage green cast; it consists of anhydrous chromium oxide. It is extremely durable, is quite fast to light, withstands acid and alkaline attack, is unaffected by sulphur and resists heat; it is reasonably low in cost. Originally introduced as a colour for the pottery industry, it is now widely used as a pigment in oil paints and water paints and as a rubber pigment.

CHURCH OAK VARNISH A recognized trade term for the best quality of indoor varnish; a short-oil varnish giving a hard film, which, as it does not soften when warmed, may be used on seats, pews, etc. Generally made from Congo or Kauri gums.

CIMENT FONDU High alumina cement made by burning a mixture of limestone and bauxite, cooling it rapidly and grinding it to a fine powder. For further details see *Cement*.

CINQUEFOIL Literally, five leaves. In tracery or arcading it is an arrangement of five foils or openings, terminating in cusps.

CIPOLLINO A highly decorative marble with a whitish ground traversed by veins or bands of green.

CISSING This is a term applied when a coat of paint, varnish or water colour refuses to form a continuous film, recedes from the surface, collects in beads and leaves the surface partially exposed. It occurs very often in graining when water colour is applied over an oily ground; it can also occur when a second coat of varnish is applied over a varnished surface which has not been flatted down, when varnishing is delayed so long that the undercoats have become unduly hard, and when paint or varnish is applied over greasy surfaces (such as surfaces which have been wax polished, or old painted surfaces, which have not been thoroughly washed down). In all these cases cissing can be prevented by "cissing down", or by rubbing the surface down with fine waterproof sandpaper.
    A delayed form of cissing can also occur in varnished work some time after application and may be caused by mixing different kinds of varnish together, by applying the varnish too vigorously or by using a brush which has not been properly worked into the varnish and which still contains turps. When delayed cissing occurs the varnish must be removed with turps and the surface allowed to dry before rubbing down and revarnishing.

CISSING DOWN This is the process employed when it is known that cissing is likely to occur, such as for example in graining when water colour is to be applied over an oily ground. The surface is rubbed over with a damp sponge lightly powdered with fine whiting or fuller's earth used very sparingly. The practice which is sometimes employed of cissing down with soap is a dangerous one which may cause damage to the work and to the superimposed varnish.

CLADDING A term derived from an old English version of "clothing"; which is applied in modern building to a thin external covering of various materials over a hidden structure of other materials (e.g., reinforced concrete).

CLAIRCOLLE or CLEARCOLE Glue size, appropriately diluted, to which a little whiting has been added. It is used on ceilings and walls to reduce the porosity and equalize the suction before a coat of soft distemper is applied. Sometimes a little alum is added to the claircolle to make the distemper work more coolly on a "hot" surface; this hardens the glue size and makes it less soluble but it makes the subsequent removal of the distemper and claircolle very difficult when the time comes for redecoration.

Claircolle should never be used under water paints or emulsion paints, although the instruction to do so is sometimes seen in architects' specifications.

CLAPBOARD A thin narrow board, usually of cleft oak, but nowadays often made from sawn deal, used for covering the exterior of timber framed buildings. The term is still used in America but is no longer as common as it was in this country; the term more generally used now is "weather boarding".

CLEAN COLOUR A term used very vaguely by painters and decorators and even by the writers of textbooks; at various times it is used to imply light colours of high light-reflective value as opposed to dark sombre colours, strong primary colour as opposed to secondary or tertiary colours, tints which consist of an uncomplicated mixture of white and a single stainer as opposed to muddy colours produced by mixing several stainers, and so on. A term of more definite meaning is "cleaner" colour.

CLEANER COLOUR Used to express a comparison between two samples of colour, in which there is an apparent difference due to the presence of less black in one than the other.

CLEANLINESS The most important factor in painting and decorating, and a vital factor in such operations as glass gilding, paperhanging, etc.

CLOUDING A defect which is sometimes apparent in varnished work due to faulty manufacture or to a measure of blooming after application.

COAL TAR Materials from which various substances such as benzene and naphthalene are distilled, from which are derived a number of dye-stuffs used in the paint industry.

COAL TAR PAINTS Phenolic resin-based paints of this kind are highly resistant to dilute acids and alkalis and also possess outstanding water resistance. Various combinations of coal tar pitch and epoxy resins (some of them two-pack materials) are produced for situations demanding resistance to heat as well as to water and chemical attack, and such paints are also eminently suitable for lock gates and chemical plant where exposure to water is severe. Before these paints are used the surface needs to be grit-blasted.

COAT The term given to a film of paint, water paint, varnish or other similar liquid decorative material, applied to a surface in one single application. A paint system consists of a number of coats, separately applied, with a reasonable interval between each to allow for drying. The painter often adds to the term in order to describe the type of coat more fully, e.g., full coat, mist coat, sharp coat, etc.

COBWEBBING   The production of fine filaments instead of the usual atomized particles when certain materials are sprayed. Normally it is regarded as a fault which can be overcome by the use of suitable solvents and by adjustment of the spray equipment, but it is sometimes used deliberately to provide a protective covering for certain articles during storage. The process is used for the protection of aeroplane engines, for example; the article is encased in a cocoon of cobwebbed lacquers prepared specially for the purpose, the cocoon then being sprayed with a complete film of lacquer.

COHESION   The forces which bind together the particles of paint or varnish into a coherent film as opposed to *adhesion,* the forces which bind the film to the surface to which it is applied.

COLD GALVANIZING   A term sometimes used to describe the application of zinc-rich primer.

COLLOID   A gluey substance of a non-crystalline semi-solid nature, the particles of which form a permanent suspension in some medium, e.g., starch, flour paste, etc. China clay, used as a flatting agent in undercoatings, etc., can be prepared artifically in the form of a colloid.

COLOPHONY   Also known as rosin. The residue which remains when turpentine has been distilled from the oleo-resin exudation of pine trees. It is a brittle and highly acid resin with low melting point, and when used alone is not capable of producing good quality finishes, but when suitably modified it is of great importance in modern paint.

COLOUR   (i) The sensation produced by waves of decomposed light upon the optic nerve. White light, or sunlight, is composed of innumerable different wave lengths or colours of light; when a beam of white light passes through a prism, or a beam of sunlight passes through raindrops, it is decomposed or split up into its constituent parts producing the familiar colour spectrum.
(ii) That property of bodies by which rays of light are decomposed so as to produce certain effects upon the eye. When light falls upon a body it may be reflected or absorbed or transmitted; in practice it never occurs that only one of these actions takes place at once, and the colour which the body appears to be depends upon the particular absorption properties it possesses. Thus the colour of a piece of stained glass will depend upon which rays are absorbed and which transmitted, and the colour of an opaque body upon which rays are absorbed and which reflected. In general, the light that is absorbed by a substance is complementary to the light that is reflected or transmitted by it.
(iii) Any one of the hues into which light can be decomposed, or a tint or

a shade, so that, for example, we term one hue red, another blue, and so on, and refer to a tint of red as pink, or a shade of orange as brown, etc.

(iv) That which is used for colouring or altering the apparent colour of a body. A pigment, for example, produces a certain sensation of colour because of the particular rays which it absorbs and the rays which it reflects. That pigment can be applied in the form of a film over an object of a different colour; for example, if a film of paint pigmented with green is applied to a length of white wood, we speak of "painting the wood green" or "applying a coat of green".

(v) The term is also used very loosely in the trade to refer to any coat of paint after the primer as a "coat of colour".

COLOUR CIRCLE Colours arranged in a graduated scale, useful in the planning of colour schemes and an invaluable help to those who are trying to develop colour sense.

COLOUR CODING The painting of objects to a recognized colour scheme in order that their contents or functions may be identified at a glance. Colour coding is widely used in industrial painting both for reasons of safety and for the convenience of maintenance staffs; moving parts of machinery and danger areas are picked out to give them prominence, and service pipes and conduit systems are coded so that throughout a factory one colour will denote a pipe carrying oil, another hot water, another cold water, and so on. Many large firms have their own identification codes, but there is a strong case to be made out for adopting a nation-wide standard, or better still for adopting an international code. The British Standards Institution issues a specification of ten recommended colours for pipe identification (B.S. 1710: 1960, with an amendment in July 1965). Colour coding is also applied to small scale industrial work; for instance, in the radio industry resistors and capacitors etc. are colour coded so that their values can be immediately recognized.

COLOUR COMBING The production of patterns by means of lifting wet colour to expose a differently coloured ground. It is done with either steel, rubber or celluloid combs, and it may be carried out in scumble, glaze, flat oil paint, coloured plastic paint or metallic paint.

COLOUR THEORIES The subject of colour is complicated by several factors, such as the fact that a person's reactions to colour stimuli is a highly individual matter, the loose manner in which colour terms are applied, the great number of imprecise terms which exist and the difficulty of relating experiment with coloured light to the effects obtained with coloured pigments. Since it is obvious that any faculty of the human mind can only reach its fullest development by undergoing some discipline and training, various attempts have been made to establish a set of principles by which the subject of colour can be approached logically and its use regulated by system as opposed to more fortuitous methods.

The basis of these systems is that the colour of a surface has three attributes, namely, hue, tone and saturation, and upon these attributes, considered in conjunction with each other, depends the position of that colour within an orderly arrangement of all possible colours. Various authorities differ in the details of their approach; in the Ostwald system the chromatic scale is divided into eight basic hues, the Munsell system rests upon ten basic hues, while other systems are based upon twelve, fourteen and so on.

COLOUR WASH A term applied to the treatment of broad areas with inexpensive materials, such as a coating of soft distemper on interior walls and limewash on both interior and exterior walls, as opposed to using better quality materials such as oil paint or oil-bound water paint.

COLUMBIAN PINE Also known as Oregon pine or Douglas fir, a softwood frequently employed in building work, and one which often gives rise to trouble in painting. It is extremely resinous and the resin exudes not only from the knots but over the whole surface, causing extensive lifting and blistering of the paint system. A further complication is that the wood presents a surface of uneven absorption, especially when used as plywood, part of the grain being hard and impervious while the other parts are very porous. A priming paint which is intended to penetrate cannot gain a hold on the hard parts, and in any case the resinous nature of the wood has the effect of retarding the drying of the primer. The most suitable primer for Columbian pine is aluminium, which has sufficient mechanical strength to seal the resin and which has good adhesion as well as presenting a film of even porosity for the subsequent coats of paint.

COMBINATION LACQUERS Nitro-cellulose lacquers into which a proportion of melamine or other polymerizable resin is incorporated. The effect is that for a short space of time after application the surface may be pulled over in the same way as a normal nitro-cellulose lacquer but that it soon becomes resistant to pullover solvents and forms a non-reversible film.

COMBING Lifting wet colour with rubber or steel combs to expose the ground, as explained in "Colour Combing". Combing is also used in the process of graining and provides a simple method of portraying coarse grain, especially of woods such as oak and pitchpine. A considerable degree of realism can be achieved by following the use of a broad toothed rubber comb (or broad steel comb wrapped in rag) with slanting strokes of a fine comb.

COMBS The combs used in the process just described take many forms. Steel combs may be bought in sets ranging from wide to narrow and from broad teeth to fine teeth. Rubber combs of various patterns are also available. Many craftsmen however, prefer to make their own rubber combs in order to get greater variation of pattern than is possible with the machine-made article. Celluloid combs for use with tinted glazes in colour combing are easily made to suit the requirements of the particular job in hand.

COMPATIBILITY The state of being compatible, whereby two things are able to exist together and agree with one another. Paints or varnishes are said to be compatible if they can be mixed together without causing gelling, coagulation or other undesirable results, and paint films which can exist together in a painting system without having undesirable effects upon each other are also said to be compatible.

COMPLEMENTARY COLOURS A pair of contrasting colours. The word "complement" can be defined as "that which completes". In dealing with paint mixtures, complementary colours are so called because each completes the other by reflecting those components of white light which the other absorbs.

COMPRESSOR A device which draws in air and compresses it to a pressure at which it will drive various tools and pieces of equipment. So that the operation of these tools may be properly regulated, a compressor is designed to provide a continuous supply of compressed air at a predetermined maximum pressure and minimum volume in cubic metres per minute. For workshop use, the most efficient and economical type of compressor is a stationary one with a large air receiver for ample air storage, but for normal painting and decorating work the portable type mounted on a handled and wheeled chassis is essential. The plant may be driven by electricity or petrol engine.

CONCENTRATED SIZE Glue size in powdered or granulated form. Because of its convenience and the fact that it is readily prepared for use it is much more popular than cake glue or jelly size. It should be protected from deterioration by storing in a dry place at an even temperature. It is important that concentrated size should be bought from a reputable manufacturer as this type of size lends itself to the inclusion of impurities which might retard the setting and lower the adhesive qualities of the material. It should be noticed that the size should be prepared with hot, but not boiling, water; if the size is made too hot it will not gell properly when cool

CONDENSATION A matter of considerable importance to the decorator The principles involved are as follows:

All air contains water in the form of vapour; this moisture is always present and is diffused throughout the atmosphere, but there is a limit to the amount of water that any given quantity of air can contain. If the temperature of the air remains unchanged its water content can be increased until the limit is reached; at this point the air is said to have reached *saturation point*, and if any more water is introduced it will no longer be held in the air but will condense. If the amount of water in the air remains unchanged but the temperature of the air is lowered, a temperature is reached at which the air becomes saturated; this temperature is termed the *dew point*, and any further cooling of the air beyond this results in condensation. As a general rule, the higher the temperature of the air the greater its capacity for holding water, and the lower the air temperature the less its capacity.

Condensation of moisture on the structural surfaces of a building occurs when the temperature of the surfaces falls below the dew point of the air which is in contact with them. This may be brought about by a surface being cold—plaster and steelwork, for instance, are good conductors of heat, and by drawing heat away from the air they tend to present a cold surface—or by abnormally high humidity, such as in kitchens, canteens, washhouses, etc., or in textile factories where humidifiers are installed to keep the air moist. Whether the condensation shows as water on the surface depends on the nature of the surface. On a non-absorbent surface the moisture will appear as droplets but on a more absorbent surface it will still form but will be absorbed. This is an important point to re-member; in a room such as a kitchen or bathroom, where the atmosphere becomes steamy at intervals, a surface coating such as soft distemper or water paint may not show condensation as much as a gloss paint, but such a coating will tend to disintegrate very quickly due to the repeated soakings it receives.

C

The problem of condensation of moisture inside buildings can only be cured by providing adequate thermal insulation and by improving the ventilation. Surface treatments applied by the decorator can only have a limited value, and depend for their efficiency upon the extent of the condensation and whether it is intermittent or constant.

This problem of condensation also arises in connection with the blooming of gloss finishes and the deposition of moisture upon surfaces—especially metal surfaces—if too long an interval elapses between cleaning and priming, and in recent years there has been a considerable increase in the staining of walls and ceilings due to the condensation of moisture in domestic chimneys.

Condensation is a factor to be considered in spray painting, too, since the sudden expansion of the air leaving the gun nozzle causes a drop in temperature which may lead to moisture deposits.

CONDY'S FLUID A solution of sodium permanganate used by French polishers as a chemical stain for wood.

CONSISTENCY The degree of density, firmness or solidity of any thick liquid. The consistency of paint is understood to mean its condition when mixed for application; too thick or "round" a consistency will be difficult to spread with the brush and will produce ropiness, while if the consis-tency is too thin the binder will be so attenuated as to lose some of its cohesive power, the opacity will suffer and the paint will tend to run. For spraying, the consistency of paint is very often slightly thinner than brushing consistency. The degree of consistency is generally determined by practical application but can be measured more accurately by means of the Plastometer or the Consistometer.

"Consistency" is also applied to the other fluids and semi-fluids used by the painter, such as fillers, paste, etc. A considerable part of the skill of the paperhanger is the ability to judge the correct consistency of paste for any given sample of paper.

CONSTRUCTION REGULATIONS Regulations introduced under the provisions of the Factories Act of 1961 to provide a complete code of safety, health and welfare for the building and civil engineering industries;

they supersede the 1948 Regulations which only dealt with building operations and which specifically excluded works of engineering construction. They lay down detailed and explicit requirements covering, amongst other things, the provision, maintenance, and examination of scaffolds, the use of lifting appliances, chains, ropes, lifting gear and hoists, the dangers inherent in excavation and demolition work, the use of vehicles, the provision of first-aid equipment and shelters, the protection against dust, fumes and poisonous compounds. Together with the Compressed Air Regulations and the Diving Operations Regulations of 1960 they form a code embracing every aspect of the industry.

CONSTRUCTION REGULATIONS—STATUTORY INSTRUMENTS
There are now six sets of regulations which together comprise a comprehensive code applying uniform requirements for safety, health and welfare to all types of construction work; the titles and numbers of the statutory instruments which relate to these are as follows:
(1)   The Construction (General Provisions) Regulations 1961 (S.I. 1961 No. 1580).
(2)   The Construction (Lifting Operations) Regulations 1961 (S.I. 1961 No. 1581).
(3)   The Construction (Working Places) Regulations 1966 (S.I. 1966 No. 94).
(4)   The Construction (Health and Welfare) Regulations 1966 (S.I. 1966 No. 95).
(5)   The Work in Compressed Air Special Regulations 1960 (S.I. 1960 No. 1307).
(6)   The Diving Operations Special Regulations 1960 (S.I. 1960 No. 688)

CONTRACTILE   Tending to contract, having the power of shortening, shrinking or drawing together. Certain painting and decorating materials are contractile, glue size and paste being examples. There is an obvious danger in allowing size or paste to dry on a painted surface as the strong shrinkage might lead to deep cracking of the paintwork. There is a danger, too, in the practice of adding size to plaster stopping in order to retard the set; the size may cause such strong contraction that the stopping is loosene and drops out.

CONTRACTION   The act of shrinking, shortening, drawing together.

CONTRASTING COLOURS   Colours which lie opposite or nearly opposit one another on the colour circle. When placed side by side they intensify one another.

CONTROLLED CRACKING   The defect of cracking in paintwork may be caused, among other things, by applying a hard brittle coating over the top of a soft, elastic coat; this principle is put to a practical use in order to obtain a wrinkled or "crackle" effect in the industrial finishing of small objects such as typewriters, etc. Of course, the process is carefully regulated, as opposed to the accidental effect from which it is evolved, and is usually carried out with stoving paints.

CONVECTION The transfer of heat through a gas or a liquid by means of movement of the heated particles; e.g., in a convection stoving oven the air surrounding the object which is to be stoved is heated, being circulated from the source of heat to the object and returned for reheating.

CONVERSION FACTORS AND TABLE See pages vii and viii.

COPAL A generic name embracing a number of resins, both fossil and recent, which are found in many tropical and subtropical regions of the world and are commonly named after the country of their origin. These resins, which are usually hard and somewhat brittle, formed the basis of most oil varnishes until the introduction of synthetic resins and are still very widely employed.

CO-POLYMER See *Polymerization.*

COPPER A reddish-coloured, malleable, ductile metal.

COPPER SULPHATE Solutions of copper sulphate in water have always enjoyed a great deal of popularity in the painting and decorating trade. They are sometimes used as a wash to discourage mould growths and provided the infected surface is allowed to dry thoroughly it is quite safe to paint afterwards. They have also been extensively used in the past to etch the surface of galvanized iron sheeting before painting, but this is not a practice to be encouraged as a black deposit of copper is left upon the surface, preventing the paint from adhering properly.

COPPER, THE PAINTING OF Failure of adhesion is often experienced when paint is applied to copper or copper alloy surfaces; in addition, the metal has a retarding effect upon the drying of linseed oil paint films (although synthetic primers are not affected) and drying oils and varnish media with a high acid content have a slightly solvent action on the copper which is sufficient to produce a green stain in the paint. Before priming, the surface should be roughened with steel wool or emery cloth to improve adhesion (in industrial processes shot blasting may be employed) and should then be de-greased by brushing down with trichlorethylene, a two-to-one mixture of benzole and acetone, or a proprietary de-greasing agent. The primer should be mixed with a medium of low acid value, such as a mixing varnish, and may be pigmented with aluminium to help to check the bleeding of any green stain.

COPPER, TOXIC PROPERTIES OF Various compounds of copper are used to repel the attack of insects and fungi. Copper rosinate, made by heating rosin with copper acetate and combining it with linseed oil, forms a durable varnish which is used in a poisonous paint for the protection of timber; copper naphthanate and similar solutions are used as a protection against woodworm, furniture beetles, etc., and there are various proprietary solutions made for the same purpose which are based on copper.

COPYING INK PENCIL   A pencil, the marks made by which are indelible and which when moistened release the viscid fluid of copying ink. This fluid bleeds through any number of coats of paint, water paint or distemper. On no account should such a pencil ever be brought on a decorative job; its use can lead to considerable damage, annoyance and expense.

CORBEL   A block of stone, often carved or moulded, projecting from a wall and supporting the beams of a roof or other feature.

CORINTHIAN   The third order of Greek architecture, the most elaborate and ornate of the three, the capital being enriched with graceful foliated forms added to the volute of the Ionic capital.

CORK PAINT   See *Anti-Condensation Paint.*

CORNER KNIFE   A broad sharp-ended knife mounted on a light wooden handle and used in a similar manner to a casing wheel for the rapid trimming of surplus wallpaper from around skirtings and architraves. See *Casing Wheel.*

CORNICE   In architecture this is a term applied to any crowning projection but the painter and decorator generally understands it as being the moulding (usually of plaster) at the junction of ceiling and walls.

CORROSION   The wasting away of a metal due to the chemical attack which it undergoes when exposed to the action of oxygen, water, acid, alkali or salts. Most of the metals used industrially do corrode but the effect upon non-ferrous metals is extremely slow compared with the rapid deterioration of iron and steel. When iron and steel corrode, rust, which is hydrated ferric oxide, is formed; this is very often due to an electro-chemical action, which can only occur when moisture is present. Efforts to check the corrosion of structural steel are directed towards coating the steel while it is clean and dry with a suitable primer of rust inhibitive qualities and building up a paint film, which will resist the ingress of moisture. These conditions, however, are not easy to achieve. Rust itself contains moisture and active rusting ingredients; its moisture content makes its complete removal from a surface very difficult, but if it is not completely removed further rusting proceeds to take place under the new paint film. As rust occupies a greater volume than its parent metal it swells when forming and eventually pushes the paint film off, leaving the metal open to the weather and allowing further corrosion to proceed very rapidly.

The subject of corrosion is highly complex and a great deal of energy and research is being devoted to it. Painters and decorators should try to keep abreast of developments in this field.

The corrosion of metals is put to practical use in the production of the pigment white lead, a basic carbonate of lead prepared by the corrosion of metallic lead with acetic acid and carbonic acid gases.

COUMARONE RESINS   Resins made by the polymerization of certain constituents of naphtha. They possess a high degree of resistance to chemicals, particularly alkalis, and are used in the formulation of alkali resistant paints and as media for paints containing metallic powder. They have a tendency to yellow both on exposure and on heating.

COUPLER   A term used in connection with tubular scaffolding; it is a fitting used to grip the external surface of two tubes in order to hold them together.

COURLENE ROPES   Polythene ropes, resistant to acid and alkali. See *Synthetic Ropes*.

COVERING POWER   A very loose term, the use of which is best avoided. It is sometimes used to refer to the spreading capacity of paint and at other times to mean the hiding or obliterating power.

CRACKING   A defect occurring in paintwork, usually due to the application of a hard drying coating over a softer and more elastic film, so that the top coating is unable to keep pace with the expansion and contraction of the undercoat. This may be because of using undercoats in too round a condition or through not allowing the undercoats sufficient drying time; it may also be caused by using driers too freely. Another cause of cracking of paintwork lies in allowing paste or glue size to stray on to it and become dry. There are various degrees of cracking, varying from the fine cracks already mentioned under the heading of "checking" to deep cracks which penetrate the entire film. In bad cases there is no remedy except to burn off the defective paint. One of the drawbacks of trying to seal bituminous paints with knotting is the cracking which is liable to occur.

CRACKLE FINISHES   Paints employed in the industrial finishing of small objects such as typewriters, radio components, etc., and which simulate such defects as cracking and turn them to decorative use. See *Controlled Cracking*.

CRADLE   A type of suspended scaffold for exterior use, in which a cradle or boat composed of wood, metal or polyester fibre is occupied by two men who have the ability to raise or lower it as required. In many cases it is the easiest, cheapest and most practicable form of scaffold for painting and decorating and maintenance work. It is especially useful over a busy thoroughfare because it does not cause any obstruction on the ground, and on a building rising above a river bed or some other feature which would preclude the use of a scaffold rising from the ground, or on very lofty buildings which would not be accessible from the ground.

Hand-operated cradles are suspended by a system of ropes passing over pulley blocks; the men occupying the cradle raise or lower themselves as required and then tie off the ropes to hold the cradle in the desired position. They fall into three main types. A fixed cradle is suspended from outriggers and is capable of upwards and downwards movement only. A travelling cradle consists of a track suspended from outriggers, with the cradle itself suspended from jockeys which are able to run laterally along the track; this type of cradle provides movement upwards and downwards and also sideways in either direction. A third type of cradle is suspended from a mobile tower; the cradle itself is fixed and only capable of upwards and downwards movement but the tower supporting the cradle can be moved sideways.

Cradles may also be operated mechanically. In many cases nowadays, especially for very lofty buildings, a winch is mounted on the cradle decking and suspension is by wire ropes; upwards and downwards movement is controlled by the winch. There is also an electrically operated type of cradle designed to be incorporated into modern buildings in the construction stage or added to existing buildings for maintenance purposes, which runs along the roof track and is placed out of sight on the roof when not in use.

CRAWLING   A very pronounced form of cissing, which is sometimes due to faulty materials or to working on an extremely greasy or oily surface. See *Cissing.*

CRAYONS   Often used in the production of figure markings in graining (and sometimes in marbling). Conté crayons are suitable for oil-colour work; for water-colour work, crayon pencils in a wide variety of colours may be bought, although some grainers prefer to make their own from a mixture of pipe clay, dry pigment, gum and glycerine. Crayon should always be tested before use to ascertain how it will behave when varnished; some varieties may be found to "work up" in the varnish, while very waxy crayons will give rise to cissing.

CRAZING   A form of cracking in which the surface is covered with fine cracks which give the appearance of a small pattern; the term is understood to mean cracks that are deeper and broader than those indicated by the term "checking".

CREEPING   Another term for *crawling,* q.v.

CREOSOTE   An oily liquid with a penetrating smell and strongly antiseptic properties, obtained by the distillation of wood-tar or coal-tar, and ranging from light brown to a tarry black in colour. It is used as a preservative for timber when for any reason ordinary paint treatment would not be suitable, especially when the timber is to be in contact with the ground (on garden fencing and posts, for example) and where protection from fungoid growths, mites and woodboring insects is desired. It is also used in the treatment of such things as telegraph posts, etc., but in such cases as this it is forced into the wood under pressure. Certain proprietary brands are marketed which are available in other colours than brown and which, when dry, may be varnished. Normally, creosote cannot be painted or varnished unless sealed with a stop-tar knotting; otherwise, it would bleed through.

CRINKLING   A fault in paintwork which takes the form of a puckering or gathering of the surface, and very often due to too thick an application of the paint or to applying paint over a greasy surface. Also termed "wrinkling".

CRIPPLES   A colloquial term for ladder brackets; by means of their use a scaffold can be erected with stave ladders and planks. They are of sturdy construction; the arms are adjustable to the angle of the ladder and are secured when adjusted by means of a chained pin. The method of fixing is to hook them over the rungs of the ladders; the safest type are those which hook over two rungs as opposed to those which rely on one rung only.

CROCODILING   An extreme form of cracking whereby the surface is so badly affected as to resemble crocodile hide.

CROSS LINING   The hanging of a lining paper as a foundation for a good quality wall or ceiling paper, the lining paper being run at right angles to the direction taken by the finishing paper.

CROSSING   The means whereby paint applied with a brush is distributed evenly over the surface. The paint is brushed on and then the brush is taken across the work at right angles to the direction of the previous stroke. Each time the work is crossed the pressure on the brush is decreased, in order to eliminate brush marks.

CROW'S FOOTING   A defect in a paint or varnish film whereby small wrinkles, similar in appearance to a crow's foot, appear; it is often caused by the formation of a surface skin.

CRUTCH   The name given to a roll of paper used by a paperhanger, when working on a ceiling, to support the folded portion of the length he is actually hanging.

CRYSTAL PAPER VARNISH   A very pale varnish made for the purpose of varnishing light coloured sanitary papers (such as marble patterns, etc.) in the decoration of kitchens, bathrooms, etc. Usually made from a spirit-soluble resin, such as damar or mastic. Although almost colourless when first applied, it tends to discolour badly as time passes and has the further disadvantage of not being particularly durable. Its use is largely superseded nowadays by the pale synthetic resin varnishes which may be obtained and which retain their clean colour far better and which are much more durable.

CRYSTALLINE DEPOSITS   Deposits which appear on the surface of plaster, brick, cement, stonework, etc., and which are due to the presence of soluble salts.
    Most building materials contain small quantities of such salts; when the materials are drying out the salts are brought to the surface and are left there in the form of a white crystalline growth as the moisture evaporates. On a surface decorated with water paint or distemper the salts may percolate through the coating and be deposited on the face, where they will

do little damage apart from presenting an unsightly appearance. If, however, the salts are deposited beneath a paint or water paint film the coating may be disrupted and flaking or peeling will take place.

When such deposits appear they should be brushed off and the surface kept under observation until no further growth occurs, before any impervious paint coating is applied. Washing off deposits is inadvisable as the water is liable to dissolve further salts and bring them to the surface. Sealing the surface with an impervious coating will aggravate the trouble. See "efflorescence".

CURTAIN COATING A method of paint application used in industrial finishing; it is somewhat similar to flow coating, the items to be treated passing on a conveyor beneath a curtain of falling paint. It produces an even coating of accurately controlled film thickness. It is simple, there is no wastage and the production rate is rapid.

CURTAIN WALL In mediaeval building, a wall connecting two towers or strong points; in a modern framed building, a thin wall between, and often in front of, the main structural members of steel or of reinforced concrete, and bearing no load.

CURTAINING Sagging; the occurrence of curtains in paint, enamel or varnish films.

CURTAINS A defect which occurs in paint coatings, particularly gloss paints and varnishes, when applied to a vertical surface. It is due to uneven application. It takes the form of a downward movement of the paint film between the time of its application and its setting which results in the formation of a thick line of paint like a slung curtain. Also known as "sags".

CUTTING DOWN A term applied to the rubbing down of a painted surface with abrasives, and generally taken to imply the grinding down of a glossy surface.

CUTTING IN Finishing off a section of paintwork in a neat line. Hence, "cutting in windows"—finishing the paintwork in a neat edge where it meets the glass of a window pane; "cutting in to a colour"—where a sharp line of demarcation is formed in parti-coloured work; "cutting in skirtings" —where the paintwork is performed neatly without encroaching on the flooring. Hence also the term "a clean cut" applied to neatly finished paintwork.

CUTTING TOOL A round brush, approximating in size when bridled to the 25mm flat paint brush, and used for the cutting in of windows, etc. Also known as a "sash tool".

CUTTLE FISH BONE Used as an abrasive for cutting down paintwork, particularly in the cutting down of varnish or enamel in between coats. It is used with water and is very clean in use; it grinds well and does not clog readily. It has a hard outer shell which must be removed before use; otherwise, the paint surface will be scratched.

D

DADO The lower part of the wall when decorated differently from the remainder of the wall.

DAMAR OR DAMMAR A soft resin with a characteristic aromatic odour, generally imported from Malaya or Siam, and soluble in turpentine. It is used in the preparation of crystal paper varnishes, map varnishes, etc. It lacks the hardness and durability required for an exterior varnish.

DAMP Dampness, whether due to humid weather conditions or present in the structure of a building, is always a source of trouble. If paint is applied while rain is falling moisture will be trapped beneath the paint film leading to blistering and flaking. Fog and mist cause considerable surface deposits of moisture which may penetrate to such an extent that even if the surface is dried off before paint is applied there is sufficient moisture present to impair the adhesion. Moisture condensing on a partly dried paint or varnish film may cause loss of gloss or blooming and during damp weather conditions the drying rate of most paint is retarded, particularly the drying of water paints and distempers.

The presence of moisture in the wall and ceiling surfaces of a building may be due to a number of factors; the chief causes of damp in building may be summarized as follows:

(a) *Damp in new building materials.* There is a considerable amount of free moisture in the brickwork, mortar, plaster, etc., of a new building which takes a long time to dry out; evidence of damp during the first year or two may be due to this rather than to any structural faults that can be rectified.

(b) *Penetration from outside.* This may be due to defective slates or tiles, damaged lead flashing or broken guttering or downspouting, or the brickwork or stonework may have become porous, absorbing the rain instead of repelling it, or in the older type of house there may be no cavity wall so that once penetration occurs there may be no barrier to the ingress of moisture, or the pointing of the building may be faulty, or in a building faced with cement rendering fine cracks may have developed in the rendering, or water may have lodged on a flat roof or parapet or may be entering because of faulty window-sill construction or through the jointing of prefabricated panels.

(c) *Rising damp.* This may be caused by a faulty or fractured damp course, or in the older type of house the absence of any damp course at all, and sometimes by the fact that soil has been allowed to encroach on the outside wall above the damp course level; moisture is drawn from the ground by capillary action and rises to a considerable height.

(d) *Condensation.* The tendency for water to condense when warm moisture-laden air strikes a cold plaster surface is increased if the ventilation is inadequate.

(e) *Condensation in domestic chimneys.* A fault which is becoming increasingly troublesome with the extended use of small domestic boilers.

(f) *Deliquescent salts.* Some of the building materials used in the construction of the house may contain mineral salts, etc., which have a special affinity for water and which remain permanently moist.

The essential thing in the treatment of damp surfaces is to find out the cause of the damp and, if possible, to remove the cause, and allow ample time for the surface to dry out before decorating. In most cases the removal of the cause of damp will be outside the province of the decorator and will definitely be a job for the builder. It must be emphasized that any surface coating applied by the decorator can only be a temporary palliative and not a substitute for curing the trouble.

While it is possible in some cases (e.g., in the case of faulty pointing or a leaking roof) to effect a complete cure, there are other cases where such a cure is impossible or impracticable. There are various measures that can be adopted to hold back the moisture, such as the fixing of lead foil, the hanging of pitch paper, etc., but except in mild cases these measures will only give a temporary relief.

In the case of rising damp, it will be found that the damp will climb beyond the level of any damp-proofing that is applied. Various proprietary damp-proofing solutions are made; it will generally be found that directions are given indicating the conditions under which these materials will be effective. Provided they are used on the type of work for which they are appropriate they fulfil the claims made by their manufacturers. But damp-proofing solutions should not be used indiscriminately; in the case of damp caused by condensation of moisture on a wall surface, for example, if the fault is wrongly diagnosed as being due to penetration of moisture and a damp-proofing solution is applied to the inner face of the wall, the effect will be to increase the amount of condensation (due to making the surface more impervious) and the trouble will be aggravated.

DAMP-RESISTING PAINTS Usually composed of a vehicle formed by dissolving paraffin wax, rosin, bitumen and gutta-percha in varying proportions in mineral solvents, with tung oil added.

DARKENING OF PAINT Often due to a chemical reaction affecting certain pigments, as, for example, when white lead paints, lead chromes or chrome greens are exposed to a sulphurous atmosphere, when black lead sulphide is formed. A similar reaction takes place when lead pigments are mixed with sulphide pigments such as vermilion and ultra-marine.

DECORATIVE CANVAS Closely woven jute canvas, attractively coloured and mounted on a waterproof backing; it is extremely durable and is a material of distinctive appearance with many applications in modern schemes, especially where a background is required for pictures, displays, etc. It is usually 0·9 metre wide and is ready trimmed. The walls should be cross lined with a tinted lining paper; the adhesive may be of a stiff flour paste but a proprietary adhesive of the PVA type is preferable; the adhesive is spread on the lined wall and the dry canvas pressed on to it. Alternate lengths should be reversed and the edges butted; any attempt to stretch the material to force the edges together will result in shrinkage and open joints. Application is by felt-covered roller; over rolling must be avoided, otherwise moisture from the paste will penetrate and stain the fabric. The canvas can also be obtained on a paper backing in rolls of tr same dimensions as wallpaper; here the normal procedure for paperhanging is followed, using a PVA adhesive.

DE-GREASING A term generally taken to mean the de-greasing of metals—the removal of grease from the metals before painting. Obviously the presence of grease would have an adverse effect upon the adhesion of the paint film and would also affect the drying and protective properties of the paint. The methods of de-greasing may be summarized as: (a) wiping over with solvent, (b) the use of trichlorethylene, (c) emulsion cleaning, (d) alkali de-greasing. The second and fourth methods are not applicable to the treatment of large areas and therefore not of interest to painters and decorators. Emulsion cleaning is used in the cleaning of machinery before painting in industrial work; rinsing with water is necessary afterwards, followed by a thorough drying.

DELAYED EXPANSION A term referring to a defect in plaster. It takes the form of a buckling or blistering of the plaster; in mild cases it consists of a slight rippling of the face but in severe cases there is a wholesale rotting and lifting of the skim coat. It is due to plaster which is suffering from the effect of "dryout" becoming wet again, and because the wetting is frequently caused by the application of decorative material the subject is an important one for the painter and decorator.

Dry-out occurs in anhydrous gypsum plasters when they do not remain wet long enough for the setting, that is their chemical hydration, to be completed. This may be caused by rapid evaporation of moisture due to a spell of hot weather, or by the absorption of moisture from the skim coat into the backing, the backing being unduly porous; sometimes, too, it is caused by lighting fires or circulating heat in order to speed up the rate of drying. The plaster becomes friable and powdery and lacks strength and hardness, but the fault may easily go unnoticed until the decoration is applied. When, however, such materials as water paint or emulsion paint are used the water which is introduced into the surface is absorbed by the plaster and the setting action which was interrupted may be resumed, causing the buckling of the surface, which is known as delayed expansion. It is important that the decorator should be aware of these facts because it sometimes happens that he is unjustly blamed for the defect when it occurs.

DELIQUESCENT SALTS Literally, this means salts which liquefy and which melt away gradually by absorbing moisture from the atmosphere. Many building materials—mortar, bricks, plaster, etc.—contain small quantities of soluble salt, but some materials, such as sea-sand, contain quite considerable quantities. When we speak of the presence of deliquescent salts in a building we are generally referring to cases where materials unduly rich in such salts have been used; the salts, being hygroscopic, attract moisture from the atmosphere and the tendency is for the affected areas either to appear permanently damp or, in certain cases, to become damp during spells of humid weather.

DENATURED ALCOHOL Methylated spirit; alcohol adulterated for industrial use with some noxious substances to render it unfit for drinking.

DENTAL PLASTER An unmodified hemi-hydrate gypsum plaster similar to plaster of Paris except that it is much more finely ground and is generally made from a pure sample of gypsum (alabaster) to produce a good pure white colour. While, as its name implies, it is prepared primarily for use in dental surgery, it has an application to painting and decorating; for those who prefer a home made plastic paint to a ready made bought mixture, dental plaster is a useful ingredient mixed in equal proportions by weight with oil-bound water paint, and for this purpose plaster of Paris would be too coarse.

DERMATITIS An inflammation of the skin which, though it cannot be classed as a serious disease, is very unpleasant and can only be cured by a long course of treatment. It can be caused, among other things, by the careless use of solvents; almost any solvent used in such a way as to remove the natural oils from the skin may produce it. Some people are more susceptible to the action of solvents than others, but the risk of contracting the complaint should be recognized. The practice of washing the hands with white spirit to remove paint splashes, common among some operatives, should be strongly discouraged, and when any process involving scrubbing down with solvent is required it is a wise precaution to use a barrier cream before starting work.

DESCALING The removal of rust and mill scale from iron and steelwork preparatory to painting it; complete removal is essential before any permanent paint film is applied.

When steel comes off the rolling mills it is covered with a layer of iron oxides known as mill scale, generally adhering tightly but in some places fairly loosely; if the layer were continuous and intact it would provide a good basis for paint but as in practice the scale is broken in places the metal is exposed and corrosion spreads rapidly, the whole of the scale eventually becoming loose. Very often it is specified that steelwork should be left to weather, unpainted, for a period of six months to allow the scale to loosen and to facilitate the process of descaling.

The principal methods of descaling are:

(a) Chipping and wirebrushing. By far the most usual method, but not an efficient one. Wire brushing is a tedious task and rust is very difficult to dislodge; the complete removal of rust and scale by this means is a practical impossibility.

(b) Mechanical chipping and brushing, by means of pneumatic hammers and rotary wire brushes. Again, not completely effective; the pneumatic tools tend to cause pitting of the surface of the metal and the rotary wire brushes tend to burnish the rust instead of removing it.

(c) Flame cleaning—rapid heating with an intensely hot oxy-acetylene flame which dehydrates the rust and dislodges the scale by means of differential expansion. Very efficient, but unfortunately very expensive.

(d) Shot blasting or sand blasting. Very effective, leaving a bright clean surface for the paint. Unsuitable for use on steelwork already erected, except when combined with a vacuum attachment to withdraw the loosened scale and reclaim the shot, when the process becomes expensive.

(e) Acid etching, and (f) passivation, are in general unsuitable for the treatment of erected steelwork.

DEXTRIN A strong adhesive derived from starch, prepared by heating the dry material to a temperature of $200°-250°C$ ($392°-482°F$), or by moistening flour with a mixture of dilute nitric and hydrochloric acids and heating it to $125°C$ ($257°F$). It varies in colour from nearly white (pure dextrin is quite white) to a dark brownish yellow and is soluble in water. It is used by the decorator when panelling with realwoods and relief materials, for fixing mouldings, strappings and similar members; it is also added at times to ordinary paste to improve its adhesiveness when fixing heavy materials.

DILUENT Strictly speaking, something used to dilute a substance making it thinner and more liquid and increasing the proportion of fluid.

The term is used rather loosely by writers on painting and decorating and may be considered in three different ways.

(a) When the term is used to describe a liquid which dilutes another fluid. For instance, in the production of cellulose lacquers, diluents are used to dilute the solvents, being cheaper than the solvents and therefore of importance in lowering the price of the product; as an example, ethyl acetate, a solvent (a liquid capable of dissolving nitro-cellulose) can be diluted with benzole (a liquid incapable of dissolving nitro-cellulose but which when added to the solvent does not cause the precipitation of the nitro-cellulose).

(b) When the term is used as a synoym for an "extender". Some text books describe as "diluents" or "diluent whites" those white pigments such as barytes, blanc fixé, terra alba, etc., which have little opacity in oil and which are incorporated into paints, among other reasons, in order to cheapen the material.

(c) When the term is used as a synonym for "solvent" or "thinner". The word "diluent" is sometimes used rather loosely to mean turpentine or white spirit in the case of oil paint or water in the case of water paint and some writers use all three terms, diluent, solvent and thinner at random without drawing any distinction between them. It is better to avoid using the term so loosely; the word diluent sounds pretentious compared with the much more expressive terms thinner and solvent, and its use contributes nothing whatever to the cause of clarity of expression.

DIP TANK The tank in which dipping is carried out, which naturally varies in size according to the object to be treated. Several factors are involved in the design of the dip tank; it must present as small a surface area as possible in order to cut down the evaporation of the paint solvents, and a means must be provided to circulate the paint continually in order to prevent settlement at the bottom of the tank. The evenness of the paint finish depends on the rate of withdrawal of the painted object from the tank, and this rate is carefully governed, the object being withdrawn by mechanical means. Generally there is a conveyor system included in the installation so that the dipping of numerous objects may take place in smooth rotation.

DIPPER A small pot or tin used whenever it is desired to hold small quantities of paint, medium, gold size or thinner for a variety of uses. Dippers may be bought which have a clip attachment enabling them to be clipped to a palette board; these are very useful in mural work for holding the thinners, and in graining or marbling work for holding medium or thinners as required. The dipper is an essential tool in signwriting; it allows a full dip of paint or gold size to be taken and the signwriting brush thus charged to be drawn across the edge of the dipper to remove surplus paint and bring the writer to a good shape. The practice of dispensing with the dipper and using a palette board instead is to be deplored, as it leads to the inefficient use of the writer.

DIPPING A method of paint application, used in mass production work, which consists of immersing the objects that are to be coated in a tank of paint and allowing them to drain during and after their removal. A wide variety of articles, ranging from motor-car bodies to quite small objects, is treated by this technique. The advantages offered by the process compared with spray application are (a) its speed, (b) low labour costs, (c) low paint losses, most of the surplus paint draining back into the tank, and (d) the fact that surfaces such as the interior of pipes and tubes which could not be reached by spray or brush are coated successfully by this method. Against these advantages are to be set the high initial cost of the dipping installation and the difficulty of coating objects of irregular or complicated shape.

DIPPING LACQUERS, DIPPING PAINTS, ETC. Paints formulated especially for dip application. The viscosity of the paint is of vital importance; it must be exactly suited to the rate of withdrawal of the object, and once fixed must not be allowed to vary. It is necessary, too, that the paint should be able to withstand the constant circulation and exposure to air.

DIRT RETENTION The extent to which dust and dirt become embedded in a dried paint film thereby masking its true colour and spoiling its appearance; it is very closely related to the hardness of the film.

DISCOLOURATION Some slight change of colour may be expected when any paint or water paint is drying; as a general rule, flat paints and undercoats tend to dry lighter, while enamels and gloss paints tend to darken on drying. It may also be expected that some slight darkening of colour will occur gradually over the passage of time, due to the vehicle darkening, etc. Anything more rapid and drastic in the way of a colour change, sufficient to constitute a fault, may be caused in a variety of ways. For instance, there is the discolouration or whitening of a paint due to bleaching, the discolouration which occurs when some substance penetrates the paint from beneath, or the darkening which occurs when certain pigments are exposed to sulphurous atmospheres, which are dealt with under the headings of *Bleaching, Bleeding* and *Darkening* respectively. Discolouration may also take the form of fading, which certain colours undergo when exposed to strong light, or "floating", whereby certain pigments separate and rise to the top of the material while it is still wet.

72

Another common cause of discolouration is the action of free alkali, which may attack the oil content of the paint causing a change of colour even though the pigments are not affected, or which may attack certain pigments and stainers such as Prussian blue, Brunswick greens, etc.

DISCORD Discord, when the term is applied to colour, is produced when the correct tonal order of colours is reversed. In the natural order of colour there is an orderly progression from yellow, the lightest, to violet, the darkest colour, all intermediate colours between these extremes becoming progressively darker in tone. If the natural order is reversed so that, for example, a pale purple is placed against a strong orange, the sensation of discord is produced.

DISPERSING AGENT In the formulation of a paint the dispersion of the pigment in the medium is bound up also with the "wetting" of the pigment. A simple mixture of pigment and medium would not produce a satisfactory paint, as the pigment particles would tend to fall through the medium and settle in a hard mass at the bottom of the container. In order that the particles may remain in a state of dispersion they must also be "wetted" by the medium. In cases where the pigment or medium is not likely to produce good wetting, dispersing agents consisting of aluminium soaps such as stearate and oleate, sulphonated oils or modified rubber are added to prevent hard settlement from taking place.

DISPERSION The state of being dispersed, i.e., diffused or scattered. To the decorator the term refers to the dispersion of a pigment in a medium or vehicle; in other words, the distribution of the particles of pigment throughout the liquid constituent of a paint.

DISPOSABLE FACE MASKS Paper face masks intended primarily for the use of doctors and nurses, but which are very useful to painters and decorators during short spells of spray painting and in situations where otherwise the unhygienic practice of sharing a respirator by several persons would need to be resorted to.

DISPOSABLE STRAINERS See *Strainer*.

DISTEMPER A term that is often used rather loosely to embrace any form of water paint or water thinned material; but this looseness is to be deplored. There is a considerable difference between distempers and water paints, both as to their composition and properties, and the nature of the preparation required before their use. It is by no means uncommon to see specifications drawn up by people who do not understand these differences and which, if adhered to, could only lead to a faulty and most unsatisfactory piece of work.

Strictly speaking, the term distemper means a composition of common whiting bound with either glue size or casein. A size-bound distemper is also known as soft distemper, because the dried coating remains soluble in water and is easily removed by washing. It may be mixed by the painter from powdered whiting, the whiting being soaked and dry stainers and glue size being added when required, or it may be obtained in paste form, semi-prepared for use. Paste distemper does not store well but powdered distemper, provided it is kept dry, may be kept indefinitely. It is desirable that 2% carbolic acid should be added to the mix to act as a preservative for the size. Size distemper, apart from its cheapness, has little to commend it. Because of its solubility it cannot be satisfactorily re-coated when redecoration is required, and it is very susceptible to damp and to the formation of mould growths. Its complete removal is necessary before any other form of decorative material can be used on the surface, and this is a dirty operation the cost of which counterbalances any initial saving in its use.

"Washable" distempers consist of whiting or other mineral white to which borax and lime are added, and are bound with casein. Casein, a product of skimmed milk, is insoluble in water but soluble in alkalis. When water is added the casein is dissolved by the alkaline action of the lime, but when the distemper is applied in a thin coating and the water evaporates the action of the lime ceases and the casein gradually reverts to its hard insoluble form. When completely hardened this distemper has a certain resistance to water which permits of mild sponging down, although the term "washable" is rather optimistic. Casein distempers are widely used in the U.S.A. under the name of calcimine.

DISTEMPER BRUSH   The brush used for the application of distempers, water paints and emulsion paints. The nature of these materials is such that a very different brush technique is needed for their application from that required for an oil paint. In general it may be said that they are best applied liberally with good firm strokes, and the size and shape of distemper brushes is governed by what has been proved by long years of experience to lend itself most successfully to this technique. Broadly speaking, although there are many different sizes and types according to local usage, the dictates of price, etc., the essential feature of any distemper brush is the length of its hair filling, its width and its weight. Flat distemper brushes, known in some areas as kalsomines, kalsoes or whiteners, vary in width from 150 to 200mm; they are supplied in three weights, 170, 198 and 227 grammes and the length of the hair filling visible above the binding varies from 110 to 150mm. The brush with the conventional shape of handle and metal binding is known as the Yorkshire pattern, but some people prefer a brush with a triangular stock and leather binding known as the Lancashire pattern. Two-knot distemper brushes consist of two knots of bristles bound with copper wire attached to a common handle, and these weigh 283 grammes; they are more popular in the South of England than the North.

Bristle is to be preferred to any other material at present available as a filling for a good distemper brush, but the supply of bristle, especially in lengths exceeding 100mm is steadily decreasing. It follows that a good quality distemper brush is bound to be an expensive item, and it is a pity that one so often sees brushes being spoiled by mishandling and by careless cleaning, etc.

DISTILLATION   The process of heating a solid or a liquid in a vessel so constructed that the vapours thrown off from the heated substance may be collected and condensed. The product of this process is termed a distillate. A number of paint materials are obtained in this way, turpentine being distilled from the semi-liquid resinous exudations of the pine tree, white spirit being a petroleum distillate, naphtha and benzole being coal tar distillates, and so on.

DISTRESSED PAINTING   A term sometimes used to describe a broken colour effect in which a glaze applied over a light coloured ground is treated with a brush-graining technique. The effect is also known by the name of "dragging".

The ground is generally white, although it may be lightly tinted if so wished; it is desirable that the ground should dry with an eggshell sheen. The glaze can consist of a proprietary glaze medium, its setting time adjusted as required by the addition of raw linseed oil or white spirit; alternatively, a home-made glaze medium can be used consisting of one part of linseed oil, two parts of white spirit and a small quantity of liquid driers. The important thing is that the glaze should remain fluid long enough to be dragged successfully but should set up without any tendency for the drag marks to flow out. The glaze is tinted with appropriate stainers of semi-transparent type.

The broken colour effect is obtained by drawing a clean duster brush, paperhanging brush or distemper brush through the glaze. The essential feature of the process is that all these brush marks should be in a vertical direction.

DOME   A roof, the base of which is a circle, an ellipse, or a polygon, and its vertical section a curved line, concave towards the interior; a cupola.

DOPE   A type of lacquer used in aeroplane manufacture for the tautening and protection of stretched linen fabric.

DORIC   The first and simplest order of Greek architecture.

DORMER WINDOW   A window projecting vertically from a sloping roof; usually the window of a sleeping apartment, hence the name.

DOTTER   A brush used in graining for obtaining the "bird's eyes", the small horse-shoe shaped dots, in the imitation of maple. The tool is generally a home made one; an old water-colour sable, the centre of which has been scorched out with a red hot knitting needle, serves the purpose admirably.

DOUBLE GILDING   A term used in glass gilding. When gold leaf is applied to glass, no matter how carefully the work has been done it will, when dry, reveal a number of blemishes such as open joints, pin-holing of the leaf and so on. It is customary on commercial work to lay in small pieces of gold over the blemishes, an operation known as "faulting", but in good quality work the whole of the gold surface is gilded a second time. The process is referred to as double gilding.

DOUGLAS FIR A softwood frequently used in joinery work.

DOWNHAUL That part of the suspension rope by which the up and down movement of a cradle or chair is controlled.

DR. ANGUS SMITH'S PROCESS A method of treating ferrous metal articles in order to prevent corrosion. It consists of heating the articles at a temperature of 149°C (300°F) as soon as they are cast, and then immersing them in a prepared solution of coal tar which is then brought to the boil and allowed to continue boiling until all the ammoniacal liquor, water and lighter oils are expelled. The articles remain in the solution for some time and are then removed and allowed to drain.

DR. ANGUS SMITH'S SOLUTION A term which is sometimes used loosely and incorrectly in the trade to refer to any black bituminous composition applied by brush.

DRAG (a) A small wire-drawn brush with a handle shaped for easy gripping with the fingers, resembling in appearance a paperhanging brush in miniature; it is used for the purpose of brush graining, as a brush to pull through the wet stain,
(b) The pull on the bristles which is experienced when paint is applied by brush.

DRAGGING See *Distressed Painting.*

DRAGON'S BLOOD The resinous product of an Asiatic tree, used as a spirit stain and yielding a deep red colour.

DRIER, ELECTRIC The use of an electric hair drier can save a lot of time in glass gilding, particularly in wintry conditions. As each stage of the gilding is completed it can be dried off rapidly and the next stage carried out, so that the work can be set out, gilded, faulted and backed up all in one operation where without the aid of a drier three separate visits probably on three separate days might be needed to reach the same stage.

DRIERS Materials which are added in small quantities either to drying oils or to paints based on drying oils in order to hasten the absorption of oxygen by the oil and thereby increase the rate of drying. They are compounds of certain metals, chiefly lead, manganese and cobalt, with fatty or other organic acids; when prepared with rosin they are known as rosinates, with linseed oil as linoleates, with tung oil as tungates and with naphthenic acid as naphthanates, naphthanates being widely used at the present day because they form very stable solutions giving a uniform drying action. Cobalt is the most active drier; cobalt and manganese commence drying at the surface, while lead is considered to give uniform drying throughout the film; generally, mixtures of the driers are employed as being more effective than any one individually.
    Driers are available to the painter in the form of paste driers, liquid oil driers and terebine. Paste driers, sometimes called patent driers, consist of

a drying agent reduced with mineral extenders and ground to a stiff paste with boiled linseed oil. Cheap qualities should be avoided as they contain large amounts of extender, the introduction of which into a paint may lead to early chalking. Liquid oil driers consist of drying agents such as lino-leates, etc., dissolved in turps and added to oil. Unlike paste driers, they can be added to dark or transparent colours without making them muddy. Terebine consists of drying agents combined with linseed oil and natural resin and thinned with turps. It is a strong drier, producing a brittle film which is liable to crack.

D

Drying oils are not sufficiently rapid in their action for the purpose of paint manufacture, and practical considerations demand that they should be accelerated, but driers should always be used with caution. An excess of driers may cause the paint to skin over the surface and remain soft underneath, instead of hardening uniformly throughout, a condition which will give rise to wrinkling and cracking; sweat-back can also be caused by an excess of driers. Moreover, the oxidation of an oil is not completed when the oil dries; the elastic film continues to change, becoming gradually harder and more brittle until it finally disintegrates. The acceleration of oxidation produced by the addition of driers hastens these changes and an excess of driers can shorten the life of a paint film considerably.

DRIPSTONE   In Gothic architecture, the projecting moulding over the heads of doorways, windows and archways for the purpose of throwing off rain; also known as "hood moulding".

DROP BLACK   A good quality bone black, produced by calcinating animal bones in closed retorts. The name refers to a former method of manufacture when the pigment was squeezed through perforated plates, forming drops. Drop black is a good intense black colour; it is generally ground in turpentine and used as a spirit colour, because if mixed with oil it retards the drying of the oil.

DRY COLOURS   Pigments which have been ground and dried and pre-pared in powdered condition for use as stainers for distempers and water paints. Pigments which are unaffected by alkali are used for this purpose. They should always be soaked throughly in water and mixed to a smooth paste before they are added to the distemper. If they were added in their dry state it would be found impossible to mix them completely and streakiness would result.

DRY-OUT   A fault which occurs in anhydrous gypsum plasters, due to the fact that they do not combine very readily with water. If they do not remain wet long enough to absorb all the moisture they need in order to achieve complete hydration, the plaster does not attain its full hard-ness and strength and in severe cases it assumes a powdery friable con-dition. Dry-out may be caused in various ways, such as by the too rapid evaporation of the water in hot weather, the absorption of water from the skimming coat into a backing which is too porous, or by the use of artificial heat to speed up the drying of the plaster. The subject is an important one for the decorator. See *Delayed Expansion*.

DRY ROT Decay in timber caused by fungi which reduce it to a dry brittle mass.

DRYING The change which takes place whereby a film of paint ceases to be a liquid and becomes solid.

There are three main ways in which paints dry: (i) by evaporation of the solvent, (ii) by oxidation of their oil content, and (iii) by a change in the structure of the medium which occurs irrespective of the oxygen supply.

In some cases a paint dries almost entirely by one or other of these ways; cellulose, for instance, dries entirely by means of the evaporation of the volatile solvent. But in most cases the drying is brought about by a combination of two or more of these causes. The traditional oil paints, for example, dry partly by the evaporation of the solvent and partly by the oxidation and polymerization of the oil.

Paints which dry by exposure to the air at normal temperatures are said to be "air dyring"; materials which need the application of heat either in convection ovens or by infra-red plant in order to develop hardness and protective powers are called "thermosetting paints" or "stoving paints". When the drying of paint is accelerated by applying a moderate degree of heat, $65°C$ ($150°F$) or less it is called "forced drying".

DRYING OILS Oils which are secreted in the seed pods of plants and in the liver and other organs of animals, which when spread out in a thin film and exposed to the air have the property of combining with the oxygen in the air to undergo a chemical change, changing from a liquid to a solid state. Such oils are the basis of oil paints and varnishes. Well-known examples of drying oils are linseed oil and tung oil; other examples are perilla, walnut, poppy-seed, etc.

DRYING TIME The length of time which elapses between the application of a coat of paint and the point at which it achieves a certain degree of hardness. There are certain recognized terms which indicate the degree of hardness achieved by a paint film; for instance, it is said to be "surface dry" when a surface skin has formed which is dry although the paint underneath is still soft and tacky, "dust dry" means that dust will no longer embed itself in the paint, but can be removed, "hard dry" means that it is dry enough for a further coat of paint to be applied, "touch dry" means that the paint will bear gentle pressure from the fingers, and "tack free' means that it is no longer tacky even under pressure. The drying time of a paint is affected by numerous factors such as the temperature of the air, the presence or otherwise of light, and so on.

DUCAT GOLD An alloy of copper and aluminium, used in imitation of gold leaf. It is supplied in books, the leaves varying in size between 82 and 120mm square. It is liable to tarnish unless protected with lacquer.

DUPLEX PAPERS Good quality embossed wallpapers, which are reinforced with an additional backing paper, the two layers being pressed together while wet. The backing paper takes a lot of the strain when the paper is pasted, with the result that there is less tendency for the embossing to be stretched and levelled out during hanging.

DURABILITY The length of time that a paint, paint system or decorative material will last before it needs to be renewed; in the case of protective materials, the length of time that they continue to be effective.

The factors affecting the durability of a paint system are:

(a) That the correct types of paint are used; that there should be an adequate build for the purpose, and that the paints should be properly compounded and of good quality materials.

(b) That the paint should be applied with a high measure of skill

(c) That the surface should be adequately prepared to remove any deposits in the way of soot, dirt, rust, etc., that would be harmful, to remove surface imperfections, and to insulate the paint system from any chemical activity of the surface.

(d) That the paint should be applied only under suitable weather conditions and not during periods of fog, rain, mist, etc. Factors outside the control of the painter or manufacturer are the conditions of exposure, the presence of polluted atmosphere, the extent to which actinic rays can penetrate to the paint, the presence or otherwise of local chemical concentrations that might affect the film, etc.

DUSTER "Duster brush" or "Jamb duster". A brush, some 100mm wide, 25mm thick and with bristles some 85mm long out of the ferrule, which is an essential part of the painter's equipment. It should be carried at all times; it is used to remove dry loose grit or dirt from a surface before paint is applied, and it should be the instinctive act of every painter to pass the duster over any surface he is painting. Far too often the duster brush is a neglected tool; it will not do its work properly if it is clogged up with dirt and dried paint. It should be washed regularly and kept in good condition.

The duster brush is frequently used as a drag for brush graining.

DUSTER "Air duster". A small compact tool for use when compressed air is available. It can be used to blow grit and dust from a surface before painting—a great advantage when places inaccessible to a duster brush are to be sprayed. The tool has several other applications to industry, such as in garage work, etc.

DUTCH ENAMEL An enamel prepared from linseed stand oil. Stand oil, which is very pale and slow drying, is obtained by heating a fine quality oil for a long period (without the addition of driers) until it has thickened or polymerized, and the production of viscous oils by this method without any appreciable oxidation taking place originated in Holland. Enamels prepared from stand oil may contain a proportion of resin to harden them, but this is unnecessary in the case of white enamel, in which the pigment which is used, zinc oxide, has a hardening effect upon the oil. Only a small proportion of pigment is added, rarely more than 600 grammes of pigment to one litre of oil; otherwise the gloss and the flow will be impaired, and for this reason Dutch enamels possess little opacity. It is therefore essential that the surfaces on which they are used should be well prepared and free from blemishes and that the undercoating should be perfectly solid. These enamels are not very easy to apply, and are rather slow drying, but they offer many advantages in compensation—they dry with a beautiful brilliant lustre, they have exceptionally good flow which results in a smooth surface free from brush marks, and they produce a very tough, durable and elastic film.

DUTCH PINK   A yellow pigment; it is obtained from quercitron, the bark of a tree found in North and Central America. The extract from this bark is precipitated with alum on to a base of alumina or Paris white.

DUTCH PROCESS   Otherwise known as the "stack process", for a very long time the principal method by which white lead was prepared. It consists of building a "stack" by setting earthenware pots containing acetic acid upon a thick layer of spent tan or manure and placing strips or coils of metallic lead over the pots; boards are then laid to form a false floor over all this and further layers of spent tan, pots of acid and strips of lead are added until the top of the brick chamber in which the stack is being constructed is reached. The stack is sealed up and the metallic lead is converted into basic carbonate of lead by a process of corrosion caused by the action of acetic acid vapour in the presence of warm moist air and carbon dioxide.

DYE   A coloured substance in the form of a liquid or a soluble solid, which is capable of imparting its colour to any porous material, such as wood or fabric, which is immersed in the solution.

E

EARLY ENGLISH   The first of the three divisions of Gothic architecture.

EARTH COLOURS   The name given to those pigments which are mined or derived from the earth, as opposed to chemically manufactured pigments. They are prepared by grinding and levigation, and are very stable and permanent. They include ochre, sienna, umber, red oxide, malachite, etc., and the range of colours obtained naturally is increased by calcining some of these materials to obtain a deeper, warmer hue, e.g., burnt sienna, a reddish brown obtained by calcining raw sienna, burnt umber from raw umber, etc.

EAST INDIA GUM   A gum resin similar to fossilized damar, used in flat lacquers.

EAVES   The projecting edge at the bottom of a roof, beyond the face of the wall.

ECRU   A name given to a creamy-yellow colour. The term is derived from a French word which refers to the colour of unbleached cloth of any kind, cotton, linen, silk or wool.

EDGE RUNNER MILL   A type of mill which consists of one or two heavy rollers revolving in a circular pan and which, although used to some extent in the production of oil paste paints, is chiefly employed in the manufacture of distempers and oil-bound water paints.

EFFLORESCENCE   A term which means, literally, "bursting out into flowers" and which is used to refer to a white crystalline deposit which forms on the surface of plaster, brick, cement, etc., giving the appearance of a white growth. It is due to the presence of soluble salts in the various building materials; the salts, dissolved in free moisture, are brought to the surface and are left behind when the water evaporates.

The salts may be wiped off or brushed off quite readily, but often continue to develop for quite a long time. If the surface has been decorated, the deposit may form on the surface of the paint film, in which case it can be brushed off without causing much damage, but generally the paint film is pushed off and broken and will flake and peel.

The treatment for efflorescence is to brush off the deposit, wipe the surface with a damp sponge, and keep the surface under observation for a few days. Should no further crystallization occur it may be assumed that it is safe to decorate. It should be noted that the crystals should be brushed off dry; if they are washed off more water is introduced into the surface and the formation of crystals will be renewed and increased. Should it be insisted that some form of decoration should be applied in spite of the risk of efflorescence, the decoration should take the form of water paint thinned with water—not petrifying liquid. On no account should an impervious paint film be applied.

EGG GLAIR   A material used in the process of gilding to prevent gold leaf from sticking to varnished or enamelled work other than where required. However hard drying the varnish or enamel may be, it retains for a surprisingly long time enough tack to allow gold leaf to adhere to it; if lettering or ornamental work is applied directly on such a finish, the edges of the gilding will be blurred and marred by the gold which adheres around them.

Egg glair is prepared by blowing a new-laid egg to separate the white from the yolk, the white of the egg being added to half a litre of lukewarm water which is then shaken up well to produce a froth. The glair is applied all over the surface that is to be gilded and is allowed to dry; it may be applied with a clean sponge which is quite adequate for normal large scale sign work, but on small scale decorative work some authorities prefer that it should be applied with a flat camel hair size brush. It is important that the glair should be applied all over the surface and not just where the gilding is to be done; otherwise, a slight difference in lustre may be detected on the parts treated with glair.

The lettering or ornament is set out in the usual way and run in with gold size which, when it has reached the right degree of tack, is gilded with transfer gold. The solvent in the gold size destroys the egg glair with which it comes in contact. When gilding is completed the egg glair is washed off with lukewarm water and a sponge, taking with it the gold which has infringed beyond the edges of the gold size. Egg glair must not be allowed to remain on the surface longer than is necessary for the gilding to be completed, because if it is left too long cracking of the paint film may take place.

EGGSHELL FINISH A rather vague term for a finish which is not completely flat or matt, but which presents instead a slight sheen or lustre, similar to the sheen on an eggshell. The precise degree of sheen which is implied by this description is difficult to determine, as the term is applied by various authorities to finishes which range from almost matt to semi-gloss; the British Standards Institution suggests in one of its publications that two degrees of eggshell finish are recognized, "eggshell flat" having slightly more lustre than a flat finish, and "eggshell gloss" having more lustre than eggshell flat but less lustre than semi-gloss.

EGGSHELL VARNISH An interior quality varnish which dries to an eggshell sheen. It may take the form of a gloss varnish which has been thinned and modified by the addition of paraffin wax, or it may be made from saponified beeswax.

Eggshell varnishes are intended for decorative effect and do not offer a great measure of protection. To obtain the best results, a coat of full-gloss varnish should be applied to the surface and allowed to dry, and the eggshell varnish applied on the following day while the gloss finish still possesses a certain degree of tack. Unlike gloss varnish which should be disturbed as little as possible, eggshell varnish should be vigorously shaken up before application and in cold weather the varnish bottle should be allowed to stand for a while in warm water before any varnish is poured out. Eggshell varnish needs to be applied quickly and confidently, each section of the work being cut in cleanly, and once applied it must not be brushed again or disturbed while setting; otherwise, "flashing" will result.

EGYPTIAN BLUE This was the first pigment ever to have been prepared by artificial means, and was for many centuries the most important blue pigment in use. It is a crystalline silicate of copper, a fine rich blue that is eminently suited to fresco work, and a small amount is still manufactured.

ELASTICITY The degree of flexibility possessed by a paint or varnish film. It is a factor of considerable importance in a varnish or gloss paint, which depends on its elasticity for its ability to conform without cracking to the expansion and contraction of the surface to which it is applied. The degree of elasticity is also an important feature of undercoats, since the application of a hard drying coating over a softer and more elastic undercoat will cause the defect known as cracking.

ELECTROLYTIC WHITE LEAD There are various methods of producing white lead by electrolysis, and the pigment which is obtained, similar in chemical composition to stack or chamber process white lead, is generally of very good colour and texture with a high degree of oil absorption. It is also sold as "flake white" as an artists' colour.

ELECTROPHORESIS An electro-chemical process which involves the migration of paint particles through a fluid under the action of an electric field, whereby under certain conditions the particles adhere to the electrode to which they are attracted. Although the electrophoretic effect was first observed more than 150 years ago, no serious attempts were made to harness it commercially until fairly recently. The process has now, however, heen considerably developed for use in a number of industries, and particularly for the application of water-thinned paints. Since 1963 it has been incorporated in the production-line treatment of motor car bodies, the metal being electrically charged as one of the electrodes in a tank containing an ammonia-stabilized water-borne paint.

The operation of the plant is fully automatic and film thickness can be accurately controlled. In particular, a uniform thickness of film can be more readily maintained on the internal surfaces of box sections and on partially screened surfaces than when conventional painting methods are employed. The process gives very good coverage of sharp corners and the paint even penetrates between spot welded surfaces. Variations in the viscosity of paint, caused by changes of temperature or concentration, which can affect the efficiency of conventional automatic and electro-static spray systems, are eliminated. "Solvent washing", whereby paint deposited in a confined box section is washed away by the condensation of solvent vapours during stoving, is also eliminated. Paint adhesion to greasy surfaces is improved by this process.

ELECTROSTATIC DE-TEARING The principle described in the next paragraph on electrostatic spraying is employed to prevent the formation of the tears and fat edges which frequently mar the finish of articles painted by the dipping process. The dipped article, after a short period of draining, is passed over a grid, and both the grid and the article are electrically charged but with charges of opposite sign. The tears and thick edges are removed by the attraction of the grid.

ELECTROSTATIC SPRAY A method of paint application which depends on the principle that, when bodies are electrically charged, those of similar charge repel each other while those of opposite charge are attracted. An electric field of very high voltage is set up through which the paint is sprayed, the atomized particles of paint becoming charged by the absorption of electrons from the ionized air; the article to be painted is earthed, so as to attract the particles of paint. By this means, the paint not only reaches the side of the article which faces the spray but also passes round to the far side of the article; this is termed the "wrap-round effect".

ELEVATION A side or end view of the vertical surfaces of an object, wall or building, which may be sketched in perspective or may be drawn to scale without reference to perspective.

ELLIPSE A regular oval.

ELM A wood used in furniture making, panelling and artistic joinery, and one which therefore lends itself to reproduction in painted treatments.

E

83

The grain markings are conspicuous; according to whether the wood is cut longitudinally or obliquely they take the form of zig-zag lines or a distinctive feathery formation known among woodworkers as "partridge breast".

EMBLEMS One of the most interesting branches of the decorator's craft is that which concerns the use of emblems and symbols as motifs for decoration, and the selection of such symbols as are appropriate for any particular building. In earlier days, when a large proportion of the population was illiterate, the visual arts of painting, sculpture, etc., were also required to serve as a medium of instruction, and the various figures could often be identified by symbols which they bore. The signs displayed by shops and business premises were also pictorial in character, bearing symbols to represent the trade in which the owners were engaged.

Not only has this symbolism persisted to the present day, but its use is still extending, as may be seen by the trade marks which modern business firms employ as distinguishing marks for their goods. The decorator who is alive to the possibilities of this traditional branch of the craft is never at a loss for suitable and appropriate mofits as a basis for design. Church decoration teems with symbolism, such as the dice, nails and thorns which are the emblems of the Passion, the keys of St. Peter, the eagle of St. John, the winged bull of St. Luke (who is also the patron saint of painters), and so on. Emblems suitable for other types of public buildings include the scales of justice, the torch of learning, the serpent and rod representing medicine, the crown, orb and sceptre of royalty, etc.

EMBOSSED WALLPAPER A paper which has been passed through rollers which mould it so that either the pattern is raised in relief or a raised background texture is produced. When these papers are being hung, care must be taken that they are not oversoaked during the pasting and that they are not subjected to undue brushing or stretching during application; otherwise, the embossing may be stretched and levelled out. See also *Duplex Papers.*

EMBOSSING OF GLASS The process of etching glass with hydrofluoric acid so as to produce a pattern or piece of lettering raised in relief. The glass must be perfectly clean, and the parts which are not to be etched are protected with acid-resist. The glass is then set perfectly level upon a bed of sawdust on a workbench—it must be laid horizontally; the process cannot be carried out on vertical or sloping surfaces—and a wall of cobblers' wax built around it. Dilute acid is poured in and allowed to remain until the required depth of etching has been obtained, when it is poured off and the glass thoroughly cleaned. See also *Acid Etching.*

EMERALD GREEN A pigment compounded from the arsenite and acetate of copper. Its brilliant blue-green colour is a useful addition to the decorator's range, but it has many drawbacks, being coarse in texture, liable to settle and, like all the copper pigments, easily discoloured. Its chief drawback, however, is its highly poisonous nature. It is rarely used nowadays for decorative work, but is included in anti-fouling paints for the hulls of ships and is also prepared as an insecticide known as Paris green.

EMULSIFYING AGENT A material added to substances which are not normally miscible in water in order to form a stable emulsion, such as the soap or glue used to emulsify an oil to form the medium of an oil-bound water paint. See *Emulsion*.

EMULSION A stable combination of two liquids which normally will not mix together, one liquid being dispersed in the other one in the form of extremely fine globules.

Various materials commonly used in painting and decorating are based upon emulsion. Oil-bound water paints, for example, are prepared with a medium consisting of an oil-in-water emulsion. Oil and water are not normally miscible; if the two liquids are shaken together the oil will split up into droplets, but when the shaking ceases the liquids separate again and the oil will float on top of the water. But if a substance such as soap or glue is dissolved in the water and this mixture and the oil strongly agitated together, the oil breaks up into minute droplets, each of which becomes coated with an envelope of soap or glue and is unable to coalesce or flow together again when the shaking ceases; the oil now remains in a state of permanent suspension in the water.

Water paint consisting of suitable pigments ground in such an emulsion, which dry firstly by evaporation of the water content and later by the oxidation of the oil (the same chemical change that takes place in an oil paint), may be thinned with water to provide a matt finish eminently suitable for interior decoration, or may be thinned with a diluted form of the emulsion, known as petrifying liquid, to produce a finish for exterior work.

Other examples of the use of emulsions in paint materials include bituminous emulsion paints, in which the medium is an emulsion of bitumen in water and which are chiefly used for exterior work, being especially useful on concrete and similar alkaline materials; wool grease emulsion paints made from an emulsion of wool grease in water and which, because they repel water, are also useful for exterior work, and others. Water-in-oil emulsions, in which the water is the disperse phase, are used in various gloss and semi-gloss paints.

EMULSION PAINTS It will be seen from the previous definition that there are many surface coatings which might very properly be described as emulsion paints, including (for example) oil-bound water paint. In practice, however, the term is now generally accepted by the trade to mean those types of water-thinned paints in which the disperse phase consists of minute droplets of synthetic high polymers. Furthermore, in recent years synthetic polymer emulsion paints have to a large extent supplanted the oil-bound water paints and have rendered such materials as washable distempers practically obsolete, and in terms of sheer volume of production they represent by far the greatest part of the water-thinned materials on the market.

Briefly, emulsion paints consist of synthetic resin polymers with the addition of suitable pigments, suspended in a continuous phase of water. They dry by the evaporation of the water, when the droplets of polymer coalesce; the final film consists, therefore, of small spheres packed tightly together. This, of course, is an extreme simplification; the development of the synthetic polymers is a highly complex field of science which has been, and still is, the subject of a considerable volume of research. The original researches in this field, carried out in Germany before and during the second world war, produced polyvinyl acetate emulsions that were crude by present-day standards but were an important step in providing an alternative for the natural products which were in short supply. At the close of the war the development passed into American hands, where experiments continued not only with polyvinyl acetate but with synthetic rubber latices based on other resins such as styrene, alkyd, etc. When eventually restrictions were lifted and production in this country became possible the concentration here was on polyvinyl acetate, the paints produced being known by the shortened version "PVA emulsions". Interest in the development of these products was due to a number of factors, not all of scientific origin, and often promoted chiefly by salesmanship. These factors were (a) the cheapness of water compared with other solvents, (b) the advantage of requiring less capital equipment, (c) the reduction of fire hazards, (d) speed of application, and (e) rapidity of drying. A state was reached when there were obvious advantages in merging the research activities of paint technologists with those of scientific workers in other industries (such as, for example, tyre manufacture). The original PVA emulsions suffered from the drawback that the resin droplets when coalesced, became extremely brittle, to overcome which the addition of a plasticizer was necessary. PVA is still very widely employed, but the original homopolymer p.v.a., externally plasticized, has been partly replaced by co-polymers of various kinds which do not need an external plasticizer. Most of these, besides being more flexible, produce a film of improved washability and alkali resistance. Acrylic emulsions, more expensive than PVA, are also available for outdoor use and for situations requiring an exceptional degree of alkali resistance. In recent years a number of "vinyl distempers" or "vinyl water paints" has been produced for indoor use where they are not exposed to any severe conditions of wear and tear; these are cheaper than PVA but not washable to the same extent. Their performance in fact is roughly similar to that of oil-bound water paints — which incidentally are cheaper in price.

The attractive qualities offered by emulsion paint may be summarized as follows:- (a) ease of application, making for reduced labour costs, (b) speed of drying, which means that further coats can be applied without much delay — a useful point where premises have to be brought back into use in as short a time as possible, (d) lack of odour during application — a useful feature in restaurants, hospitals, etc., (d) resistance to alkaline action, making them suitable for use on new plaster, cement, asbestos sheeting, etc., (e) ability to withstand washing and scrubbing shortly after application (except in the case of vinyl water paints). Emulsion paints possess other features which need to be accepted critically and with some reservations, e.g., (f) Tolerance of damp. The structure of the dried film permits the passage of moisture vapour (a property more marked in matt and eggshell finishes than in semi-gloss or glaze types). For this reason they are useful for decorating new property but the risk of breakdown is always greater on a damp surface than on one which is reasonably dry and it is unwise to make too great a demand on the material. (g) Resistance to mould growth. They contain nothing which provides the nourishment needed for mould spores to develop, but on the other hand they are not fungicidal and will not destroy any fungoid growths already present. (h) Resistance to bleeding. Many types of emulsion can be used successfully over coatings of bitumen, creosote, etc., but they do *not* seal the surface; if oil paint is subsequently applied the solvents may penetrate the emulsion and the painted surface may be discoloured by bleeding.

There are certain purposes for which emulsion paints are not suitable. They should never be used on bare metal as the free acids they contain will attack non-ferrous metals and their water content will promote rusting of ferrous metals. They have no power to bind down loose or powdery material. Although they are tolerant of moisture they may be susceptible to damage when exposed to severe conditions of condensation.

It should be noted that emulsion paints do not penetrate the surface to which they are applied to any marked extent. For this reason emulsion paints do not possess powers of adhesion comparable with those of oil paint or even with those of an oil-bound water paint. On the other hand it does mean that emulsion paints are very effective in sealing the absorbency of a porous surface.

Emulsion paints may be applied by brush, roller or spray. The liquid paint must be protected from frost and must not be applied at temperatures lower than 4°C. They may be used on both interior and exterior work, but vinyl water paints are for interior use only. On the grounds of economy they are frequently used in the trade as undercoats for gloss paint, but this is still a very questionable practice particularly on outdoor work.

EMULSION VARNISH   A clear untinted emulsion glaze which is used to give a washable finish to wallpaper. It is not to be confused with a paper varnish of the traditional gloss type. It is intended for use on ordinary wallpapers of the distemper coated type, whereas a paper varnish is intended for oil coated sanitary papers. It is applied with a broad flat brush, not a varnish brush. It is applied direct to the paper, whereas when paper varnish is being used the paper needs to be sized to prevent discolouration from the oil in the varnish staining the paper. The finish is an eggshell sheen as opposed to the gloss finish of a paper varnish. It is intended to improve the durability of ordinary wallpaper by making it easy to clean down; it is not intended to replace paper varnish as a finish for sanitary papers in steamy atmospheres.

ENAMEL   Originally meaning a vitreous compound with which articles of metal or porcelain are coated by fusion, the term is used in several connections to refer to a hard, smooth, glossy coating.

The word is now used rather loosely in the painting and decorating trade. Until recently its meaning was more precise; it was applied specifically to a material made with a limited quantity of finely ground pigment in a medium of linseed stand oil with or without the addition of resins; such materials, which possess little opacity and are rather slow drying, produce a very durable film of considerable smoothness and lustre and are described under the heading of "Dutch Enamels". A distinction was drawn between these enamels and the materials with greater powers of obliteration made with a higher proportion of pigment in a varnish medium, which were known by such names as "hard gloss paints", etc.

Nowadays, with the increased use of synthetic resins and of highly opaque pigments such as titanium and antimony oxides, there has ceased to be any clear cut distinction between the materials variously termed enamel, enamel paint, hard gloss paint, full gloss paint, gloss enamel, etc., and the term "enamel" is generally taken to imply a superior quality of full gloss paint.

Various materials are used for specific purposes (e.g., see "Bath Enamel") and in the field of industrial finishes there are a number of thermosetting enamels.

ENCAUSTIC PAINTING　An ancient method of painting, practised by the Greeks and Romans, whereby melted beeswax was applied, the colours being blended with heated spatulae.

END FINISHER　A small type of check roller used in graining, which allows the top and bottom angles of panel work to be completed without leaving a gap.

END GRAIN　The pattern seen when a piece of wood has been cut across the grain. The end grain of wood is considerably more absorbent than any face which runs parallel with the direction in which the fibres run. This is because the cells which conduct moisture up the trunk from the roots have been cut across, leaving their open ends exposed in the form of pipe-like ducts; these ducts act as capillary tubes, through which liquids will rise. It is essential when painting timber that end grain should be properly primed to check this absorption; otherwise, moisture will enter and will be conveyed into the very heart of the wood no matter how well the rest has been painted. Because of its great absorbency, end grain should, whereever possible, be primed twice.

ENTASIS　A slight curving outwards of the shaft of a column, introduced to correct the optical illusion whereby the column appears to be concave.

EPON　The name under which epoxy resins are marketed in the U.S.A.

EPOXY PAINT　A two-pack material forming a thick coating with high resistance to chemicals, alkalis, etc. It chalks fairly rapidly outdoors, but further breakdown is slow. It possesses excellent properties of adhesion to concrete, and is used as the basis of floor finishes. See *Epoxy Resins*.

EPOXY RESINS　These are recently developed resins with properties of outstanding importance in the manufacture of paint. They are made by reacting epichlorhydrin and diphenylol propane together and are used in the production of a wide range of both air drying and stoving finishes. The features which they offer include a very high resistance to alkalis, extreme hardness combined with great flexibility and toughness, excellent adhesion and resistance to abrasion. They are rarely used on their own but are combined with other resins or resin-forming materials to produce stoving finishes with considerable chemical resistance, high grade air drying varnishes and paints, etc.; when combined with suitable amines as "curing" or polymerizing agents a surface coating is produced which, at normal air drying temperatures or at the slightly higher temperatures obtained by forced drying, has the durability and chemical resistance of a stoved finish —a factor of great importance when the object to be painted is sensitive to heat or too large to be treated in a stoving oven. Paints based on epikote resins have been successfully used in the treatment of new concrete, the protection of metals exposed to strong acids, alkalis, detergents, etc., and in the aircraft industry and in a wide variety of other conditions.

EPOXYESTER PAINT   A single pack material designed to resist mild chemical attack. It is resistant to water, acids, oils and to many solvents, but is usually adversely affected by alkalis.

EROSION   The wearing away of the top surface of a paint film, by means of chalking, etc.

ESTER COPALS   Soft copals of high acid value, such as Congo copals, esterified in the same way as the rosin described in the next paragraph.

ESTER GUMS   Glyceride esters of naturally occurring acid resins; generally the term is understood to refer to rosin esters. They are of very low acid value, and because they do not "feed" with basic pigments they are used in the preparation of mixing varnishes and enamel media; they are also used in nitro-cellulose lacquers.

ESTER INTERCHANGE   A chemical reaction which occurs when two or more resins are heated together under suitable conditions; a factor of great importance in the varnish industry, as it produces films with better performance than the natural resins. Other examples relating to the paint industry are (a) when linseed and tung oils are heated together, a range of new glycerides is produced; (b) when polyamide resin is introduced into an alkyd resin cook, an ester and amine interchange takes place whereby a thixotropic alkyd paint is produced.

ESTERS   Compounds formed by replacing the hydrogen of an acid by a hydrocarbon radical of the ethyl type. Examples relevant to the painting trade include a number of materials used industrially as solvents, such as ethyl, propyl, glycol, amyl and butyl acetates (the latter two being the chief solvents used in the manufacture of nitro-cellulose lacquers), ethyl carbonate, ethyl, amyl and butyl formates and lactates, etc.

ESTIMATE   A contractor's statement of the sum for which he will undertake a specified piece of work, based essentially on his knowledge of the length of time required to perform the various operations of the trade and his judgment of the area covered by a given quantity of material.

ETCH PRIMER   See *Pre-treatment Primers.*

ETCHING   See *Acid Etching.*

EVAPORATION   The process whereby a liquid is transformed to a vapour.

EXPANDED POLYSTYRENE or FOAMED POLYSTYRENE   A material prepared in such a form that it can be applied by the decorator to improve the thermal insulation of structural surfaces and thus help to eliminate condensation and minimize the occurrence of pattern staining. It is extremely light in weight and is available in various forms and several thicknesses to suit varying purposes. The usual forms in which it is supplied are as follows
(a) In sheet form, in various thicknesses, for application to plastered walls and ceiling surfaces, after which the surface can be hung with wallpaper or decorated with water paint or emulsion paint; it should be noted that oil paint is not a suitable material to be applied directly to foamed polystyrene because of the damaging effect of the solvent upon the plastic.
(b) As a moulded coving, which enables the decorator to add a cornice to a room at the junction of the wall and ceiling surfaces; such coving may be finished with a coating of water paint or emulsion paint.
(c) As acoustic tiles of various dimensions and thicknesses, which present a pleasing appearance even when no further decorative coating is applied.
(d) As acoustic tiles in ready decorated form with a simple geometric pattern applied in colour to the surface.

All these materials are very easy to handle and can readily be affixed with the special adhesive supplied by the manufacturers. In some cases it is necessary to seal the plastered surface with a coat of alkali-resisting primer before fixing the polystyrene.

The surface of the foamed polystyrene is easily dented and damaged; when wallpaper has been superimposed, and re-decoration is necessary, no attempt should be made to use a knife for stripping the old paper; the paper should be well soaked with water until it is loose enough to be pulled away by hand.

While the main purpose of the material is to reduce condensation, it also provides a good measure of sound insulation, and also by retaining the heat in the room helps to cut down on fuel costs. Expanded polystyrene is available in large slabs of considerable thickness, some of them patterned with a cross cut design for ornamental effect, as well as in the forms stated above. The fixing of such slabs, however, is usually carried out by constructional staffs rather than by the decorator.

EXPOSURE RACK   A frame upon which painted panels are exposed for durability tests. The panels are generally arranged at an angle of 45° and facing due south so that the full severity of the weather and the action of sunlight is encountered.

EXPOSURE TESTS   Tests carried out by paint manufacturers in order to determine the durability of paint products under various conditions of exposure. Panels painted with the material under test are mounted on exposure racks in various parts of the country, generally in chemically pollut atmospheres, coastal districts and other places where the conditions destructive to paint are severe, and an overall assessment of the material is arrived at by keeping the several panels under observation. Similar exposure stations are set up abroad by manufacturers engaged in overseas markets.

EXTENDED ELEVATION   The elevations of the several wall surfaces of a room arranged so as to read as a long continuous strip; this device is useful in preparing working drawings for decoration.

EXTENDERS   Materials which have little or no opacity when mixed with varnish or oil, and which are incorporated into paints for a variety of technical reasons, such as to prevent the settling of heavy pigments, to harden the film, to increase the body, to arrest the flow, and in some cases to cheapen the material. Among the principal extenders used are barytes, blanc fixé, China clay, asbestine and silica.

EXTENDING SCAFFOLD BOARDS   Scaffold boards which can be adjusted in length.

EXTENSION LADDER   A ladder consisting of two or more sections, each of the standing ladder type, made so that the height can be adjusted by telescoping the sections. Each section can be used separately if desired. The two main types are (a) the hook-and-clip catch type, which is ropeless, and (b) the rope-operated, safety catch type, which is operated by means of pulleys. Type (b) is heavier and stronger, and should be used where a considerable height is required. Extension ladders consisting of two sections are used for heights of up to 15 metres, and of three sections for heights of up to 22 metres.

EXTENSION SPRAY HEAD   A device used in industrial finishing to enable the interior of small necked vessels, tubes, pipes, etc., to be sprayed. The head can be arranged to give a disc spray, cone spray or fan spray as required.

F

FABRIC WALL HANGINGS   Among the fabrics used as wall hangings are fine materials such as silk, tapestry and velvet, coarser materials such as canvas, hessian and jute and coated fabrics which include American cloth and Lancaster cloth, rexine which is a nitro-cellulose coated fabric, and polyvinyl chloride coated fabrics such as Texturide, Vynide, Stormur, Lionide, Lionclad, Suwide, Galon, etc.

FACADE   The face or elevation of a building.

FAD   A pad used in the application of French polish.

FADDING   The application of polish by means of a fad.

FADING   The loss of colouring matter in a painted surface, which may be due to ageing, weathering or exposure to sunlight. Colours which fade under the action of sunlight are known as "fugitive" colours; the lakes are notorious in this respect. Certain colours which are tolerably fast to light when used at full strength will fade badly when reduced to a tint with white. Fugitive colours tend to fade more in flat finishes than when protected by a gloss medium. Sometimes a paint which is chalking gives the appearance of fading but the colour may be restored by the application of a coat of varnish.

FALL   The suspension rope passing through the pulley blocks in a suspended chair or cradle.

FALSE BODY   A condition whereby a paint appears to be full-bodied but undergoes a sharp drop in viscosity when agitated or brushed out, resuming its original condition when the agitation stops; the condition is often seen in flat oil paints, in which it may be produced by the addition of such materials as aluminium stearate, bentonite, etc., and is a feature of such materials as transparent glaze medium. False body should not be confused with thixotropy, although it appears to be a similar condition. When thixotropic materials are subjected to the shearing action of a brush there is a lapse of time before the original viscosity is resumed, during which the brushmarks flow out; in the case of false body, the original viscosity of the materials is resumed immediately the shearing action ceases, and brushmarks do not flow out.

FANLIGHT   A glazed oblong or semi-circular window over a door; so called because in the late eighteenth century, when they became a popular feature in English architecture, such windows had glazing bars radiating from the centre like a fan.

FANTAIL OVERGRAINER   A long-handled brush the bristles of which are splayed out into the shape of an open fan, used in graining.

FAST TO LIGHT   A term meaning that the paint or pigment so described will not fade on exposure to light.

FASTENING   The binding down of loose particles of pigment, etc. For example, the water-colour pigments used in graining are loosely bound by the addition of stale beer, vinegar or fuller's earth, but will not withstand any vigorous rubbing; before any further working in the form of overgraining, etc., can take place, they must be bound down with a coat of varnish and turps in equal quantities, applied with speed. This process is described as "fastening" the graining colour.

FAT EDGES   A fault in application whereby a thick ridge of paint occurs on a corner or arris; it can be avoided by laying off at the corners with an almost dry brush. The fault may also occur on an article coated by dipping due to the paint accumulating at the edges when draining.

FATTENING A thickening up of fluid paint which sometimes occurs in the interval between its being mixed and being put into use. Probably the term conveys very little to those who are only accustomed to using ready mixed paints, but those who remember when most paints were mixed on the job will recall it as a very expressive phrase, suggesting very forcefully the fatty feel of the paint under the brush   when for some reason it was kept too long before use.

FATTY ACIDS The acid components obtained by the hydrolysis of fats; they are used in the preparation of alkyd resins, driers, etc. Vegetable oils, such as linseed oil, consist chiefly of the glycerides of fatty acids; the smoothness with which white lead paint works and the toughness of the dried film are due to the lead soap formed by the chemical combination of the lead with the fatty acid.

FAULTING A term used in glass gilding. When the gold leaf has been laid in, a number of blemishes reveal themselves as the mordant dries; some of the joints will be open, in some places the leaf will be seen to be pinholed and here and there cracks will have opened. Before the leaf can be fixed with the backing up paint it is always necessary to inspect the work and touch in the blemishes, where they occur, with further pieces of gold leaf. This operation is known as "faulting".

FEATHER The characteristic figuring found in mahogany (and certain other woods) when the timber is cut from the topmost part of the tree trunk through the actual base of the main branch.

FEATHER, THE USE OF A feather is frequently used by grainers to put in the more open grain markings of wood such as walnut, etc,; when used with a dragging motion through wet stain it produces effects which cannot be obtained by other tools such as overgrainers, etc.

FEATHERED EDGE The irregular joint invisible beneath the completed decoration obtained by the process described in *Feathering*.

FEATHERING A method of producing joints in lining paper, etc., in such a way as to avoid showing a distinct edge or ridge. When the paper is applied to the surface the last few inches are folded back at right angles to the surface; when the paste has dried out the projecting fold of paper is firmly seized and torn off, leaving a joint which is imperceptible beneath the completed decoration. The method is also of value when it is desired to cover only a small portion of a surface with lining paper, such as when covering a stain or making a neat and tight finish after making good the defective plaster on an external angle.

FEEDING A defect whereby a paint thickens up to an unusable consistency; a feature of the fault is that although the paint has become very thick it loses its opacity, and that any attempt to thin the paint with solvents tends to make it become thicker still. It is due to the mixing of incompatible materials, such as, for instance, when lead or zinc based paints are mixed with a varnish medium of high acid value instead of a proper mixing varnish, or when two different types of ready mixed paints incompatible with each other are mixed together.

FELT BLOCKS   Thick pads of hard felt sold by decorators' merchants for use as rubbing blocks. When a surface is being sandpapered down, the common practice of holding the sandpaper across the flat of the hand is very inefficient; pressure is only applied by the finger-tips, with the result that the abrasive action is unevenly distributed; and it is practically impossible to rub into the corners of panels. If the sandpaper is wrapped around a rubbing block, the abrasive face outwards, the task or rubbing down is made easier and an even pressure is exerted over the whole working surface of the sandpaper; it is possible to sandpaper the corners of panels just as effectively as the centres and the whole work is performed better and more quickly.

FELT COVERED ROLLER   A broad roller, the drum of which is encased in a long cylinder of thick felt or in several short cylinders placed end to end, which is sometimes used by the paperhanger as an alternative to the papering brush in the hanging of delicate papers such as flocks, satins, etc., which are easily scratched or damaged by normal handling, and which is also used for pressing down certain materials such as vinyl wallpapers, Realwood leathercloths, etc., to expel air bubbles.

FELTING DOWN   The process of rubbing down a recently painted surface with powdered pumice and a piece of thick felt, with water as a lubricant; generally it is done with the intention of rubbing down a gloss varnish or enamel coating to a matt surface prior to the application of a second coat of gloss. To some extent it has been superseded by the fact that modern alkyd paints do not need to be flatted down before a second coat of gloss is applied. When flatting down is still required it has largely given place to the use of waterproof sandpaper which is considered to be cleaner in use, there being less likelihood of traces of grit remaining on the surface to mar the next application of gloss paint. Nevertheless it is doubtful whether rubbing down with waterproof sandpaper flats the surface as effectively as felting down with pumice and, provided the surface is properly washed off and is rubbed over with a tack rag before being revarnished, there is no reason why any grit should remain to cause trouble.

FIBRE   A slender filament of which the tissues of plants and animals are composed; the substances composed of vegetable or animal tissue which form the raw materials of textile manufacture.

FIBRE BOARDS   Materials made from pulped wood fibre or other vegetable fibre, used to form a rigid lining construction for walls and ceilings, and which provide thermal and sound insulation to the structures in which they are employed. They range from thick loosely compacted boards of the type used for acoustic purposes to hardboards closely compacted under high pressure.

FIBRE BRUSHES   Brushes in which the filling consists of vegetable fibre derived from the Mexican agave plant. This fibre possesses none of the spring or elasticity of bristle, but because it is not affected by alkalis it is very suitable for a cheap form of brush which can be used for the application of limewash, cement paints, etc., and for washing down with alkaline materials, all purposes which are extremely harmful to bristle brushes.

Vegetable fibre is also used as an adulterant, being mixed with bristle to produce cheaper brushes than those made entirely of bristle. Mixture brushes do not, however, work so easily as those composed of 100% bristle, nor do they produce so good a finish; this is because the fibre does not taper as bristle does and therefore does not help the paint to flow to the tip, nor does it possess the flag which is so characteristic of bristle and which contributes so much to the laying-off of the paintwork. Brushes containing a high proportion of fibre tend to become matted in use and are noticeably lacking in spring.

F

FIBROUS PLASTER High relief decorative plaster work which is used to form cornices, mouldings, wall panels, decorative swags, ceiling centrepieces etc., and which is cast by the plasterer from reverse moulds on the bench and then fixed in position on the site. Although it appears to be solid it is really a thin layer of plaster strengthened with scrim and wooden laths; the plaster used is generally of the hemi-hydrate type, such as plaster of Paris, retarded by the addition of glue size. Because of the porous nature of the plaster and the thinness of the shell, fibrous plaster units are often considerably more absorbent than the surrounding areas of ceiling or wall plaster against which they are set; they should therefore be given a coat of sealer or an extra coat of primer, otherwise when painted they may dry to a different colour from the adjacent plaster due to the variation of porosity. Difficulty sometimes arises from the fact that the moulds used in preparing fibrous plaster are coated with oil to facilitate the removal of the cast; this may retard the drying of the paint.

FILLER (a) A composition used to fill surface indentations, fine cracks, etc., in order to produce a perfectly smooth and level surface prior to painting. It may take the form of Japan filler or water filler. The former consists of slate powder, silica, powdered pumice and similar materials ground in Japan gold size or can be made from paste white lead, gilders' whiting and gold size; a home made water filler can be mixed with equal parts of good class water paint and fine plaster of Paris, but excellent proprietary brands are obtainable in powder form, ready to be mixed with water. Water filler tends to work more easily than Japan filler; on the other hand, the rubbing down of water filler, which must be done with dry sandpaper, entails considerable dust, whereas Japan filler is rubbed down wet and is much cleaner. Both types of filler may be applied in thick paste form with the knife or may be thinned for brush application; Japan filler may also be prepared for spray application.

The term "filler" is often loosely and incorrectly used nowadays to include materials used for the stopping of large holes and cracks
(b) The term filler is also used as an alternative name for "extender", a mineral pigment having no opacity in oil (see "Extender"). The term is sometimes loosely and wrongly used in this connection to refer not only to the extender but to the pigmentary content of a paint in general.

95

FILLET A small flat band between mouldings separating them from each other; also, the top member of a cornice.

FILLETER A very long-haired signwriting pencil with a squared end, used for running in bands and fillets with colour.

FILLING (a) The process of achieving a perfectly smooth level surface, prior to painting, by the use of filler.
(b) When a wall surface is broken up by various mouldings and members, the term "filling" is applied to the main portion of the wall between picture rail and dado rail.
(c) In speaking of brushes, the filling is the bristle, animal hair, fibre or synthetic filament which forms the brush head.

FILLING KNIFE A broad knife used for the application of filler when filling and levelling a surface prior to painting. The knife should be reasonably stiff but flexible at the tip. It is essential that the edge should be perfectly true and free from any twists, kinks or other defects, otherwise each stroke of the knife will produce a ridge in the filler, which will defeat the purpose of the operation; it is therefore desirable that the filling knife should be kept solely for that purpose and not used for stripping wallpaper, burning off, etc., and that the edge of the knife should be protected, when not in use, in a sheath of stout paper or leather.

FILM THICKNESS The degree of protection afforded by a film of paint depends to a great extent on its being of adequate thickness, recent experiments having revealed a direct relationship between the thickness of the film and the duration of the protection. It has been established that the thickness of the dried film on a steel structure needs to be at least 0.127mm to ensure a satisfactory level of protection. The thickness of a single coat of paint applied by brush by a competent craftsman may be said to vary between as little as 0·017mm and as much as 0·050mm depending upon the type of paint, the conditions of application and the quality of the brushwork. The thickness of a normal four-coat system on new work may therefore be as low as 0·076mm and will hardly exceed 0·102mm, from which it will be seen how easily it may be worn away by even mild abrasion. Of course, the thickness of the film is not the only criterion; no useful purpose would be served by trying to build up the requisite thickness in one heavy coat of paint. The film should consist of primer, undercoats and finishing coat, each allowed to become thoroughly hard and designed to form a well-balanced, adhesive and protective whole. It is important, too, that a satisfactory film thickness should be maintained by undertaking regular re-painting before the old film has deteriorated too badly.

FINENESS OF GRIND An important quality, in any pigment, the durability, spreading power and hiding power of a paint depending to a great extent upon the fineness of the particles.

FINGERING A term used when a new paint brush, instead of maintaining a good shape and clean chisel edge, splays out into a bad shape. A brush tends to finger through being wrongly used, as for example by being used edgeways, or through not being properly treated during the breaking-in period.

FINIAL A scaffold fitting designed to hold a horizontal tube directly above the vertical tubes to form a guard rail or barrier. Two types are available, a fixed type to make a right-angled joint and a swivel type for a joint at an angle other than a right angle.

FINISH (a) The final coat in a paint system; the coat which is intended to provide the required colour, texture and degree of gloss, and which offers resistance to the corrosive effects of the atmosphere, the destructive effect of sunlight and to the peculiar conditions met with in special circumstances such as in bakeries, breweries, chemical works, etc. The extent to which the finish fulfils these requirements depends upon the previous coatings being suitable, adequate and properly applied.
(b) The term is also used in a general sense to indicate the appearance of the finished work, e.g., "flat finish", "gloss finish", "textured finish", "crackle finish", etc., and in a still more general sense "good finish", "poor finish", etc.; it can also be used loosely to describe the type of finishing material, e.g., "synthetic finish", "bitumen finish", etc.

FIRE POINT The temperature at which a substance will ignite and continue to burn when brought into contact with a small flame.

FIRE-RETARDING PAINTS Paints applied to combustible materials such as timber, fibre board or fabric for fire protection purposes. No paint will render an inflammable material flameproof, but fire-retarding paints can make such a material less readily ignitable, can delay and minimize the spread of flame across the surface and may prevent the material from continuing to burn after the source of heat has been removed; in these ways the seat of the outbreak is localized and occupants of the building given time to escape. Fire-retarding paints arrest the spread of flame by acting as a sealer or buffer coat, sealing off the more inflammable material beneath by cutting off the supply of oxygen. To a lesser extent, when used on wood or fibre board their effectiveness is due to a chemical reaction with the cellulose content of these materials.
The ability of a paint to retard the spread of flame varies according to its composition; for instance, the use of certain pigments such as lithopone and titanium dioxide increases this capacity. Another factor is the degree of pigmentation; in general, the resistance to flame spread is improved as the proportion of pigment is increased, but a point is reached when the paint is so highly pigmented as to crack under the influence of heat, releasing inflammable gases from below. Fire-retarding paints may be roughly classified as follows:
Class I. Materials of very low flame spread. Silicate or water glass paints, consisting of alkali resisting pigments and extenders in a medium of silicate of soda or other alkaline silicates, which become insoluble on drying; also plastic paints based on calcium sulphate plaster.
Class II. Materials of low flame spread. These include flat oil paints

97

pigmented with lithopone and oil-bound water paints pigmented with lithopone. In addition there are various materials such as borax, magnesium phosphate, vermiculite, etc., which can be added to both oil paints and water paints to improve their fire resistance, and white lead oil paints containing such materials come into this class. Oil paints can also be given increased resistance by the addition of chlorinated rubber.

Class III. Materials of medium flame spread. Ordinary varnish paints and oil paints without the addition of such materials as borax, etc.

FIRST COAT The first coating applied in any painting system; it may be the primer coat or a sealer or binder coat.

FISH OILS Oils derived from fish or fish organs; very often they possess a disagreeable odour and are liable to yellowing upon exposure; their weathering properties are poor. In the U.S.A. the term is generally used to refer to menhadin oil, which is combined with perilla and tung oils to produce finishes which will withstand fairly high temperatures.

FITCH A word derived from a Dutch word meaning polecat, and originally applied to a brush made from the fur of a polecat; nowadays the term is used to refer to a brush, generally composed of hog hair, set in a metal ferrule and attached to a long slender wooden handle. Fitches are made in various graded sizes, and are supplied in three types—flat fitches which are squared at the end, round fitches which have a cylindrical section and taper slightly at the tip, and the filbert type, which have a tip shaped like a finger end. They are most useful brushes with a variety of applications; they are essential for all classes of decorative work, mural work and so on, and are widely used in sign work, etc. They are also a useful adjunct to the tool kit of the ordinary painter and decorator as there are many occasions when small touches of colour can be applied more easily with a fitch than with any other tool.

FIXATIVE A liquid which is applied over charcoal, crayon, chalk or black lead pencil drawings in order to prevent them from becoming blurred; it is usually applied by means of a diffuser, two hinged tubes of metal, one of which is dipped in a bottle of fixative and the other placed in the mouth of the operative, the act of blowing upon the latter tube producing a fine spray, or by means of a small hand-operated atomizer like a scent spray.

The term is also used rather loosely sometimes to refer to pastes of various kinds, latex solutions and similar materials used in the hanging of wallpapers, Lincrusta and other wall coverings.

FIXED CRADLE A cradle which can be operated upwards and downwards but not in a sideways direction.

FLAG A characteristic feature of bristle—hog hair—whereby the tips of the hair split into two or three separate strands. This has a great bearing on the quality of brushwork produced with a bristle brush; not only is the bristle strong and resilient enough to enable oil paints to be applied firmly and vigorously, but it also possesses a softness at the tip, due to the flag, which allows the paint to be laid off lightly and the brushmarks eliminated. As bristle is worn down the tip continues to split, so that the flag is continually being renewed; for this reason a bristle brush maintains its characteristic properties throughout the time it is in use.

FLAKE WHITE White lead of very fine quality produced as an artists' colour by a process of precipitation.

FLAKING A defect primarily due to poor adhesion, whereby the paint film lifts from the underlying surface and breaks away in the form of brittle flakes. The conditions which give rise to flaking may develop in a number of ways. Moisture is often the cause of the trouble; it may be present in the surface before it is painted or may find an entry into the surface after painting, through open joints or building defects, and may be drawn out by the action of heat or sunlight, causing the paint film to lift, or a film of moisture may be present upon the surface while painting is in progress, due to condensation or because the surface is exposed to rain, frost or fog, thus preventing the adhesion of the paint.

Flaking may also occur due to the surface being in a loose or powdery condition when painted; for example, the paint may have been applied over rust or upon old paintwork which was chalking badly and not properly prepared, or upon loose distemper or weak, crumbling plaster.

Sometimes flaking may be due to the nature of the surface or to the use of an unsuitable primer, such as when paint fails to adhere to the highly polished surface of a dense plaster such as Keene's or to the greasy surface of certain non-ferrous metals. If dirt and grease are not removed from an old painted surface before re-painting is commenced flaking may result, and if decoration is begun before efflorescence has ceased to form on a surface the paint film may be fractured and flaked by the eruption of the salts. Water paints which are repeatedly re-coated without suitable preparation are liable to build up a film of considerable thickness which eventually tends to flake; when water paints are exposed to steamy atmospheres they are subjected to the stress of alternate wetting and drying which causes expansion and contraction movements and eventually weakens their adhesion.

Flaking also results when either water paints or oil paints are applied over a coating of glue size.

FLAMBOYANT FINISH A type of industrial finish very popular for the treatment of such items as cycle frames, etc. The article to be painted is given one or two coats of metallic paint, usually aluminium; it is then lightly sprayed with a semi-transparent coat of very pure bright colour and finished with a coat of clear lacquer. It is generally carried out with stoving paints.

FLAME CLEANING A very effective method of cleaning and preparing steelwork; it consists of applying an intensely hot oxy-acetylene flame to the surface. Its effectiveness is due to several factors, which may be summarized as follows:
(a) It loosens rust and scale by means of differential expansion, that is to

say the scale is heated more rapidly than the parent metal to which it is attached and therefore expands more quickly, thus being caused to flake off.

(b) The rust is dehydrated by the process; all the contained moisture, which causes rust to cling so tenaciously to the parent metal and which, if the rust were not completely removed, would cause further rusting to develop beneath the new paint film, is rapidly driven off by the intense dry heat of the flame and the rust converted to a dry powder which is easily removed by wire-brushing.

(c) Convection currents and heat radiation from the treated surface prevent impurities suspended in the atmosphere from settling before the steel is painted.

(d) The metal is still in a warm expanded condition when the paint is applied, so that as it cools the paint tends to be drawn into the irregularities of the surface, promoting good adhesion.

(e) Under certain circumstances work can be carried out during damp weather conditions which would bring other forms of preparation to a standstill.

An essential part of the treatment is that the priming paint must be applied while the steel is still hot; unless this is done the whole advantage of the process is lost. While flame cleaning is considerably more satisfactory than manual or mechanical scaling and wire brushing, it is also unfortunately far more expensive.

FLAMMABLE See *Inflammable*.

FLASH A gloss streak in a flat or eggshell finish.

FLASH DRY A term used in industrial finishing. To flash dry a coating is to allow most of the volatile solvents to evaporate from a sprayed coating before re-spraying or stoving.

FLASHING A defect which occurs in flat and eggshell finishes, taking the form of glossy streaks or patches which mar the appearance of the work. It is generally due to faulty application of the material, such as when flat oil paint has been applied without due regard to keeping the edges alive so that wet paint is brushed into material which has partially set, or when an attempt is made to touch up slight misses in material which is setting. Flashing often occurs at the intersection of stiles and rails in woodwork which is being finished in flat varnish or flat enamel, due to careless brushwork at the joints.

The tendency of flat paints to flash is increased if the grounding is unduly absorbent or of uneven porosity, factors which cause the finish to set too quickly making it difficult to keep the edges alive. Flashing may also be caused by the use of too much oil or unsuitable thinners in the finishing material.

FLASHPOINT The temperature at which the material gives off a vapour which will ignite on exposure to a flame.

When the flashpoint of a substance is known the extent of its inflammability may be assessed; for instance, a liquid is stated to be inflammable

100

if its flashpoint is below $65 \cdot 6°C$ ($150°F$), and if its flashpoint comes within the range of normal summer atmospheric temperature it is stated to be "highly inflammable" and it becomes subject to certain transport regulations. Under the terms of the Highly Flammable Liquids and Liquefied Gases Regulations, which came into force in June, 1973, a liquid is classed as "highly flammable" if its flashpoint is $32°C$ ($89 \cdot 6°F$) or less.

FLAT (otherwise MATT)   Possessing no gloss, sheen or lustre.

FLAT BRUSH   Colloquial term for a distemper brush.

FLAT ENAMEL   A finishing material intended for use where a finish free from gloss is required on surfaces subjected to constant handling, where a flat oil paint would rapidly become finger marked. It possesses similar properties of flow to a gloss enamel, for which reason it dries with a smooth satin-like surface, but it is made with an excess of volatile thinners and is not so full-bodied as a gloss enamel, working more easily under the brush. It is applied in a full flowing coat and care must be taken to avoid flashing. Whereas most flat finishes are applied over a semi-gloss ground, the grounding for flat enamel should be a flat or eggshell undercoat.

FLAT OIL PAINT   A finishing paint for indoor use presenting a matt surface restful to the eyes. It is composed of pigments of high reflective power such as lithopone or titanium, ground in a good quality drying oil or varnish medium of a type which is not readily absorbed by the surface to which it is applied. The absence of gloss is due to several factors such as the fact that generally the proportion of pigment is high and the vehicle content low, the flatting effect which lithopone exerts upon oil, and the inclusion of other suitable flatting agents and extenders.

   Flat oil paint should be applied liberally with 125mm or 100mm wall brushes, it should be crossed and laid off as soon as possible after application and should not then be disturbed any further. Care must be taken to keep the edges alive. The ground coat should be dry and hard, and should possess a fair degree of gloss, presenting at least a semi-gloss finish. It is sometimes desirable, when treating large areas, to retard the setting of a flat oil paint by the addition of a small quantity of transparent glaze medium.

FLAT VARNISH   A varnish made to dry to a matt surface by the inclusion of waxes, metallic stearates, etc., with volatile solvents added to reduce the viscosity imparted by these materials. It is generally thinner than gloss varnish and brushes more easily. It should be applied quickly and fairly liberally; care is needed to avoid flashing and each section of the work should be cut in cleanly so that no part receives a double application. Flat varnish has little protective power and is chiefly used for interior work. Its durability is increased and a more uniform result obtained if it is applied over a coating of full gloss varnish, preferably while the gloss varnish retains a little tack. Some brands of flat varnish need to be warmed immediately prior to application; the manufacturers' instructions on this point should be noted.

F

FLATTING A flat finish for walls and ceilings; it is made from paste white lead mixed to a very thin consistency with turpentine; no oil is added but a small quantity of varnish or gold size may be included. The work is grounded out with an extremely oily undercoat, and the following day while the undercoat still retains some degree of tack the flatting is applied. The grounding is softened to some extent by the solvent in the flatting and the excess oil serves to bind the flatting very firmly. The application of flatting requires considerable dexterity if flashing is to be avoided; should flashing occur there is no alternative but to ground the work out again. Because of this difficulty flatting has been completely superseded in general practice by more modern finishes such as flat oil paint.

The term flatting is also sometimes used rather loosely to mean the flat undercoating used as a grounding for gloss paint or enamel.

FLATTING DOWN Rubbing down a painted or varnished surface with fine abrasives to produce a smooth surface free from gloss. See also *Cutting Down*.

FLATTING VARNISH An undercoating varnish used when a two-coat varnish system is being employed. It is a short oil varnish containing a high proportion of hard resin, and is designed to produce a hard, quick-drying film which can be flatted down with powdered pumice or waterproof sandpaper within a few hours of application without risk of scratching or "sweating up".

FLINT A hard crystalline mineral, consisting of almost pure silica, used in the manufacture of certain grades of dry sandpaper and waterproof abrasive paper of the type employed by painters and decorators.

FLOATING A defect in painting taking the form of a discolouration which occurs during the drying of the film. It is caused by the pigments separating and rising to the surface while the paint is wet. The defect is most common in greens, blues and brown shades, and is accentuated if the paint is over-thinned. If the paint has not been applied evenly the discolouration appears in patches. In extreme cases the defect is known by the term *flooding*.

FLOCCULENCE A term used to describe the puffy or woolly texture which a paint sometimes develops due to faulty mixing.

FLOCK FINISHES Finishes obtained by spraying finely shredded rayon or similar textile fibres on to an adhesive ground to produce the effect of baize or suede. These materials are chiefly used in industrial finishing on small articles such as the insides of spectacle cases, the lining of cutlery drawers and instrument cases, the undersides of table lamps, etc., although they have occasionally been applied to the treatment of wall surfaces.

FLOCK GUN A special type of spray gun and container designed for the application of textile fibres used in producing flock finishes. The gun can also be used for such purposes as applying French chalk to rubber goods, granulated cork in anti-condensation treatments, etc. It is used solely for dry materials.

FLOCK PAPERS Wallpapers with a pattern of raised pile, produced by printing the pattern in adhesive medium, such as varnish or glue, on to which, when tacky, finely shredded wool or rayon fibres are blown. The effect is that of velvet or tapestry hangings. Flock papers, which first came into vogue towards the end of the 16th century, are now being produced by machinery and are within the price range of a much wider public than ever before. These papers need careful treatment in hanging to avoid damaging the pile; the surface to which they are applied must always be lined.

FLOGGER A brush used in graining for the purpose of imitating the pores of certain hardwoods. It has a broad thin handle into which is set a row of long bristles so as to form a thin lightweight brush about 125mm long and some 75 to 100mm wide. Freshly applied oil stain or water stain is stippled by striking it with the flat side of the flogger in a series of sharp strokes, working from the base upwards.

FLOODING An extreme form of floating, in which the pigment particles rise to the surface of a film of paint in such a way that the colour of the dried film, although uniform over the entire surface, differs considerably from the colour when first applied.

FLOOR PAINT Highly pigmented paint in a hard varnish medium, resistant to chipping. Most modern floor paints are based on epoxy resins and they are supplied either as one-pack or two-pack materials.

FLOOR STAIN A variety of materials can be used for the treatment of floor boards, etc., including oil stains, water stains, spirit stains, chemical compositions such as solutions of potassium permanganate, and so on. The essential thing is that they should be able to penetrate the surface of the wood; otherwise, they will soon be worn away in places by the constant passage of feet. Glue size, which is sometimes used as a preparatory coat before staining, should not be employed under floor stain as it prevents penetration and is also liable to be softened by buckets and other wet household implements placed on the floor. Proprietary brands of spirit stain are often used much too thickly, presenting an unpleasant, treacly appearance and being liable to chipping. Varnish stains consisting of a mixture of varnish and oil stain generally present a muddy appearance; better results are obtained by applying the stain and varnish as separate coatings.

FLOOR VARNISH A hard, quick-drying varnish, in which resistance to abrasion is of more importance than clear colour.

FLOTATION Another term for *floating*. Also used in the sense of *air flotation* to mean a process in the preparation of certain pigments whereby the dry pigment particles are conveyed by an air stream into a device which separates them into grades ranging from coarse to fine, due to the heavier particles settling first.

FLOUR PASTE A fixative used in the hanging of wallpaper. Flour consists of gluten and starch. The paste is made by mixing pure wheaten flour with a little cold water, beating it to a smooth creamy batter and then scalding it by pouring boiling water on to it very quickly, stirring vigorously all the time. By this means the flour is cooked, the molecules being partially broken down by fermentation or heat. Flour paste can be prepared as a powder which keeps indefinitely by mixing flour and water to form a dough which is fermented at about 43°C (110°F) and then cooked, dried and pulverized.

FLOW   The extent to which a material can flow out after application to produce a smooth surface free from brushmarks.

FLOW COATING   A method of paint application in which paint from a tank with a circulating system is poured or hosed on to the object to be painted, the excess paint being allowed to drain off. It is used for objects of an awkward shape that makes them unsuitable for dipping.

FLUID   A substance composed of particles that move freely in relation to one another, hence "fluidity", the ability to flow freely.

FLUID HOSE   The tubing which, in spray equipment, conveys paint to the gun. The fluid hose is usually coloured black to distinguish it from the air hose, which is coloured red.

FLUID NEEDLE   That part of a spray gun which stops and starts the flow of paint.

FLUID NEEDLE ADJUSTMENT   The adjustment controlling the movement of the needle of a spray gun, and hence the amount of paint which can pass.

FLUID REGULATOR   A device incorporated into circulating paint feed systems, a regulator being provided at each fluid outlet in order to maintain constant and correct fluid pressure at each spray gun.

FLUID STRAINER   A device fitted either to the fluid inlet of a spray gun or to the fluid outlet of a pressure tank in order to strain the finishing material before it enters the fluid passages.

FLUID TIP   That part of a spray gun which meters and directs the fluid into the air streams. Fluid tips are available in a number of nozzle sizes to permit materials of different types and varying viscosities each to be sprayed satisfactorily, taking into account the type of paint feed (e.g., suction feed or pressure feed).

FLUID VALVE   A valve incorporated in a spraying system in order to turn the supply of fluid on or off.

FLUORESCENT PIGMENTS   Coarse crystalline materials, usually the sulphides of calcium, barium and strontium, which have the property of glowing in the dark after they have been activated by exposure to light.

The length of time that the glowing remains visible varies considerably and depends to a great extent upon the medium in which the pigment is dispersed.

FLUSHING (a) The application of paint to the inside of a hollow article by means of pouring it in or pumping it through, the excess being allowed to drain off.
(b) A term used in paint manufacture to refer to a process whereby an aqueous pigment paste is treated in such a way that the water is replaced by oil.

FLUTTERING SPRAY A defect in spray painting, the paint leaving the gun in a jerky fashion; it is caused by air leaking into the fluid line, which may be due to a variety of reasons.

FLY ASH Fly ash, or pulverized fuel ash, is the residue left by the combustion of the pulverized coal that is used as the fuel in power stations, etc. The fine ash is collected for use as the lightweight aggregate in certain types of concrete and is sometimes incorporated as a constituent of lightweight screeds and building blocks; it is also used as an artificial form of pozzolana.

The composition and properties of fly ash vary considerably according both to the type of fuel from which it is derived and the type of plant in which the fuel was burnt; it sometimes contains a high proportion of unburnt fuel. In general it can be stated, however, that any concrete or building blocks containing fly ash are usually highly alkaline, even more so than Portland cement, and will rapidly attack and destroy any oil paint that is applied to their surface.

Pozzolana is a natural volcanic ash found near Rome, the peculiar properties of which largely accounted for the excellence of ancient Roman mortar and concrete. The term is used in modern concrete technology to denote a material either natural or artificial which is added to concrete to retard its hardening and to increase its resistance to chemical attack.

FOAM-IN-PLACE SPRAYING The application of a polyurethane material directly to the structure of a building to form a continuous coating of rigid foamed texture for thermal insulating and sound deadening purposes. The equipment consists of a twin-headed spray gun, two pressure feed tanks of 25 or 50 litre capacity with stainless steel fluid passages and fittings to resist corrosion, an air transformer and an air compressor. The polyurethane material and the appropriate catalyst are fed to the gun in the required proportions, the fluids blending as they emerge from the gun. See *Catalyst Spraying*.

FOLLOWING THE TROWEL A technique often employed on anhydrous gypsum plasters in order to improve the adhesion of paint. Considerable trouble is experienced in the decoration of plasters in this group, particularly Keene's and Parian; because of their slow rate of setting they are frequently trowelled by the plasterer to a smooth glass-like surface to which paint does not readily adhere, and this fact, coupled with the presence of moisture in the plaster, often leads to the failure of the decoration through flaking and peeling.

Following the trowel consists of applying a sharp coat of paint to the newly plastered surface as soon as it is firm enough to bear the weight of the brush. The setting of a gypsum plaster is due to the plaster and water combining chemically by a process of crystallization, and at a certain stage in this process a slight suction is exerted; the object is to apply the sharp coat early enough for it to be drawn into the surface as a result of this action. Ideally it should be applied within two or three hours of the plastering being completed and if through any circumstances a much longer time has elapsed the idea of following the trowel should be abandoned.

The sharp coat is made of white lead with just enough oil, gold size or varnish to bind it, well thinned down with turps or white spirit; it is essential that the proportion of oil be kept very low or the hydration of the plaster may be prevented. After the paint has been applied the plaster must be given adequate time to dry out thoroughly before any normal painting is commenced, and on no account must it be imagined that following the trowel offers a means of carrying out the decoration any earlier. When the surface is ready for further painting it should be sand-papered down lightly to remove any loose material or efflorescence which may have formed.

It is important that the technique of following the trowel should be used only on plasters which are acid (e.g., Keene's, Parian, anhydrite, etc.,) to which no lime has been added. Used on an alkaline surface it may result in the formation of a powdery layer of plaster, not properly hydrated, which is not strong enough to support paint. There is also a danger of alkaline attack. To decide whether the technique may safely be used a scraping of the plaster should be mixed with a suitable chemical indicator and the resultant colour noted. While the process of following the trowel is usually adopted to promote adhesion, it may also, by delaying the setting of the plaster, prevent the defect of "dry-out", which is caused by the too-rapid loss of moisture in the initial drying stages. Such undue loss is most likely to occur in warm dry weather and it is at such a time, therefore, that the technique is most valuable.

Opinions differ as to whether following the trowel is an effective measure or not. When it fails in its object, however, it is frequently found that faulty methods have been employed, either by making the paint too thick or too oily, by applying it too long after completion of plastering, or by following it up too quickly with the subsequent decoration. It should be noted that following the trowel is a suitable technique when the finished decoration is to be in oil paint or oil-bound water paint, but is not suitable when silicate paints are to be used.

FOOTNER PROCESS A method of cleaning scale from steelwork and providing a good surface for painting by means of phosphate pickling.

FORCED DRYING Speeding up the drying of a material by the application of a moderate degree of heat.

FORD CUP A form of viscometer, used to determine the viscosity of paints, enamels, varnishes, etc., which is calibrated to conform to the cups used in the laboratories of the Ford Motor Company. It is a cup with an accurately machined orifice; the cup is filled with the material under test and a stop watch is used to record the time from the moment when it is allowed to flow to the point at which the stream of liquid breaks into droplets.

FOSSIL GUM   Resin, used in the manufacture of varnish, which is found buried in the ground, having been secreted in trees which lived so long ago as to have now become extinct.

FOXY   Hot unpleasant colour; so called from the colour of the fur of the red fox.

FRENCH CHALK   A hydrated silicate of magnesium sometimes incorporated in paint to help to keep the pigments in suspension. French chalk is also used occasionally in signwriting; it is dusted over the gilder's cushion at intervals in order to prevent the surface from becoming greasy and causing the gold leaf to stick, and it is sometimes applied to a signboard by means of a pounce so as to provide a guide when the signwriter is using untinted gold size and to prevent the gold from adhering beyond the edge of the letter.

FRENCH OCHRE   A good quality opaque ochre of bright yellow colour and good staining strength.

FRENCH POLISH   A spirit varnish composed of shellac dissolved in methylated spirits, with other spirit-soluble gums sometimes added.

FRENCH POLISHING   The production of a rich high-gloss finish by means of the application of several thin coatings of French polish, a "rubber", consisting of a pad of cotton wool wrapped in two layers of calico, being used to apply the material. In the final states the shine is due to friction rather than to the quantity of polish applied.

FRENCH POLISHING MOP   A round dome-shaped brush, composed of squirrel hair, used in "bodying-up" French polish, i.e., in applying the preliminary coating.

FRESCO   A painting carried out with lime-proof pigments mixed with limewater, the colour being applied directly on to a freshly laid surface of lime plaster. The surface sets and hardens by a process of carbonation, a hard layer of insoluble calcium carbonate being formed which binds the colours firmly together in a durable film. The technique of fresco painting presents many difficulties, due to the limited number of colours that can be used, the fact that the colours lighten very considerably as they dry, and the necessity for applying only as much of the ground as can be painted in one day, since anything in excess of this films over and gives a patchy appearance to the work; nevertheless some of the greatest achievements in the history of art have been carried out in this medium. Fresco painting is permanent in a dry climate, but is not suitable for work in damp industrial regions, as the film, although insoluble in water, is readily attacked by weak acids.

The term is often wrongly used to describe any form of mural painting indiscriminately.

FRET PATTERN Sometimes called a "key-pattern"; an ornament consisting of straight lines intersecting at right angles. The term is derived from an early French word, *frettes,* meaning a grating.

FRIEZE In classic architecture, the middle division of the entablature. In ordinary domestic architecture, the horizontal band beneath the cornice and above the picture rail.

FROGS A colloquial term referring to skins and other foreign bodies in paint which needs straining.

FROSTING A defect taking the form of a fine wrinkling on the surface of a drying film of paint, giving a frosted appearance. It is generally due to faulty material, the oil content of which has not been properly prepared.

FROTHING Frothing occurs when certain materials are shaken or agitated and is very often a sign that the material has been handled too roughly. A creamy froth appears on varnish, for instance, if the material is poured out of the bottle carelessly, or if the bottle is shaken up, or when a brush is worked into the varnish and scraped out on the edge of the paint can. In all these cases the froth, once formed, takes a very long time to clear, and is detrimental to the quality of the finished work. The froth consists of minute air bubbles, and when a coating of the varnish is applied the air bubbles burst as the material is drying, causing pinholing of the dried film and the defect known as "delayed cissing"; the film thus presents a roughened surface instead of a smooth gloss finish, and allows moisture to penetrate instead of offering a resistant coating.

Another example of the unfortunate effect of frothing is provided when glue size, applied to a sanitary wallpaper as a preparatory coat before varnish, is brushed on so vigorously as to develop a froth. Here again the frothing denotes pinholing of the film, and in this case the effect is that the size ceases to be an effective buffer between the varnish and the fibres of the paper, the varnish penetrates the pinholes and strikes into the paper, causing a blotchy brown stain in the form of a cluster of tiny speckles.

FUGITIVE COLOURS Colours which fade when exposed to light. The lake pigments are notorious in this respect. Some colours which are reasonably fast to light when used at full strength develop fugitive tendencies when reduced with white. Fugitive colours fade much more quickly when used in flat paints than when incorporated into gloss paints or protected by a varnish coating.

FUGITOMETER A device comprising a humidifier and an arc light which approximates to daylight, and in which the combined effects of moisture and light reproduce to some extent the conditions of weathering. Samples of paint applied to small panels are inserted in the instrument, part of each panel being covered with a mask to exclude the light. After a period of exposure a comparison of the two portions of a panel reveals the amount of fading which has taken place, providing a test by which samples of paint can be compared with one another.

FULL COAT A single coating of paint, enamel or varnish applied as thickly as is possible without detriment to the quality of the work and the satisfactory performance of the material, as opposed to a "bare coat" or a "starved coat", in which the material has been applied too thinly.

FULL COLOUR Rich pure colour, as opposed to tints and greyed hues.

FULL GLOSS A term used about enamels, varnishes and paints meaning that they possess a high-gloss finish when dry, as opposed to semi-gloss, eggshell or matt finishes.

FULLER'S EARTH A kind of clay or marl of highly absorbent properties, composed chemically of hydrous silicate of alumina, so-called because it is used in the "fulling"—i.e., the cleaning and felting— of cloth. It has various applications to the painting trade. It is used in the preparation of linseed oil, as a means of clarifying the oil. It is also used on the site by the painter and the grainer. In graining it is used as a binder for water stains; in many respects it is superior to the traditional stale beer, as it is less likely to cause damage to the superimposed varnish and also prevents the stain from cissing, which makes for clean, speedy working. In normal painting practice fuller's earth is used to prevent cissing, which is likely to occur when paint, stain or varnish is applied to greasy surfaces or to surfaces which have been standing so long as to have become very hard; the surface is wiped over with a damp wash-leather sprinkled with the fuller's earth and then allowed to dry.

FULLY TRIMMED MATERIAL Wallpaper, ceiling paper, coated fabric or any other kind of wall hanging which is supplied in a form ready for immediate use, without any selvedge. It is usual for fully trimmed hand hangings to be individually wrapped in cellophane or a protective paper wrapper, in order to keep the material tightly rolled and to protect the edges from damage during transit. Naturally, it is rather more expensive to supply materials in this form than to produce them in the conventional manner, but the extra cost is heavily outweighed by the fact that no trimming is necessary, with the consequent saving in labour cost. Furthermore, a perfectly cut edge is assured, which is by no means always the case when trimming is carried out by hand. It is reasonable to suppose that eventually all materials will be supplied ready trimmed, and that the trimming of wallpapers will soon be a thing of the past.

FUME PIGMENTS Pigments with extremely fine texture, such as zinc oxide, antimony white, carbon black, etc., which are produced by the process of sublimation. In this process the raw material from which the

F

pigment is produced is volatilized by roasting it in the presence of air, forming dense fumes; the fumes are drawn into chambers where they condense and settle in the form of a light powder.

FUMED OAK Oak which has been stained by exposure to the fumes of ammonia, a process which leads to considerable darkening of the figuring.

FUNGICIDAL PAINTS Oil or water paints containing mercury salts or other poisonous substances to make them resistant to the formation of fungoid and mould growths. If such paints are to be used in breweries, bakehouses or other premises where foodstuffs are prepared, the advice of the paint manufacturers should be obtained to avoid risk of contamination of the food.

FUNGICIDES Substances which destroy fungi. They are used in several forms in the painting trade, as antiseptic washes for the cleansing of surfaces which have become infected with mould growths, as penetrative solutions and stains for the treatment of timber and other building materials, which are to be exposed to conditions giving rise to fungoid growths, and as ingredients in fungicidal paints.

FUNGOID GROWTHS The term fungus covers a wide variety of plant forms which includes moulds and mildew as well as growths such as toadstools, etc. All fungi are alike in that they are destitute of chlorophyll and so are unable to synthesize food from simple substances; instead, they obtain nourishment from various organic substances. While some of them are parasites, attacking living organisms, the ones which concern the painter are saprophytes, which attack dead organisms and break down the organic compounds which are present into simple forms in order to feed upon them. They thrive upon such materials as glue size and flour paste, the oil content of paint and the oils and caseins contained in water paints and distempers, and their growth is encouraged by the presence of warmth and humidity. They are a frequent source of trouble in premises such as bakehouses, breweries, dairies and conservatories.

Fungus spores can be carried considerable distances by the wind and can infect plaster and timber which has hitherto been perfectly free from such growth. The spores can lie dormant for a very long time, ready to germinate should the conditions favourable to their development occur for even a short period. All the indications are that trouble from mould growths is becoming increasingly prevalent.

The presence of fungoid growths is denoted by the appearance of spots or patches of varying colours such as black, green or fluffy white; pink and purple patches are also common, especially in greenhouses. The treatment consist of stripping all infected paper or paint (the paper, etc., being burnt to prevent the spreading of the spores), finding out the cause of any damp and taking steps to cure it, and sterilizing the infected surfaces and surrounding areas with a suitable antiseptic wash, used in accordance with the makers' instructions. Where conditions especially favourable to fungoid growths exist, as in breweries, etc., paints containing fungicidal agents may be used, precautions being taken to avoid contamination of foodstuffs with poisonous substances.

A lot of the trouble caused by fungoid growths on ordinary domestic work is due to very obvious mistakes, such as applying wallpaper over newly plastered or damp surfaces. It should be noted, too, that the same reasons which give rise to fungoid growths in decorative materials can give trouble to the painter in other ways; brushes made from animal hair or vegetable fibre, if put away damp, are very liable to be attacked by mildew.

FUNNEL An essential piece of equipment in any painter's kit whereby such operations as filling a blow lamp may be performed without spilling the fuel in the dangerous wasteful manner sometimes seen.

FURS The furs used in heraldry are depicted by conventional patterns, and the most common are ermine and vair. Ermine is shown as a white ground with black spots which represent the animal tails. In the early heraldic records the tails are drawn with more realism than is shown in the conventional form which is usually favoured today. There are certain variants of ermine; *ermines* has a black ground with white spots, *erminois* has a gold ground with black spots, and *pean* has a black ground with gold spots.

Vair is a pattern representing the stitching together of squirrel furs, as used in cloak linings. In the earliest records vair is depicted as a series of straight horizontal lines alternating with horizontal wavy lines, but later became conventionalized into a geometric pattern of bell-like shapes of blue and white in alternate spaces. There is a variant called counter-vair. Vair is always blue and white, but the same pattern is frequently found in other colours when it is termed "vairy" of the colours concerned. Another fur, potent, originally derived from vair, is depicted as a pattern of crutch shaped skins in blue and white, potent being an old English word for a crutch or walking staff. There is a variant known as counter-potent.

G

G

GABLE The triangular portion of a piece of wall between the enclosing lines of a sloping roof.

GABOON A hardwood very similar to mahogany, showing the same fine grooving as mahogany, but generally lighter in colour. Used extensively in making plywood and often encountered by the painter.

GALVANIZED IRON, GALVANIZED STEEL Iron or steel sheeting which is protected from corrosion by means of the application of a layer of zinc, the low cost and ease of application of which compares favourably with other forms of metallic coating. Although the zinc is sometimes deposited by electro-plating, the more usual process is that of hot dripping, in which the sheets are prepared by pickling and washing before being immersed in molten zinc, known commercially as "spelter".

When it is new, galvanized iron is a difficult material to paint satisfactorily unless the correct priming procedures are adopted. The difficulties arise partly from the smooth greasy surface which offers very little key to a paint film, and partly from the fact that the zinc coating has an embrittling effect upon the oil content of any paint applied to it; for these reasons the paint film tends to peel and flake off in small fragments very soon after application. In recent years calcium plumbate primer has been developed specifically to overcome this problem, and it is now recognized as the standard treatment for galvanized iron. It is applied directly to the metal without any prior etching process and without waiting for the surface to weather.

It is important to notice that paints containing lead should never be used for priming galvanized iron as they react unfavourably with the zinc coating. Primers based on zinc chromate, zinc oxide or zinc dust produce no such reaction, but will peel and flake if applied directly to the surface; before they are used it is essential to degrease the surface and then apply a phosphoric acid wash or an etch primer. The old time craftsman painter used to set great store by home made recipes for etching the surface prior to painting, and placed great faith in washes of vinegar and solutions of copper sulphate, copper chloride, zinc sulphide and the like, and for some extraordinary reason this tradition has persisted to the present day; it is astonishing how many people insist on experimenting with recipes handed down from the past. For this reason, and because such recipes are still seen in old-fashioned trade literature, it is emphasized that treatments of this kind may indeed etch the surface and improve the adhesion of the paint for a time but will definitely lead to an early breakdown of the paint system and will in many cases actively stimulate corrosion.

GARNET A vitreous mineral used as the grit in making waterproof sandpaper of the yellow type employed by painters and decorators.

GARNET LAC A spirit-soluble resin similar to button lac but produced in a thick flat cake.

GAS BLACK A black pigment of the carbon black type, produced by the incomplete combustion of natural gases. It is an intense black colour with good staining properties; when reduced with white it yields a brownish grey colour.

GAS CHECKING A form of webbing or surface wrinkling which sometimes occurs when paints containing vegetable oils or derivatives from such oils are dried in an atmosphere containing the products of coal gas combustion (e.g., in a gas fired stoving oven).

GAUGED LIME PLASTER Lime plaster to which a small quantity of plaster of Paris has been added to accelerate the set and to prevent shrinkage cracking.

GEL A semi-solid colloidal solution; hence "to gell"—to assume a semi-solid condition.

GELATINE A transparent substance which forms a strong jelly in water, obtained from connective animal tissues, such as skin, tendons, bones and horns. In its dry state it is horny and flexible.

GELATINE CAPSULES Hollow cylindrical capsules of dry gelatine which are often used instead of isinglass to make the mordant for glass gilding. For this purpose one capsule is dissolved in half a litre (500ml) of hot, almost boiling water. The advantage of using such capsules is that the gilder is not likely to be tempted to make the mordant too strong, as so often happens when he is using shredded isinglass, the hollow capsule giving a deceptive appearance of size.

GELATION Becoming semi-solid.

G

GELLING As gelation.

GESSO A composition of whiting and glue used for the execution of relief work on woodwork or plaster. Although it can be modelled with the fingers or with a modelling tool, and may also be carved when dry, essentially it is a brush-applied material, and finished gesso work should possess the free fluid sweeps and the smooth textureless appearance of brushwork. A gesso composition of plaster of Paris and glue or size is also used at times to produce a smooth grounding on woodwork prior to the application of paint.

GHOSTING A colloquial term sometimes used to denote pattern staining, whereby dust and dirt accumulate on the plastered surface of a ceiling in such a way as to show the arrangement of the joists and lathing underlying the plaster. It is due to the difference in thermal conductivity between the plaster and the wood or metal of which the joists are composed, dirt being deposited on those areas which offer the readiest passage for the transmission of heat. See "Pattern Staining" for a fuller description.

GILDER'S COMPO A composition used to form relief ornament of the type favoured in the Victorian period for the enrichment of picture frames, etc. It is made up from glue, rosin and linseed oil, stiffened with sifted whiting to a dough-like consistency, and is pressed into wooden or plaster moulds from which it takes a sharp impression. While still in the mould the back of the material is cut to a level surface ready for attachment to the surface which is to be decorated.

GILDER'S CUSHION A pad from which the gilder works when applying loose leaf gold. It consists of a flat wooden board padded with felt and covered with a tightly stretched skin of chamois leather. One end of the pad is fitted with a stout parchment screen to shield the leaves of gold from draughts; when not in use the screen is folded down to lie flat upon the pad. A few leaves of gold are emptied from the book into a corner of the draught screen, and one leaf at a time is withdrawn and placed on the centre of the cushion as required. The underside of the wooden board is fitted with two soft leather straps, one of which is a thumb strap by which the gilder holds the cushion and the other serves to hold the gilder's knife. The chamois leather face of the cushion must be kept free from grease, otherwise the gold leaf will stick to it and tear instead of lifting cleanly; this is achieved by lightly dusting it occasionally with French chalk.

GILDER'S KNIFE   A long thin knife used in the process of gilding with loose leaf gold; its purpose is to cut the separate leaves of gold into strips of whatever width is required. A leaf of gold is brought to the centre of the cushion and the knife drawn backwards and forwards across it to cut it. The blade is not sharpened; it it were sharp it would cut the chamois leather cushion, and in any case a sharp edge is not needed for such a malleable metal as gold. The knife is balanced so that when it is laid on a flat surface the blade is lifted clear and is not in contact with the surface. It is essential, if the knife is to cut the gold cleanly and not tear it, that the blade should be quite clean and free from grease; it should be dusted at intervals with French chalk and should on no account be handled or fingered. A gilder's knife is usually about 250mm in overall length, the blade being about 150mm long.

GILDER'S MOP   A round bushy squirrel hair brush used to press gold leaf into place in the recesses and hollow contours of carved work and enrichments.

GILDER'S TIP   This is another item of equipment, along with the cushion and knife, used in loose leaf gilding. It is a small brush composed of a single line of badger hairs fastened in a cardboard handle consisting of two thin sheets of card glued together, and it is used to pick up the gold leaf from the cushion and transfer it to the surface which is being gilded. In order to do this the badger hair must be slightly greasy, a condition which is achieved by the gilder drawing the tip across his cheek or across his hair.

GILDER'S WHEEL   A device used for applying lines in gold leaf or for gilding single members of beads and mouldings. It consists of two wheels mounted on a handle, one wheel holding a roll of ribbon gold and the other wheel a padded one which presses the gold into contact with the mordant. Generally, the lining is carried out directly upon a varnished surface when the varnish has achieved a degree of tack suitable for gilding.

GILDING   The application of gold leaf to any surface by means of an adhesive or *mordant*.

GILL SANS   A name given to a sans serif alphabet designed by Eric Gill. In sans serif letters the short cross line, which terminates the unconnected strokes in Roman lettering, is dispensed with. In designing this style Eric Gill was probably influenced by the letters produced by Edward Johnston for the London Underground in 1918, both these designers being concerned to raise the standard of lettering above the level which had become common in the nineteenth century. Gill sans letters are of more uniform width than the modern German sans serif versions; the only points come at the feet of the V and W, and the M is square with the middle strokes descending half-way.

GIRDER   A large heavy beam capable of carrying both concentrated and uniformly distributed loads.

GLAIR   See *Egg Glair*.

GLASS EMBOSSING   The treatment of glass so that lettering or ornament is etched or otherwise hollowed deeply into the surface; when viewed from the other side this gives the pattern the appearance of being raised or embossed. Glass embossing may be carried out by the process described under the heading *Acid Etching* or by sandblasting.

GLASS FIBRE, PAINTING OF   Glass fibre is being increasingly used in the construction of vehicle bodies. The moulds in which the components are manufactured are lined with a wax or water-soluble material called a "parting agent" which facilitates the extraction of the completed mouldings. Unless all the parting agent is completely removed it will affect the drying and hardening of the paint system and may lead to flaking. As a general rule, more filling is required on a glass fibre surface than on a metal surface.

GLASS GILDING   The application of gold leaf to glass. The work is carried out in reverse so that the gilding is viewed through the glass. Loose leaf gold is employed for the purpose, the tools being the cushion, knife, tip, and a camel hair size brush; the mordant is isinglass or gelatine dissolved and cooked in hot water. The essence of the work is scrupulous cleanliness.

GLASS, PAINTING OF   When paint is applied to glass, either in the form of painted letters or an all-over coating to obscure the glass, the results are often disappointing and the film begins to peel after a short time. This is due to (a) the smoothness of the glass and the fact that it provides no "key" for paint, (b) the fact that glass is prone to condensation which affects the adhesion of the paint and (c) the fact that glass is a good conductor of heat and the paint is therefore subjected to frequent and rapid changes of temperature affecting its adhesion.

The success of the operation is more likely to be assured if certain points are observed. These are as follows: (a) The glass must be scrupulously clean before paint is applied; in particular it must be free from all trace of grease. A thin coating of whiting helps to clean the glass and to reveal any greasy areas. (b) Thick coatings of paint must be avoided, as thick coats are more liable to peel; thin coats are more successful. For lettering work, some firms produce tubes of extra-opaque colour specially for glass writing. (c) The medium of the paint must be of an adhesive or tenacious nature—thickened oil or damar varnish in preference to raw linseed oil. Alkyd resin varnishes or gloss paints are very useful in this respect and under present-day conditions are generally the most suitable materials to use. (d) The tenacity of the paint can be improved by adding a small quantity of silica to impart some degree of "tooth". (e) Genuine turpentine is more suitable than white spirit as a thinner, being less likely to be greasy.

It should be noted that the colour of the glass itself, usually a greenish hue, modifies the appearance of any paint which is applied. A little crimson lake added to the paint helps to correct the colour. A small sample of paint should be applied and the colour examined before the whole of the work is laid in.

GLASSPAPER An abrasive for dry rubbing down, consisting of fused alumina bonded by means of hide glue or resin to stout cartridge paper.

GLAZE A transparent or semi-transparent coating which is used to modify or enrich a previously applied colour. There are several ways in which glazes are employed in decorative work. One of the simplest is to relieve the plainness of broad wall surfaces finished in solid colour by applying a coat of delicately tinted glaze all over the surface and stippling it evenly with a hair stippler; the effect of this is to give a richness and depth which cannot be achieved with opaque colour alone. Glaze can also be used in the production of broken colour effects, by means of rag-rolling, combing, rubber stippling, etc.; it can be used to accentuate the highlights on relief work, the carving or modelling being coated with tinted glaze, stippled and then wiped over with a soft rag; further examples include the glazing of plastic paint followed by wiping to expose the highlights, and the use of glaze in blended effects. The term "glaze" also refers to some of the thin coatings used in graining, such as the wash of Vandyke brown which is applied over figured oak graining and which is manipulated to produce lights and shadows, the thin washes of colour employed in obtaining mottled effects, flogging, and so on. Oil-bound water paint, suitably thinned with petrifying liquid and water, may be used as a glaze over a ground of a different colour in order to produce broken colour effects in water media.

As a general rule, it may be said that too wide a difference should not exist between the glaze colour and the ground colour in any type of glazed work; otherwise, the work will appear crude and coarse.

GLAZE COAT Any transparent or semi-transparent coating used to modify an existing colour without obscuring it.

The term is also sometimes used as meaning any transparent finishing coat, for example varnish or flat varnish, or a clear emulsion coating giving sheen to a surface, and so on.

GLAZE MEDIUM A transparent material which may be tinted with oil stainers in order to produce glazed and broken colour effects. There are two types of glaze medium, both of which are based on light amorphous pigments such as china clay, aluminium stearate, etc., which have little or no opacity in oil. One type, known as the fixed glaze type, is prepared with a medium such as gold size and may also contain beeswax, and is deliberately formulated so as not to flow out after application; this type is used for effects such as rag-rolling and colour combing, where it is necessary that the crispness of the pattern should be retained. Although the material appears very thick it brushes out most easily; it possesses "false body" in that it decreases its viscosity when agitated but reverts to its former viscosity directly the shearing action ceases. The other type, known as the flowing or merging type, is prepared with a medium which flows out readily after application; this type is used for shading and blending of colours.

Glaze medium is sometimes added to flat oil paints in order to retard the set when large surfaces are being painted or when blending of colours is to take place, and is sometimes added to graining colour to prevent the markings from flowing out.

GLOSS   The brightness or lustre of a painted surface; the extent to which it will reflect light, ranging from flat (absence of gloss), through the stages of eggshell sheen and semi-gloss, to the degree of smoothness and brilliance which is described as full gloss.

G

GLOSS METER   A piece of apparatus for determining the degree of gloss of a painted surface. In general, the glossier a paint the more light it will reflect. The gloss meter works on the principle of directing a beam of light on to a painted panel and allowing the reflected beam to excite a galvanometer. The more light is reflected the higher will be the galvanometer reading. The reading is usually expressed as a percentage of the gloss that would be obtained with a glass panel painted at the back.

GLOSS PAINT   A rather vague term, which may mean any paint which is mixed to dry with a fair degree of gloss. More correctly the term is applied to a paint consisting of pigments ground up in a varnish medium with the addition of driers and thinners and with reasonably good hiding power and fairly rapid drying and hardening, as opposed to an enamel of the pigment/stand oil type. The pigment used would be of small particle size in order to give a smooth gloss finish; the varnish might be a blend of linseed, tung or dehydrated castor oil and either natural or synthetic resins.

GLOSSING UP   The appearance of glossy patches on a flat paint finish due to the surface being handled or subjected to polishing.

GLUE   An adhesive substance made by boiling animal hides, hooves or bones. It consists of gelatine and chondrin, a substance derived from cartilage and which is similar to gelatine except that it does not form as firm a jelly; the adhesive properties of the glue depend on the proportion of chondrin which it contains. Glue made from skins is superior to that obtained from bones. The best quality of cake glue is called Scotch glue.

The chief application of glue in the paint industry is as a stabilizer in the manufacture of washable water paints, strong Scotch glue being dissolved in water and made into an emulsion with linseed oil.

GLUE SIZE   A weak form of glue with several applications to the painting and decorating trade. It is available to the decorator as cake glue, jelly size or "concentrated" size; concentrated size, which is size in granulated or powdered form, is the most popular because it is easily prepared for use, stores well and dissolves quickly. A good quality of size should be insisted upon; poor qualities contain impurities which are not

117

readily apparent but which affect the setting and adhesive properties of the material. Size should not be mixed with boiling water or it will not gel properly when cool.

The main use of size nowadays is as a preparation for paperhanging; it helps to equalize the porosity of the surface to which it is applied, and it gives "slip" to the paper without which it would be difficult for the paper-hanger to slide it into the required position. It should be noted that a common error is to make the size too strong; its purpose is not to stop the suction completely but to level it up, and too strong a coat may lead to the paper remaining wet for an undue length of time, with excessive shrinkage and springing of the joints when drying.

Glue size is also used as the binder in soft distemper, and in claircolle as a preparation for distempering, although its importance in these respects has declined with the introduction of modern surface treatments. Another use for size is as a thin coating to act as a buffer coat for various purposes. Open textured wallboards, fabrics, lining papers and other fibrous materials need such a buffer coat before oil paint is applied, as linseed oil has an embrittling effect upon the fibres, but it is essential that the size should be very thin, preferably applied hot, and should not form a continuous coating over the surface. Size is also used as a buffer coat on sanitary wall-paper before a varnish coating is applied, to prevent the oil in the varnish from "striking" into the paper to discolour it. Here again the size is used very thinly; two coats are applied (one in an upwards direction and one horizontally to minimize misses) and the first coat should be applied hot.

Size is a very useful material when properly used but can do a lot of damage when wrongly used. It is *not* suitable for use under oil paint (except on fibrous materials as already mentioned), or under water paints or emulsion paints. Splashes of size allowed to dry upon painted wood-work disrupt the paint film badly.

GLYCERINE or GLYCEROL A colourless sweet liquid which is a compound of alcohol. It is contained as an ester in all vegetable oils and is released when a vegetable oil is saponified or decomposed by alkaline action. It has many applications in paint manufacture, such as, for example, when glycerine and phthalic anhydride are heated together in the production of an alkyd resin or when glycerine and rosin are fused to produce ester gums.

Glycerine is a hygroscopic material and when it is mixed with water it resists the tendency of water to evaporate. This fact is used in various ways; glycerine is added to artists' water colours as a plasticizer, and it is also used by the scene painter to plasticise the distemper colours used on canvas backcloths and by the decorator wishing to retard the setting of plastic paint in order to carry out modelling.

GLYPTAL RESINS Alkyd resins; "glyptal" is the trade name applied to alkyd resins produced by the American company which was the first to develop them.

GOLD BRONZE A light coloured bronze powder made from a copper alloy, mainly used for decorative purposes on interior work. It can be obtained with the powder mixed in medium ready for use, or with the powder and medium separate to be mixed immediately before it is required, or if desired can be applied in powder form over a ground of tacky gold size. It tends to tarnish unless protected by lacquer.

GOLD LEAF Metallic gold beaten out into the form of a very thin leaf or sheet. It is supplied in books in which the individual leaves of gold are separated by thin leaves of tissue paper dusted with Armenian bole to prevent the gold sticking to it. Each book contains 25 leaves of gold, each leaf measuring 82·5mm square. It is sold either as loose leaf gold or transfer gold. Loose leaf gold, as its name implies, consists just of the thin squares of leaf unattached to anything else; in this form, which is intended for tip and cushion work, the leaf is very fragile. Transfer gold is more robust and easy to handle, each leaf of gold being attached to a thin sheet of waxed tissue paper large enough to leave a margin all round it, and is intended for outdoor sign work and any other type of gilding in which the draughts or the nature of the work preclude the use of loose leaf gold. Transfer gold is also available in the form of rolls of various widths known as ribbon gold, for use with the gilder's wheel.

Gold leaf is available in various shades ranging from pale to deep, and in various thicknesses, extra thick leaf being used when the work is to be exposed to very severe conditions or is in some inaccessible place that cannot often be reached. English gold leaf, of twenty-three or twenty-four carat, is reckoned to be the best quality, being more dependable and consistent than foreign leaf. Gold leaf can be readily distinguished from cheap substitutes by holding it up against a strong light when it appears green, whereas alloys, and Dutch metals appear reddish or blue-black according to their composition.

GOLD SIZE An adhesive material used as a mordant for gold leaf, the leaf being applied when the gold size has attained the requisite degree of tack.

Gold size is available in two forms; there is "oil gold size", which is a slow-drying composition prepared from a linseed stand oil or a naturally thickened linseed oil tinted with yellow ochre and thinned to workable consistency with boiled linseed oil or varnish, and there is *Japan gold size*, sometimes termed "writers' gold size", which is a quick drying short-oil varnish.

Oil gold size is used for the gilding of large wooden or metal letters and carved woodwork, and on broad areas of wall surface which are to be gilded in solid gold. The work must be painted so that its absorption is completely satisfied and so that it presents a hard, smooth semi-gloss ground for the gilding. The gold size, which has a tendency to form sags, curtains and thick edges, must be brushed out evenly, and steps must be taken to prevent dust from settling on the surface. Twenty-four to thirty hours must elapse before it is tacky enough to gild, and it may retain its tack for several days. It is not suitable for use with alloys and metals other than gold as these react with the oil and become discoloured.

Japan gold size is used for lettering, lining and ornamental work on which a sharply defined outline is required, and for any gilding work which is to be carried out *in situ* in a position where exposure to dust or weather conditions would affect the gold size before the gold was applied. The proportions of oil and driers can be adjusted so that it dries at varying speeds, and writers' gold size is sold at such rates as 1-hour, 4-hour, or 20-hour size. Generally speaking, the longer the gold size takes to tack up the brighter and more lustrous the gold will appear; the drying speed is selected according to the circumstances ruling on the particular job in hand. For outdoor signwork in inclement weather a quick-drying size presents obvious advantages. The drying speed suggested on the label is only intended as a rough guide and the actual length of time required before the material tacks will fluctuate according to weather conditions; for instance, a 1-hour gold size may take considerably longer to tack up in dull humid weather but may take much less than an hour to harden if exposed to a burst of hot sunshine. For this reason it is necessary to test the hardness of the gold size at frequent intervals, laying the gold whenever the right degree of tack has been reached before proceeding to run in any more gold size. The material is ready for gilding when the back of the forefinger can be lightly laid upon it without leaving any mark. On lettering work a small quantity of tube lemon chrome is added to the gold size so that it can be seen more clearly; too much stainer should not be added or the drying will be retarded. If it is found necessary to thin Japan gold size pure turps should be used, as the material reacts unfavourably with white spirit.

Japan gold size has various other uses besides being a mordant for gilding. It is used as a binder for coachpainters' colours and spirit colours which are ground in turps, it can be added to oil paint as a drier or a hardening agent, it can be incorporated in stopping and filling compositions as a hardener and it can be thinned with turps to provide a sealer coat for various purposes such as coating woodwork prior to staining, etc.

GOTHIC The term used to describe the pointed style of medieval architecture prevalent in Western Europe between the 13th and 14th centuries.

GOTHIC LETTERING Otherwise known as "Old English"; a style of lettering sometimes used by signwriters which is derived from medieval manuscript lettering.

GOUACHE A method of painting on paper with opaque colours mixed with water, honey and gum, and much favoured by some designers.

GRAINING A reproduction of the decorative qualities of natural wood grain, achieved by manipulating semi-transparent glazes over a painted ground of solid colour.

GRAINING COLOUR The term used by the painter to mean a thin stain, scumble or semi-transparent glaze which is brushed on to a grounding of solid colour and which is dragged, combed or otherwise manipulated to produce brush graining or figure graining.

GRAINING COMBS Steel combs with teeth of varying widths, and pieces of rubber, cork or linoleum with the edges serrated to form openings of various widths, which are used to reproduce the plainer kinds of wood markings and which are used in combination with various other effects in figure graining.

GRAINING HORN A short piece of celluloid or perspex over which a piece of folded rag is doubled and which is used by the grainer to "wipe out" or lift wet graining colour in order to reproduce grain markings. It is a less painful and more hygienic substitute for the old-time grainer's method of using his own thumb nail, allowed to grow unnaturally long for the purpose.

GRAINING PAPER A material used as a means of imitating wood grain. It consists of absorbent paper embossed with the features of a particular type of wood grain. The surface to be grained is painted in a suitable ground colour and allowed to dry; it is then laid in with scumble and while the scumble is wet the paper is pressed into contact with it, the absorbency of the paper removing some of the stain.

G

GRANITE A hard igneous rock, composed of feldspar, quartz and mica used in building. Granite occurs in various shades of pinky-red, blue-grey and green-grey; some varieties present a coarse mottled appearance while others show a mass of fine spots. The appearance of the rock is sometimes imitated in paint by a simple process known as *graniting*.

GRANITING The imitation of granite in paint. The work is grounded out in red or grey and when this is dry the surface is sponge stippled with black, blue-grey, red and white, the darkest colours being applied first. For the fine spotted varieties brush spattering is used instead of sponge stippling.

GRANULATED CORK A material used in anti-condensation treatments, its effectiveness being due to the fact that cork is a poor conductor of heat so that a thick layer of cork forms a buffer coat which insulates the surface. The surface to be treated is coated with a strongly adhesive material consisting of white lead, stand oil and gold size and the granulated cork is either thrown on to the tacky surface by hand or sprayed on by means of a special type of spray gun. Another form of treatment is provided by mixing finely granulated cork in a suitable medium and applying it in the form of a thick coating which is then stippled. See also *Anti-condensation Paint*.

GRANULATED SIZE Concentrated size.

GRAPHITE A black pigment consisting of carbon in crystalline form. Natural deposits of graphite, which is also known as "plumbago" or "blacklead", are found in various parts of the world and a very pure quality is produced artificially by calcining anthracite coal or coke residue in electric furnaces. In appearance, graphite is dark grey with a metallic lustre rather than black. The particles of which it is composed take the form of very thin hexagonal flakes, similar to the flakes of metallic bronze powder, and because of this it possesses great opacity and resistance to moisture penetration. Its outstanding property, however, is its tremendous covering power, one litre covering as much as 40 square metres; it brushes out to such a thin film that it has little value when used alone but it can be incorporated with other pigments to make them work freely. When mixed with red lead or silica it produces an excellent protective coating for metal work.

GRASS CLOTH   A term with two very different meanings. From the early 19th century until recently, a rather coarse fabric used sometimes as a chea wall hanging; in recent years, a highly sophisticated and expensive material used in high-class decoration. Modern grass cloths consist of the long trailing stems of plants of the convolvulus type, dried and hand-dyed, wove with metallic thread and mounted on a thin ricepaper backing. See *Japanese grasscloths.*

GRAVITY BUCKET   A type of paint container which is hoisted by block and tackle and from which the paint is fed downwards through a fluid hose to a spray gun below. Gravity buckets are seldom used nowadays. A less cumbersome type of gravity feed container with a capacity of 10 litres is available for use where large quantities of material have to be sprayed and where pressure feed cannot be employed.

GRAVITY FEED CUP   A small paint container which is attached directly to the top or side of a spray gun, so that when the gun trigger is pulled a stream of paint is fed by the force of gravity into the air stream. There is an orifice in the lid of the cup by which air enters to replace the paint as it is used.

GRAVITY FEED TYPE GUN   A spray gun which can be fed from a gravity feed cup. The air cap for such a gun should be of the suction feed type. Gravity feed guns with ½ litre (500ml) capacity cups are very useful for decorative spraying; they would, of course, be impracticable for any large-scale work because of the low pressure employed, the fact that they would need frequent re-charging with paint and the fact that they could not be tilted to any great extent because of stopping up the air hole in the cup lid. A range of smaller type guns is available for a variety of purposes, being employed in many industrial finishing processes and as touch-up guns; very small gravity feed guns of the pencil type are made as artists' air brushes.

GREEN   One of the three primary colours of light, and one of the three secondary colours of pigment mixture, obtained by blending blue and yellow. The green pigments used in the painting trade include chrome greens and Brunswick greens made by blending chrome yellows with Prussian blue, chromium compounds such as chromium oxide and Guignet green, cobalt green, copper compounds such as emerald green, and terre verte or green earth.

GREEN EARTH (Terre Verte) A natural earth pigment found in many parts of the world, especially in the Verona district of Italy. The colour is chiefly due to the presence of silicate of iron. It is a rather dull colour, variable in strength and tone like most of the earth colours, and possesses little opacity. The better qualities are supplied as artists' tube colours; inferior grades are used in the preparation of green lakes.

GRINDING The use of mills and runners of various types to reduce pigments to a state of uniform fineness.

GRINNING A term used when a coat of paint fails to obscure the surface to which it is applied; the ground which shows through is said to be "grinning through". This may be due to the paint being applied unevenly or too thinly, or may be because too great a difference of tone exists between the grounding and the coat which is being applied. Painted lettering and ornament and stencilled decoration will often grin through several coats of paint unless proper steps are first taken to reduce the difference of tone. As a general rule the use of the term "grinning" is applied mainly to finishing coats which have failed to obscure the under-coats properly.

GROIN An architectural term for the edge formed by the intersection of curved vaults, or the fillet or moulding which covers this edge.

GROUND A rather loose term used in a great number of ways to describe a surface to which paint is to be applied; for instance, to denote the condition of the surface (e.g., "The application of a hard brittle film over a soft *ground* will cause cracking", "The *ground* for gilding should be hard and non-absorbent"), to denote a colour which is to be completely covered (e.g., "A delicate raw sienna glaze on an ivory *ground*", "The room was *grounded* out in white"), to indicate the background or prevailing colour upon which a design is to be painted (e.g., "A sprig pattern in gold on a crimson *ground*"), to suggest the texture of a surface (e.g., "Painting with a dry-brush technique on a stippled *ground*"), and so on.

GROUND BRUSH Known as a "pound brush" or a "4/0". A heavy substantial brush of the old-fashioned round shape, with bristles projecting some 150mm beyond the binding. Before such a brush can be used it needs to be bridled with string, i.e., bound with string in extension of the original binding. When properly bridled and broken in, a ground brush spreads paint very evenly, and there are still many craftsmen who prefer this type to the modern flat metal-bound brush. As the brush wears down in the course of its use, the bridling can be taken off a few turns at a time, so that the brush preserves its shape and its ideal working length for a very long time and will far outlast its modern equivalent.

GROUND COAT An opaque coat of paint over which it is intended to apply a further coating or treatment; for instance, the opaque coating which is used as the base for a glaze or scumble coat in broken colour effects, or the oily coat of paint which serves as the base for a thin flatting.

GROUND COLOUR   The general background colour upon which a design is painted or stencilled or a piece of lettering executed. The term is also sometimes used very loosely to mean the first coat of paint in any paint system.

GROUNDING   A term used in many districts to mean specifically the solid colour which is the base upon which graining colour is applied and which shows through the graining colour as the lightest part of the wood which is being imitated; for instance, "medium oak grounding" to denote a buff colour suitable as the base for medium oak graining, "mahogany grounding", and so on.

GROUNDS   Wallpapers to which a coat of background colour has been applied and allowed to dry before the pattern is printed upon it, as opposed to those on which the pattern has been printed directly upon the uncoated paper.

GUARD RAIL   A protective rail placed around the working platform of a scaffold in order (together with the toe boards) to prevent the fall of persons, materials or tools from the platform. Under the Construction Regulations it is required that guard rails shall be provided on every working platform (with certain exemptions which are listed) from which a person might fall a distance exceeding two metres (6ft.6ins). The height of the rail is to be between 0·9m and 1·14m (3ft and 3ft 9ins) and the distance between the guard rail and the toe boards shall not exceed 0·76m (30in).
   N.B. At the time of this edition going to press the Construction Regulations have not been converted to metric measurements. Until such time as they are converted it should be noted that the figures given in feet and inches in brackets are still legally binding.

GUIDE COAT   A very thin coating of spirit colour which is applied to a surface which has been filled and levelled, in order to indicate whether the filling has been completely and thoroughly carried out or whether there are still some indentations which require further filling. The guide coat is generally composed of turps tinted with Prussian blue or drop black; it is brushed on to the surface and allowed to dry, and the surface is then carefully rubbed down with fine sandpaper stretched over a rubbing block. The thin colour is removed from the flat surface but is not dislodged from any cavities which remain, and by this means the position of such cavities is revealed.

GUIGNET'S GREEN (also called VIRIDIAN)   A fine brilliant green with an almost metallic lustre, which is permanent to light, stable and inert, and unaffected by sulphur or alkalis. It consists of a hydrated oxide of chromium. It is almost transparent in oil and makes an excellent glaze colour. It is used as artists' colour, being rather expensive for general use, but it is also mixed with zinc chrome in order to produce "permanent green" and is employed, too, in the tinting of water paints.

GUILLOCHE   A type of ornament consisting of inter-twisted or inter-laced bands.

GULES   The heraldic tincture red.

GUM   A viscid substance exuded from certain trees in the same way as resin, but differing from resin in that it is soluble in water but insoluble in organic solvents. In the paint industry, however, the term is used in a wide and general sense to include both resins and gums.

GUM ARABIC   A product of acacia used in the preparation of artists' water colours.

GUM THUS   A material which exudes naturally from American pine trees, and is essentially the same material as the oleo-resin from which turpentine and rosin are distilled.

GUMWOOD   A wood which is native to the Southern parts of the U.S.A. The grain resembles the figure of rosewood, and is sometimes imitated by grainers. It can be grained in either water or oil media, working with raw umber and drop black on a ground colour composed of white lead, raw umber and raw sienna.

GYPSUM   A soft pinky-white rock consisting of a hydrous calcium sulphate.

GYPSUM CEMENTS   A name sometimes used as a synonym for anhydrous plasters.

GYPSUM PLASTERBOARD   A building board consisting of a layer of set gypsum plaster enclosed between two firmly attached sheets of heavy paper. Various types are manufactured, including gypsum baseboards and gypsum lath which are designed to receive a skimming of gypsum plaster, insulating gypsum plasterboard which is faced on one or both sides with a thin veneer of aluminium foil, and water-repellent plasterboard; the type of most interest to the painter is that known as gypsum wallboard, which is faced on one side with a grey paper suitable for the reception of plaster and on the other side with an ivory paper which is suitable for immediate decoration with oil paint, water paint, emulsion paint or wallpaper applied directly to the surface.

GYPSUM PLASTERS   Plasters used in building, which are derived from natural gypsum. They are produced by calcining the crushed rock in order to drive off the water of crystallization; when the gypsum is roasted at a moderate temperature ($170°C$, $338°F$) three-quarters of the contained water is driven off, the product being known as hemihydrate plaster; heating the gypsum to a temperature of $400°C$ ($752°F$) drives off the entire water content, and anhydrous plaster is obtained. Neat hemihydrate plaster, commonly known as plaster of Paris, sets very quickly and is used as a material for stopping holes and cracks; for use on large areas it needs to have a retarding agent added during manufacture and is then known as a "retarded hemihydrate plaster"—often called a "hardwall" plaster. Anhydrous plasters can be modified in various ways during manufacture, the products being classified either as anhydrous gypsum plasters or as Keene's or Parian cement.

The characteristic of all gypsum plasters is that they set by a process of crystallization whereby the water added to them by the plasterer combines chemically with them to replace the water of crystallization driven off during manufacture. They expand slightly as they set and are chemically neutral. For further details of the various types see under the appropriate headings—e.g., *Anhydrous Gypsum Plaster*, etc.

H

HAIR CRACKING   When the term is used to refer to the degree of cracking of a paint, it implies the presence of fine cracks occurring irregularly and at random, and not deep enough to penetrate the top coat.

HAIR CRACKS   Very fine cracks occurring at random in a surface which is to be painted, particularly in plaster work. Lime plasters especially, unless gauged with plaster of Paris, are liable to shrink when drying and to develop a mass of fine hair cracks; these are not particularly noticeable until paint is applied, but then they become very conspicuous due to the absorption of the medium into the cracks. There are filling materials suitable for filling hair cracks, but when the surface is extensively affected it is difficult to fill all the cracks satisfactorily, and it is often more economical to size and line the surface with lining paper.

HAIR STIPPLER   A type of brush with several applications to painting and decorating. It consists of a flat rectangular base plate into which several rows of wire drawn bristles are set, the rows being so close together that the bristles present a flat level face of the same area as the base. The base is in two parts consisting of a flat rectangle of wood to which a thin plate of either aluminium or ebonite is attached in order to keep the wood dry and prevent it from warping. Various sizes are available but the most usual sizes are those with a base plate measuring 175mm by 125mm or 150mm by 100mm. Each stippler is provided with two interchangeable handles, secured to the base with a thumb screw; one of these is a long handle projecting well beyond the base, and the other is a bridge or arch handle.

The purposes of the hair stippler are as follows:
(a) To level out the newly applied coat of paint and to eliminate the brushmarks from it.
(b) To blend colours together in order to obtain a gentle gradation where a blending of colour from light to dark is required.

(c) To level out an area of tinted glaze before any broken colour effects such as rag-rolling or rubber stippling are commenced.

The method of use is that when an area of suitable dimensions has been laid in with paint or glaze, the surface of the wet material is patted or struck several times with the face of the stippler, the brush being used with short sharp clean strokes, each stroke largely overlapping the previous one. It is essential that the stippler be used systematically with a series of strokes travelling in a straight line across the painted surface, followed by another series travelling in a straight line below it and slightly overlapping the previous series, and so on; if it is used in a haphazard fashion with a series of circular movements there is a strong tendency for some small areas to be missed, and these show up very prominently in the finished work. A hair stippler is generally used with flat or semi-flat materials, such as oilbound water paint, flat oil paint, semi–gloss paint or glaze; it would, of course, be quite unsuitable for use with a gloss paint as it would disturb the even flow of the material and produce minute pits and hollows that would detract from the gloss.

The method of cleaning a stippler after use is not always clearly understood; the correct method is as follows: (a) A piece of lining paper or newspaper is laid down flat and a few drops of the appropriate solvent (water for a water paint, white spirit for an oil paint or glaze) poured upon it. The stippler is gently tapped on the solvent so as to loosen the paint in the tips of the brush. (b) Once the cleaning operation has begun the stippler must on no account be turned face upwards, otherwise softened paint may flow down into the base of the brush from whence it will be difficult to dislodge it and where it will tend to set hard and stiffen the bristles; moreover, when washing commences, if water flows down into the base plate it may cause the base to warp and buckle. (c) The stippler is then washed with warm water and soap; the tips of the bristles only are dipped in the water, the stippler is kept face downwards, and the soap worked into the brush with the fingers until the paint is loosened. The washing continues until the soapsuds produced are clean and frothy, indicating that all oily material has been removed. Hot water should not be used, as it has a harmful effect on the bristles. Under no circumstances should the stippler be completely immersed in water so as to wet the base plate. (d) The tips of the bristles are rinsed in clean water to remove all the soap. (e) The stippler is well shaken to remove as much moisture as possible and is then hung up to dry with the bristles pointing face downwards. No attempt should be made to dry the stippler by artificial heat as this will lead to the base plate becoming warped.

HAMMER FINISHES Industrial finishes, used on a variety of products ranging from office equipment to toilet articles, which give the appearance of hammered metal but with the irregularities of the surface not as pronounced. They offer the same advantages as wrinkle finishes without the drawbacks, such as the tendency to harbour dirt. They are usually produced by stoving processes owing to the difficulty of obtaining a hard film with an air drying paint. One of the methods used commercially is to apply a stoving metallic paint, allow the solvents to flash off, and to spatter the surface with highly volatile thinner before the paint is dry. Special guns are available with two separate fluid feeds, allowing two materials to be applied simultaneously to produce a hammered effect. In this country this method is being superseded with a one-coat hammer finish in which silicones are used to produce the hammer effect within the film itself.

HANDBOARD A stout piece of wood, usually about 300mm square, on which the painter mixes small quantities of plaster of Paris when making good the cracks and holes in plaster work. The handle consists of a sturdy piece of dowelling fastened centrally on the back at right angles to the board.

HANGING EDGE The hanging edge of the door is the edge which is hinged.

HARD DRY A term which is used rather loosely to denote the degree of hardness attained by a film of paint. It can mean that the film is hard enough to be rubbed down and for a further coat of paint to be applied by brushing. In the case of a finishing coat it implies that the film is hard enough to be handled without damage.

HARD GLOSS PAINT A full gloss finishing material consisting of fine textured pigments ground in an oil varnish medium prepared from natural or synthetic resins and heat-treated drying oils (as opposed to a Dutch enamel in which the medium is linseed stand oil). The pigments, driers and thinners are the same as for an oil paint.

HARD STOPPING A material for stopping the holes and cracks in timber; it can be prepared in various ways, such as by mixing stiff paste white lead with whiting and Japan gold size, by mixing white and red lead with gold size, or by stiffening linseed oil putty with red lead powder. A hard stopping for iron work can be prepared with red lead powder and gold size or boiled oil. On good quality work a hard stopping, which dries hard throughout its mass, is always preferable to ordinary linseed oil putty, which hardens slowly and tends in time to shrink and crumble.

HARDBOARD A type of building board available in the form of large sheets and extensively used as a lining for walls and ceilings and for such purposes as the erection of exhibition stands, shop fitting, the facing of signboards and the flushing of doors. It is composed of wood pulp, wood fibre or other vegetable fibre together with suitable fillers and bonding agents, and is densely compacted under high pressure to present a smooth hard polished surface. Some types of hardboard possess very little porosity while others in spite of their polished appearance are extremely porous; some types contain oil in their composition and require a special primer and filling treatment if they are to be brought to a good quality enamel finish. Because of the varying composition and texture of different brands it is advisable to consult the manufacturers' instructions about the painting of any particular type. Hardboards are hygroscopic and it is therefore advisable that the back and edges should be painted before fixing in order to prevent the penetration of moisture.

HARDNESS   The extent to which a paint film can resist the impact of a hard object without denting and the extent to which it will stand handling without sustaining damage. Various tests such as the scratch test, the mechanical thumb and the hardness rocker are used by manufacturers in order to assess with accuracy the hardness of a paint film after a certain length of time.

HARDWALL PLASTERS   Gypsum plasters of the retarded hemi-hydrate type are commonly known as hardwall plasters, but the term is not precise and is sometimes applied also to certain plasters of the anhydrous group.

HARDWOODS   All timbers obtained from broad-leaved trees are called hardwoods and nearly all the coniferous trees are classed as softwoods, but certain broad-leaved trees such as the horse chestnut, the willow, the poplar, etc., are actually quite soft. Generally speaking, softwoods are timbers of fairly rapid growth, while hardwoods grow more slowly and consequently have a finer, closer grain. Sometimes, when hardwoods such as mahogany and oak are to be painted, difficulty is experienced due to the closeness of the grain resisting the penetration of the primer, which results in poor adhesion. For this reason the primer for a hardwood should be mixed with a greater proportion of thinner, and a reduced proportion of oil compared with that used for a softwood, and it is an advantage to replace some of the oil with a mixing varnish which will promote adhesion and hardening of the primer. In the case of a ready mixed primer, extra thinners should be added to assist penetration.

HARMONY   A scheme or colour combination which presents a pleasing appearance because it is composed of colours which lie close to one another on the colour circle and are used in their proper tonal order.

HAWK   The name given over a wide part of the country to the handboard used in making-good defective plaster. See also *Handboard*.

HAZINESS   A term sometimes used for blooming.

HEARTWOOD   The older, inner part of a tree trunk, impregnated with colouring matter, oil, tannin, resin and mineral by-products. Heartwood markings are the grain markings seen when the log is sawn along its length from bark to bark. In graining, the heartwood is mainly employed in situations where it would be used by the woodworker, such as the rail of doors, etc.

HEAT-RESISTING PAINTS   To some extent the term is self-explanatory, as it obviously implies paint which will withstand the effects of heat, but the actual choice of a heat-resisting paint for any particular purpose will depend upon the conditions which prevail and the temperature range likely to be encountered. The temperatures reached in radiators and pipes fed by normal hot water heating systems are not as a rule sufficiently high to cause serious difficulty, provided the finish is elastic enough to cope with the expansion and contraction of the metal and that soft undercoats are avoided. The temperatures reached in steam radiators and pipes are much higher and are more likely to present difficulty, and the painting of industrial premises includes the treatment of such items as metal smoke stacks, flues, exhausts, boilers, furnace installations and coke ovens which may reach an extremely high temperature, often in combination with other highly corrosive and destructive conditions.

Oil paints tend to become brittle under the influence of constant heat and this, together with the expansion and contraction of the metal, makes them liable to flake. There are also various pigments which fade or darken under the action of heat. In general it may be said, therefore, that the medium used in heat-resisting paints contains a minimum of oil and is usually composed of synthetic resin, and only those pigments which are unaffected by heat are employed. Heat-resisting paints may be classed under three headings as follows:

(i) Paints withstanding temperatures of up to 93°C (200°F). Ordinary alkyd resin paints, pigmented with titanium oxide, synthetic reds, yellow oxides, Monastral blue, etc., are successful up to 93°C (200°F); they will, in fact, withstand temperatures up to 120°C (250°F), but there is some loss of gloss and some discolouration of the lighter shades.

(ii) Paints withstanding temperatures of between 93°C (200°F) and 260°C (500°F). These include: (a) Acrylic resin based paints which will stand temperatures of up to 150°C (300°F) for fairly long periods without deterioration even in the presence of severe conditions such as on smoke stacks exposed to acid fumes. They may be pigmented with titanium oxide and earth colours, Monastral blue, chromium oxide, etc., but organic reds and lead pigments are excluded. (b) Heat-resisting bituminous enamels in black, aluminium and certain colours, which withstand temperatures of up to 260°C (500°F) and are used for boilers, smoke stacks and for asbestos cement flue pipes subjected to rapid attack by acid condensates. (c) Cyclised rubber paints which, suitably pigmented, will withstand temperatures of 200°C (400°F), although yellowing occurs after 120°C (250°F) has been reached. (d) Graphite in sodium silicate paint, up to 150°C (300°F). (e) Red iron oxide and zinc chromate in linseed oil paint, up to 260°C (500°F). (f) Aluminium and other metallic paints which will withstand temperatures of up to 150°C (300°F). In this connection it may be noted that when metallic paints are used on pipes and radiators they reduce the emissivity to a considerable extent; in the case of steam pipes carrying live steam to various parts of a factory this may be an advantage by cutting down heat losses, but in the case of hot water systems for heating domestic and public buildings it can lead to a marked reduction in the efficiency of the radiators and heating pipes.

(iii) Paints withstanding temperatures above 260°C (500°F) and up to 540°C ($1\,000^{\circ}$F). In some of the newer heat-resisting paints an inorganic medium is used in place of an organic medium. Such paints are based upon silicone resins or butyl titanate resins tinted with earth colours, aluminium powder, etc.; the resins decompose when heated and leave a firmly adherent film of inert residues of silica or titanium oxide. These paints have great resistance to heat but a less certain resistance to weather; they may withstand up to 315°C (600°F) on exterior surfaces such as chimney stacks and up to 540°C (1 000°F) on interior surfaces. Their resistance to atmospheric corrosion is increased if they are pigmented with zinc instead of aluminium but this reduces their heat resistance from 540°C to 400°C (1 000°F to 750°F). It is essential, if they are to be efficient, that the metal to which they are applied should be perfectly clean, and they need to be brought to a temperature of 260°C (500°F) very shortly after application in order to cure them. They withstand a constant temperature better than a fluctuating one, and it is found that when they have been exposed to heat for any length of time they are liable to break down rapidly should the heat be withdrawn due to a temporary closing down of the plant.

HEAVY BODIED   A term applied to a material of thick consistency or to a very viscous material, generally one that leaves a thick coating when dry. Sometimes the term is used in a misleading and incorrect sense to refer to a material of high opacity.

HEMIHYDRATE PLASTERS   Plaster derived from the rock gypsum, and obtained by crushing the rock and heating it at a temperature of 170°C (338°F), a process which drives off three-quarters of the water of crystallization. The plaster thus formed is commonly known as plaster of Paris. When mixed with water it sets or hydrates very quickly, the water combining chemically with it to replace the crystalline water driven off during manufacture so that the plaster reverts to its original composition. Plaster of Paris sets so quickly that its use is limited mostly to the pointing of holes and cracks, but if a retarding agent is incorporated during manufacture a form of plaster suitable for skimming large surfaces and yet capable of setting very rapidly is produced; this is known as retarded hemihydrate plaster, often called "hardwall" plaster.

In common with all gypsum plasters, hemihydrate plasters expand slightly when setting and are chemically inert. Theoretically they contain nothing which would set up an unfavourable reaction with any oil paint which is applied upon them, but it must be remembered that they may be contaminated by alkaline materials brought forward from the backing, and that sand and lime may have been added to them by the plasterer; they should therefore be tested for alkalinity before any paint is applied.

HERALDRY   The science connected with the correct use of armorial bearings; hence, *heraldic charges,* the conventionalized symbols used in heraldry; *heraldic colours,* the colours used in heraldry, known by their Norman-French names, viz.. azure (blue), gules (red), purpure (purple), sable (black), vert (green); *heraldic painting,* that part of the decorator's work concerned with the representation of heraldic devices; and so on.

HESSIAN   A coarse cloth made of hemp and jute; it is sometimes used as a wall hanging, in which case it is hung dry, the wall being pasted and the hessian pressed into contact with it and well brushed out. If after hanging it is to be painted it should first be coated with weak hot size to insulate the fibres from the oil in the paint. But in recent years the coarseness of the weave has been turned to advantage, and decorative hessians have been produced for use in highly sophisticated schemes. These modern hessians are usually supplied on a stout paper backing, the colour of the paper serving sometimes to throw the weave and texture into prominence.

HIDING POWER   The opacity of a material, its ability to obliterate the surface to which it is applied.

HOG HAIR   Animal hair, generally obtained from the neck, shoulders and back of the wild boar, used in brush manufacture. Because of certain outstanding features, such as its taper, curve, serrated surface and flagged end, it is a particularly useful filling for paint brushes. See also *Bristle*.

HOLIDAYS   A colloquial term for misses or areas left uncoated with paint due to carelessness on the part of the operative.

HORSE HAIR   Animal hair obtained from the manes or tails of horses and used in brush manufacture. It is inferior to bristle in every way, possessing neither the stiff root end, the fine taper, the flagged tip, the resistance to water nor the resilience and springiness of hog hair. It is used as an adulterant or substitute, being mixed with other hair, such as bristle, in order to produce a cheaper brush, but brushes containing more than a small proportion of horse hair are too soft and floppy to be of much use.

HOSE   Flexible tubing through which gases or liquids can be conveyed to a given point. for example, the fluid hose and the air hose in spray equipment, the hose feeding an inflammable gas to a blow-torch, etc. In some cases it is desirable that hose should be colour coded to prevent confusion; very often in spray equipment the fluid hose is brown or black and the air hose red, and when oxyacetylene equipment is being used for flame cleaning etc., red hose is used for acetylene and black hose for the oxygen.

HOT SPRAYING   A spray painting process in which paint or lacquer is heated just before application in order to reduce its viscosity, so that in effect heat is used instead of the addition of volatile solvents in order to bring the paint to spraying consistency.

Several advantages over normal cold spraying methods are claimed for the process. Heated paint has improved flow characteristics, giving a smoother finish, and is independent of fluctuation in atmospheric conditions since the temperature and the viscosity of the material are controlled. The solvent lost from the material is much greater—up to 80% in hot spraying compared with some 20% in cold spraying—so that the applied paint film has a very high solid content and therefore gives greater build, with consequent saving of costs if required. In addition, the applied film regains its viscosity so rapidly as to reduce the tendency for sags and runs to form, there is less tendency for orange peeling to occur since there is less solvent to be expelled from the film, and the coverage of surface imperfections is improved since the lower solvent content means that there is less shrinkage in the film.

There are also certain distinct economies to be considered; there is obviously a saving on the amount of thinners used, but in addition there is a significant saving of paint since heated paint requires less air for its atomization and consequently there is a marked reduction of overspray and spray rebound.

Various types of hot spray equipment are on the market, for use both with stationary spray plant and mounted as portable units.

HOT SURFACES To the painter the term "hot" is applied to any surface which is unusually absorbent or porous.

HOT WIRE SPRAYING A term sometimes applied to metal spraying, a process in which steelwork is sprayed with a molten metal, such as zinc or aluminium, in order to receive protection from corrosion. The metal to be sprayed is drawn into the form of wire which is fed into a specially designed pistol operated by gas and oxygen. While zinc and aluminium are the two metals most usually sprayed there are several other metals, such as tin, copper, brass, cadmium, etc., which may be used for certain specific purposes, and in fact any metal which can be drawn into wire and melted by oxy-gas equipment can be sprayed.

In the treatment of structural steel the process is mainly used for spraying the steel before erection, but it can also be used for steelwork *in situ* and in fact several important contracts have been carried out by this method.

Although hot wire spraying is a specialized trade and is not carried out by painters and decorators, it is still a matter of interest and concern to them, as the durability of the coating is enhanced if it is painted immediately after application and repainted at regular intervals. The sprayed deposit has a matt surface ideally suited to the reception of paint. See *Metal Spraying.*

HUE Another name for colour, e.g., red, orange, yellow, green, blue, etc.

HUMID Moist, damp; hence humidity, moisture.

HUNGARIAN ASH A beautiful silky wood, a little deeper and richer than common ash, with a fine curly grain and strong high-lights and shades. It is grained in raw umber and raw sienna on a ground of pale cream.

HUNGRY The painter speaks of a hungry surface when he means that the absorption of the surface has not been completely satisfied by the previous coats of paint so that it appears patchy and uneven.

HYDRO-ADDITIVE PAINTS Primers, undercoatings and finishes which have been developed for application to surfaces on which moisture is present. The principle involved is that if certain organic materials are added to paint the surface tension of the wet paint film is reduced; when this occurs the paint is able to displace the water present on the surface to which it is applied and is able to spread over the surface in its stead. The organic material used for the purpose is stearine amine, derived from stearic acid. It should be noted that these paints are only effective in the case of surface moisture; they cannot function and are not intended to function on wood or any other material which is saturated with water, and the effect of applying them to such a material is exactly what would occur with a conventional paint system, namely that there would be no possibility of adhesion and the paint film would be forced off by the pressure of the contained moisture.

HYDROFLUORIC ACID   The type of acid used in glass embossing and etching.

HYGROSCOPICITY   The property of taking up moisture from, and giving out moisture to, the atmosphere. The term has a bearing upon various aspects of a painter's work, such as, for example, when deliquescent salts are present in a building and, being hygroscopic, cause the surface to appear permanently damp or to become damp during spells of humid weather.

HYPALON PAINT   A chemically resistant paint similar to neoprene paint (q.v.) except that it is available in a wider range of colours.

I

IDENTIFICATION COLOURS   Colours used to denote the function of the object painted with them—e.g., the colours used to call attention to a hazard, such as a dangerous piece of mechanism — or to identify the purpose or the contents of conduits, cables or pipes in a building. See also *Colour Coding*.

ILMENITE   A lustrous black substance, a titaniferous iron ore, which is the principal source of titanium oxide.

ILMENITE BLACK   A black pigment derived from the mineral ilmenite and used in the preparation of fillers and undercoatings for the painting of machinery, motor cars, etc. It is also sometimes added to other paints to improve their resistance to heat.

IMITATION GLASS EMBOSSING   A method of obtaining a matt finish in glass gilding in order to imitate the appearance of gold upon glass that has been etched. It is produced by pencilling in with clear varnish those parts of the lettering or ornament which are to appear dull, and allowing the varnish to dry before proceeding to apply the gold leaf.

IMITATION LEATHER   The appearance of tooled leather can be imitated in a paint treatment by the use of plastic paint, which is manipulated in various ways to produce the desired pattern and emboss and is then grounded out with bronze paint. A scumble of umber glaze is then applied and the surface wiped with a soft cloth to expose the metallic paint on the raised portions of the work.

IMITATION LEATHER WALLPAPERS Embossed papers coated with metallic paints and scumbles to suggest antique leather hangings, and ranging in quality from cheap leatherettes to high class hand-scumbled productions.

IMITATION STONE PAINTS Paints intended to present the texture and appearance of stone. They consist of an aggregate of granulated stone or silver sand, held in suspension in either a flat oil medium or an emulsion medium and suitably pigmented. Imitation stone paints are produced by several of the leading paint manufacturers for both interior and exterior use. Generally they are supplied ready for use, and they should be applied in a thick coating. On no account must they be over-thinned; otherwise, the finish will be patchy and uneven. They may be applied either by brush or by spray and usually two coats are necessary, the porosity of the surface having previously been sealed with a suitable primer; if the stone paint is applied by brush, each coat should be stippled. After application, as the second coat is drying off, the paint may be scored with a blunt steel tool such as a screwdriver to represent the joints in the stonework; the joints are afterwards picked out in flat oil colour to enhance the effect.

The spreading capacity of imitation stone paint is low, that of the second coat being even less than the first because of the texture produced by the first coat.

Imitation stone paint can also be produced by hand. The surface, suitably sealed, is painted with a highly viscous compound (e.g. white lead and varnish) and when this is tacky, dry sand is thrown on to it; using two or three colours of sand gives a variegated effect. The joints are scored with a screwdriver and picked out in paint.

In recent years, a much improved version of stone paint has become available. Most leading manufacturers now produce a texture paint consisting of emulsions or co-polymers derived from synthetic rubber with a suitable aggregate added; many of these are thinned with water and are adapted to both brush and roller application.

IMPACT RESISTANCE The extent to which a paint film can withstand a sudden blow.

IMPASTO In mural painting, the application of paint in a thick layer.

IMPENETRABLE VARNISH A term sometimes given to sealers such as stop-tar knotting, etc., which are used to prevent such materials as bitumen, tar, creosote and certain colours from bleeding through and spoiling a newly applied paint film.

IMPERVIOUS Impenetrable; not allowing passage or entrance; for instance, when we speak of a film of paint as being impervious to moisture we mean that it will not allow moisture to pass through.

IMPREGNATING VARNISHES Varnishes which are designed to penetrate the material to which they are applied, such as, for instance, electrical insulation varnishes designed to impregnate the cotton fabric covering of coil or armature windings.

IMPREGNATION The saturation of a substance or a surface with some other material; for example, we speak of a surface which is heavily charged with machine oil or grease, thereby presenting difficulties in painting, as being *impregnated* with oil. Sometimes building materials such as timber, etc., are impregnated with fluids for preservative or fire-resisting purposes, the fluid being forced in under pressure in order to penetrate deeply.

IMPRISONED MOISTURE Free moisture which is trapped beneath the surface of such a material as wood or plaster by an impervious film of paint and which can only escape by forcing the film away from the surface.

INCOMPATIBILITY Materials which are unable to subsist together are said to be incompatible. There are many instances affecting painters' work; for example, it may generally be said that paints based on synthetic resin media do not mix satisfactorily with those based on natural drying oils, which may be due to incompatibility either of media or solvent or both, and for the same reason it is often unwise to mix together different brands of paint, water paint or emulsion. There are also certain pigments which react unfavourably if mixed together—for example, white lead and sulphide pigments such as ultramarine—and pigment mixtures of this kind would be incompatible.

INDENE RESINS Synthetic resins similar to coumarone resins.

INDEPENDENT SCAFFOLD A scaffold used chiefly for painting and decorating and general repair work on existing buildings (although also used for masons' work on premises in course of erection) which does not depend upon the building for support. An independent scaffold used by painters generally consists of two rows of standards or a series of prefabricated frames with the inner row placed as close to the building as possible allowing for projections such as cornices, etc.; the standards or frames are connected longitudinally with ledgers upon which transoms are coupled to support the working platform. Although no load is carried by the building, it is essential that the scaffold should be adequately tied in to the building throughout its length.

INDIAN INK A waterproof ink consisting of a dispersion of carbon black in water with an organic binder, and used by decorators in the preparation of working drawings and perspective drawings for decorative schemes.

INDIAN RED A deep red oxide pigment tending towards purple-brown, which is prepared by the calcination of crystalline ferrous sulphate. It possesses good staining power, spreading power and opacity, is permanent and will mix with all other pigments without either affecting them or being affected by them.

INDIAN YELLOW   Otherwise called puree. A pigment prepared from animal sources and now no longer made.

INDIGO   A fine rich blue pigment of subdued tone, formerly obtained from vegetable sources but now produced artifically; used in decorative work, mural painting, etc.

INDUCTION HEATING   A method of raising the temperature of a painted object in order to speed up the drying time of the paint on the same principles employed in stoving processes. The painted article is placed within a series of copper coils, and an electric current passed through the coils produces a magnetic field which induces a secondary current in the article itself, causing it to heat up very rapidly.

INDUSTRIAL FINISHING   Generally taken to mean the painting of machine made articles under controlled conditions at a factory, as opposed to the painting of structures and buildings carried out on the site. It includes many techniques which could not be applied to the painting of structures.

INDUSTRIAL PAINTING   The painting of industrial premises, once regarded by the painter and decorator as being largely unskilled work but now recognized as a highly organized business covering a vast range of interesting and important operations.

INDUSTRIAL PAINTS   Usually understood to mean paints formulated for factory use on machine made products, as opposed to decorators' paints intended for use on the site.

INDUSTRIAL SPIRIT   Similar to methylated spirit; like methylated spirit, it is denatured to prevent its being used for drinking, but not to such an extent as to interfere with its technical properties; it is available only for manufacturing purposes.

INERT   Lacking the power of reacting chemically with other substances; for example, "an inert pigment", a pigment which can be mixed with other pigments or paint materials without affecting them or being affected by them; "an inert plaster", a plaster which does not exert any chemical action upon the superimposed paint; and so on.

INFLAMMABLE. Now often referred to as flammable.   Capable of being ignited, kindled, set on fire.
   While there is no paint which will render an inflammable material completely flameproof, there are a number of coatings which can make a material less easily ignitable and can delay or minimize the spread of flame. See *Fire-retarding Paints.*
   The term also has a bearing upon the use, storage and transport of paint solvents. A liquid is termed "inflammable" when the flashpoint, i.e., the temperature at which the liquid begins to give off a vapour which will ignite upon exposure to flame, is below $65 \cdot 6^{\circ}$C (150°F); and under

the terms of the Highly Flammable Liquids and Liquefied Gases Regulation which came into force in June, 1973, a liquid is classed as "highly flammable" if its flashpoint is $32°C$ $(89·6°F)$ or less.

INFRA-RED STOVING A modern technique by which heat is transferred to a painted article by radiation from a hot surface in order to accelerate the drying, and which has many applications in present-day industrial finishing. The term infra-red indicates the location of this type of radiation in the complete electromagnetic spectrum, just below visible red, the wave length of infra-red rays being beyond that of the visible spectrum. The transfer of heat by infra-red radiation is a familiar phenomenon in nature, half the total energy emitted by the sun being in this form.

The oxidation and polymerization of a paint film is a chemical reaction which is accelerated as the temperature of the reactant rises. The efficacy of infra-red radiation on a painted metal article is due to various factors, which include: (a) the radiation being partially absorbed by the paint to raise its temperature directly, partially reflected by the paint and partially transmitted through the paint film; (b) the radiation which is transmitted through the film striking the metal and being absorbed, transmitted and reflected by the metal itself; (c) the radiation which is absorbed by the metal causing the temperature of the metal to rise and some of this heat being transferred by conduction to the inner part of the paint film; and (d) the radiation reflected from the metal being partially absorbed by the paint film as it passes through again. These factors constitute the difference between infra-red stoving and stoving in convection ovens, which relies on surface heating.

The source of infra-red energy may be plant operated either by gas or electricity. In infra-red gas ovens the radiation is emitted from a black steel plate heated to a dull red heat. In electrical plant the emission may be from tungsten lamps running at a lower temperature than that used for lighting, with reflectors to concentrate the radiation on to the painted object, or from sheathed-wire heating elements mounted in trough-shaped reflectors. In general, it may be said that the former provide almost instantaneous heating up or cooling down while the latter are more robust, although the selection of one or other of these systems for any particular purpose is guided by several other factors.

The design of infra-red drying installations includes many possible arrangements. There are small portable and adjustable lamp units available for spotting and general repair work in garages and workshops, and large banks of lamps or heating elements mounted on a mobile chassis which are very often arranged to face a movable aluminium reflector screen so that articles of widely varied size and shape can be accommodated, but the equipment is chiefly used for large scale repetition work in industrial painting processes, and ovens are designed to meet specific requirements, very often with the painted articles mounted on a conveyor assembly moving at a predetermined rate. In fact, a correctly designed plant arranged to suit the contours of the painted articles is essential if the full possibilities of infra-red heating are to be realized; otherwise, the efficiency will be marred by wasted energy due to stray radiation, uneven distribution of radiation, and cooling caused by stray currents of air in the heating zone.

Generally, paints specially formulated for infra-red drying and based on synthetic resins are employed, although the technique can also be used with oil-bound paints to evaporate the solvents quickly and can also be used with cellulose paints and wood finishes. There are, of course, numerous applications of infra-red heating outside the sphere of paint finishing.

INGRAIN PAPERS Wallpapers, the characteristic of which is their "oatmeal" or "woolly" texture. They consist of stout substantial pulps to which wood chips and fibres of various kinds have been introduced during manufacture in order to impart the texture; colour is sometimes added during manufacture or the paper may be coated with colour afterwards.

INHIBITIVE PIGMENTS Pigments, which, when used in direct contact with iron or steel, inhibit or retard corrosion. Included among such pigments are zinc chromate, zinc dust, red lead, white lead, lead chromate, basic lead sulphates, etc.

INHIBITORS Materials added in small quantities to compounds of various kinds in order to arrest or delay the onset of a chemical reaction. Examples relating to the painting trade include anti-oxidants incorporated into paints to prevent them from skinning in the containers and arsenic or antimony compounds, used as restrainers in acid pickling solutions to prevent the metal from being unduly attacked.

INLAY A decoration formed by inserting different materials into a groundwork and leaving the surface level. For example, in cabinet making the term is properly applied to the process of scooping shallow holes in the surface of solid wood and filling them with contrasting materials, but it is also used to refer to veneered work where the thin veneer is laid in separate pieces, a decorative pattern being produced by arranging the pieces so that the grain markings are in varying directions or by using pieces of assorted colourings. In painters' work inlaid effects are produced in various ways. For instance, a technique very similar to that of the cabinet marker's can be used when woodgrain wallpapers are hung with bands of contrasting colour or grain pattern inserted, or when Lincrusta is employed to form decorative panels by arranging separate pieces with varying direction of grain. On the other hand, the representation of inlaid effects in graining involves a very different technique whereby all the work of one particular colour or direction is grained, fixed with varnish, and allowed to dry before the next stage is proceeded with, each colour being treated separately.

INSECTICIDAL PAINT A paint containing an additive which forms a bloom on the surface and which destroys any insect which alights upon it. The most advanced of these paints, introduced in 1964, is lethal to flies, wasps, moths, ants, cockroaches, mosquitoes, silver fish, fleas, etc;. but is harmless to children, domestic pets and livestock and is suitable for use even where food is prepared. The performance of the paint is not affected in any way by the additive, and the surface may be washed repeatedly without reducing the potency of the insecticidal materials, which remains unimpaired for the entire life of the paint film.

INSECTICIDE   A preparation for killing insects. Insecticides are sometimes incorporated into paints and distempers with the object of providing a surface which will be lethal to house flies, bluebottles, cockroaches and other insect pests. Coatings of this kind are most useful not only on domestic properties but in restaurants, hospitals, farm buildings, dairies, etc., where the frequent use of an insecticide spray in the atmosphere is either objectionable or inconvenient. Proprietary materials are now available which are designed to remain active for a considerable period of time, the insecticide content being gradually discharged at a controlled rate to form a crystalline bloom on the surface of the material. These materials are available in the form of flat oil paints, semi-gloss paints and furniture lacquers, and even when the surface is washed down and the bloom removed, a fresh coating of bloom soon forms. There are also preservative fluids which are available for the treatment of structural timbers and for other wooden constructions which for various reasons cannot be maintained by regular painting, and these give protection against the attacks of wood-boring insects, exterminating pests such as the furniture beetle and the deathwatch beetle by destroying the eggs, larvae and beetles and preventing re-infestation by making the wood unpalatable to larvae.

INSERT CONTAINER   A device used in spray painting equipment consisting of a thin light metal vessel which is placed inside a pressure feed tank; the paint is placed in the insert container instead of being poured directly into the tank. The use of these containers presents many advantages; it makes the cleaning out of the tank a much simpler and quicker operation, makes the process of changing from one colour to another very much easier, and allows batches of paint to be prepared and strained in advance so that no time is wasted when the tank becomes empty and requires replenishing.

INSOLUBLE   Incapable of being dissolved—hence *insolubility* of a material—the fact that it cannot be dissolved. For example, shellac which is soluble in methylated spirit but is insoluble in turpentine, petroleum spirit or oil, is dissolved in methylated spirit to form knotting, so that when the methylated spirit evaporates it acts as an insoluble sealer coat to prevent the natural solvents present in resinous knots from bleeding into the oil when paint is applied to new wood.

INSULATING BOARD   A fibre building board of cellular composition with good thermal insulation and sound-absorption properties. It is made from a fibrous pulp similar to that used in the manufacture of hardboard, but instead of being compressed into thin sheets it is only lightly squeezed between rollers prior to being dried off in a drying tunnel. It is supplied either in large sheets or in the form of tiles in thicknesses ranging between 12mm and 25mm. Wallboard, which is similar in composition but is not so thick, is supplied in large sheets, and there are also acoustic boards in the form of small panels made with insulating board which sometimes has other materials added and is sometimes perforated to increase its sound absorption.

Insulating boards are occasionally supplied in ready-decorated form, but as a general rule some form of decorative treatment will be required after fixing. Their spongy open texture makes them extremely porous and a thin sealer coat is necessary as a primer. For an emulsion paint finish a thinned coat of the emulsion will serve as a satisfactory sealer; for a water paint finish either a thin primer of the type recommended for the particular brand of water paint, or alternatively a coat of water paint well thinned with petrifying liquid, should be used. For a flat oil finish a thin oily primer is required, but since oil paint has an embrittling effect upon vegetable fibres it is desirable that a liberal coating of very weak hot glue size should be applied before the oil primer is used, in order to penetrate the fibres and insulate them from the oil in the paint. Before applying the glue size, the nail heads should be touched in with zinc chromate primer to prevent their rusting. The texture of these boards does not lend itself to a gloss paint finish. When insulating boards are being used for acoustic purposes they should not be decorated with oil paint as this reduces their acoustic properties; suitable treatments are suggested under the heading *Acoustic Materials.*

INSULATING VARNISH   A type of varnish used in electrical work for the treatment of coils to prevent the entry of water, which would break down the insulation.

INTENSITY   The purity of a colour, sometimes called the "saturation" or, in American terminology, the "chroma". The spectrum colours are the most intense; the intensity of a pigmentary colour is reduced or weakened if it is mixed with white, black, grey or another colour.

INTERLACING   A form of surface decoration in which a number of strands or ribands are interwoven to produce a symmetrical design, as in Celtic art.

INTERMIXING   Mixing together, intermingling. In the painting trade, the term usually refers to the mixing together of two or more ready mixed materials, such as when the colour of a paint is modified by the addition of a quantity of another colour, or when flat and gloss materials are mixed to produce an *eggshell* finish. Intermixing of different brands of paint is most unwise, as the media may react together unfavourably; even with paints of the same brand, unless it is particularly stated by the manufacturer that intermixing is permissible, such intermixing may lead to gelling, fading, etc., due to the incompatability of various pigments.

INTERNAL MIX GUN   A type of spray gun which mixes air and paint within the air cap and is used with small air compressors delivering a restricted volume of air at a comparatively low pressure. The gun is suitable for spraying such materials as multicolour paint; it is not suitable for paints containing absasive particles nor for very quick drying materials.

INTRADOS The inner curve or soffit of an arch.

INTUMESCENT PAINTS Fire retarding paints of a type which swell upon heating to form an insulating coating. They are usually coarse textured and are not generally considered to be capable of increasing the fire resistance grading of a structural element.

INVISIBLE MOISTURE Moisture which is always present and is diffused throughout the atmosphere. The amount of invisible moisture in the air is constantly varying, depending upon the temperature; when the air according to its temperature contains as much vapour as it can hold in invisible state it is said to be saturated, any further addition of vapour becoming visible as cloud, fog, mist, etc., or any drop of temperature causing the vapour to be condensed. See *Condensation.*

IRIDESCENT FINISHES Industrial finishes which give the appearance of *shot silk,* the hues changing with variations in the contours of the painted surface and with variations in the direction of viewing. They are produced with dyestuffs giving a semi-transparent film, in conjunction with non-leafing varieties of aluminium paste or powder.

IRON A malleable tenacious metal, with the chemical symbol of Fe, used extensively in every walk of life. Its relevance to the painter takes two main forms. (i) Iron and steel (which is iron combined with carbon in various proportions) when used for structural purposes present considerable problems to the painter and the paint manufacturer due to the rapidity with which they corrode. (ii) A number of painters' pigments are derived from iron oxides; for example, red oxide, siennas, ochre, etc.

ISINGLASS A very pure form of gelatine prepared from the swimming bladders of certain kinds of fish, chiefly the sturgeon (from which Russian isinglass is produced) and the cod and the hake (from which North American isinglass is derived). When cooked in boiling water it forms an extremely strong jelly. It is used as a mordant in glass gilding in the proportions of a small pinch of isinglass to half a litre of boiling water. The mordant needs to be strained before use; otherwise, it may cause a cloudy film to occur between the gold and the glass.

ISOMETRIC PROJECTION A method of projecting the plan and elevations of a room, building or other object in order to present a three-dimensional picture for use as a working drawing. The lines of the plan are drawn at an angle of 30° from the horizontal, vertical lines are projected on the same scale as the plan, and the whole of the work can be carried out with a 60° set square and a T square.

ITALIAN WALNUT A variety of walnut, the characteristic features of which are its curly formation, close and well-defined mottle and broad bands of contrasting tone. It is usually grained in Vandyke brown and black on a ground of warm buff.

ITALIC ALPHABET   A lower case alphabet of sloping characters, derived from a cursive style developed in Italy in the 16th century. It is a beautiful alphabet which is ideally suited to the technique of the writing pencil, and is particularly useful for anything in the nature of lengthy inscriptions, being a compressed style which occupies a comparatively small space.

IVORY   The hard white substance of which the tusks of an elephant are composed. To the painter it represents a delicate colour similar to that of piano keys, deeper in tone than off-white and cooler than cream, although the term is rather vague. Old ivory is a much warmer colour approximating to the deeper colour of antique ivory carvings.

IVORY BLACK   A fine artists' colour produced by calcining ivory chippings in air-tight retorts. Although some is still prepared in this manner the term is now generally used to refer to the highest quality of bone black.

J

J

JAMB   The side post of a doorway, window, etc.

JAMB DUSTER   A brush used for dusting preparatory to painting. See *Duster*.

JAPAN   A glossy black enamel based on ashphaltum and drying oils. See *Black Japan*.

JAPAN BLACK   Same as black Japan.

JAPAN DRIER   Otherwise known as terebine; a liquid drying agent consisting originally of a quick-drying varnish composed of soft copal, linseed oil and litharge, but now more usually composed of a heavy boiled oil saturated with lead and manganese to which rosin is sometimes added.

JAPAN FILLER   A composition consisting either of materials such as slate powder, pumice powder, or silica ground in Japan gold size, or of paste white lead, whiting and Japan gold size, which is used to fill shallow indentations and to produce a smooth level surface prior to painting. The filler may be applied in thick paste form with a filling knife, thinned down for brush application, or mixed for spray application. When hard it is rubbed down wet with pumice or waterproof sandpaper. A Japan filler as a general rule gives more durable results than a water filler. Machinery painting very often involves the use of a filler to level out the roughness of the castings, and a Japan filler is essential for this purpose as it withstands vibration whereas a water filler is quickly dislodged.

JAPAN GOLD SIZE Sometimes called "writers' gold size". A mordant or adhesive for gold leaf, consisting of a short oil varnish containing a high proportion of driers. It is used for the gilding of lettering, lining and ornamental work in which sharpness and clarity of outline are desirable features and for any gilding which is to be done in situations where there is a possibility of dust or weather conditions affecting the work before the gold is applied. It can be obtained in various drying speeds, such as 1-hour size, 4-hour size, etc., the variation in drying time being achieved by adjusting the proportions of oil and driers; as a general rule, the longer the drying rate the more lustrous the gilding appears. Japan gold size is also used as a binder for spirit colours, as a drier in paint, as an ingredient in fillers and stopping compositions and as a sealer coat for various purposes. See *Gold Size*.

JAPAN WAX An ingredient of oriental lacquer, derived from the berries of the sumac trees of Japan and China.

JAPANESE GRASS CLOTHS AND SILK CLOTHS These are among the more luxurious decorative materials available at the present time, and in recent years they have been imported in fair quantity. Actually, these are traditional materials that have been used in the decoration of shrines and palaces in Japan for many centuries, and the weaving of these materials is a peasant craft. Grasscloth is made from the inner core of the slender stems of wild honeysuckle, and was originally hand-treated by splitting and knotting and was mounted on to a backing of rice paper. Because the work was carried out in the home with natural products, there was considerable variation of colour and texture and no two weaves were ever exactly alike. Now that the commercial possibilities of the material have been grasped, modern methods of production have been applied, the colouring is carefully supervised, and a much more robust backing paper is used. Even so, there are many different ways of treating the material by interlocking the fibres with cotton or metallic strips or by cutting the grasscloth into square or diamonds to achieve parquet or basket weave effects, and the individual nature of the product is one of the distinctive features which appeals to people.

The wall surfaces are cross lined before the finishing material is applied. Trimming is carried out with a razor or a very sharp knife and straightedge, about 16mm being taken from each edge. The material is cut very carefully to length before pasting. Any part that needs cutting after pasting requires careful handling, because unless the scissors are very sharp they are likely to produce a ragged untidy edge. After pasting the material is allowed to become supple before hanging, but oversoaking must at all costs be avoided. A felt covered roller is used to press the material into contact with the wall, care being taken not to stretch it. No attempt can be made, of course, to match up the weave along the joints; the individual appearance of the lengths is part of the effect which is sought after and prized. Naturally, the appearance is improved if the lengths are centred on each wall. Sometimes the joints are covered with beading. Both grasscloths and silk cloths are supplied in rolls 2·44metres long by 0·9metres wide.

JAPANNERS' GOLD SIZE A synonym for Japan gold size.

JAPANNING The application of a stoving black Japan finish.

JARRAH An Australian hardwood now being widely used in building
and furniture making. It is so close grained that normal wood primers
will not penetrate; it should be primed with a thin aluminium primer or
synthetic primer.

JASPÉ PAPERS Wallpapers with a soft irregular pattern giving the
appearance of the surface having been combed or brushed.

JAUNE BRILLIANT An artists' colour prepared from cadmium, vermilion and white lead.

JELLY SIZE One of the forms in which glue size is made available to the
decorator. Apart from the drawback of being bulky, this is quite a
convenient form for the material since it is easy for the painter to judge
the amount of water necessary to thin it. The stiffness of the jelly gives
an indication of the strength of the size; it should have a gummy consistency and should not feel "short" when rubbed between thumb and
forefinger. A good quality of jelly size needs very little added water, only
enough to prevent burning when the size is heated. A disadvantage of
jelly size is its tendency to putrefy in warm weather.

J

JIB DOOR A door which is flush with a wall and which is painted or
papered in the same manner as the wall so as to make it inconspicuous
or indistinguishable from its surroundings.

JIB SCAFFOLD Alternative term for cantilever scaffold.

JOINERY The lighter and finer aspect of woodwork as distinct from
carpentry; it includes built-in furnishing fitments as well as doors,
windows, staircases and panelling.

JOINT The place at which two things are joined together, e.g., the
joints of wallpaper.

JOINT PIN An internal connection used in scaffolding for joining two
metal tubes together, end to end; it is fitted with a screw by which it can
be expanded to grip the inside of the tubes firmly.

JOINT ROLLER A roller used to press down the edges of wallpaper in
order to make the joints less conspicuous.

JUTE The fibre from the inner bark of certain plants, from which is
derived a coarse fabric, available in various colourings or in a natural finish,
which is sometimes used as a wall hanging. Prepared or backed jute fabric
is hung like wallpaper, being applied with a stiff paste on a cross-lined

surface, unprepared jute is usually hung dry, the wall surface being pasted and the fabric rolled on and well brushed out. It is an extremely hard-wearing material which withstands brushing and scrubbing. When jute fabric is to be painted after hanging it should be treated first with a coat of hot weak size to insulate the fibres from the oil in the paint, because of the hardening effect of drying oils upon the fibre; some varieties are, however, supplied specially for overpainting without any further preparation. In recent years highly attractive jute fabrics have been produced suitable for modern decorative scheming.

K

KALSOMINE or KALSO   A name used in some parts of the country to indicate a flat whitewash brush.

KAOLIN   China clay; a porcelain clay derived principally from the decomposition of felspar, and used in the paint industry as a base for lake pigments and in the preparation of ultramarine blue, and also as an extender and as a flatting agent.

KAURI GUM   A fossil resin, obtained from New Zealand, which is used in the manufacture of varnish, being easy to run and combining well with oil. There is also a recent resin called bush kauri.

KEENE'S CEMENT   An anhydrous gypsum plaster of the hard-burnt type—composed, that is to say, of calcium sulphate to which an accelerator has been added. It is used where a hard, compact smooth plaster surface is required; sometimes when a softer grade of plaster has been used for the main body of the work Keene's cement is used to form external angles, mouldings and arrises. It is very often trowelled to a hard glass-like surface which offers poor reception for paint, and may be subject to the defect known as *dry-out*. Unless lime has been added by the plasterer Keene's cement exerts no harmful chemical effect upon paint. See also the notes under the headings *Anhydrous Gypsum Plasters* and *Dry-out*, and for a possible treatment to improve paint adhesion see *Following the Trowel*. Keene's is also sold under various proprietary names such as Astroplax, Pixie Keene's and Superite.

KEROSENE   The correct word for what is usually described as paraffin.

KEY   A surface is said to present a "key" for paint when it exhibits a slight degree of roughness which helps the paint to adhere. A perfectly smooth surface does not provide any key; for example, paint does not readily grip the close-trowelled surface of Keene's cement or the hard smooth surface of a film of shellac knotting. The failure of paint to adhere to a smooth hard surface is the reason for rubbing down a varnished or enamelled surface with pumice or waterproof sandpaper before applying fresh coatings of paint, and there are many instances of treatments such as etching or grit-blasting metal surfaces to make them provide a key for paint.

KING POST   A vertical post extending from the ridge of a roof to support the tie-beam below in the centre of its length.

KNIFE FILLER   A filling composition mixed to the consistency of a stiff paste so that it can be applied with a broad filling knife.

KNIFE FILLING   The application of knife filler in order to fill surface indentations; the filler is drawn across the surface with a broad knife with a flexible blade and a perfectly level edge. It is an operation which calls for considerable skill and patience.

KNIVES   Essential items of a painter's equipment, comprising a broad knife for general purposes such as stripping wallpaper, a broad knife with a perfectly true edge for filling, a chisel knife for working in narrow spaces, a putty knife for the application of stopping and a palette knife for mixing small quantities of colour and for colour matching. Other knives used in specialized departments of the trade include stencil knives, gilders' knives, etc.

KNOCKING UP   A term used to denote the mixing up of paint; probably dating back to the time when paint mixing was an arduous process involving the beating up of stiff paste pigments.

K

KNOTS   Hard cross-grained disfigurements in timber which are formed where the parent stem puts out the shoots which develop into branches. Since the resin ducts run parallel with the growth, the resin which is in the knots flows to the surface of the timber. If the exposed surface of the knots is not sealed before paint is applied the resin, being the same substance from which turpentine is obtained, bleeds into the paint film to cause staining and in severe cases exudes in the form of sticky unsightly tears. The most effective treatment in the case of large knots is to cut them right out and plug the holes with sound wood. Where this is impracticable an alternative method is to cut the knot back below the surface and fill the cavity with a water filler which when hard is sandpapered down to the level of the surrounding wood. The normal method employed where the knots are small and not too troublesome is to seal them with shellac knotting, although occasionally metal foil is used as the sealer.

KNOTTING   A solution of shellac in methylated spirit which is used to prevent resin from exuding from the knots in woodwork and softening and affecting the paint film. The knotting should be applied sparingly and allowed to extend well beyond the edge of the knots, being feathered off so as not to leave a prominent ridge. It is better to apply two thin coats rather than one thick one, as there is a tendency for the spirit evaporating from a thick film of knotting to develop pinholes through which the resin can pass, and in any case it is difficult to avoid the formation of a ridge.

Cheap grades of knotting should never be used as they are frequently adulterated with colophony (rosin), a material which is readily suluble in paint oils and thinners, and they are therefore incapable of holding back the resinous matter from the knots.

Knotting should be kept in air-tight containers to prevent the thickening and darkening which takes place on exposure to air.

A variety of knotting known as stop-tar knotting, consisting of shellac and methylated spirit with the addition of a plasticiser, is used to prevent materials such as creosote from bleeding into paint.

KNOTTING BOTTLE A metal container with a glass lining, with a wide neck in which a close fitting stopper is inserted. The stopper is pierced so as to grip the handle of a small soft-haired brush, the brush and stopper being firmly joined together to form a complete unit; thus, when the stopper is replaced in the neck of the bottle the brush is suspended in the knotting.

It is most desirable that knotting should be used from a properly made container of this kind; the common practice of using discarded varnish tins and other makeshift receptacles is very unsatisfactory. Even the heaviest tin plating used for protecting the iron of cans is disintegrated in the presence of knotting, and if there are any imperfections in the lining the corrosion which takes place is very rapid indeed. This causes the knotting to become contaminated with soluble iron salts, and also sets up an electrolytic action which affects the resin by producing acidic substances. It used to be the practice for knotting to be supplied by the manufacturers in large earthenware jars; nowadays it is often sold in metal cans but the metal has been specially protected with a lining of mineral wax. It is not generally realized that when the knotting is transferred to smaller containers for use on the site its properties are often adversely affected.

L

LAC A resinous substance secreted by an insect and from which such materials as shellac are derived. It is collected from the twigs and branches upon which the insects have swarmed.

LACQUER In its original sense the term refers to the material used in oriental lacquer work. This is a thick emulsion derived from the sap of a type of tree native to China, and is purified to produce a natural varnish which requires darkness and a cool damp atmosphere to make it dry. The varnish is applied in thin coatings which dry to a tough dark durable film which takes a fine polish. The art of lacquer ware was introduced in China but was perfected in Japan, and consists of the skilful application of as many as thirty or even forty thin coats of the varnish. Burmese lacquer and Indian lacquer are somewhat similar materials obtained from vegetation native to those countries.

Nowadays the term is used much more widely. It is applied, for instance, to certain varnishes made by dissolving various gums—chiefly shellac—with suitable volatile solvents; these materials are used in the furniture industry and in various industrial finishing processes but are not sufficiently elastic or durable for general use in building work, although hard dark spirit varnishes are sometimes used for floor treatments. There is a wide range of cellulose lacquers used in the motor car industry, the furniture industry and in many industrial finishes. Wood polishing by cellulose lacquers is a significant development which has reduced the amount of hand work entailed by French polishing, and hot spraying lacquer processes are widely used. Pale clear cellulose lacquers are frequently used on polished metal to minimize tarnishing; clear lacquers, however, are not resistant to sunlight and are unsuitable for exterior use on wood. Metallic lacquers are produced by pigmenting clear lacquers with "bronze" and other metal powders. There are also transparent coloured lacquers made by introducing spirit-soluble dyes. Certain types of lacquer with considerable resistance to sea water, acids and alkalis are made with chlorinated rubber.

LADDER (1) A portable device consisting of two long upright members connected by rungs or steps by which a person may climb to points which cannot be reached from the ground. Ladders may be classified under two main headings: single-section ladders, constructed as a single unit, and extension ladders consisting of two or more sections which can be telescoped so as to adjust the height. Single-section ladders may be of the pole ladder type or the standing ladder type. A pole ladder, otherwise known as a builders' ladder, has semi-circular stiles made by sawing a straight pole down the centre, and is used for general building work and wherever a robust ladder or a ladder of considerable length is required. A standing ladder has rectangular stiles and is used where lightness is required. Standing ladders are obtainable in lengths of up to 8 metres, and pole ladders in lengths of up to 20 metres or even more on occasion. Extension ladders may be of the hook-and-clip catch type or of the rope-operated safety catch type. Rope-operated ladders are heavier and stronger and are to be preferred when considerable lengths are required.

Wooden ladders are made with softwood stiles and hardwood rungs; metal reinforcements are provided under the rungs and long ladders have a metal reinforcement sunk in the stiles. There are also metal ladders made from aluminium alloy, which offer the advantages of lightness, strength and freedom from deterioration and decay but which are a hazard when used in the vicinity of exposed electrical equipment.
(2) A colloquial term used to describe a fault in painting. The fault is due to a failure to lay off properly, and consists of a narrow strip of work, missed in the final laying off, in which brushmarks at right angles to the direction of the laying off are exposed.

LADDER BRACKET A wrought iron bracket which rests upon the rungs of a ladder and supports one end of a scaffold plank; by the use of two of these brackets a light temporary scaffold can be erected between two ladders.

Several types of bracket are available; the safest type is that which has two sets of hooks so that the weight is not resting upon one ladder rung only. It is desirable that the hooks should be adjustable to fit ladders of varying rung spacings. The arm which supports the plank is hinged so that when in position it lies horizontally whatever the inclination of the ladder, and it is useful if there is sufficient latitude in the adjustment to allow the bracket to be fixed either in front of the ladder or behind it, whichever is more convenient. The pin securing the arm should be fastened with a short chain so that it cannot be detached or lost.

Ladder brackets are particularly useful for operations such as signwriting where the work is of such short duration that it does not justify the erection of a more elaborate scaffold. They are especially valuable for operations on wall panels or gable ends where the height of the plank needs to be altered frequently as the work proceeds.

Ladder brackets are sometimes known by the term "cripples".

LADDER STAY A device which hooks on to the top rungs of a ladder so that the end of the ladder is held at a distance of about 300mm away from the vertical surface instead of resting directly upon it.

LAKE COLOURS Pigments prepared by precipitating soluble organic dyes on to a mineral base such as alumina, Paris white, China clay, etc. and fixing them chemically to form an insoluble compound. Some authorities say that the term is derived from the word "lac"; others maintain that it comes from the word "lacca", which was used by medieval dyers for the coloured scum which formed in the dye vats. Originally a large number of brilliant pigments were prepared in this way from natural mineral or vegetable dyestuffs; most of these are now obsolete but pigments prepared from cochineal, logwood, madder and indigo are still used to a limited extent. Many of the natural lakes suffered from the disadvantage of fading badly when exposed to sunlight and were very liable to bleed.

By far the greatest number of the lake colours now used are prepared from the products of coal-tar distillation. They represent a most important group of pigments and are produced in a vast range of colours covering the whole spectrum, the variation in colour being due chiefly to slight modifications in the arrangement of the constituent atoms of carbon, hydrogen, nitrogen and oxygen. The chemistry of these materials is very complex.

LAMBSWOOL Lambswool is used as one of the covering fabrics for paint rollers. It is softer than a pile fabric, and is generally considered more suitable than the latter for the application of gloss and semi-gloss paints by roller. Comparative tests seem to indicate that the consumption of paint and the labour costs are both lower with lambswool rollers than with rollers covered in pile fabrics.

LAMINATED LEAD A form of lead sheeting sometimes used in the treatment of damp surfaces.

LAMP BLACK A black pigment consisting essentially of free carbon, produced by the incomplete combustion of waste coal-tar products. It is not so intense a black as carbon black, but makes a fine bluish grey when reduced with white.

LANCASHIRE PATTERN DISTEMPER BRUSH See *Distemper brush.*

LANCASTER CLOTH A washable coated cotton fabric of the oilcloth type, sometimes used as a wall hanging where a hard-wearing waterproof finish suitable for bathrooms, kitchens, canteens, etc., is required. It is hung with a stiff flour paste or proprietary paste on a previously crossline surface, a felt covered roller being used to press out all the air bubbles.

LANOLINE Cholesterin-fatty matter which is extracted from a sheep's wool. Lanoline is a constituent of certain proprietary compounds used as temporary protective coatings for steelwork, such coatings being employed when for some reason it is necessary for a time lag to occur between the cleaning and de-scaling of the steel and the application of the paint coatings.

LAP The word is used by the decorator both as a verb and as a noun. Used as a verb, "to lap" means either to apply a coat of paint in such a way that it partially overlaps the edge of a section previously painted so that there is a double thickness of paint along the edge, or to apply wallpaper, metal foil, canvas or any other form of wall hanging in such a way that the edge overlaps the previously hung piece. Used as a noun, the word "lap" applies to the double thickness of material, whether it be paint, wallpaper, foil or anything else, which exists along the joint when the edge has been allowed to overlap.

L

LAPIS LAZULI A semi-precious stone consisting of a rich blue silicate of alumina, lime and soda, from which ultramarine blue was formerly prepared.

LAPPED JOINT A term employed when wallpaper, metal foil, or some form of fabric is hung in such a way that the edges overlap, as opposed to a butt edge, where the edges meet without overlapping.

LATEX The milk-like juice of the rubber tree, often used instead of the cured crude rubber for such purposes as the preparation of adhesives, etc. Artifical latex, which is a water dispersion of reclaimed rubber, resembles latex but is softer and tackier, and is often used in the manufacture of adhesives; it is produced by swelling and dissolving the rubber in an organic solvent, treating it with an organic acid or ammonia and then emulsifying it.

Latex has several applications in the painting and decorating trade. Adhesives based upon it are used for many purposes, including the fixing of solid backed relief materials such as Lincrusta-Walton, the cementing of lead and aluminium foil in the treatment of damp surfaces and the sealing of stains, the hanging of Realwood panels and the fastening of canvases and calicos. Latex adhesives are especially useful when heavy impervious materials are to be fixed on a non-porous ground such as a painted surface, because a flour paste adhesive trapped between the two surfaces is unable to dry and tends to cause blisters to form, whereas a latex glue is quick setting.

Latex is also used in the formulation of a variety of paints and emulsions for use where a high degree of chemical resistance is required, such as, for example, in styrenebutadiene emulsions, and in the acrylic emulsion paints which are employed as exterior coatings for concrete, cinder block, asbestos shingles and similar purposes.

LAYING GOLD A term used to indicate the process of applying gold leaf to a surface. When transfer leaf is being used, the process consists of holding between the thumb and forefinger of one hand the waxed tissue to which the leaf is attached, placing it so that the gold is brought into contact with the gold size which has been allowed to assume the correct degree of tack, and then rubbing the back of the tissue with the ball of the thumb of the other hand, rubbing to and fro with short firm strokes of about an inch in each direction till the leaf has completely parted from the tissue and is firmly adhering to the gold size with no pinholes to mar the surface. The laying of loose leaf gold involves the use of a gilder's cushion in the corner of which several leaves are placed; the process consists of taking each leaf in turn with the knife, spreading it flat on the surface of the cushion, cutting it approximately to size, lifting each piece with the gilder's tip and bringing it into contact with the mordant.

LAYING IN A term which is generally understood to mean painting or otherwise covering a surface as a preparation for some further treatment. For instance, we speak of a surface being laid in with gold size preparatory to gilding, of a wall being laid in with glaze medium which is subsequently manipulated to produce a broken colour treatment, of a surface being laid in with plastic paint prior to texturing, etc.

LAYING OFF Part of the technique of applying paint by brush; it is the action of finishing off an area of paintwork with very light strokes of the brush in order to eliminate brushmarks.

The competent painter who takes a pride in the quality of his brushwork applies several brushfuls of paint with firm vigorous strokes; having laid in a suitable area in this way he "crosses" the work without recharging the brush in order to distribute the paint evenly, and at this stage he uses a somewhat lighter touch; with lighter strokes still he takes the brush across the area with diagonal strokes; finally he "lays off", using only the tips of the bristles and working rapidly with the lightest possible touch. The general rule when woodwork is being painted is that the wood is laid off in the direction of the grain; walls are laid off vertically and ceilings are laid off with strokes running parallel to the main window. Water paint calls for a different technique and is usually laid off with long semi-circular strokes.

LEACHING To "leach" is to make a liquid percolate through a substance in order to dissolve and remove some soluble matter that happens to be there. The term is frequently used in painting and decorating to describe operations aimed at getting rid of some offensive material; for example, we speak of leaching out deliquescent salts from plaster by washing with copious quantities of water, leaching out stains from a surface by swabbing liberally with solvents, and so on. Sometimes the effect of using a water paint containing a soluble dye upon a surface which still contains moisture is that the moisture, seeking to escape, causes colour to leach out of the paint.

LEAD A soft heavy blue-grey metal, with the chemical symbol Pb, obtained chiefly from the mineral galena. It is the basis of a great many paint materials, including the following: *White lead,* a basic carbonate of lead and a pigment of great importance. *Red lead,* an oxide of lead, also a most important pigment. *Orange lead,* similar in composition to red lead. *Sublimed white lead,* a pigment consisting of basic sulphate of lead. *Lead acetate,* otherwise known as "sugar of lead", a white crystalline salt formed by the reaction of lead oxide and acetic acid which is used as a paint and varnish drier and as a precipitating agent in the production of certain synthetic dyes. *Lead borate,* a white crystalline compound used as a drier in paints and varnishes. *Lead chromate,* the basis of a group of pigments. *Litharge,* which is lead monoxide, used as a drier.

LEAD CHROMES A group of pigments based on chromate of lead, ranging in colour from very pale primrose yellow, through lemon, gold and orange to red, and known by various names such as lemon chrome, primrose chrome, chrome yellow, orange chrome, chrome red, Derby red, Chinese red, etc. Lead chromes possess the properties of brilliant strong colour, good opacity, considerable staining strength and moderate price, and they have useful rust-inhibitive qualities. They are fairly permanent though apt to fade in strong sunlight. When used in conjunction with Prussian blue and Monastral blue they produce a wide variety of green shades. Lead chromes become discoloured if exposed to atmospheres containing hydrogen sulphide or if mixed with sulphide pigments such as ultramarine or vermilion. They are also sensitive to alkalis.

LEAD COLOUR The painter's term for a grey coloured paint, generally in reference to a grey undercoat.

LEAD FOIL Thin sheet lead which is available in various forms and has several applications to painting and decorating.

Lead foil sheets are sometimes used in the treatment of damp surfaces and for sealing stains of various kinds, the sheet being attached to the wall with a fixative consisting of either paste white lead and gold size or red lead and gold size and then pressed into close contact with the wall by means of a roller. Fixing commences with the topmost sheet and proceeds downwards, each sheet being allowed to overlap the previous one slightly. There is also a paperbacked lead foil produced for use on damp surfaces, and this is attached with a latex glue.

Lead foil is also used as a masking material in certain kinds of glass sign work and in glass embossing. When employed in the production of painted glass signs the foil is attached to the glass with weak gelatine size

L

and firmly pressed down. The design is traced in reverse on the back of the foil, which is then cut with a sharp knife, the letter shapes being lifted out. The exposed glass is painted, two coats usually being required to obtain a solid job, after which the remainder of the foil is removed leaving the letters clear and sharp. When lead foil is used for glass embossing, the whole of the glass is coated with Brunswick black and allowed to dry; the surface is then laid in with beeswax and the foil pressed firmly into contact with it. The design is traced on the foil in reverse, the foil is cut and the parts to be embossed are removed. The exposed portions are gently cleaned off with white spirit to remove the beeswax and Brunswick black, a wall of tallow is built up round the edge of the glass and acid is poured in and allowed to etch the exposed parts of the glass.

Another use for lead foil is the production of stencil plates, especially for such purposes as stencilling a pattern on a curved or moulded surface or for stencilling lettering on the curved stiles of ladders, etc., because the metal can be pressed into close contact with the contours of the surface.

LEAD FREE A term used to describe a paint which is sufficiently low in lead content to satisfy the exacting requirements which make it permissible in places where the use of lead would constitute a grave danger, such as in a food-producing or packing factory.

LEAD PAINT This is defined in the Lead Paint (Protection Against Poisoning) Act, 1926, as being any paint, paste, spray, stopping, filling, or other material used in painting which, when treated in a manner prescribed by rules issued by the Secretary of State, yields to an aqueous solution of hydrochloric acid a quantity of soluble lead exceeding, when calculated as lead monoxide, five per cent of the dry weight of the portion taken for analysis.

LEAD PAINT (PROTECTION AGAINST POISONING) ACT, 1926 An act of Parliament which was passed on 15th December 1926, and which came into force on 1st January 1927, for the purpose of improving provision for the protection of persons employed in the painting of buildings against the dangers of lead poisoning.

Part 1 of the Act deals with the regulations which might be issued by the Secretary of State regarding the form in which lead compounds are used, the application of lead paints by spray, the rubbing down of painted surfaces, the medical examination of operatives, the provision of washing facilities and the use of protective clothing. Part 2 defines the limitations upon the employment of young persons in painting. Part 3 links the terms of the Act with certain provisions of the Factory and Workshop Act of 1901. Part 4 states that every employer of painting and decorating labour is required to register his name and business address with H.M. Inspector of Factories in the district in which his office is situated, to keep a register of all persons employed by him on painting operations and to maintain a record of all contracts and painting work that he undertakes. Part 5 deals with the power vested in the Inspector of Factories, under the Factory and Workshop Act of 1901, to visit a site and to take samples of any substance which he suspects contains a lead compound. Part 6 defines the application of the Act to Crown employees. Part 7 defines the expression "lead paints". Part 8 is concerned with the title of the Act, the date on which it became operative, etc.

LEAD PAINT REGULATIONS These are regulations governing the use of lead paints, made by the Secretary of State under the terms of the Lead Paint (Protection Against Poisoning) Act, 1926, and dated 6th September 1927. They came into force on 1st October 1927. They are divided into two parts, Part I defining the duties of employers and Part II the duties which operatives are expected to observe. The main provisions of the regulations may be summarized as follows:

Part I. Lead compounds must be used in paste form or in the form of ready mixed paints; they must not be used in dry powder form except in the case of read lead powder used for making small quantities of hand mixed stopping. Lead paints and compounds, when kept either on the workshop premises or on a site, must be stored in containers clearly and legibly marked as containing lead. Lead paint must not be applied by spray in interior painting. No painted surface other than that of iron or steel is to be rubbed down or scraped by a dry process, no painted surface of iron or steelwork is to be rubbed down or scraped by a dry sandpapering process, and all debris produced by rubbing down is to be removed before it has been allowed to become dry; these regulations do not apply, however, if it can be proved that there is no lead paint contained in the surface.

A sufficient supply of water, soap, nail brushes and towels must be provided for all persons using lead paint or coming in contact with lead paint, with at least one bucket or basin for every five persons. Suitable arrangements must be made for the outer clothing of the operatives to be taken off during working hours and steps taken to prevent the outer clothing from becoming soiled with lead paint; where possible the clothing is to be kept outside the apartment where painting is in progress.

When in the opinion of the Chief Inspector of Factories the incidence of lead poisoning among operatives is excessive, the employer must make arrangements for his employees to undergo periodic medical examination.

Every operative is to be supplied on engagement, and on the first pay day of every year, with a copy of the prescribed leaflet giving health instructions on the use of paint. A copy of the regulations is to be displayed in every workshop and on every job or contract on which more than twelve persons are engaged.

Part II. Overalls or protective clothing must be worn all the time work is in progress; overalls must be removed at mealtimes and must be washed at least once a week. Painted surfaces are not to be rubbed down in a manner contravening the terms of the Act. Steps must be taken to prevent ordinary clothing from being soiled or contaminated with lead paint. Every operative must clean and wash his hands before taking food and before leaving the premises where he is working. Every operative shall present himself for medical examination when required to do so.

LEAD POISONING An occupational disease to which those employed in making or using certain lead products are liable; at one time it was a common complaint among painters but in recent years its incidence has

L

decreased to insignificant proportions. Lead poisoning is caused by continual absorption of lead into the system over a long period, due chiefly to inhalation of lead dust or spray or to transference of lead from the hands to the mouth, although some authorities state that lead can also be absorbed through the skin. The symptoms are weakness, constipation and severe abdominal pains (painters' colic) followed by sickness and palpitation. In its more advanced stages it leads to anaemia and loss of weight; in chronic cases it may cause palsy or paralysis. One of the features of lead poisoning is the gradual weakening of the muscles which leads to the condition known among painters as "drop-wrist".

LEAD RESTRICTED   A term used to describe a paint which contains less than 5 per cent of soluble lead, such a paint being often spoken of as "lead free within the meaning of the Act".

LEAD SOAPS   Organic compounds which are formed by the interaction of lead pigments and driers with the fatty acids of the drying oils used in paint. When viewed through a microscope the lead soap is seen to radiate outwards from the particles of pigment in a fibre-like manner; in a heavily pigmented paint the particles are so close together that the fibres intertwine, an action which reinforces the film and imparts great toughness and elasticity. The formation of lead soaps is one of the specially desirable features of a lead paint, producing a waterproof film which expands and contracts in conformity with the surface to which it is applied giving a tough, durable, protective coating.

LEAD STOPPING   A material for stopping up holes and cracks in timber, etc., to which hardness is imparted by the addition of lead. The term covers various compositions, such as a mixture of stiff white lead paste, whiting and Japan gold size, or white lead, red lead and gold size, or linseed oil putty mixed with red lead powder, and a lead stopping for ironwork can be made with red lead powder mixed with gold size or boiled oil. For good quality work a lead stopping is far more satisfactory than the usual stopping consisting of linseed oil putty, which takes a long time to harden and is liable to shrink and crumble.

LEADED ZINC   A pigment, used more freely in the U.S.A. than in this country, which consists of a variety of zinc oxide containing a certain amount of basic lead sulphate, the proportion of lead varying from 5% to 45%. It possesses good weathering properties and it has greater opacity than zinc oxide, although its colour is not so good.

LEADINESS   The defect which occurs when a paint pigmented with aluminium powder loses its initial lustre and develops the dull appearance of weathered lead sheeting.

LEADLESS PAINTS   Paints which are free from lead content, and which are not subject to the Lead Paint Regulations. Logically, it might be expected that the term referred to any lead-free paint for any purpose, but in practice its meaning is restricted, and it is generally understood to refer to primers, undercoats and finishes for normal domestic house painting. The British Standards Institution gives details of a suitable composition for a leadless primer for indoor use, containing linseed oil and white spirit, lithopone and titanium white, a tinting pigment, a mineral suspending agent, barytes and driers. Leadless undercoatings are perfectly suitable for indoor use, but some care is needed when using them for exterior work, as they are more susceptible to moisture than lead-based paint. It is important that leadless finishing paint should be used in places liable to strong concentrations of sulphurous materials; trouble is frequently encountered, for instance, in the decoration of hairdressing saloons, etc., because of the presence of steamy vapour combined with fumes from the chemicals used in the various processes, which rapidly discolour lead-based paints.

LEAFING A term used to describe the behaviour of certain pigments with a flaky or laminated structure when mixed in a suitable vehicle and applied as a paint film. Aluminium powder and graphite are outstanding examples of materials possessing this property. The minute flakes of which they are composed, although heavier than the vehicle, have a tendency to float to the surface and arrange themselves parallel to the surface, overlapping each other and forming continuous layers several flakes in depth with a thin film of vehicle between each layer. This phenomenon resembles the way in which leaves falling from a tree in the autumn overlap one another on the ground, and it is this resemblance which gives rise to the term.

The leafing properties of aluminium, graphite, etc., have an important bearing upon the characteristics of the paint film of which they are a part. The individual flakes, although very thin, offer a barrier to the passage of moisture, which can only penetrate the film by means of finding a path across and around the edge of each flake and, since the surface area of the flakes is very great compared with their thickness, it follows that the film has very considerable resistance to moisture penetration. Another feature of such a film is its opacity, and this in turn may serve to improve the durability of the paint since the overlapping flakes in the upper layers of the film tend to protect the underlying layers of medium. In the case of aluminium paints, the overlapping layers form a continuous film, which is an effective sealer to prevent the penetration of bitumen, creosote, soot, bleeding reds, etc., and which is also a useful sealer-primer for timbers with a high resinous content such as Columbian pine, etc.

LEATHER The skins or hides of animals cured by the chemical action of tannin.

LEATHERCLOTH A term used to cover a wide range of coated fabrics which are embossed and coloured to present the texture and appearance of various kinds of leather. These materials are available in differing weights and qualities which make them suitable for a variety of purposes such as upholstery, car trimmings, coverings for tables and shelves, and wall hangings, the latter, of course, being of most interest to the decorator. Leathercloth is being used on an increasingly large scale in interior decoration because of its attractive appearance and because it is tough, durable,

L

157

hygienic and resistant to most household chemicals. It is eminently suitable for the treatment of public buildings, such as restaurants, hotels, hospitals, schools and offices, and is also used in the finishing of aircraft and caravan interiors.

Modern leathercloths usually consist of PVC-coated fabrics (polyvinyl chloride), these being more fire resistant than the earlier types coated with nitro-cellulose material. They are supplied in rolls of varying width, generally either 533mm, 762mm or between 1036 and 1275mm. They are usually applied with one of the many proprietary adhesives which are available. If paste is used for fixing them, it *must* contain a fungicide. In some circumstances the adhesive is applied to the back of the leathercloth, while in other cases it is better for it to be applied to the wall and the dry leathercloth pressed into contact with it; the exact details of hanging will depend upon the recommendations of the manufacturers of the particular product in use and also upon the nature of the job.

The term "leathercloth" is sometimes employed rather loosely to describe almost any kind of coated fabric, including oilcloths such as Lancaster cloth and American cloth, but this looseness is best avoided as it can lead to ambiguity.

LEATHERETTE A type of embossed wallpaper which is coloured, lacquered, metalled and bronzed in various ways to represent antique Spanish and Venetian tooled leather hangings. The term is generally understood to refer to the cheaper kinds of imitation leather paper.

When leatherette papers are being hung, care should be taken to avoid oversoaking them, otherwise they may stretch and the relief be to a great extent lost; it is important that the paste should be perfectly fresh, as any metal or bronze used in the finish of the paper would be badly affected by the acid content of sour paste.

LEDGER A term used in scaffolding, particularly in tubular metal constructions. The ledgers are the main horizontal members which tie the scaffold longitudinally and support the transoms and putlogs. It is very important for the stability of the scaffold that the ledgers should be checked in course of erection to see that they are perfectly horizontal, and they should be coupled to the standards with load-bearing couplers.

LEMON CHROME A pale yellow pigment belonging to the lead chrome group. See *Lead Chrome.*

LEMON YELLOW A very pale yellow pigment made by precipitating barium chloride with sodium bichromate. It has an advantage over lead chrome in that it is not discoloured in the presence of sulphuretted hydrogen, but has the drawbacks of being available only as a very pale tint and being less opaque than lead chromates, and it is used principally as an artist's colour.

LEVELLING A term sometimes used to mean obtaining a smooth level surface by the use of fillers.

LEVELLING-OFF COAT A fluid applied by spray over a final coating of nitro-cellulose lacquer in order to soften it and allow the irregularities to smooth themselves out.

LEVIGATION A process used in the preparation of certain pigments such as earth colours, red oxides and mineral whites. Wet levigation has been practised from the earliest times; the plant consists of a mixing tank, below which is a further series of tanks, each tank being of greater size and capacity than the previous one and each placed at a lower elevation than the previous one. The lump ore or crude pigment is agitated with running water in the mixing tank, and the water carrying the pigment particles in suspension overflows into the lower tanks. As each tank is reached the rate of flow is reduced due to the increased capacity, and in each case the heaviest and coarsest particles settle at the bottom. When the final tank is reached the particles that remain are those of the finest and smallest size. By this means the pigment is automatically separated into grades. The particles are allowed to settle, the water drained off, and the pigment removed from the tanks, dried and ground in a suitable medium. Dry levigation is a process by which dry ground pigment is passed into an air stream and through a device which grades the particles; this process is also known as "air flotation".

LICHEN A type of plant consisting of a combination of alga and fungus which is found on building stone and masonry in rural districts and which the painter and decorator is sometimes called upon to remove; its removal can be effected with a solution of 125 grammes of zinc or magnesium silicofluoride to 5 litres of water.

L

LIFE The length of time that a paint or other decorative material continues to serve its purpose completely and adequately. Not to be confused with terms such as "pot life" and "shelf life", which refer to the length of time that a material will remain in usable condition before application.

LIFTING A term used to describe the softening and wrinkling up of a dry film of paint or varnish which sometimes occurs when a further coat is applied over it. This is particularly likely to occur when materials which need a very powerful solvent to bring them to a workable condition are being used, or when materials containing a solvent which is incompatible with the previous coating are being applied: for example, when a material such as a chlorinated rubber paint is used over an unsuitable primer, when cellulose is applied over soft oil paint or when certain finishing materials are used over unsuitable undercoats. Lifting can also occur, of course, if a coat of paint is applied before the previous coat has been allowed enough time to dry and harden properly.

LIGHT FASTNESS The extent to which a paint, pigment or dyestuff will retain its colour on exposure to light.

LIGHTWEIGHT STAGING A form of strongly constructed staging which is 460mm wide (the width of two planks) and is available in lengths of from 3 to 7 metres. It is designed so that the amount of sag or deflection when it is fully loaded is negligible, although it is only supported at each end. For this reason it is invaluable for roof work in factories, when it can be used to span the trusses without any further support and provide a broad rigid runway without causing any obstruction to the floor below. Used as a trestle scaffold, it reduces the number of trestles necessary. It is only half the weight of the equivalent quantity of scaffold boarding.

LILY BRISTLE The highest quality of natural white bristle, usually understood to refer to Siberian white bristle, which is now unfortunately no longer obtainable.

LIME Calcium oxide occurring abundantly in nature, chiefly in combination with carbon dioxide as calcium carbonate in chalk, limestone etc. Its importance as a building material has lasted from ancient times to the present day, and it is widely used in mortars and cements, internal plastering and external renderings. It is produced by heating limestone or chalk to a high temperature in a kiln to drive off the carbonic acid gas, the residue being known as quicklime. The addition of water causes this material to slake with the production of much heat. Hydrated lime, which is made by grinding quicklime, slaking it under controlled conditions with water, and sifting it to a fine powder, is easier to handle and is more reliable.

From the decorator's point of view, the interest of lime as a building material is largely bound up with its capacity for destroying oil paint. Pure lime itself is not particularly harmful, but it becomes very destructive when contaminated with even small quantities of soluble alkalis, such as soda or potash.

LIME BLUE Originally this was a term applied to a copper blue, but now it is used to describe a very cheap form of ultramarine blue, made by grinding the lowest grade pigment with terra alba or by striking a synthetic dye on a white base. Lime blue is a weak stainer that is not affected by alkali, and is used for tinting or correcting the colour of distemper and limewash. It is generally supplied as a powder which needs to be soaked in water by the painter before it is added to the distemper.

LIME GREEN A limeproof pigment used for tinting distemper. It can be made by reducing, with white, a material produced at a certain stage in the manufacture of ultramarine blue, and can also be made by striking a dye such as malachite green on green earth.

LIME PLASTER A type of plaster used as a thin skimming coat for walls and ceilings, which is usually applied over a rough lime/sand backing. It is produced by slaking quicklime by means of adding water to it, the milk of lime which is obtained being sieved and allowed to mature for a fortnight, when it fattens up into what is known as lime putty, or it can also by made from a hydrated lime which is soaked to lime putty by mixing with water and then is allowed to stand for a time. The process by which lime plaster dries and hardens is a dual one combining both evaporation and carbonation; while the water is evaporating the plaster is gradually absorbing carbon dioxide from the atmosphere to form a firm compact layer of calcium carbonate, similar in composition to the limestone or chalk from which the lime was originally derived, the depth of the layer depending on the extent to which carbon dioxide can penetrate.

The factors involved in the successful decoration of lime plaster surfaces are as follows:

(i) The plaster must be allowed to dry out completely before the surface is sealed with an impervious layer of paint; otherwise, the paint film will be forced off in the form of blistering and flaking. The length of time that this will take depends to a great extent upon the type of construction, i.e., whether the plaster is applied to plasterboards, wooden or expanded metal lathing, old porous brickwork or new brickwork containing a large quantity of water; much will depend, too, upon whether the drying conditions are favourable or otherwise.

(ii) The plaster must be allowed adequate time to carbonate before it is sealed; otherwise, it will be prevented from ever attaining its proper hardness and strength, and a permanently weak skin will be the result. Carbonation is a very slow process which cannot be hastened.

(iii) For practical purposes all lime plaster should be regarded as chemically active, because even if the lime putty itself is relatively harmless it becomes strongly alkaline if contaminated by sodium and potassium salts brought forward from the backing; the effect of alkaline attack upon an oil paint is to saponify the oil, causing the film to become soft and sticky and causing oily runs to develop. For these reasons the decoration of lime plaster should be delayed until the surface is reasonably dry, the initial decoration should preferably be undertaken with a p.v.a. emulsion or a water paint both of which materials have a certain tolerance for damp, and before oil paint is used on the surface a priming system consiting of two coats of alkali resisting primer is generally advisable. Wallpaper should not be hung until the surface is thoroughly dry, and then the preparation consists of sandpapering down to remove mortar splashes and nibs and applying a coat of alkali resisting primer.

Other characteristics of lime plaster which affect the painter are as follows:

(i) The plaster, if not properly gauged and worked, tends to shrink when drying and develops a mass of fine hair cracks, called surface crazing.

(ii) If the lime has not been properly slaked the plaster is liable to the defect of "popping" and "blowing" due to the presence of pockets of unslaked lime which, when attacked by moisture, slake after the surface has set and erupt to cause pits and craters.

(iii) Lime plaster finishes usually possess a fairly high degree of suction.

(iv) Lime plaster rarely develops efflorescence, and gives less trouble in this respect than any other type of plaster.

LIME PUTTY Lime Plaster.

LIME-RESISTING COLOURS Colours which are not affected by the presence of active alkali, and which are therefore suitable for use on newly plastered surfaces, cement, concrete, asbestos-cement sheeting, etc. Colours which are not limeproof are liable to bleach or discolour under such conditions whether in the form of oil paint, water paint or distemper, and for the initial decoration of these surfaces the safest policy is to use a range of colours limited to creams, buffs and browns.

Pigments which can be relied upon to be practically limeproof include yellow ochre, all the brown earth pigments, all types of black, green earth and chromium oxide among the greens, cobalt blue, ultramarine and Monastral among the blues, and oxides of iron among the reds.

LIME WATER A bucket of water into which a small pat of lime putty has been mixed is frequently used in the washing down, rubbing down and preparation of old paintwork, particularly in kitchens and similar places where there are deposits of grease. Some people object to this on the grounds that any residue of lime left on the surface may have an adverse effect upon the new paint but provided the lime water is not allowed to dry on the surface and is thoroughly rinsed off with clean water after use, there is no reason why it should raise any difficulty. Lime water used in this way has a less positive action upon grease than sugar soap but is milder in its action upon the paint.

LIMED OAK Oak which has been pickled by the application of a coating of lime, which is subsequently brushed off the surface but allowed to remain in the grain. The surface is usually left unpolished.

The painter and decorator is sometimes called upon to match the woodwork of a room to an existing suite of limed oak furniture or to carry out a scheme in limed oak, and there are various methods by which the effect can be reproduced. When the woodwork consists of real oak, whether in the form of solid wood or of sheets of thin veneer used as panelling, the treatment usually resolves itself into staining the work to the required depth of colour and applying one or two sealer coats, usually of clear shellac varnish; a paste of white material is then prepared stiff enough to cling in the grain and this is either brushed or knifed across the surface in such a way as to fill the pores, the surplus material being removed from the face either with a soft cloth or a squeegee. The white paste can be made up with a proprietary brand of watermixed filler or with an oil-bound water paint.

When Lincrusta has to be matched to limed oak it presents a smooth face and after it has been stained to the required colour it may be found that a paste of flat oil paint mixed with glaze medium clings in the surface better.

Softwood doors and architraves can be matched to limed oak very successfully by painting them with a suitable ground, incising the grain pattern by a "needle oak" process with proprietary cutting tools, staining to the required colour, and filing the grain with stiff water paint or flat oil paint and glaze medium. Alternatively, a straightforward graining technique may be used on a smooth painted ground with a graining colour composed of glaze medium tinted with flat oil white, which by judicious combing, cross-combed with a fine toothed steel comb and supplemented where necessary by light figuring, can be made to achieve a passable representation.

LIMER A large fibre brush used for limewashing. It may have either a flat or a round head, and is designed to be fitted to a long handle, for use on factory work and industrial painting.

LIMEWASH An inexpensive form of treatment for brickwork, plaster, stonework and similar surfaces, both interior and exterior, which has been used for thousands of years in many parts of the world and which is still employed in this country on farm buildings and domestic properties, especially in rural districts. It needs to be recoated at fairly frequent intervals, but its renewal is easy and cheap, and it very often presents quite a pleasing appearance. It also has the advantage of preventing the accumulation of lichen and mould growths and discouraging the presence of insects and vermin. For these reasons it has enjoyed widespread use in the treatment of factories and industrial premises for a very long time.

In its simplest form limewash consists of newly slaked lime mixed with water. When freshly mixed it is thin and semi-transparent, but it becomes opaque when dry. Lime blue is generally added to correct its slightly dingy colour and give a clean white, but it can also be tinted with a variety of limeproof dry pigments. There are, however, a huge number of recipes in which binders and waterproofing agents are added to improve the properties of limewash. In rural districts it is common practice to add organic matter of various kinds, and there are several recipes calling for the use of such materials as casein, linseed oil, starch, etc. Probably the most satisfactory mixtures are those based on lime and tallow, applied cool; upon lime, glue and salt, applied hot; and upon lime and Portland cement mixed to a thick slurry.

Limewash is applied by brush or by a limewash sprayer designed for the purpose. Under the terms of the Factories Act, 1937, limewash coatings used on industrial premises must be renewed every fourteen months.

LINCRUSTA A low-relief composition made with oxidized linseed oil with suitable filling agents added. The most familar form of Lincrusta is that of wood effects and imitations, which are supplied in plain buff or putty colour to be stained and varnished after hanging, or in ready decorated form. There are also patterns available in ready decorated form giving the appearance of glazed tiles, and it has also been produced in the form of ornamental patterns, leathers and plastic textures.

LINENFOLD Panelling carved in low relief with a stylized representation of folded linen, developed by woodcarvers in the sixteenth century. Certain modern decorative materials such as Lincrusta are sometimes supplied in a form which reproduces the effect of linenfold panelling.

LINER A long haired brush, which may be sword shaped or may terminate in a chisel edge and which is usually set in a quill, used in the production of fine lines in paint. Liners are commonly used in coachpainting but are not often used by painters and decorators.

LINING (a) The application of paint in the form of a narrow line of regular width. In painting and decorating this generally refers to running a line by means of lining fitch and straightedge for such purposes as separating a dado from a wall filling or for lining out panels on walls or ceilings, although for picking out the mouldings on doors or around signboards it is customary to use a sable writer. In commercial painting various methods of lining are employed, including the use of sword liners and lining pencils, transfers, masking tape or mechanical lining tools.

(b) The hanging of a backing paper in order to provide a good foundation of even porosity for the reception of good quality wallpapers or relief goods, to provide a better surface for the reception of wallpaper on badly cracked or uneven walls and ceilings, or to provide a surface of regular absorbency for the reception of paint or distemper.

LINING FITCH A brush used in conjunction with a straightedge in the production of narrow lines in paint, the method of lining most commonly used by the painter and decorator. It is made of hog hair and is set in a tin ferrule mounted on a long thin wooden handle which is tapered down to a narrow end. The working edge of the brush is slanted, and the ferrule is slanted in a parallel direction.

Lining fitches are available in various sizes, the smallest being capable of producing a line 1·5mm wide. They are also sold with varying lengths of bristle. In general, it may be said that the shorter the bristle, the easier it is for the beginner to achieve a reasonably straight line, but that the man who accustoms himself to working with a short brush will never gain real proficiency and speed; fitches with longer bristle carry more paint and require recharging less frequently. A bad practice adopted by some painters is to cut down the bristle very short so that it cannot splay outwards at all, making it easier to use the fitch but also making the work tediously slow. The correct method of using the fitch is to hold it very lightly so that no weight rests on the bristles and therefore there is no tendency for them to splay outwards; the fitch, charged with colour is then drawn rapidly along the whole length of the straightedge; with practice this produces the cleanest quickest lining.

LINING PAPER Plain paper applied for the purposes mentioned in paragraph (b) under the heading *Lining*. It is available in varying weights and qualities. White lining paper of a pulp type is used prior to the hanging of ordinary wallpapers, stouter brown lining papers are used for the reception of heavy relief materials and for rough walls, and there are linings faced with calico or muslin for use on badly cracked surfaces or for jointed boardings. A brown lining paper coated on one side with tar, known as pitch paper, is sometimes used as a treatment for damp surfaces. Coloured linings are still available but are not so widely used as they were before the war.

Any piece of paperhanging work is improved by the use of lining paper, which provides the ideal surface for its reception, but in some cases lining is absolutely essential; lining paper should always be hung prior to the hanging of relief materials, delicate or expensive papers, and papers with a lustrous finish that reflects the light and therefore shows up the imperfections in the surface, and when wallpaper is to be hung on previously painted surfaces or upon surfaces treated with damp-proofing solutions or lead foil.

LINING PENCIL   Sometimes known as a "rigger". A type of signwriting brush with extremely long hair set in a quill, and used chiefly by coach-painters for the rapid production of fine lines in paint. The best variety is made from sable. The operative holds the brush by the quill, charges it with colour, and applies it to the work by means of a deft flick of the wrist.

LINING TOOL or LINING WHEEL   A device used for the production of narrow painted lines in industrial finishing, such as, for example, the lining of bicycle frames, metal furniture, etc. It consists of a paint container and a system of wheels or wipers which transfer the paint to the work. Generally the wheels may be changed to provide lines of varying widths. Usually a guiding device is incorporated to ensure the production of an accurate straight line.

The same principle is applied on a much larger scale in road lining machines, with which white or coloured lines can be painted on roads by unskilled labour.

LINOLEATES   Drying agents produced by fusing linseed oil and metallic oxides.

LINOXYN   The tough leathery substance of which a dried film of linseed oil is composed. When a film of liquid linseed oil is exposed to the air it undergoes a chemical change, absorbing oxygen and becoming the solid substance known as linoxyn; this action is commonly described as drying.

LINSEED OIL   A vegetable drying oil obtained by crushing the seed pods of the flax plant; until recently it was the principal and indeed practically the only oil used in the binding of paint and the manufacture of varnish, and although this is no longer the case, due to the introduction of a wider range of media, it is still a material of major importance in the paint industry and to the painter and decorator. It was always considered that oil derived from the Baltic provinces of Russia was superior to any other, having a higher iodine value and therefore greater drying properties; this source of supply no longer contributes to the world market and the chief producing countries are now Argentina, the U.S.A., Canada and India.

Raw or crude linseed oil as expressed from the pods needs refining in order to rid it of mucilage before it is fit for use as a paint medium, and what the painter and decorator describes as "raw linseed oil" is actually a refined oil. In this form it is a pale yellow colour which becomes paler with age and with exposure to light. It possesses the property of working very easily under the brush and mixes readily with other paint materials. When exposed to the air in a thin film it absorbs oxygen and "dries" in three or four days, the drying being chiefly due to the process of oxidation. Since this is too slow for practical purposes the rate of drying is accelerated by the addition of suitable drying agents. Linseed oil, like most vegetable oils, is a compound of glycerine and certain fatty acids; a small quantity of the fatty acid exists in a free state and the degree of acidity is expressed as the "acid value" of the oil. When exposed to the action of alkalis linseed oil is readily decomposed, free glycerine being released, and the film becoming sticky and soapy; this phenomenon is known as "saponification". Because the oil is so sensitive to alkaline attack it is unsuitable for use as a medium for paints which are to be applied directly to new Portland cement, lime plaster, concrete and similar chemically active surfaces.

Raw linseed oil can be modified in various ways. Its property of absorbing oxygen can be increased by heating it for several hours at a high temperature in contact with the air and adding a small quantity of driers; in this form it is known as "boiled oil", which is much darker in colour than raw oil, more viscous, quicker drying and more resistant to moisture; boiled oil also produces a harder and more glossy film, but it is doubtful if it is as durable. The action of heat produces polymerization, the oil increasing in viscosity as the heating continues. Stand oil is a thickened oil produced by heating a high quality refined oil for a considerable period without the addition of driers, and is a pale slow-drying material with a high degree of flow. Blown oil is produced by blowing air through a heated oil, which causes it to thicken rapidly and become much darker in colour.

LINTEL　The horizontal beam or stone over a door or window.

LIQUID　Matter which is in a fluid state but which is relatively incompressible.

LIQUID DRIERS　Driers used for the purpose of accelerating the oxidation of an oil medium, which are prepared in liquid form as opposed to the paste or powder forms which are also available. They include terebine and liquid oil driers; as a general rule, liquid oil driers are the safer of the two in use, being more elastic and less likely to cause cracking of the paint film.

LIQUID OIL DRIERS　Liquid driers made by dissolving linoleates with turpentine and reducing them by the addition of linseed oil or wood oil, the process being carried out cold. They are very pale in colour and can therefore be added to whites and light colours without causing discolouration. They are safer in use than terebine because of their greater elasticity. A variety known as "strong liquid driers" is also sold, which is darker in colour than the normal liquid oil driers and is very much more powerful; this type should be used with caution, as an excess may lead to cracking of the paint film.

LITHARGE　A monoxide of lead, prepared by oxidizing metallic lead in a current of air at a high enough temperature for the oxide to be melted as it forms, which is used as a drier for paint. It is employed in the production of boiled oil and terebine.

LITHOPONE　A white pigment of great importance in the paint industry, produced by the co-precipitation of zinc sulphide and barium sulphate. It is a very pure white and it possesses a high degree of opacity, ranking next to titanium white in this respect. It works well in an oil, varnish or water medium, and is not affected by acidity in the medium. It has excellent spreading capacity. Lithopone is widely used in the preparation of interior coatings such as flat oil paint, egg shell and semi-gloss finishes, undercoatings, waterpaints and emulsion paints. It disintegrates rapidly when subjected to outside exposure, causing chalking and cracking of the paint film, and is therefore unsuitable for use in exterior finishes.

LITMUS   A vegetable dye which is sensitive to acid and alkali, becoming red in the presence of an acid and blue in contact with an alkali. The dye is obtained from lichen and the chief source of supply is Holland.

LITMUS PAPER   A type of unsized paper stained with litmus; books of litmus paper containing a number of small leaves can be obtained very cheaply from a chemist, and provide a useful and convenient method of determining the alkalinity or otherwise of a surface which is to be painted.

LIVE EDGES   A term used to denote the fact that the edges of a previously applied area of paintwork are sufficiently fluid to allow newly applied paint to blend into them without showing any lap. It is important when large areas are being painted that the edges should be kept "alive" so that no joints or laps are apparent in the work.

LIVERING   A defect in paint whereby the paint thickens partially or completely into a jelly-like condition resembling raw liver and becomes unusable. It is caused by a chemical reaction within the paint itself; Prussian blue and certain of the lakes are liable to react with linseed oil to form soaps, and zinc oxide and acidic varnish media react similarly. The fault may also be caused by adding an unsuitable type of thinner or some other incompatible ingredient to a paint. A further cause is the continued oxidation and polymerization of the varnish medium of a paint in the container during storage.

LOCK RAIL   A term used to define one of the horizontal members of a door construction, namely the member upon which the lock or handle is mounted.

LOGWOOD   The wood of a small tree, the campeachy, which is a native of Central America but is also grown in the West Indies and South America and which is used as a dyestuff. The material owes its name to the fact that it is imported in logs. Campeachy wood is hard and yellow but turns red on exposure to air; the sapwood is cut away and the heartwood is cut into chips from which the dye is extracted. The colouring matter is a crystalline substance and is nearly colourless but when combined with oxygen it becomes red; when applied on a suitable mordant it produces dark red, blue and dense black colourings.

Logwood, the only natural mordant dye still used commercially, is employed by the decorator in making up water stains. Sixteen parts of logwood to one part of cream of Tartar produce a rich rosewood stain, and sixteen parts of logwood to one part of potassium chromate gives an ebony stain.

LOMBARDIC   A type of alphabet characterized by bulging shapes, derived from a style employed in medieval manuscript writing.

LONG OIL   A term applied to a varnish or varnish medium indicating that it is composed of a high proportion of oil and a low proportion of resin. A long oil varnish is defined by the British Standards Institution as being an oleo-resinous varnish, other than an alkyd, comprising not less than $2\frac{1}{2}$ parts of oil to 1 part of resin by weight. Such varnishes are durable, elastic and capable of withstanding considerable changes of temperature; they are generally slow drying and are less lustrous than varnishes with a higher resin content. All exterior quality varnishes are of the long oil type. Long oil alkyds are alkyd resins in which the amount of oil included as a modifying agent exceeds 60%.

LOOSE LEAF GOLD   Gold beaten into very thin leaves measuring 82·5mm square and supplied in books containing 25 leaves each. The individual leaves are kept separate from one another by being interspersed with thin sheets of tissue paper which are dusted with Armenian bole to prevent them from sticking to the gold; the gold itself, as its name implies, is loose, that is to say it is not fastened down in any way to any substance which would make it easier to handle, as opposed to transfer gold in which the gold leaf is attached to a waxed tissue. Loose leaf gold is used by the decorator for such purposes as glass gilding, the gilding of carved or modelled work, and the gilding of large wooden or metal letters of the type which can be taken down and treated in the workshop instead of being gilded *in situ*. Gold in this form is very delicate and susceptible to the slightest draught or current of air; it is generally applied by means of the tip and cushion. It produces a much more brilliant lustre than transfer gold.

LPG BLOWTORCHES   An abbreviation for "Liquefied Petroleum Gas Blowtorches". See *LPG Containers*.

LPG CONTAINERS OR CYLINDERS   Steel cylinders containing a hydrocarbon such as butane, propane, etc., in compressed, and therefore liquefied, form; when released from compression the substance vaporizes to produce a flammable gas. The cylinders are supplied for domestic use in situations where no piped gas supply is available, and they also have many applications in the industrial field. The particular application in which they are most familiar to painters and decorators is as a fuel feed for the blowtorches used for burning-off old paintwork. For practical purposes the domestic type of container which supplies sufficient fuel for about thirty hours of continuous burning is used; the outlet from the container is connected to the blowtorch by means of a flexible tube. For situations where such a large and heavy container would be too unwieldy, a small container of approximately the same size as an ordinary blowlamp is available, and in this case the torch is screwed directly on to the outlet to form a complete and rigid unit; this piece of equipment, being completely portable in one hand leaving the other hand free to manipulate the scraper, gives sufficient fuel for about three hours continuous burning. In both cases, as soon as the blowtorch valve is opened a steady flow of the flammable gas is released. Blowtorches operated by such gases offer the same advantages as the acetylene blowtorch, in that the handpiece is light in weight and easy to handle, the torch lights instantly when the valve is opened, and, provided propane, as opposed to butane, is used there is no loss of force in cold weather; special burner nozzles can be fitted for windy conditions.

LPG cylinders are usually hired on a rental basis, empty containers being returned to the supplier for replenishment in exchange for refilled cylinders as needed. It is desirable that only sufficient cylinders for immediate requirements should be kept on a site. If for any reason it is necessary to maintain a stock of cylinders either on a site or in a workshop, certain safety precautions are essential. A definite area should be reserved for the storage of the cylinders and every cylinder must be returned to this area at the end of each day's work; the local fire brigade headquarters should be notified that LPG containers are being stored on the premises and the brigade should be informed of the exact location of the storage area. Strict observance of these rules is necessary because in the event of an outbreak of fire the explosive nature of the cylinders presents a serious hazard; firemen unaware of the presence of such containers face the added danger of explosion.

LUMIGRAPHIC   The trade name used for fluorescent pigments.

LUMINOUS PAINT   Paint which is activated by daylight and continues to glow in the dark. It consists of a crystalline fluorescent pigment bound by a synthetic resin medium. One type, in which the pigment is either zinc sulphide, cadmium sulphide, or a combination of both, produces a glow which is fairly bright at first but which soon declines; another type, based upon cadmium fluoride, strontium sulphide or a combination of both, gives a glow which is not so bright in the initial stages but which persists for a longer time. Oleo-resinous varnish media are unsuitable because the metallic drying agents in them react with the pigments. A pronounced reaction takes place when any of these pigments is brought into contact with lead, and it is most important when luminous paints are to be used that they should not be applied directly upon a surface or old paint film containing lead. For the same reason it is desirable that a new brush should be employed for their application rather than a brush which may previously have been used in a paint containing lead. Special undercoats based on titanium are supplied. Luminous paints may be applied by brush, roller or spray; they may be used for sign work but their value in this field is limited by their poor flowing properties and the coarse nature of the pigment particles.

There is another type of luminous paint which is radioactive and which is used for picking out the figures or markings on watches, compasses, etc., but this is a specialist application with no bearing upon the painter and decorator's work.

LUSTRE Brightness, gloss or sheen. The term is often used to describe the quality of gloss and the extent to which light is reflected by a varnish, enamel or gloss paint finish.

LUSTRE FINISH A term used for a nitro-cellulose lacquer tinted with spirit soluble dye to give a sparkling effect when used on a bright metal.

LYMNATO A type of decorative effect obtained by manipulating a spray gun in such a way as to produce a continuous irregularly shaped line of paint in a colour contrasting with the ground; a low air pressure is used so that the paint, instead of being atomized, emerges from the gun in a thin continuous stream.

M

MACHINE PRINT Wallpaper in which the pattern is printed from cylindrical rollers. The paper is fed into the printing machine as a continuous roll from a large reel; it passes over a revolving drum to which the printing rollers are attached, and the drum and the rollers revolve in unison. A separate roller is required for each colour in the design; the paper passes under each of them in turn and the printing of all the colours is completed in one operation, after which it goes through a drying chamber. The majority of the vast quantities of wallpaper produced today are machine printed; such papers possess the obvious advantage of being cheaper to produce in large quantities than hand-printed papers. The standard length of an English machine-printed paper is 10.05 metres.

MADDER A shrubby climbing plant, the *rubia tinctorium,* from the root of which a red dyestuff is obtained; the dye itself is also known by the name madder, although another name for it is alizarin.

MAGENTA A brilliant crimson colour, named after an Italian city with a flourishing silk industry.

MAGNESIUM A silvery white metal which itself is comparatively weak but which can be mixed with aluminium, zinc and manganese to produce magnesium alloys of considerable strength. These alloys are largely employed in the manufacture of aircraft parts. Most of the magnesium alloys are rapidly corroded by salt, especially when in sheet form. The treatment for them consists of a degreasing and cleaning process followed by a pre-treatment aimed at producing a surface layer rich in chromates which will give a high resistance to corrosion and provide a good base for paint. The priming paint is based upon zinc chromate or a mixture of pigments with zinc chromate predominating. Subsequent coatings, which because of the highly corrodible nature of the material need to be developed to a good film thickness, vary according to the purpose for which the metal article is to be used, but paints containing lead are quite unsuitable for the purpose.

MAHLSTICK   Sometimes called "maulstick". A wooden rod with a round pad at the end, used by signwriters and decorative artists as a rest upon which the hand holding the brush or writer is steadied. The most convenient pattern is tapered and is divided up into two or three separate sections, each section being fitted with brass jointing-pieces. The pad at the end should be covered with a piece of clean chamois leather so as to prevent damage to the painted surface of the signboard.

The position of the mahlstick should be varied according to the stroke which is being executed. Generally speaking, the mahlstick should be at right angles to the direction of the stroke. A great many people adopt a rigid attitude and never shift the position of the mahlstick, thereby robbing themselves of most of the value of the tool. It sometimes happens that due to a misunderstanding of the purpose of the implement students develop the habit of using the mahlstick solely as a sort of straightedge along which the writing pencil is drawn to form straight lines; this practice should be firmly discouraged since it prevents the student from attaining a proper brush technique.

MAHOGANY   A light hardwood; one of the best known and most widely used of the hardwoods. The original Spanish mahogany which in the 18th century became so popular for the production of furniture was introduced into Britain in the first place as a ballast cargo from Cuba and Central America; it is now rare, its place having been taken by another species from Central America and by African mahogany from Nigeria and Ghana. Spanish mahogany is very close grained with a fine silky texture and is often beautifully figured particularly where forking of the stem occurs to produce the "crotch". Central American and African mahoganies are lighter in colour and coarser in texture. A number of other tropical woods which bear some resemblance to it in colour, grain and texture are sometimes described as mahogany but strictly speaking only woods of the true mahogany or *Meliaceae* family are entitled to the name.

Mahogany is important to the painter and decorator in two connections. In the first place the wood is widely used for constructional purposes, advantages in its favour being the fact that it shrinks very little when drying and also the fact that when dry it is very durable and largely free from twisting and warping; it is employed in the construction of doors and panelling, in high class joinery work of all kinds and in the production of veneers. A white lead primer of the traditional type is suitable for mahogany but some difficulty may be experienced due to the closeness of the grain resisting penetration by the paint; adhesion is improved if the primer is thinned with up to 10% of white spirit.

In the second place the popularity of mahogany in the making of furniture means that it is a wood that the decorator is often called upon to imitate by graining. It can be reproduced in either oil or water medium, but it is generally agreed that the effect of its characteristic silky appearance is achieved more faithfully in water medium. A common fault in mahogany graining is the use of a rather unsuitable pink ground, upon which the necessary richness of colour can only be obtained by means of a too-warmly coloured reddish glaze; far better results are achieved if the warmth is introduced into the ground colour and the glaze colour is kept on the cool side. A suitable ground can be made up with Venetian red,

M

burnt sienna and ochre, or Venetian red and orange chrome and the glaze
may consist of Vandyke brown, Vandyke brown and mahogany lake, or
mahogany lake and blue-black. There are innumerable methods of producing the figure; it is usual to build it up in stages, using the flogger to
produce the pore marks, a feather, a sponge or a mottler, coupled with
overgrainers, to produce the main figure, and a mottler to produce the
final faint mottling, all the work being softened with the badger.

Mahogany is a wood that takes a high degree of polish and the decorator
is often called upon to finish such items as mahogany doors and shop
facias in French polish.

MAHOGANY FEATHER The highly decorative figuring which occurs at
the forking of the stem.

MAIZE A type of corn indigenous to the American continent and grown
also in Southern Europe, India and Australia, which besides being used for
food has important secondary products such as starch. It forms the basis
of dextrine, which is a fixative used in the hanging of heavy relief goods.
Maize starch has strong adhesive qualities but has very little "slide" and
is not therefore used in ordinary paperhanging operations. It is applied with
a knife or trowel, being too thin for use if mixed to a brushing consistency.

Corn oil, obtained from maize, is used in the U.S.A. as an addition to
linseed oil in the preparation of paint.

MAKING GOOD Cutting out and repairing defective plaster or Portland
cement work to present a sound surface prior to decoration; the term is
often included in painting specifications, and implies that any loose or
crumbly material should be removed and any holes or cracks raked out,
and the cavities then patched in with sound material.

MALACHITE A green mineral, consisting of basic carbonate of copper,
which occurs in many parts of the world, particularly in the Urals, in
Germany, France, England, the Belgian Congo, Rhodesia and Australia.

MALACHITE GREEN A green pigment, used as an artists' colour, prepared by grinding and levigation of the mineral malachite.

MALEIC ANHYDRIDE Used in the production of certain types of alkyd
resins to give very pale varnishes of good durability, the maleic anhydride
taking the place of phthalic anhydride as the acid component.

MANGANESE A diatomic metallic element which in various compounds
has several applications to the paint industry. Manganese salts are important as drying agents, manganese dioxide being used in the same way as
litharge or red lead, and manganese sulphate, borate and oxalate being used
in the manufacture of very pale boiled oils and varnishes. Manganese is
also present in certain pigments such as sienna, umber, manganese brown
and manganese black.

MANHELP A handle, the length of which is adjustable, which may be attached to various types of brushes in order to reach places that would otherwise be difficult or inaccessible.

MANILA   (a) A type of hemp used for making rope; hence "manila rope" used in rigging cradles and other forms of scaffolding.
(b) A natural resin found in the Philippine Islands; the fossil resin is fairly hard but the recent resin is soft and is used in spirit varnishes, being freely soluble in alcohol.

MANTLING   Decorative scrollwork or drapery in heraldic painting, derived from the silken mantle worn by medieval warriors to prevent the heat of the sun from striking directly upon their armour. The mantling is usually depicted in the principal colours of the charge but there are certain exceptions, e.g., the Sovereign's mantling, which is gold lined with ermine.

MAPLE   A tree of the same family as the sycamore, the wood of which is used as a decorative veneer and is also employed in furniture making and to some extent for flooring and stair treads. Maple wood is very light and clean in colour and is characterized by a beautiful silky silvery mottle, but when exposed to air and light it darkens to an unattractive yellow colour. The grain markings are indistinct; sometimes the outer parts of the wood are dotted with "birds eyes" where tiny branches have sprung.

  The graining of maple is usually carried out in water medium on a ground of white or ivory, a very thin glaze of raw umber and raw sienna being used. After the glaze has been mottled and softened with the badger, grain markings may be inserted with a crayon. "Birds' eyes" are put in with burnt sienna by means of a maple dotter; they can also be put in with the finger-tips or with a piece of rough cork, but these devices produce an unnatural effect.

MAPLE DOTTER   A simple tool with which the small horseshoe shaped "birds' eyes" can be inserted in maple graining. A useful dotter can be made by singeing the centre out of a water colour brush with a red hot needle; dotters can also be cut from pieces of rubber, chamois leather, felt, etc.

MAQUETTE   A small three-dimensional model. Interior designers very often use maquettes of rooms, including furniture, etc., either instead of perspective drawings or in addition to drawings in order to give their clients a clear indication of the probable appearance of a completed scheme.

MAR RESISTANCE   The ability of a film of paint, varnish or lacquer to undergo the conditions for which it was designed without showing signs of damage—for instance, the ability of a bar counter finish to withstand the contact with alcoholic liquids, or the ability of a furniture lacquer to resist damage by normal wear and tear.

M

MARBLE Strictly speaking, a metamorphized and recrystallized limestone or dolomite capable of taking a high polish. In the building trade, however, the term is used freely to describe any crystallized calcium carbonate rock which displays a pleasing pattern and colour when cut and polished.

MARBLING A surface treatment by which the texture, pattern and broken colour effect of polished marbles are imitated in paint. The work is prepared and grounded out in a suitable colour, and the marbling is generally executed with opaque oil colour, blended and softened as required although glazes are sometimes used to give added depth and the appearance of translucency, and crayons are sometimes used for the veining.

MARINE PAINTS, MARINE VARNISHES, ETC. Materials formulated especially for the protection and enrichment of ships, especially ocean going vessels, and to some extent for application to harbour installations in seaports. The conditions of exposure which such materials are expected to withstand are very severe and it is seldom possible to ensure that the materials will be applied under suitable circumstances; it is rarely possible, for instance, for a ship to be in dry dock long enough for a treatment comprising complete rust removal followed by the application of a thorough anti-corrosive system to take place, nor can it always be arranged for the repainting of the superstructure to be preceded by adequate preparation.

The various parts of a ship each present their own particular problems demanding a paint system specially designed to meet their needs. The whole of the steel structure is subjected to the severe corrosive effects of exposure to salt water, sea air and strong sunlight, the topside also being attacked by continual wetting and drying and those parts which are at waterline level being liable to physical damage due to the impact of tugs and lighters. The paint for the funnels may have to withstand high temperatures. The underwater painted surfaces must not only resist corrosion but also combat the accumulation of marine growth and barnacles. A further factor influencing the manufacture of marine paints is that they need to be elastic enough to withstand considerable climate changes ranging from arctic to tropical conditions within a few days.

The term "marine paints" also covers the compositions used for painting the holds, cargo tanks, etc.

MARKING The term used in industrial finishing for the application of trade marks and coding devices or the application of the scale markings on instruments, etc.

MAROUFLAGE The method of affixing a painted canvas picture to a wall surface by cementing it with white lead and gold size or oil.

MARQUETRY Inlaid work. The term is usually applied to inlaying with fine woods, ivory or metals, but the painter and decorator can use the technique of marquetry to produce patterns and decorative motifs with low-relief materials such as Lincrusta, or with thin wood veneers.

MASK (a) Some object, such as, for example, a sheet of paper or a piece

of sheet metal, which is placed on a surface to prevent paint from encroaching on to it when an adjacent surface is being painted. The term is generally used in connection with spray painting rather than with other forms of paint application; for instance, the technique used for decorative spraying is similar to that used for edge stencilling, but the paper used to define the pattern in decorative spraying is referred to as a mask, whereas in the case of edge stencilling it would normally be termed a stencil plate.
(b) Term commonly used to mean a respirator.

MASKING PASTE A paste which is used to mask off certain areas of a surface before paint is sprayed, and which, after the paint has dried, is sponged away. There are various proprietary emulsion types of paste available, or a home made paste can be prepared from a mixture of whiting and flour made into a stiff paste with glycerine and glue size. When working on a cellulose ground a paste made from whiting, glycerine and soft soap can be used. It is most essential that such pastes should be thoroughly cleaned off the surface as soon as it is reasonably possible; otherwise, there is a serious risk that they will cause cracking of the ground coat.

MASKING TAPE A material sold in rolls of varying widths for the purpose of masking out prior to spray painting. Gummed paper and cellotape are sometimes used for the purpose but these tend to disturb the ground coat and pluck it off when they are being peeled away. Proprietary masking materials consisting of pressure-sensitive adhesive paper or linen tapes are safer, although more expensive. These are flexible and can be made to conform to the contours of almost any desired shape.

MASTIC A jointing or sealing compound which is plastic when applied and which should retain the property of yielding and movement throughout its life. Mastic generally consists of bitumen, tar, resin, rubber or oil with the addition of some inert fibrous or powdered filler. If the joint is to remain waterproof the mastic should be of a form which will adhere firmly to the sides of the joint.

MASTIC CEMENT A sealing compound made from litharge and boiled oil which sets harder than most other types of mastic.

MASTIC VARNISH A spirit varnish made from a natural resin called gum mastic, which is used for varnishing oil paintings; because it possesses the property of becoming brittle when ageing it can when old be removed by friction, without damaging the picture, which can then be revarnished.

MATCHING Making two things correspond—for example, matching one colour to another, or matching a wallpaper so that the pattern on one piece is accurately joined at all points to the pattern of the piece previously hung.

MATT Flat; substantially free from gloss or sheen.

MATT FINISH A finish which presents neither gloss nor sheen.

175

MATT GOLD A term usually used in connection with glass gilding, where certain areas of gold may be made to present a matt effect which contrasts with other highly burnished areas. Such an effect is seen when the gold leaf is applied to an area of glass which has been etched or sandblasted, and the effect can be simulated on a piece of plain glass by coating in the area which is to appear matt with clear varnish and allowing it to dry before the gilding is commenced.

MATTING AGENT A material used to decrease the gloss of a paint film; it may be a material which is soluble in a medium or it may take the form of a solid extender such as magnesium carbonate, asbestine or colloidal china clay.

MATURING The process whereby varnishes are clarified and improved by storage.

MAULSTICK See *Mahlstick.*

MECHANICAL CLEANING The preparation of surfaces by mechanical means, as opposed to manual methods, prior to painting. In the field of industrial painting this includes the use of pneumatic hammers and chisels, rotary wire brushes, flame cleaning and certain shot blasting processes. The methods employed in coachpainting and industrial finishing include grinding, sanding, steam cleaning, buffing, rumbling, etc.

MEDIA The plural of *medium.*

MEDIUM The medium, or vehicle, is the liquid component of a paint, in which the pigment is dispersed or suspended and which enables it to be spread upon a surface. Once the paint is applied to a surface the medium acts as a binder to hold the pigment particles together in a cohesive film and to make the film adhere to the surface. These two factors militate against one another so that if the cohesive properties of the medium are too great the adhesion of the film is weakened. The functions of a medium are thus interdependent, and can be defined as (i) to support the pigment particles during storage without undue settling taking place, (ii) to provide fluidity whereby the paint can be readily applied, (iii) to dry as a film which effectively binds the pigment particles, and (iv) to provide good adhesion to the substrate. The nature of the medium also affects the degree of gloss or sheen possessed by the film and the extent to which it will be resistant to water penetration.

The earliest paint media were mucilaginous extracts of animal or vegetable origin, followed by the egg-yolk, glue or milk used in tempera painting and the fixing of pigments with slaked lime in fresco painting. The medium in soft distemper is a weak solution of glue, and that of the glazes used in water-colour graining is a solution of sugar.

Present day water media consist of oils or varnishes emulsified with water in the case of oil-bound water paints, and droplets of synthetic high polymers dispersed in water in the case of emulsion paints. In the case of oil paints the traditional medium is a vegetable drying oil such as linseed oil which can readily be mixed with suitable pigments, driers and thinners on the site by the operative, but there are distinct limitations to its use. In modern paints a wide range of media is available, many of them based on synthetic resins blended with drying or semi-drying oils, which can only be blended under carefully controlled factory conditions. It is in the development of media that the most striking advances in paint technology have been made.

MEGILP A substance which is added to graining colour to prevent it from flowing together and to help it to retain its sharpness of definition after it has been combed or figured. Old-time grainers who prided themselves on possessing their own private recipes used some curious materials as megilp, including limewater, jellied soap, and a concoction of beeswax dissolved in hot linseed oil. Modern paint products include various materials such as transparent glaze media, scumble glazes, etc., that serve efficiently as megilps and are less likely to disrupt the film than home made recipes. Megilp should always be used in moderation; an excessive quantity thickens the graining colour and produces an unpleasant relief effect which detracts from the smoothness of the finish and gives a patchy appearance when varnished.

MELAMINE RESINS Etherified condensation products of melamine with formaldehyde. Alkylated melamine finishes are characterized by good adhesion and a high degree of impact, heat and chemical resistance; they are used in the finishing of motor cars and kitchen and office equipment. Acid catalysed melamine resin finishes are used as air-drying and force dried finishes for metal and wood.

M

MENHADEN OIL An oil sometimes used in paint manufacture, derived from a fish of the shad family, common on the Atlantic coast of North America.

MERCURY Sometimes known as quicksilver. A very heavy metal which at ordinary temperatures takes the form of a bright silvery liquid. Various materials used in painting processes are derived from it. Water-soluble salts such as mercuric chloride are strongly poisonous and are incorporated into fungicidal paints, wood preservatives of various kinds, and marine paints for discouraging the growth of barnacles, etc., on ships' hulls. Mercuric sulphide is sublimed to produce the fine red pigment known as vermilon. It should be noted that although the salts of mercury are virulent poisons, vermilon, being insoluble, is free from toxic properties.

METAL A material belonging to a class of elementary substances which usually present in varying degrees certain characteristic properties such as high electrical and thermal conductivity, great opacity, high reflectivity of light, malleability and ductility.

METAL SPRAYING A process whereby molten metal is sprayed to form a protective coating for iron and steelwork. A specially designed type of spray gun is used and the metal is fed in in the form of thin wire (or sometimes in powdered form), melted in an oxy-acetylene or oxy-hydrogen flame and blown out in finely divided form by an air blast. Any type of metal that can be drawn into wire and melted in an oxy-gas blowpipe can be sprayed, and a wide range of metals including aluminium, brass, bronze, cadmium, copper, cupro-nickel, iron, lead, molybdenum and tin are used for various purposes; aluminium, cadmium and zinc appear to offer the greatest protection. It is essential that the surface to be sprayed should be absolutely clean and shot blasting is usually employed to obtain a suitable surface.

Metal spraying is a specialized industry and the process is carried out by firms devoted to this particular branch of industry. The subject has been the basis of considerable research. The interest of the process to the painter lies not in the application of the molten metal but in the painting systems which follow it. Metal spraying, which has been used on some contracts of immense scale for the protection of structural steelwork in exposed conditions, always produces a matt surface which is porous and which is ideally suited for the reception of paint. Apart from the very considerable degree of protection afforded by the metal spraying itself, the addition of a single coat of paint applied in the usual manner increases the effective life of the coating for a number of years. If the surface is washed down and the coating of paint renewed at regular intervals the total cost of the anti-corrosive treatment assessed over the whole of its life is very much lower than that of normal steelwork protective treatments.

The choice of paint to be used on a sprayed metal surface is still the subject of experiment. Experience seems to indicate that lead-based paints and the cheaper varieties of bituminous paints are unsuitable. Good results have been obtained with chlorinated rubber paints and paints containing co-polymers of vinyl chloride and vinyl acetate.

METALLIC CAR FINISHES   Finishing paints which incorporate flake aluminium to provide a sparkling effect. They contain less coloured pigment than normal paints and in fact without the addition of the aluminium they would lack opacity. Light rays penetrate the surface of the paint film and are reflected at different angles by the minute metallic particles, which means that the contours of the vehicle produce apparent differences of colour from one surface to another.

Metallic finishes for car bodies were used on a small scale in this country in the early 1930's but soon became very unpopular because of the difficulty of matching the existing finish when repairs were necessary, and for many years they have hardly been used at all. In recent years, however, due to the influence of the American market, they have been reintroduced on a considerable scale. In the U.S.A. more than half the current car production is in metallic finishes, and this is reflected to a lesser extent in the British and Continental markets.

The increasing popularity of these finishes has brought problems to vehicle painters called upon to finish and re-spray repair work. These problems are accentuated by the fact that many people are unaware of the factors involved in achieving a satisfactory colour match. Since the layering of the aluminium flakes affects the appearance of the paint film, it follows that the apparent colour of the finish can be altered by varying the spraying technique. Briefly the most important factors are the viscosity of the paint and the air pressure on the spray. The wetter the paint whilst spraying, the more the flakes will tend to sink in and settle, whereas when the material is sprayed dry the flakes are trapped in the surface of the film. Matching an existing sample of metallic colour thus resolves itself into the following considerations:- (a) Viscosity of the paint; the higher the viscosity, the deeper the colour; therefore to lighten the colour, add more thinners. The use of a fast thinner will lighten the colour still further; a slow thinner blended with a retarder deepens the colour. (b) Air pressure; the lower the air pressure, the deeper the apparent colour; therefore to lighten the colour, increase the pressure. (c) Gun adjustments; spreader control — a narrow fan pattern gives a deeper colour, a wider fan pattern a lighter colour; position of gun — the gun held close to the surface gives a deeper colour, further away gives a lighter colour. The colour matching must be carried out in strong daylight, and adjusting the variable factors should produce a satisfactory match without the addition of pigment tinters. Tinting with additional pigments, if necessary at all, should be kept to a minimum.

METALLIC LEAD PRIMER   A primer for iron and steel, consisting of fine particles of metallic lead in a suitable medium. Under certain conditions it may be preferred to traditional metal primers if there is likely to be a long delay between priming and painting. It is especially valuable in situations where chemical attack is heavy.

METALLIC PAINTS   Materials made by mixing aluminium powder or bronze powder with a quick-drying varnish medium of low acid value. Aluminium powders of the leafing variety have a wide application both in priming paints for wood and in finishing paints for locations where a high degree of reflectivity of light is required; non-leafing powders are used in certain satin or silk-effect finishes. Bronze powders, made from alloys of copper and zinc or aluminium vary in colour from pale lemon gold to deep copper bronze. The powder and medium may be supplied either mixed ready for use or separately to be mixed by the decorator immediately prior to application; ready-mixed metallic paints tend to lose their lustre when stored for long periods.

Metallic paints, being heat resisting, are often used for heating pipes and radiators, although it is not generally appreciated that they reduce the radiation of heat to quite a marked extent. They are liable to discolouration if exposed to acid, alkali or sulphurous fumes. They are sometimes glazed to produce decorative effects and sometimes varnished for protection; before glaze or varnish is applied they should receive a buffer coat of thin shellac lacquer to insulate them from the oxidizing effects of the oil in the superimposed material.

METALLIZED PANELS   Panels made of a plastic material, which has been embossed and finished with a metallic coating to simulate the appearance of hammered copper, brass, pewter, etc.; some of the panels are heavily embossed to form replicas of historic repoussé metal work patterns such as the spirals and bosses, enriched with coloured enamels,

M

that were such a typical feature of Celtic art. The metallic surface retains its lustre without tarnishing and can be wiped clean when necessary with a damp cloth. Prior to the application of the panels the wall surface should be well prepared and all nibs and irregularities removed; it is usually an advantage to hang a lining paper first. The panels are fixed with an adhesive supplied by the manufacturers, and are pressed firmly into position by hand

METHYLATED SPIRIT   Alcohol prepared for industrial use; in the painting trade it is used as a solvent for shellac in knotting, spirit varnishes and French polish. Mineralized methylated spirit consists of a mixture of nine volumes of "plain" spirit with one volume of wood naphtha or wood spirit, with the addition of a small quantity of mineral naphtha to make the liquid unpalatable. Colouring matter in the form of methyl violet is also added. When added to water a white opalescence is produced. Industrial methylated spirit, widely used as a solvent, consists of 95% ethyl alcohol and 5% crude naphtha, without the addition of any mineral naphtha or colouring matter. No opalescence is produced when it is mixed with water. Considerable restrictions are imposed upon its sale and supply.

MICA   The name given to a group of silicates which are distinguished by their perfect basal cleavage, which causes them to split readily into thin flakes, and their vitreous pearly lustre. Mica is used in paint manufacture to impart "tooth" and to increase the bulk of the product. The shape of the particles produces a leafing effect similar to that of aluminium powder or graphite, which helps to keep the paint in suspension and gives improved resistance to moisture penetration. Mica is also used in the manufacture of wallpaper.

MICA PAPERS   Wallpapers or ceiling papers in which the ground or the pattern is printed with mica, giving a silvery satin sheen.

MILDEW   A white fluffy form of mould which, like all fungoid growths, thrives under damp and humid conditions and is liable to infect and feed upon the organic matter contained in a number of decorative materials such as oil paint, water paint, distemper, paste, wallpaper, etc. New paint brushes attacked by damp during storage are particularly prone to develop mildew growths. The term is also used in a general way to describe the rotting of paper, cloth and fabrics by fungi or moulds. See also *Mould Growths.*

MILKINESS   A term used to describe a defect whereby a film of lacquer or varnish which should be transparent presents a whitish translucent appearance. Its most general application is to a fault similar to blooming in cellulose or spirit finishes, caused by working under damp conditions.

MILL SCALE   A thin skin or layer of iron oxides which covers the surface of hot-rolled steel when it leaves the rolling mills, produced by the rapid oxidation of the white-hot metal in contact with the air. Mill scale is also present on the surface of new wrought iron. When first formed it adheres tightly to the parent metal but in course of time it generally becomes loose and flaky and provides an unstable basis for a paint system.

Mill scale usually has a laminated structure, and examination under a microscope reveals the fact that it consists of three separate layers each composed of a different iron oxide, with ferrous oxide (FeO) in contact with the steel, magnetite (Fe_3O_4) above this, and ferric oxide (Fe_2O_3) on the outside face. The thickness, composition and structure of the mill scale vary considerably according to the nature of the steel to which it is attached, the conditions under which steel was rolled and the thickness of the finished steel section. These differences have a pronounced effect upon the way in which the mill scale behaves when the steel is exposed to weathering, and this in turn has a great bearing upon the pre-painting treatment. If it were possible to apply a white lead/linseed oil priming paint to the steel while it was still hot on leaving the rolling mill, a coating would be formed which would provide good protective qualities for as long as the scale remained intact. Such a course is rarely possible, however, because of the way in which it would slow up steel production at the mill. Furthermore, the process of cutting the steel to the required lengths and drilling it for fixing, together with the scoring to which it is subjected while being handled by cranes in transit, all lead to the film of scale being disrupted. Where the scale is broken, the presence of moisture causes a galvanic action to be set up between it and the exposed steel and corrosion spreads rapidly, loosening the scale and, of course, lifting the paint film.

The manner in which mill scale is loosened by exposure to air and moisture suggests a method by which it can be removed prior to painting, and it is a common practice for engineers to specify that structural steel shall be left unpainted and allowed to weather for a period of some six months prior to scraping, wire brushing and painting. There are several drawbacks to this course, however. As already indicated, the rate of loosening varies considerably according to such factors as the type of steel, the thickness of the sections, etc.; it also happens that those parts of the structure which are sheltered in any way weather much more slowly than those exposed to the full severity of the atmospheric attack, and the extent to which the atmosphere is polluted also has a bearing on the rate of weathering; for these reasons, the weathering of the structure does not proceed at a uniform rate, and in practice it is found that while in some areas the mill scale may have loosened satisfactorily, in other parts it will still be clinging tightly to the surface, and in other parts again it may have disintegrated completely and considerable rusting may have developed, leading to an appreciable loss of metal.

It is now generally recognized that the only sound basis for a painting system for structural steelwork is to carry out complete removal of the mill scale before painting. The method most widely used is chipping and wire brushing, by hand, which in some circumstances may be the only practicable method on erected steelwork, but which for various reasons rarely results in complete descaling, and leaves a partially descaled surface which is a bad foundation for paint. Better results are obtained with pneumatic chisels and hammers and rotary wire brushes, but the use of these tools may result in the steel being pitted, and rust may be burnished over instead of being removed. A very effective method of removal, although an expensive one, is that provided by flame cleaning, which loosens the scale by means of differential expansion and which also de-hydrates any rust which is present. Shot blasting also results in the

M

complete removal of scale and leaves a surface which is more receptive to paint than is bare metal. Modifications of the shot-blasting process which can be used on erected steel include wet sand-blasting and a proprietary type of shot blasting which incorporates the use of a vacuum attachment to reclaim the shot. The efficiency of grit blasting is reduced if the steel has been allowed to rust before it is treated.

Complete descaling before erection can be carried out by pickling, a process whereby the steel sections are immersed in an acid bath of suitable concentration; the layer of ferrous oxide which is closest to the steel is dissolved and the remainder of the scale flakes off. Inhibitors are added to the acid to prevent undue attack upon the steel itself.

MILORI BLUE   Highest quality Prussian blue.

MINERAL   Any inorganic substance with a definite chemical composition, found in the ground.

MINERAL GREEN   Malachite.

MINERAL ORANGE   Another name for red lead.

MINERAL WHITE   Also called terra alba; sulphate of lime derived from gypsum.

MINERAL WHITES   A term used in paint manufacture to indicate those substances which are used as extenders to increase the bulk and give *tooth* to paint, including barytes, barium carbonate, strontium white, Paris white, mineral white, satin white, magnesite, alumina, China clay, asbestine, mica, silica and slate powder.

MISCIBILITY   The ability of two or more substances to mix and form a single homogeneous phase.

MISSES   Areas which have been left uncoated with paint, generally through carelessness.

MIST (or SPRAY FOG)   The haze which results from finely divided particles of paint (atomized paint) rebounding from a surface which is being sprayed or being projected into the air beyond the edge of a surface through overspray. A high-pressure spraying system produces more mist than an air-volume system (although the mist so produced tends to settle in the form of a fine dust whereas the less finely atomized paint particles produced by the air-volume system are larger and wetter and are more difficult to remove). The reduction of spray mist is one of the great advantages offered by the airless spraying and hot spray processes.

While a certain amount of spray mist is inseperable from the use of high-pressure spraying equipment, the quantity of mist commonly seen when spray painting is in progress is usually quite excessive and is due in a great measure to incorrectly regulated pressures.

MIST COAT A term used in spraying to denote a very lightly applied coating. The actual nature of a mist coat is subject to considerable variation. When spraying vertical surfaces it is often an advantage, both with cellulose and synthetic resin paints, to apply a mist coat to help the main coating to hold up, and the technique is to apply the paint over an area of convenient size with rapid strokes of the gun so as to form a thin coating (which need not necessarily be a continuous film) and then immediately follow up with a full coat applied at normal spraying speed. When a cellulose surface which is in good condition is being resprayed a mist coat is very often used to help to create a firm bond between the old film and the new coating, and in this case the mist coat is made up with some three parts of thinners to one part of paint. For touch up and minor repair work on cellulose finishes a mist coat consisting of thinners alone is very often sprayed over the finished repair to help it to blend into the background.

MIXING VARNISH A type of varnish of low acid value, which can be added to lead or zinc pigments, etc., without risk of *feeding*.

MOBILE TOWERS Towers constructed from tubular scaffolding or pre-fabricated frames and mounted on castor wheels. They are most useful in painting and decorating, especially for ceiling work; they enable a large ceiling area to be painted from a small working platform using only a small quantity of scaffold, and they occupy very little space where other types of scaffold would obstruct the whole floor area. Unfortunately, accidents involving the use of mobile towers are very common, most of them due to the tower tilting or overturning. The essential safely pre-cautions include the following.

M

The height must not exceed three times the base length; a tower should never be moved while people are on the platform; a tower should only be moved by pressure applied to the base and men on the platform should never try to move the tower themselves by pulling on roof trusses, etc.; castor wheels should be firmly attached to the tubes so as not to drop out while the tower is being moved; and the castor wheels must be locked before work commences to prevent the tower from being accidentally moved.

MOCK UP A term frequently used by architects and interior designers to mean a scale model prepared in full colour to show in three dimensions what the effect of a proposed scheme of decoration or similar project will be.

MODEL A representation or pattern in miniature, in three dimensions, of something to be produced on a larger scale.

MODELLING (a) Fashioning, shaping or moulding a pliable material in order to produce relief, as, for example, when plastic paint is worked with modelling tools in order to produce a relief motif.
(b) Form seen within a contour; representation by use of light and shade, as distinguished from drawing in outline.

MOIRE   Wallpaper with a watered silk effect produced by means of a delicate emboss.

MONASTRAL BLUE   The proprietary name for a phthalocyanide pigment with several distinctive features. Monastral blue is completely insoluble in oils and organic solvents. It is a very powerful stainer having double the strength of Prussian blue, it is immune to acid or alkaline attack, it is resistant to heat up to a temperature of some $200°C$ ($400°F$), and can therefore be used in heat-resisting paints and stoving finishes, and since it does not react with oil media it does not feed or liver. It is an intense blue colour and is fast to light in the stronger shades although liable to fade if reduced to a very pale tint.

MONASTRAL GREEN   A pigment dye with similar characteristics to Monastral blue.

MONOCHROME   Of one colour only; hence "monochromatic painting"— painting in tints and shades of one colour only. The form and contours of a three-dimensional object can be represented in monochrome by carefully placing the tints and shades to indicate which parts of the object are exposed to the light and which are in shadow.

MONTAN WAX   A hard wax-like material obtained from lignite or peat, sometimes described as bitumen wax.

MOP   A soft camel hair brush used in the gilding of carved, moulded or modelled work for the purpose of pressing the gold leaf into the quirks and crevices.

MORDANT   A term derived from the French word *mordre* meaning to bite; hence a mordant is a substance capable of biting or gripping some other material. It has two connotations in the painting trade.
(a) A chemical solution used to etch the surface of galvanized iron or other zinc coated surfaces or any other non-ferrous metal in order to provide a *key* to improve the adhesion of the paint.
(b) An adhesive substance used to attach gold leaf to a surface—for example Japan gold size, or old-oil gold size or, in the case of glass gilding, isinglass or gelatine.

MOSAIC   A pattern or pictorial composition produced by setting small pieces of differently coloured glass, marble or stone into a bedding of cement, and owing its effectiveness very largely to the play of light reflected from the various facets. Mosaic effects have sometimes been reproduced in plastic paint by decorators.

MOTHER OF PEARL   The iridescent pearly substance which forms the internal layer of many kinds of sea shells. At one time it was widely used in glass sign work, providing a pleasing contrast when placed alongside gold leaf, and supplies can still be obtained from decorators' merchants for this purpose.

MOTIF   The dominant feature or device in a decorative composition.

MOTTLER   A type of brush used in graining for the purpose of mottling; various sizes are obtainable. The filling usually consists of hog hair, although other types of hair are sometimes used. The handle is thin and rectangular in shape and is made of tin plate packed with either wood or a compressed fibre composition.

MOTTLING   (a) A term used in graining to describe the representation of the highlights and shades which are a characteristic feature of natural wood. Mottling is generally carried out in water medium as a glaze which is superimposed on figure graining, but it may on occasions be executed in an oil stain.
(b) A defect in a sprayed film which appears in the form of a uniform series of imperfections of roughly circular shape.

MOULD GROWTHS   Mould is the general non-scientific term for a wide variety of fungi which in the presence of damp attack many kinds of animal and vegetable substances. Since a great many decorative materials contain organic matter, such as vegetable oils, glue size, casein, paste, paper, etc., it follows that under suitable conditions these may all become infected and provide nutriment upon which mould growths will thrive. Infection is particularly likely to occur in premises such as bakeries, breweries, dairies, etc. The spores may be carried by wind or air currents and may travel a considerable distance, infecting plaster and woodwork far from the original seat of the trouble. There was a sharp rise in the incidence of mould growth as a problem affecting decoration as a result of the war, when premises which had been blitzed lay derelict for long periods, fungoid growths developing unchecked and the spores being carried by the wind to spread the infection over a wide area.
     When mould is encountered the first essential is to discover the cause of any damp which is present and to take adequate steps to prevent its recurrence; the treatment is then to remove all infected matter by means of scraping, burning off or stripping, avoiding any undue disturbance which would cause the spores to be blown about and distributed over a large area; the debris is then destroyed by burning. After this the infected area is washed down with a suitable fungicide, several proprietary types of which are on the market, and is then kept under observation for the period of a week; should the growth show any sign of recurring the surface should be washed a second time with the fungicide. Two applications are usually sufficient to check even the most persistent growth. The surface may then be decorated; a fungus or mould resistant paint may be used or, alternatively, the priming coat may be thinned with naphtha, which has good fungicidal properties. If the surface is to be papered a small proportion of carbolic acid should be added to the size.

MOULD STAINS   The disfigurements caused by mould or fungoid growth.

MOULDINGS   Ornamental and continuous lines of projections or grooving used to embellish the face of a structure and showing, in profile, a complex

M

series of curves; they may, for instance, form part of a cornice, may surround the panels in a piece of woodwork, may surround a door or may be part of a capital or arch, etc. Any individual part of a moulding is called a member, and any member which is ornamentally carved is said to be enriched.

MUFFLE A pad of cloth tied and secured round the top of the stile of a ladder in order to prevent its damaging or marking the surface upon which it rests.

MULLIONS Vertical posts or uprights dividing a window into two or more lights.

MULTI-COLOUR PAINT (Also known as multi-fleck paint, flecked paint, etc.) A type of material which enables several colour combinations to be applied simultaneously in one single application. The colour particles or globules remain separate in the dried film, being insulated from each other by an aqueous colloidal solution which prevents them from merging. The finished effect resembles that of spatter (q.v.), in appearance, although the spots of colour do not stand out in high relief as in spatter.

Paints of this kind are by no means new, but although they have been on the market for many years they have until recently made little appeal to the public. In recent years, however, there has been a marked change in this respect, and multi-coloured paints are now popular and are being widely used, especially in the decoration of public buildings such as schools and office blocks. They are also employed to some extent in industrial finishing and in the production of household equipment.

The essential feature of these materials is that they can only be applied satisfactorily by spray; brush or roller application produces a streaky finish. In Denmark, two-colour brushing paints of a kind have been marketed; they consist of a coarse emulsion of white spirit-soluble paint in an acrylic emulsion paint. Normal spray equipment can be used provided the air pressure is kept low, but the best results are achieved by use of a spray head of the internal-mix type. Airless spray plant is unsuitable since the high pressure disturbs the particle shapes. The paint can be applied direct on most types of surface but is not suitable for use on expanded polystyrene. On new surfaces the use of a primer coat to promote adhesion is generally recommended. Previously painted surfaces may require the application of a sealer coat. In this country the use of multi-coloured paint is restricted to interior surfaces, although in countries with a dry climate it is also used for exterior work; even on inside work it should not be applied when humid conditions prevail, as excess moisture interferes with the film-forming properties.

A coating of multi-coloured paint applied according to the manufacturer's instructions builds up to a thickness three or four times as great as that of a conventional paint film. For this reason the coverage is low, averaging at about 3 square metres per litre. The shelf life of the material, when stored in 5 litre containers, is reckoned to be from four to six months; deterioration is more rapid when large containers are stores. The coating becomes touch-dry in one-and-a-half to two hours and hard-dry in six to eight hours. Intermixing of two different colours of the same brand by the decorator is not impossible, but is difficult because any vigorous stirring would affect the particle size.

Various claims are made for the product. It is said that because the coating does not develop a charge of static electricity the surface does not attract dust and dirt, and therefore remains cleaner than a conventional paint film and is resistant to grease and oil stains. The material dries to a hard film with fairly high resistance to abrasion, and can be washed with soap and water or with solvent cleansers. It is claimed that if the paint surface is damaged, small local repairs can be carried out with the spray gun and that such repairs are difficult to detect; this would depend to a great extent, of course, upon the length of time that had elapsed since the initial coating had been applied. It is sometimes said that the greater film thickness helps to mask surface irregularities, but this is a debatable point; there seems no reason why a single coating of multi-coloured paint should be more effective in this respect than the equivalent thickness of a three or four coat system in conventional paint, and in any case the paint, however thick, must necessarily follow the contours of the surface.

The main objection to multi-coloured paints is on aesthetic grounds. The colour flecks look very attractive when seen on a small colour sample but when the paint is used on a large area the results can be disappointing; there are obviously physical limits to the size of the colour particles, and the flecks are too small to be effective when used on a large expanse of wall, being quite out of scale. Similarly, some of the colour combinations are pleasing when seen in isolation on a small shade-card sample but are most disagreeable when used on a large area.

MULTIPLE JET CAP   An air cap, or that part of a spray gun which directs the air into the stream of fluid in order to atomize it, comprising 5, 7, 9 or more orifices as opposed to the conventional type of cap with only 3 orifices. The advantages provided by a multiple jet cap include better atomization of viscous materials such as synthetics and greater uniformity of spray pattern.

M

MULTIPLE PLATE STENCILS   Stencilled patterns produced by means of the design being cut from two or more plates accurately registered one to another. Various features can be obtained in this way which would not be possible with single plate stencils—for example, a pattern may be produced in which no ties are obvious and blank spaces are filled, or in which outline treatments are achieved.

MUNSELL COLOUR SYSTEM   A system of colour definition based on hue, value and chroma, hue distinguishing red from blue, green from yellow, etc., value being related to the lightness or darkness of the colour, and chroma being the strength of the colour.

The system was devised by Albert H. Munsell, an American artist, with the object of replacing vague and confusing colour terms with a clear and specific method of notation. He set himself to describe colour psychologically, ie., in terms of visual sensation, without concerning himself with the physical variables involved; his method was to establish a series of coloured shapes varying equally in all directions, in the domain of colour, in terms of visual appearance.

It is obvious that terms such as "light blue", "dark green", "shell pink", etc., are much too vague and imprecise to give any real indication of what is intended; the reason the terms are vague is that they do not supply sufficient data to describe the colours adequately. Munsell's system provides all the information required, because it describes colour by a three-dimensional notation. The clarity of this system can be illustrated by a simple analogy; if we were to attempt to describe a wooden box it would not be sufficient merely to say that the box was 900mm long; it would still not be sufficient if we added a second dimension and said it was 900mm by 600mm wide. By adding a third dimension, however, and saying that the box measured 900mm by 600mm by 300mm deep, we provide a complete description. Munsell defined the three dimensions or "variables" of colour as being *hue* (that which distinguishes red from yellow, green from blue, etc.), *value* (the lightness or darkness of a colour as related to black and white) and *chroma* (the strength or purity of the colour). These he constructed into a three-dimensional colour solid, often termed the "Munsell Colour Tree", which has a vertical axis passing from black to white through a graduated scale of greys. Radiating from the axis there are horizontal branches graded from neutral grey to full colour or hue. There are ten basic hues, consisting of five principal hues (namely, red, yellow, green, blue and purple) and five intermediate hues (namely, yellow-red, green-yellow, blue-green, purple-blue and red-purple). Each of the ten basic hues is divided into ten parts, to make a circular scale of a hundred finely graded hues.

The Munsell system enables any colour to be described precisely, which is far more satisfactory than the use of vague terms such as dove-grey, willow green, etc. What is more, it is flexible enough to permit of further expansion. A complete Munsell reference for a colour defines the hue, the value and the chroma in that order; for example, a colour corresponding to what is sometimes known vaguely as Georgian green has the Munsell reference of 7·5 GY 7/4; 7·5 GY refers to the basic hue of green-yellow, 7 to the value of a scale of ten ranging from black (0) to white (10), and 4 refers to the chroma on a scale ranging from neutral grey to full strength at any given value level. Neutral greys, having no hue or chroma, are specified by the value figure prefixed by "N", e.g. N6.

MUNTINS The vertical parts of a framed or panelled joinery construction which lie between the panels and span the distance between the various horizontal rails.

MURAL DECORATION From the latin *murus,* a wall; the adornment of walls by means of surface decoration in oil colour, water colour or fresco, by mosaics or by carvings in wood, stone, terra-cotta, marble, etc. The term is also understood to include the decoration in similar manner of vaults and ceilings. To the painter and decorator, mural painting implies a composition carried out in some material such as oil paint, oilbound water paint or emulsion paint, applied either directly to the wall or to a fabric such as canvas which is then affixed to the wall; it consists of a complete composition, design or picture which may occupy a large area of wall space, a whole wall or a series of walls extending around a room, and as such it is an integral part of the background decoration of the room as opposed to an easel picture or other movable object. Present-day mural treatments include the hanging of photographic reproductions of scenery and aerial views which are prepared in the form of large sheets, and decorators' merchants stock a range of coloured scenic reproductions printed for hanging as mural decorations.

N

NAIL HEADS The nails used to fix building boards in position may rust if water paint or distemper is applied directly upon them; rusting may also occur if they are sunk below the surface and the cavity filled with a water filler. If the boards are primed with oil paint after fixing, this difficulty does not arise, but if they have been primed before fixing the nail heads should be touched in with primer before any waterbased material is applied.

NAIL HOLES The cavities in woodwork, etc., where nails have been punched down should be filled with a hard stopping after priming and before any subsequent coats are applied.

NAIL STOCK BRUSH A brush with a binding of leather or strip metal which is secured by nails to a wooden handle.

NAPHTHA A volatile and highly inflammable solvent, water-white in colour and with a disagreeable odour, which is used in the preparation of various kinds of paint products and which is obtained by the distillation of coal-tar, petroleum or shale oil. It is sometimes used in priming paints and stains for woodwork because of its penetrative powers and its fungicidal properties, being especially useful for timber with a high resinous content and for primers to be applied to areas which have been infected with mould and fungoid growths. As a primer, however, its use should be restricted to bare unpainted surfaces, as it exerts a powerful solvent action which dissolves normal paint films and might therefore dissolve any previous coatings. Naphtha is widely used by paint manufacturers and incorporated into anti-fouling paints, certain quick-drying synthetic media and various kinds of bituminous materials.

NAPHTHALINE An aromatic hydrocarbon obtained by the distillation of coal-tar. It is used as a starting material in the production of phthalic anhydride and in the preparation of dyestuff intermediates.

NAPHTHANATE DRIERS Drying agents, widely used in modern paint manufacture, obtained by fusing metallic salts with naphthenic acid.

NAPLES YELLOW A pigment composed of lead and antimony; originally it was found occurring naturally on the slopes of Vesuvius. It is now obsolete; present-day "Naples yellow" is an imitation prepared by tinting zinc oxide with cadmium and ochre.

NATURAL ORDER (OF COLOUR) The order in which colours of maximum purity will occur if arranged in a circle so as to progress from the lightest tone to the darkest, e.g., yellow, orange, red, purple, violet, blue, blue-green, green and back to yellow, yellow being the lightest colour (nearest to white) and violet the darkest (nearest to black). If black is added to the light colours and white to the dark colours so that yellow becomes the darkest colour and violet the lightest, the natural order is reversed and a circle of discords is produced in which each hue is discordant with its neighbouring hue.

NATURAL OXIDES Oxides of iron occurring naturally in many parts of the world and prepared for use as pigments by a simple process of grinding and levigation.

NATURAL RESINS Substances of vegetable origin derived from the exudations of various types of trees, as opposed to synthetic resins produced artificially, which are used in the production of varnishes and paints.

NEAT Unadulterated.

NEEDLE OAK A name sometimes given to the method of imitating oak grain by means of cutting or incising the paint film or the underlying wood with patent tools.

NEGATIVE STENCIL A stencil pattern designed so that the background is cut out and the ornament forms the ties.

NEOPRENE A form of synthetic rubber produced from butyl chloride which may be valcanized with zinc oxide.

NEOPRENE PAINT A paint usually supplied as a two-pack material, based on the synthetic rubber substance known as neoprene (q.v.) and used in situations where a high resistance to weather and chemicals is required. Although generally applied as a multi-coat system, it can be used as a single coating where there is no splash or spillage, provided care is taken to avoid misses. It forms a tough rubbery coating, but is available only in black or grey.

NEUTRAL The state of having no definite or determinate character— hence, for example, "neutral plaster", a gypsum plaster which because it is free from lime and is therefore non-alkaline has no harmful chemical effects upon a superimposed paint, "neutral colour", a colour in which no single hue quality predominates, etc.

NEUTRALIZE To render inoperative or ineffective, to counteract. For example, when a surface has been stripped with a caustic paint stripper the residue of alkaline material which remains may be neutralized by

washing the surface with a weak acid solution such as vinegar; the difficulty, of course, lies in determining at what point true neutrality is
attained and when the substance present in the surface shows a reaction
of neither acidic nor alkaline character, and for this reason the painter's
attempts to neutralize a surface are usually of a loose and non-scientific
character.

NEWEL An upright post, at the top or bottom of a staircase, supporting
the handrail; also applied to the central shaft from which the steps of a
winding stair radiate.

NIBS Small particles of foreign matter such as pieces of paint skin or
coagulated medium, grit, etc., embedded in a paint film and projecting
above the surface so that they feel rough to the touch and mar the appearance of the surface. The term can also be applied to minute specks of
roughness present on a surface which is about to be decorated, e.g., small
specks of grit or mortar, etc., on a plastered wall.

NICHE A recess in a wall hollowed like a shell to hold a statue or ornament.

NIGROSINE A blue-black dyestuff, obtained from aniline hydrochlorates,
used in spirit stains to produce black.

NITRO-CELLULOSE MATERIALS Lacquers, enamels, etc., produced
from nitro-cotton, which is prepared by treating cellulose in the form of
cotton fibre with nitric and sulphuric acids. The other ingredients are the
solvents and diluents used to dissolve the nitro-cotton and maintain it in
solution, the plasticisers added to give flexibility, and various resins which
impart gloss and adhesive properties. See *Cellulose*.

N

NO-FINES CONCRETE A mixture of concrete consisting of coarse
aggregate and cement without the admixture of sand.

NON-BLEEDER GUN A spray gun fitted with an air valve which shuts off
air when the trigger is released, the trigger controlling both air and fluid.
This type of gun is used with compressor units having a pressure controlling device.

NON-REVERSIBLE MATERIAL A material which when dry is not
softened up by the application of further coatings.

NON-YELLOWING PAINTS Paints recently developed with improved
pigments and media to provide a finish which will maintain its whiteness
longer than conventional alkyd resin paints. They are intended for interior
use.

NORMAN The architectural style of the 11th and 12th centuries, also
called English Romanesque.

NOTIFICATION OF DISEASES Under the terms of the Factories Acts of 1937 and 1948 and of the Lead Paint (Protection Against Poisoning) Act, 1926, every medical practitioner attending or called in to visit a patient whom he believes to be suffering from certain diseases, including lead poisoning, is required to notify the case to the Chief Inspector of Factories, the Ministry of Employment.

NOZZLE The opening in the fluid tip of a spray gun. When spraying heavy coarse or fibrous materials a large nozzle size should be used to prevent clogging; viscous materials require small nozzle sizes to facilitate thorough atomization. The nozzle size also varies according to the type of feed, suction feed or pressure feed, which is being used, and is identified by a letter stamped on the collar of the needle and on the outer edge of the fluid tip.

NUMERALS The symbols employed to express a number. The numerals in normal usage in this country are incorrectly described as Arabic numerals but are actually of comparatively recent origin.

NUT OIL Walnut oil.

NYLON A general term for a wide range of recently developed materials which while having no exact counterparts among natural products are similar in chemical composition to proteins. Nylon can be produced in many forms such as powders, sheets, solutions and yarns, the latter being at present of most interest to the painter and decorator. Nylon can be produced in several ways; a common method is to react adipic acid and hexamethylene together under heat to form a polymer which is then extruded to form a continuous filament, the filament then being drawn out or stretched to give the material the properties of a textile fibre. The outstanding properties of the fibre are its very high tensile strength, lightness in weight, elasticity, resilience, resistance to abrasion, low moisture absorption, rssistance to alkalis and oils, and immunity to mould or fungoid growth and insect attack.

NYLON BRUSHES Brushes with a filling composed of nylon filament. Because of the scarcity of hog hair, the possibility of using nylon as an alternative is a matter of great interest especially as none of the other alternative types of filler apart from nylon can be used successfully on their own for ordinary paint brushes.

Nylon brushes offer several definite and distinct advantages over other types of filler. In the first place they are most remarkably hard wearing and resilient; comparative tests have proved that when bristle brushes and nylon brushes are subjected to a similar degree of hard usage for an equal length of time the length of the nylon has only been decreased minimally when the bristle has been completely worn down. In the second place, nylon is considerably cheaper than bristle and the gap in price is constantly widening as bristle becomes more and more scarce. In the third place, nylon is not adversely affected by any known paint solvent, nor is it affected by alkaline materials.

On the other hand, in its present state of development nylon has not yet become a satisfactory filling for a paint brush. When dipped into the paint kettle the brush does not become charged with paint as effectively as bristle, and when charged it does not spread the material efficiently, which means that the painter cannot produce an even level coating; in addition, the rate of application is slowed down. Nor can paint be laid off satisfactorily, and this results in a coarse, ropey finish. Attempts have been made to improve the spreading qualities of the filament by grinding it down to produce an artificial taper, and a further refinement has been to form an artificial flag at the tip of each length of filament; naturally however, when the flag is worn away it cannot be replaced, whereas the flag of a hog hair bristle is constantly renewed throughout the life of the bristle. A further disadvantage is that the springiness of nylon filament leads to far more paint being splashed about than when a bristle brush is used.

There seems little doubt that the attractive qualities of nylon will give rise to further endeavours to improve its performance and it may in due course become an acceptable brush filling. It should be noted, however, that nylon brushes are quite unsuitable for the application of creosote or any material of an acidic nature.

NYLON FABRICS The use of nylon in the manufacture of carpets, rugs, upholstery fabrics, soft furnishings, etc., is of great importance to-day to the interior decorator, although there is no indication of its ousting the more traditional textiles. Nylon does not absorb dyes as readily as wool; consequently, its colouring often appears duller and less rich than that of a woollen material.

NYLON ROPES Strong alkali-resistant ropes; their high degree of stretch makes them capable of absorbing shock loads, but is not a desirable feature in ropes intended for use in suspended scaffolds. See *Synthetic Ropes.*

O

O

OAK A hardwood of the greatest interest and importance to the painter and decorator. The oak is a tree of the genus *Quercus,* which is widely distributed throughout the world; there are some 250 different species, of which the best known and most important commercially are the European oaks, which include English oak, Austrian oak, American oak and Japanese oak. "Australian oak", however, is quite unrelated.

At one time the oak covered large areas of Great Britain, and was an important factor in its economy. Quite apart from its vital role in the development of the nation's sea power, it was the material that the Anglo-Saxon people turned to for domestic building, it was the timber used in the fine roofs, the benches and the stall work that were such important features of medieval churches, it was widely used in Tudor domestic building not only in the main structures but also for panelling, and at least from Norman times up to the Restoration in the 17th century it was the principal wood used for furniture. Although the last period in which extensive planting took place was the Napoleonic wars, it would appear that the long tradition of the use of oak coupled with the beauty and the distinctive grain of its timber have made an indelible impression on the tastes of the British people so that to this day there is a constant demand for oak effects in decorative work, a steady market for wallpapers, relief goods and veneers for the simulation of oak panelling, and a call for the painted and grained imitation of oak which exceeds that of any other type of wood imitation.

The colour of natural oak varies from a rich honey colour to a yellowish brown. The heartwood grain markings, although similar to ash, are far more rugged and varied in shape, and a peculiar feature is that the outer edges of the elliptical curves are sharply spiked and tend to open out into spoon-like shapes at the extremities. Due to the breadth of the medullary rays, oak wood presents a most beautiful silver-grain or flash when cut on the quarter. The wood takes stain well but shows to better advantage if left unstained so that its unrivalled natural colour and grain are not obscured.

Oak graining is generally carried out in oil graining colour, which should afterwards be overgrained in Vandyke to develop the subtle variations of highlight. Much of the commercial graining that is seen is hopelessly crude in colour, due to the fact that the ground colour is too muddy and the stain made too warm in an effort to redeem it. For natural oak a ground colour of white and raw umber alone may be used, for medium oak and pollard oak the white may be tinted with raw umber and golden ochre, for dark oak burnt umber and golden ochre stainers are used and for antique oak the pigments are burnt umber, ochre and black. The stainers used to make the graining colour for each of these types are respectively raw umber, raw umber and raw sienna, burnt umber and raw sienna, and burnt umber and black. The grain markings may be produced by the wipe-out process or by pencilling in with a one-stroke writer. The characteristic pore markings are sometimes added by means of a check roller. An excellent imitation of oak can be produced with patent graining wheels of various kinds which are used to cut or incise the grain markings and pores into the ground colour or into the wood itself prior to staining.

Oak timber is used for various constructional purposes, including door frames, window frames, sills, staircase treads and risers. The painting of these and similar oak surfaces is complicated by three factors: (i) the wood contains a high proportion of tannin which may retard the drying of the primer coat, (ii) the close grain prevents penetration of the primer, thus affecting adhesion, unless the primer is thinned down with 10% of white spirit or turpentine to assist penetration, (iii) the pronounced and open pores cannot be bridged satisfactorily with undercoatings or finishes, the paint tending to recede from the edges of the gaps; this necessitates filling the pores after priming, and a filler composed of paste white lead and gold size or powdered slate and gold size is recommended for the purpose. Gypsum filler does not accommodate itself sufficiently to the movement of the timber.

When oak is used for exterior doors and gates the wood is very often given a preservative treatment of boiled oil so as not to obscure the natural beauty of the grain, the oil being applied copiously and the surplus wiped off after a lapse of some two hours, the work being then rubbed briskly with a soft cloth to produce a slight sheen. It is important that the wood should be thoroughly clean before the treatment is undertaken, and that the finish should be maintained in good condition by periodic re-oiling. For interior work the recently developed catalyst wood finishes give excellent results. It should be noted that wherever iron, in the form of wedges or nails, is in contact with newly cut oak a blue-black stain of the same composition as writing ink rapidly forms, due to the action of the wood's natural tannin upon the metal.

OAK COMBING ROLLER   Alternative term for check roller.

OAK GRAIN FINISHER   A small brass roller with fluted lines running along the drum, mounted on a wooden handle. It is used for finishing the lines made by a check roller by carrying them right into the angle at the edge of a panel.

OAK VARNISH   The term given to ordinary grades of short-oil varnish for interior work, made from less expensive resins than church oak varnish.

OBECHE   A tree found in tropical West Africa producing a soft light timber which is also known as Nigerian whitewood or West African satinwood and which is used in coach building, plywood manufacture and for shelving.

OBLITERATING POWER   Opacity.

OBLITERATION   Obscuring or effacing any previous markings, pattern or colour on a surface.

O

OCHRE   A yellow earth pigment derived from sands and clays found in many parts of the world including Britain, France, Italy, India and America, and consisting of a mixture of silica, alumina and hydrated oxide of iron. Like all earth colours, ochre is a variable pigment, subject to considerable differences in colour, texture, opacity and staining strength from one sample to another. It is one of the oldest pigments known, having been used from the very earliest times. It is prepared by grinding and levigation and produces a rather dull brownish yellow which is stable, permanent and fast to light but which is rather a poor drier.

OFF-WHITE   A term applied to a material which is obviously not a pure white but which is so close to white that it cannot be called by any definite colour name.

OIL   A viscid liquid, greasy or soapy to the touch, which is lighter than water, insoluble in water, soluble in ether and usually soluble in alcohol. The term covers three classes of substance, as follows:
(i) Fatty or fixed oils, of vegetable or animal origin. These can be subdivided into three groups, namely, (a) drying oils, such as linseed oil, tung

oil, poppy seed oil, etc., which when exposed to the air absorb oxygen and undergo a chemical change whereby they become tough leathery solids; (b) non-drying oils, such as castor oil, olive oil, palm oil, tallow, etc., which ferment on exposure; and (c) semi-drying oils such as croton oil, grape seed oil, etc., which are intermediate between the other two.
(ii) Mineral oils, distilled from peat, shale, etc., which are used as illuminants.
(iii) Essential or volatile oils, which are chiefly of vegetable origin and are used in medicine and perfumery.

The oils used as binding agents in the manufacture of paint and varnish, which are clearly of most interest to the painter and decorator, belong to the first class, i.e., the fatty oils, and in particular to the group known as the drying oils, although certain non-drying oils (e.g., castor oil) can be processed in such a way as to develop a structure similar to that of tung oil whereby they can be usefully incorporated into paint media.

OIL ABSORPTION The quantity of oil required to convert a specific quantity of dry pigment to a stiff paste. This factor is of fundamental importance in paints and enamels as it affects such properties as the consistency, opacity, gloss, etc.

OIL-BOUND WATER PAINT A decorative material consisting of a good quality pigment such as lithopone and sometimes also titanium oxide, suitably tinted, which has as its binding agent an emulsion of oil in water or in some cases an emulsified oil varnish. The material is supplied in paste form and is beaten up immediately prior to use; it is thinned with water or, if required for outside use or on very absorbent surfaces, with petrifying liquid, and is applied with a broad distemper brush. The drying and hardening of an oil-bound water paint is a two-fold process; initially it dries by the evaporation of the water content and is firm enough to stand recoating within 24 hours, but this is follwed by the more gradual oxidation of the oil content. Several weeks may elapse before maximum hardness is achieved and when this stage is reached the material is insoluble in water and is to some extent washable.

Oil-bound water paint is a first-class modern product, reasonable in price and available in a wide range of attractive colours. It presents a smooth surface with a pleasing matt finish, and provided the correct preparation is carried out it can be relied upon always to give excellent results. It is a most useful material for the decoration of new buildings for the following reasons:
(i) It has a certain tolerance of damp and allows the surface to breathe thereby permitting a decorative coating to be used on new plaster work without prejudicing the drying out and carbonation of the plaster.
(ii) It is reasonably resistant to alkaline action.
(iii) It provides a firm surface which can be subsequently redecorated with any type of finish without the necessity for stripping the water paint and without risk of failure.

OILCLOTH A fabric coated with white lead ground in oil which is used principally as a covering for floors and tables, but which has also sometimes been hung as a wallcovering.

196

OIL FILLER   See *Japan Filler,* for which this is an alternative term.

OIL GLOSS   A straight linseed oil paint composed of a pigment such as white lead tinted as required with paste or liquid oil stainers, with the addition of driers, and thinned to working consistency with linseed oil and turps, the degree of gloss depending upon the proportion of oil. Boiled oil gives a higher degree of gloss than raw linseed oil but in neither case is the gloss comparable with that of a hard gloss paint. Oil gloss was formerly used very widely for areas such as stucco fronts, fencing and under-eaves, for which a high gloss paint was considered too expensive; its use has now considerably declined. It should be well brushed out to avoid thick coatings; otherwise, it tends to skin over and produce a film which wrinkles and which remains permanently soft.

OIL GOLD SIZE   Oil gold size is a mordant for gilding consisting of a thickened or partially oxidized oil. Formerly it was prepared by exposing linseed oil to the air for long periods in shallow vessels until it became fatty; at this stage it was pigmented with ochre, driers were added and it was then thinned down with boiled oil or varnish. Modern ready made oil gold size is prepared from stand oil and is supplied pigmented ready for use. It is available in varying drying speeds; as a general rule the slower its speed of drying, the more lustrous the finished gold will appear. It is used in the gilding of carved or modelled work, for gilding large wooden or metal letters and for large areas where a solid gold background is required for lettering or decoration. It must be applied over a surface which has been adequately sealed to render it non-absorbent and must be well brushed out because of its tendency to creep and develop ridges and fat edges. After application it must be protected from any possible settling of dust until such time as it is tacky enough to gild. It is not suitable for sign work or decorative work where sharply defined shapes are to be produced, nor for areas where it would be exposed during the drying period to the effects of the weather. It possesses the great advantage of holding its tack for a considerable period, thereby making it easy to apply the gold evenly. It should not be used as the mordant for metals other than gold leaf or for bronze powders because of the discolouration which takes place due to the oxidation of the oil.

O

OIL LENGTH   The ratio of oil to resin in a varnish medium.

OIL PAINT   A paint in which the binder consists of a drying oil or an oil varnish and which dries by the oxidation or polymerization of the binder, as opposed to water paints in which the binder is an emulsified oil dispersed in water and which dry initially by evaporation, distempers which are bound with such materials as casein or glue size and which dry by the evaporation of the water content, emulsion paints which are bound by the coalescence of synthetic resin particles, etc.

OIL VARNISH   A varnish composed of drying oil and resin, together with driers and thinners, as opposed to a spirit varnish or a water varnish.

OILING IN A process carried out after a surface has been filled and levelled; the substance used is actually a half-and-half mixture of varnish and turps, not oil. When the filling has been completed satisfactorily, thoroughly rubbed down and is quite dry, a thin coat of varnish and turps is applied and allowed to dry. The object is to seal the porosity of the filler. Failure to oil in results in ropey brushwork due to the uneven absorption of the subsequent coats of paint, thereby destroying the whole object of the filling process. It is not generally realized that work which has been properly filled and oiled in requires no further rubbing down, thus ensuring a saving of time.

OILING OF WOODWORK A treatment whereby hardwoods such as oak, teak, etc., are coated with oil as a preservative. The wood should be dry and should be well cleaned down before treatment. Boiled linseed oil is applied copiously and after two hours the surplus oil is wiped off. A further oiling is carried out after 48 hours, and thereafter at weekly intervals for five or six weeks. The final application should be followed by a brisk rub down with a soft cloth in order to produce a sheen. Periodically the work should be cleaned down and re-oiled to maintain it in good condition. The first coating of oil should be thinned with some 15 per cent of white spirit or turpentine or some 10 per cent of naphtha in order to ensure its penetrating the wood. The subsequent coats should be of neat oil

OITICICA OIL An oil obtained from the nuts of a tree found in Northern Brazil; of the various oils which have been used or suggested as an alternative to tung oil, oiticica oil is the one approximating most closely to tung oil in its properties. It possesses the same properties of webbing, frosting and wrinkling; on heating it polymerizes in a similar manner but takes longer to gel; and varnishes made from it are not quite so durable or resistant to water as those made from tung oil.

OLD OIL GOLD SIZE The same material as oil gold size; the terms are interchangeable.

OLEO-RESIN Some confusion exists about this term, which is not always used with a clear understanding as to its meaning and which is apt to be interpreted in several differing ways. Strictly speaking, an oleo-resin is a natural mixture of a volatile or essential oil and resin; it is derived from the exudations of various types of trees and is semi-fluid in form, solidifying on exposure to air but remaining soft and plastic. In some cases, oleo-resins are used as plasticisers to prevent spirit varnishes from becoming too brittle; this is so in the case of Elemi, which is found principally in the Philippines, and Capaiba, found in South America. An oleo-resin called Gum Thus, which exudes from American pine trees, is used to a small extent in varnishes but is essentially the same resin from which turpentine and rosin are produced. Canada balsam, Venice turpentine, Strasbourg turpentine and Bordeaux turpentine or Gallipot are similar oleo-resins derived from conifers in Canada, the Tyrol, the Vosges region and Southern Europe respectively.

A tendency is growing for the term oleo-resin to be used to describe any varnish composed of a fusion of vegetable drying oils and natural or synthetic resins. This probably arises from the fact that the word oleo is derived from the Latin word *oleum* meaning oil, and this particular usage has become sufficiently widespread to be included in at least two standard works of reference.

OMBRE EFFECTS   Blended colour effects produced by the use of tinted glaze medium.

ONE-COAT PAINTS   A type of finish offered by various paint manu-facturers to appeal to the customer who is anxious to eliminate labour costs and obtain as economical a job as possible. Such paints are formu-lated with high-opacity pigments, and in some cases are thixotropic. Their success depends largely upon the condition of the existing finish; clearly they are most likely to be satisfactory where the existing surface is free from defects. Under these circumstances many established finishes would be equally successful in obliterating in one coat although possibly their use would demand a higher level of application skill than the one-coat finish. Where the existing finish is damaged or in poor condition, some form of pre-treatment is required and the one-coat finish offers no particular advantage. On new surfaces a primer is required together with a sufficient degree of undercoating to provide enough "build" for the finish. Even where conditions are suitable for the material it must be realized that because a single coat is thinner than a full paint system it provides less protection.

ONE-STROKE   (Also called one-stroke brush or one-stroke writer.)
A sable hair brush set in a metal ferrule; the "length out" of the hair is shorter than that of the normal signwriting brush, and the width is usually greater; the ferrule is splayed out and flattened so that the brush itself is flat in shape and is chisel edged. One-strokes are available in several widths and are designed to produce work with short rapid strokes; they are extremely useful for ticket writing and poster work.

O

ONYX   A variety of quartz with variously coloured layers, formerly a very popular subject for marbling.

OPACITY   The obliterating power or "hiding power" of a paint, i.e., its ability to obscure the colour of the underlying surface. The opacity of a paint depends upon the nature of the pigment (for example, titanium has much greater opacity than any other commercial white pigment) and upon the amount of pigment used in relation to the medium.

OPAQUE   The opposite of transparent; impenetrable to the sight.

OPTICAL MIXTURE   To the painter and decorator dealing with pigmentary colours, this term describes the effect produced when small intermingled though separate specks of colour are viewed from a distance. Thus, if a surface were painted yellow and then spattered with blue, at a certain distance the separate primary colours would no longer be distinguishable and the effect would be that of a vibrant bright green. Optical colour mixtures are usually more brilliant than the plain allover coatings produced by a mechanical mixture of the same colours.

OR The heraldic term for gold.

ORANGE CHROME An orange pigment made by treating normal lead chromate with caustic soda or quicklime.

ORANGE LEAD Also known as orange mineral. A pigment similar to red lead but paler in colour. It is manufactured by oxidizing white lead, whereas red lead is made by oxidizing a material called massicot, which is the yellow monoxide of lead.

ORANGE PEELING A fault in a spray applied paint film, taking the form of an uneven surface which resembles the outside of the skin of an orange. There are several possible causes of the fault and they are all generally bound up with incorrect methods of application. Incorrect thinning of the paint, or using paint in so viscous a condition that when it strikes the surface it will coalesce but cannot flow out, will lead to orange peeling; so also will using too low an air pressure so that the paint is not properly atomized and cannot flow out after application. Holding the gun too far from the work and using too high an air pressure, especially when spraying lacquer, is another cause, due to the solvent evaporating before the material has had time to flow out; if, on the other hand, the gun is held too close to the work, the solvent is dried out too rapidly because of the action of the compressed air striking the surface. Careless working resulting in overspray or in overloading a surface which is setting up is a further cause of orange peeling.

ORANGE SHELLAC The best quality of shellac.

ORBITAL SANDER A sanding machine for the rubbing down of flat surfaces; the rubbing face consists of a felt covered platform measuring about 175mm by 75mm, to which a waterproof abrasive paper is clipped; when in action, the platform moves with a circular motion similar to the movement of the hand in manual rubbing down.

ORDERS A system of parts, ornaments and proportions of columns distinguishing the various styles of architecture, especially the Doric, Ionic, Corinthian, Tuscan and Composite styles of classical architecture.

ORGANIC COLOURS Pigments consisting essentially of carbon compounds; they are produced by precipitating organic dyestuffs or by coupling organic intermediates.

ORIEL WINDOW A window projecting from an upper storey and supported by a bracket or corbelling. Commonly used in late Gothic civil architecture.

ORIENTAL LACQUER   A thick milky emulsion obtained from the sap of the *Rhus vernicifera,* a tree which is native to China. The emulsion is heated to purify it and forms a natural lacquer which will dry readily in darkness provided the atmosphere is cool and damp, but which remains tacky indefinitely if exposed to light and warmth. See *Lacquer.*

OSTWALD THEORY   The theory of colour and light as related to the craft of a painter, explained in a book entitled "Letters to a Young Painter on the Theory and Practice of Painting" by a German scientist, Wilhelm Ostward, who lived from 1853—1932. An English translation of the book appeared in 1907. Ostwald attempted to establish absolute values for artists' pigments. The Ostwald colour circle is based upon eight basic hues, namely yellow, orange, red, purple, blue, turquoise, sea green and leaf green.

OUTRIGGER   The horizontal or almost horizontal tubes projecting outwards from the face of a building, to which are attached the pulley blocks from which a cradle is suspended.

OVAL BRUSH   See *Varnish Brush.*

OVERGRAINER   A brush used in graining for the purpose of producing a series of parallel lines, in thin glaze colour, either in oil or water media. It is a thin long-haired brush with a filling of hog hair set in a metal ferrule; very often the ferrule is packed with wood or with cork composition. The width may vary; the usual widths are 38mm and 63mm. The overgrainer is charged with colour and is then passed through an ordinary hair comb in order to break it up into separate strands. In addition to the normal type of overgrainer there are variations known as pencil overgrainers and fantail overgrainers which are especially useful for certain types of wood grain.

O

OVERGRAINING   A process carried out with thin glaze over the top of figure graining in order to simulate the subtle light and shade effects seen in natural wood. It is usually carried out in a water medium such as Vandyke brown but oil medium may also be employed. Though often omitted on the grounds of economy, it is very necessary if an accurate representation of true wood grain is desired, for it is impossible to convey a really natural effect in one single figuring operation.

OVERSPRAY   A term used in spray painting to mean paint which travels beyond the confines of the area which is to be painted. Excessive over-spray leads to uneconomical working through loss of paint, and overspray falling on a previously painted surface is a frequent cause of orange peeling.

OVOLO   A convex moulding much used in Classic and Renaissance archi-tecture, often carved with the egg and dart or egg and tongue.

OX HAIR   Hair obtained from the ears of oxen, used as the filler for various kinds of artists' brushes and fine brushes used for lettering, lacquering, etc.

OX HAIR BLENDER   A flat chisel-ended brush set in a metal ferrule at the end of a very long slender handle. The hair is only short and the brush itself quite a small one. It is used for blending light and dark colours in the production of shaded effects in lettering.

OXALIC ACID   A sour highly poisonous acid derived from vegetable matter which is often used for bleaching out natural woods such as oak, although it is not as useful or effective as the proprietary bleaches which are available.

OXFORD OCHRE   A soft transparent ochre with a peculiar brownish-yellow tone found in pockets in the ironstone deposits which occur over a large part of Oxfordshire. The supply is now practically exhausted.

OXIDATION   A chemical process whereby substances take up or combine with oxygen. Of importance to the painter in connection with the oxidation of metals, etc., when exposed to the air, the oxidation of vegetable drying oils, and so on.

OXIDES   Compounds formed by the union of chemical elements with oxygen.

OXY-ACETYLENE EQUIPMENT   Equipment involving the use of a mixture of oxygen and acetylene to produce an intensely hot flame, such as, for example, flame-cleaning equipment.

OZONE   A condensed form of oxygen containing 3 atoms to the molecule, whereas the oxygen molecule only contains 2 atoms. It is present in very small quantities in the lower atmosphere, its occurrence being probably due to electrical action and particularly to the electrolysis of water; its presence is supposed to explain the bracing effect of sea air. Ozone is a powerful oxidizer attacking and destroying organic matter, bleaching vegetable colouring matter and attacking most metals. It has a pronounced effect upon paints applied in coastal districts or exposed to marine atmospheres, causing the initial drying to take place at a rapid rate but also accelerating the whole process of oxidation and thereby hastening the ultimate break-down of the film through chalking and perishing.

P

PAINT   A substance consisting of finely powdered insoluble materials, chiefly pigments, suspended in a liquid binding medium, which is applied in liquid form and which when exposed to air or under the influence of heat has the power of changing to a dry adherent film.

PAINT AGITATOR   A device fitted to a pressure feed tank in a spray painting outfit as a means of stirring up the paint in the tank. The agitator may be connected to a manually operated handle which the operator turns when stirring is required, or it may be mechanically operated.

PAINT CAN or PAINT KETTLE   The container in which paint is placed ready for brush application. A wide range of sizes and shapes is available. Some paint cans are straight sided; others are tapered, which makes for easy stacking and storage. The smaller types of can are to be preferred for good quality finishes such as enamel; the larger types are more favoured by the industrial painting contractor. The desirable features of a paint can are that it should be treated to prevent rusting, that it should have a fairly sharp lip to facilitate the removal of surplus paint from the brush, that it should be robust enough to withstand repeated burning out and cleaning and that it should have a lip shaped to prevent paint running down the outside face.

PAINT COLOURS FOR BUILDING PURPOSES A British Standard with this title was introduced in 1973 and issued under the number B.S.4800. It consists of a range of 88 colours, including black and white, and supersedes the previous B.S.2660 range of 101 colours.

PAINT HARLING A process used for the protection of the exterior steelwork of steel-clad houses, which has been employed more extensively in Scotland than elsewhere. The process is carried out in four stages, as follows:
(i) The surface is carefully prepared and cleaned, and all loose bolts, rivets, etc., made good.
(ii) A rust inhibitive priming coat is applied and allowed to dry hard.
(iii) A thick coat of paint composed of paste white lead, stand oil and gold size, pigmented to the desired colour, is applied and allowed to become tacky.
(iv) Paint-coated granite chips are thrown on to the tacky surface by hand, and the whole surface then allowed to dry hard. The granite chips are coated with paint in a concrete mixer some eight hours before they are to be used.
   Paint harling produces an extremely durable finish even when used in very exposed conditions. For the best results the work should be carried out by men trained in this operation and the process should be carefully organized and supervised. When the surface becomes dingy due to accumulated soot and grime, it can be washed down to remove the dirt and a coat of paint applied by spray. If the harling itself is damaged the affected area is cleaned down to the bare steel and a further application of primer, thick paint and granite chips applied to match up to the surrounding area.

P

PAINT PUMP A fluid pump driven by compressed air and used to convey paint to the spray gun directly from the large drums in which the paint is delivered to the site. It is a useful time-saving device on large-scale painting contracts.

PAINT REMOVER A liquid which is applied to a painted surface in order to soften the old paint and bring it to such a condition that it can be stripped off. It may take the form of a caustic paint remover, which is an alkaline material acting by saponifying the binder medium in the old paint film, or a spirit paint remover, which consists of a solvent material powerful enough to dissolve the old coating. Spirit paint remover is the

more expensive of the two but in nearly every case it is a far more satisfactory stripper to use. Paint remover is employed where burning off would
be an unsuitable method of stripping, such as on surfaces like plaster or
metal which are good conductors of heat, or on delicately carved or
moulded work, on narrow glazing bars in close proximity to glass, on woodwork which is to be restored to its natural condition and where scorch
marks would be disastrous, and in localities where inflammable materials
are stored.

PAINT SHAKING MACHINE or PAINT REJUVENATOR A machine into
which tins of ready mixed paint which have been kept in stock for a considerable time may be clamped and subjected to a vigorous agitation, thus
restoring the contents to their original condition without a lengthy period
of manual stirring.

PAINT TESTING All paint materials are subjected to vigorous testing by
the manufacturers to ensure the maintenance of the quality of existing
lines and to develop new products with improved properties. Tests are
carried out under actual normal working conditions approximating as
closely as possible to the conditions which pertain on the site; in addition,
a number of techniques have been evolved for testing some specific aspect
of a paint's performance and for providing a reasonably reliable assessment
of its properties without a great deal of delay. The following are some of
the tests in common use.

Durability. The durability of a paint is tested on small panels placed on
exposure racks in various parts of the country and subjected to the effects
of the sun, rain, frost, etc. Because of the length of time required to gain
information by this method, use is also made of accelerated weathering
tests in which the panels are placed in a rotating drum and exposed to a
constant succession of ultra-violet irradiation from a carbon arc and saturation with a water spray in order to simulate rapidly the conditions leading
to breakdown.

Viscosity. This is tested by means of the flow cup in which the rate of
flow through a standard sized hole is measured, or by a torsion viscometer
or paddle viscometer in which a cylinder on wire or a paddle is immersed
in the material, rotated, released and the amount of overswing measured,
or by a falling ball viscometer in which the passage of a metal ball through
the material is timed.

Opacity. The hiding power of a paint is tested on cards or boards divided
into chequered or striped patterns in black and white, or by the use of
opacity meters or by means of a device whereby a tapering space between
two glass plates is filled with paint and the point at which the material
ceases to be transparent is noted.

Colour. Comparisons of colour are made with the human eye, which is
more sensitive than instruments, although for some purposes use is also
made of colourmeters or spectrophotometers.

Drying time. This is tested by sprinkling a painted surface with sand and
noting at what point the sand can be dusted off without injury to the surface. Use is also made of a device known as a mechanical thumb which
simulates the twisting action of the human thumb pressed down on to a

painted surface. The drying time may also be ascertained by a form of scratch test in which a pointed needle is drawn through a paint film alongside a graduated scale and the point at which the film ceases to flow together is noted.

Hardness. This is tested by a form of scratch test in which weights of increasing value are placed on a needle travelling across the paint film until scoring takes place; another instrument for the purpose is a hardness rocker, which consists of two hoops, a pendulum and a calibrated scale, the number of pendulum swings being governed by the tackiness or otherwise of the surface; the mechanical thumb is also used.

Adhesion and elasticity. These are measured by means of the bend test in which a strip of painted metal is bent around a hinge, or by a drop test in which weights are dropped on to a painted panel. A simple test is to score the surface with a knife or coin.

Water resistance. Tests are used to note how much water is absorbed by a paint film and also to what extent the paint allows the passage of moisture.

Further tests are listed in B.S. 3900.

PAINTER'S COLIC   A disease contracted by the absorption of lead into the system over a long period. See *Lead Poisoning*.

PAINTING CONDITIONS   The outside factors prevailing at the time that paint is applied and which might be expected to have a bearing on the life of the paint film, e.g., the atmospheric conditions such as rain, frost, or dew on exterior work, or the condensation of moisture or the presence of large quantities of dust in the atmosphere on indoor work.

PAINTING MITTENS   These have been developed to facilitate the painting of metal railings, pipes, etc. They consists of lambswool mittens with a polythene lining, which the operative wears like a glove; by rubbing his mittened hand backwards and forwards over the surface the operative is able to spread the paint. While this is probably the most primitive form of paint application ever invented, it must be admitted that painting railings by brush application is not a pleasant occupation and leads to the clothing and skin being spattered with paint splashes; the use of mittens results in less splashing.

PALE   Weak in colour.

PALETTE   (i) a flat board, generally with a thumb piece, used by artists as a tablet on which to mix colours.
(ii) The range of pigments used to carry out a piece of decorative work; for example, we say; "In painting this mural the decorator restricted himself to a palette of lemon chrome, ultramarine blue and Indian red" or "To imitate this marble we use a palette of raw sienna, burnt sienna and indigo blue", etc.

PALETTE BOARD   A plain piece of board used by the decorator as a substitute for an artist's palette on which to place small quantities of colour and to carry out colour mixing.

PALETTE KNIFE　A knife with a very flexible blade, used for mixing or matching small quantities of colour. Many sizes are available. The decorator usually employs a palette knife with a blade of between 100mm and 300mm in length, with its two edges parallel, and terminating in a semicircular end. The artist generally employs a shorter and smaller type of palette knife with the edges tapering and terminating in a sharply rounded end.

PALIMPSEST　A manuscript on a previously used parchment or other material from which the original writing was erased to make room for the new script. The term is also now applied to illuminated manuscripts and monumental brasses which are turned over and used on the reverse side. In recent years the term has been used even more loosely to describe any example of a surface or ground which has been re-used, and in this sense it can be applied to a decorative painting carried out on the reverse side of a canvas or painted panel.

PANEL　A distinct compartment raised above or sunk below the level of a wall, ceiling or door surface. The term is also loosely applied to an isolated piece of ornament or an isolated and free-standing piece of rigid material such as hardboard or wood upon which a sample of some decorative effect can be executed for demonstration purposes.

PANELLING EFFECTS　The treatment of flat surfaces such as walls or ceilings in order to give the impression of panelling. The term includes the hanging of relief materials to imitate the appearance of actual wood panelling, the hanging of wallpaper in such a way as to form compartments of one pattern surrounded by a stiling of a different pattern, the application of plastic paint so that compartments of one type of texture are surrounded by a stiling of a different texture, the division of a wall into panels of texture or pattern separated from one another by real or imitation wooden stiles and rails, etc.

PANTOGRAPH　A device used for making exact copies of a drawing on a larger or smaller scale.

PAPER　A thin flexible substance made up of the interlaced fibres of rags, straw, wood, etc.

PAPERHANGING　The technique of applying wallpapers to areas such as walls, ceilings, etc.; the term also includes the hanging of relief materials, real and imitation wood veneers, fabrics such as silk, tapestry, canvases, grasscloths, etc., and coated fabrics such as American cloth, rexine and PVC fabrics.

PAPERHANGING BRUSH　Also termed "papering brush", "putting on brush", "sweep", "laying on brush", "smoothing brush", and "paperhanger" A brush used in the application of wallpaper for the purpose of laying on and smoothing the paper down into its correct position. It is usually, although not always, a wire drawn brush; that is to say, the separate tufts of bristles are set into individual holes in the wooden handle and secured on the reverse side of the base piece with wire binding. The handle is shaped to fit the hand comfortably and snugly and is usually about 250mm in length and 63mm in depth. The "length out" of the bristles is normally between 63mm and 75mm.

The bristles are set in rows and the brush graded accordingly; a one-row or two-row brush is usually suitable for light and delicate papers, a three-row or four-row brush suitable for papers of average weight and consistency, while brushes with more than four rows of bristles are generally suitable for very heavy papers and relief materials. This, however, is not an invariable rule. Very fine brushes intended for delicate papers are sometimes made with three, four or five rows of bristle, but the tufts are very small and are so closely packed that there are as many as thirty-five in a row; on the other hand, a single-row brush made with very big strong tufts and only about eight tufts to the row is sometimes sold for heavy papers.

A conscientious paperhanger intent upon the quality of his work would never restrict himself to using only one papering brush, but would wish to carry two or three of different types, selecting them carefully so as to equip himself to deal with any kind of paper from the most delicate to the heaviest and coarsest.

PARAFFIN   A colourless, tasteless, odourless, solid fatty substance produced from the dry distillation of coal, shale, lignite, peat, etc. In Great Britain the word is applied quite inaccurately to a substance properly called kerosene, which is an oil distilled from petroleum, coal or bituminous shale.

PARAFFIN BLOWLAMP   A blowlamp constructed for use with kerosene. The fuel is drawn up a brass tube from inside the body of the lamp, the tube being curved round in a U-shape around the nozzle. Kerosene does not vaporize as readily as petrol; an essential feature of a paraffin lamp is therefore a pump which is used to build up the pressure when lighting and maintain pressure during operation. The running costs of a paraffin lamp are very low, being about half those of a petrol lamp, and the lamp is more satisfactory than a petrol lamp in windy weather. On the other hand, the nipple tends to clog up very easily with a carbon deposit, and a paraffin lamp needs more time spending on its maintenance than a petrol lamp, which helps to outweigh the difference in cost between the two fuels. Nevertheless, it must be said that when properly maintained a paraffin lamp gives an excellent flame. A poorly maintained lamp does not burn the fuel completely and tends to deposit a light smearing of greasy matter on the surface which is being stripped; it is therefore essential that the surface should be thoroughly rubbed down before priming, preferably by a wet process.

PARAFFIN WAX   A white translucent material obtained by the fractional distillation of petroleum; it is crystalline in structure, resistant to both acids and alkalis, is soluble in mineral oils and is slightly soluble in turpentine, crystallizing out on standing. It is used in the manufacture of flat varnishes and also as a stiffener in spirit paint removers.

PARAPET A low or breast-high wall or fence provided as a protection on balconies, bridges, terraces and flat roofs. A parapet is an essential feature in the erection of outriggers for the suspension of a cradle from a flat roof; if no parapet exists, a dummy parapet must be provided in order to cant the outriggers.

PARCHMENT The skin of calves, sheep, goats, etc., prepared for painting and manuscript writing.

PARCHMENT SIZE A clear weak size made by boiling scraps of parchment and straining the resultant liquid. It is sometimes used by the decorator to even up the lustre of a gilded surface and protect the surface from the accumulation of dirt. The size is applied with a soft squirrel hair mop. When it becomes soiled it can be washed off, taking the deposit of dirt with it, and a fresh coating of size laid on.

PARGETTING The covering of the exterior of a building (including the timbers) with a tough lime plaster mixed with ox-hair; sometimes it is decorated in moulded or combed patterns.

PARIAN CEMENT A hard burnt plaster of the anhydrous group, similar to Keene's cement and subject to the same painting techniques.

PARIS WHITE The finest grade of ordinary whiting, used as an extender in some cheap kinds of oil paint.

PARTI-COLOURED Partly of one colour, partly of another; variegated.

PASTE An adhesive substance. Pastes for paperhanging include flour paste, hot and cold water paste powders, cellulose, starch and dextrine. In recent years a very large range of adhesives has been developed for use with modern decorative materials; they are based upon synthetic rubber, acrylic, PVA, etc., and are carefully formulated for specific purposes; some are air-drying and others set on contact.

PASTEBOARD A hinged and folding board, usually supported on a trestle, employed by the paperhanger as a surface upon which to lay wallpaper during the operations of shading, cutting up, pasting and folding. The standard length of a pasteboard is 1·83 metres. There is no standard width. Most pasteboards are far too narrow to permit clean and careful working. For best results a pasteboard when opened should give a width of at least 610mm but quite a number of patterns are on sale which fall to as low as 530mm wide.

PASTE COLOURS The name given to the range of the commoner pigments such as ochre, Venetian red, burnt umber, etc., when ground in oil and supplied to the decorator in the form of a stiff paste for use in hand mixed paints.

PASTE DRIERS or PATENT DRIERS Drying agents mixed with extenders such as barytes, China clay, whiting, etc., and ground to a stiff paste with boiled linseed oil for use in hand mixed paints. They are generally quite safe in use as they are mild enough to be added to paint without the risk of causing cracking, although if used in excess they may lead to chalking. They are perfectly satisfactory when used with light colours but when added to dark colours or to semi-transparent pigments they tend to produce a muddy effect.

PASTE FILLER A filling composition mixed thickly enough to be applied by knife.

PASTE POWDERS Proprietary materials consisting of flour paste prepared as a powder which keeps indefinitely; they are chemically neutral and will not stain or discolour wallpaper. Hot water paste powders are mixed in a similar manner to ordinary flour paste, being beaten to a batter with lukewarm water and then scalded with boiling water; the precise details of mixing vary according to the particular brand. The paste should be left until cool before use. Cold water paste powders are useful where a supply of hot water is not readily available or when a supply of paste is urgently needed for immediate use. They are generally made by sprinkling the powder into a quantity of cold water, stirring all the time, and are ready for use within twenty minutes of mixing.

PASTEL COLOURS Colours in which the purity is reduced by the addition of grey.

PATCH PAINTING or PATCH PRIMING The touching in or priming of localized areas in order to bring them forward to a state corresponding more closely to the surrounding areas. It may happen, for example, that in preparing a piece of woodwork such as a window frame it may be necessary to burn off the sill while the remainder of the work only requires rubbing down; in this case the sill will be patch primed to compensate for the loss of film thickness compared with the adjacent work. Similarly, if painted plaster work is being prepared for repainting and any patches are laid bare, or if a local area has been made good or replastered such as, for example, round a newly fitted fireplace, the rubbing down is completed and the work allowed to dry out, after which the bare patch is primed to stop porosity before any coating is applied to the whole wall.

P

PATCHING UP Making good defects in a structure such as holes in plaster work, etc., or repairing a damaged area of decorative work in such a way as to make it correspond with the surrounding areas.

PATENT DRIERS See "Paste Driers".

PATENT KNOTTING A solution of shellac in methylated spirit used to seal the resinous content of knots. (See "Knotting".)

PATINA The gloss produced by age or by continuous hand polishing on woodwork.

PATTERN COMBING   The manipulation of wet tinted glaze with steel graining combs in order to produce a free-hand pattern by exposing the ground colour.

PATTERN ROLLER   A fairly wide roller the drum of which consists of a cylinder of rubber, cork or wood which is cut away in parts so as to form a pattern raised above the surrounding areas. The roller is charged with colour from a shallow tray, the surplus paint removed, and the roller then passed in a vertical or horizontal line across a previously painted surface. Some care is needed to produce an even and regular application of paint, but provided the choice of colours is suitable a pleasing result can be obtained, the main objection being the repetitive effect of numerous lines of pattern.

PATTERN STAINING   A disfigurement which occurs principally on ceilings and which takes the form of some localized areas becoming much darker than the remainder of the surface. It is commonly seen on plaster ceilings where the shape and pattern of the underlying joists and lathing is clearly revealed; it is also seen on ceilings constructed with building boards even when the surface has been skimmed with plaster, the position of the nails used in fixing the boards being indicated by local darkening.

Pattern staining is due to the deposit of smoke and dust particles on the surface and this is caused by the difference in thermal conductivity between the plaster or building board and the wood or metal of which the joists, laths or nails are composed. The trouble usually occurs on ceilings above which there is another room which is normally at a lower temperature or above which there is a roof loft or open space. It is commonly supposed that the disfigurement is caused by the passage of air through the plaster, but this is not so; the actual cause is that the air on the upper side of the ceiling seeks to become equal in temperature to the air in the room below, and, when the warm air of the room strikes the ceiling, heat is transferred from one side to the other. But plaster is a better conductor of heat than wood; where wooden laths and joists exist, therefore, the passage of the heat is obstructed, but in the spaces between the laths the passage is clear. More heat can therefore pass through the spaces and consequently more dirt is attracted to these parts. In cases where the underlying structure is of metal, however, or where expanded metal lathing has been used, it is the areas backed by the metal that are the better conductors of heat, and it is to these areas that most of the dirt will be attracted. In the same way, the metal nails securing building boards are apparent because they provide an easier path for the passage of heat than do the surrounding areas.

The only real cure for the trouble would be to equalize the temperature on both sides of the ceiling, which is usually impracticable. To some extent the trouble can be alleviated by insulating the spaces between the joists above the ceiling with some material such as slag wool or vermiculite, or by lining the face of the ceiling with a building board of low thermal conductivity. Surface treatments such as could be applied by the decorator do not provide a thick enough coating to be effective; to a very limited extent, however, a textured surface, such as a coating of plastic paint or a heavy relief paper, will break up the surface sufficiently to make the regularity of the pattern staining less obvious.

PATTRESS A colloquial term for the wooden base of a gas or electric light fitting or an electric light switch.

PEELING A fault which is similar in all respect to flaking and is caused by the same factors, namely inadequate preparation or the use of unsuitable material. (See "Flaking".)
Peeling of wallpaper, in the sense that the edges of the paper become loose and begin to curl away from the underlying surface, may be due to careless pasting as a result of which the edges are starved of paste, or may be caused by inadequate preparation whereby the surface to which the paper is allied bears a deposit of loose dry powdery material (e.g., incompletely washed off distemper).

PENCIL A term which is often used rather loosely; decorators very often apply the term to any kind of signwriting brush, and some people go so far as to describe any small form of artists' brush as a pencil. It is more accurate to reserve the term "pencil" for a signwriting brush of the long-haired variety terminating in a point, as opposed to a "writer", which is chisel edged. The best type of pencil is made from red sable, although ox hair pencils are made for use on rough surfaces. The sable may be set in quill or in a metal ferrule.
To avoid any possible confusion between the signwriting brush and the familiar instrument used for drawing, a good habit to cultivate is that of always referring to a black lead pencil by its full name.

PENCIL OVERGRAINER An overgrainer consisting of a series of small pointed brushes similar to writing pencils set in a row along a metal bound wooden stock. Several sizes are available in varying widths. The best kind has pencils of sable hair, but this makes an expensive brush. The pencils should be spaced irregularly so as to give variation of width between the lines. Pencil overgrainers are excellent for the imitation of many woods, being particularly useful for American walnut.

P

PENTIMENTO A term for what occurs when coatings of oil paint become more translucent with the passage of time due to a change in the refractive index of the medium. The process is a very gradual one.

PERILLA OIL A very useful drying oil obtained from Manchuria and the East Indies; it is superior to linseed oil both in drying rate and polymerization rate.

PERISHING The breakdown of a paint film through age, resulting in loss of flexibility, adhesion and cohesion and revealed by the development of such conditions as chalking, cracking, flaking, etc.

PERMANENT Fadeless, fast to light; a term used in describing pigments.

PERMANENT GREEN A mixture of viridian, which is a hydrated oxide of chromium, with cadmium yellow or zinc chrome.

PERMANGANATE OF POTASH Used by the French polisher to make a water stain for wood; a very weak solution is used to give oak colour and a slightly stronger solution mixed with a little ammonia to give walnut.

PERMEABLE Penetrable; allowing the passage of fluids; e.g., water paints and PVA emulsions are said to possess a certain degree of tolerance for damp because if used on a plaster surface which is not completely dry the moisture can pass through the film and escape without forcing the film away from the surface, a property which is due to the permeability of the film.

PERPENDICULAR The phase of English Gothic architecture prevalent during the 15th and 16th centuries.

PERSPECTIVE DRAWING The representation of solid objects as the eye actually sees them, i.e., with receding parallel lines converging to a point on the horizon or eye level, so that distant objects appear smaller than objects of the same size closer to the viewer. Perspective drawings are widely used by interior designers and decorators in order to convey to a prospective client an impression of the actual appearance of a finished scheme.

PETRIFYING LIQUID A thin emulsion which is used instead of water when thinning down an oil-bound water paint for exterior use or for use on a very hot, absorbent surface. It is usually composed of the same materials as those used in binding the water paint; the effect of its use is therefore to increase the binder content of the paint.

The nature and properties of petrifying liquid and the correct method of its use are very often completely misunderstood. A great number of painters confuse petrifying liquid with primer and imagine that the two materials are interchangeable; in particular, when a specification calls for an application of primer, followed perhaps by two coats of water paint, petrifying liquid is very often used quite wrongly for the purpose. It should be clearly understood that petrifying liquid used alone is not capable of sealing absorption or binding down any loose particles or flaking material on a surface. Another common fault concerns the treatment of new plaster surfaces which may not be completely dry; petrifying liquid should not be used as the thinner for water paints on these surfaces as it reduces the permeability of the paint. Its use on outdoor work, however, is essential if an early breakdown is to be avoided. It should also be used when a water paint is to be employed in the form of a glaze on broken colour work, as over-thinning with water reduces the paint to an underbound and potentially powdery condition.

PETROL A fuel used for internal combustion engines and as a heating fuel, obtained by refining natural petroleum. Its chief use to the painter as distinct from its normal use in motor vehicles is as a fuel for blowlamps and for the operation of spray plant.

PETROL BLOWLAMP A lamp designed to use petrol as its fuel; a cotton wick inside the lamp draws the petrol up a brass tube to the nozzle which, being hot, causes the fuel to vaporize. When the lamp is warm, pressure is maintained automatically, and there is therefore no necessity for a pump; some patterns of petrol lamp are, however, fitted with a pump, which is used to increase the pressure when the lamp is first being lighted.

Although petrol is more expensive than kerosene, and the running costs of a petrol lamp therefore higher, a petrol lamp is cleaner in operation and requires less time to be spent in stripping it down and cleaning for maintenance purposes. It tends to lose its pressure in windy weather; this can be prevented to some extent by the use of an asbestos-lined metal wind-shield which, however, adds to the weight of the lamp.

PETROLEUM A natural oil composed of hydrocarbons occurring at several places in the earth's crust, and from which are derived lubricants, fuels for heating, lighting and power, and a wide range of chemical products such as solvents, plastics, synthetic rubber, synthetic fibres, dye-stuffs and pigments.

PETROLEUM (CONSOLIDATION) ACT, 1928 Under the terms of this Act, "petroleum" includes petrol products and oil made from coal, shale, peat and other bituminous substances. "Petroleum spirit" is petroleum which has a flashpoint of below 73°F ($22 \cdot 8^{\circ}$C), when tested in the manner described in the Act. This means that many of the solvents used in paint may be affected by the Act. The provisions laid down include the following:
(i) A licence must be obtained if more than 3 gallons (3 gallons = $13 \cdot 638$ litres) of petroleum spirit are to be kept in storage.
(ii) Either the containers themselves or the store must be clearly marked with the words "Petroleum spirit" and "Highly inflammable".

PHENOL Carbolic acid.

P

PHENOL FORMALDEHYDE RESINS Also called phenol resins and P.F. resins. These materials, produced by the interaction of phenol and formaldehyde under a variety of conditions, were the first synthetic resins to be made on a large scale. The earliest phenol resins were thermosetting, suitable for moulding but insoluble in oil. The next stage was to cook the resins with rosin at a fairly high temperature, the acidity of the rosin being neutralized by the introduction of glycerine, which produced "reduced" or "modified" P.F. resins which have a tendency to yellowing but which are used in undercoatings and gold sizes. From these were developed a class of rosin-free resins, known as "100 per cent" or "pure" phenolic resins, which are highly water resistant and durable and which if cooked with tung oil possess very good resistance to alkalis and to the destructive effects of industrial and marine atmospheres.

PHOSPHATING The name given to various processes which have been developed to increase the corrosion resistance of bright sheet steel and light-gauge sections and to limit the spread of rust from damaged areas and edges; these processes are widely used in the automobile and similar industries and are adapted to the large-scale production of sheet metal articles to prevent rust creep from damaged parts. The metal is degreased and freed from rust and is then treated, either by dipping or spraying, with a solution of metal phosphates and phosphoric acid. In the "thin coating" or "accelerated" process the metal is immersed for five minutes at $75°$ to $85°C$ ($167°$ to $185°F$), or subjected to power spraying for one minute; in the "thick coating" process used for nuts, bolts and castings the metal is immersed for an interval of 15 to 60 minutes at boiling point. The thicker coating which is produced is unsuitable for articles to be finished in high gloss paint as it causes an appreciable loss of gloss.

The application of phosphating to structural steelwork has been limited by the difficulties of handling heavy plates and sections, but plant is now in operation in which heavy steel components of up to 10 metres in length can be phosphated.

PHOSPHORIC ACID WASHES Surface washes for the preparation of structural steelwork and domestic fittings prior to painting; various proprietary brands are available. They are usually in concentrated form and require diluting with three parts of water before use. They are used cold and are applied either by brush or spray; after application they are allowed to remain on the surface long enough to react with any light rust which is present, and the residue is then removed with hot water washing. In their present stage of development their usefulness on structural steelwork is very limited, although their performance is improved if the surface is first freed of heavy rust and scale by mechanical cleaning.

PHOTOMURALS Photographs, either in monochrome or in full colour; generally photographs of outdoor scenes or of buildings or aerial photographs. They can be hung directly to the wall surface or mounted on a hardboard backing and then framed. In some cases the paper is limp enough to be hung with ordinary paperhanger's paste, but when the mural is on a very stiff backing it is better to use latex rubber glue as the fixative.

PHTHALIC ANHYDRIDE A substance which when combined with glycerine forms the basis of alkyd resins.

PHYSICAL CHANGE A change which takes place whereby a substance undergoes an alteration in form and sometimes in volume but no alteration of weight or chemical composition occurs, as opposed to a chemical change in which a new substance is formed. For example, water which is in liquid form can undergo a physical change and become a solid substance, ice, under the effect of cold, and can become a gas, steam, under the effect of heat. In neither case is the change permanent and when the temperature rises above the freezing point or drops below the boiling point of water the substance reverts to its liquid state.

As an illustration of the difference between physical change and chemical change, if a piece of iron is melted, made to expand or contract, or magnetized, it undergoes a physical change. If it is made to rust, i.e., to oxidize, a chemical change occurs.

PICKING OUT (or PICKING IN)   Treating a small localized area in some special way that distinguishes it from the surrounding areas: e.g., treating one individual member of a moulding or cornice with a different colour from the remainder, treating some individual piece of ornament in order to emphasize it by comparison with the surrounding surfaces, etc.

PICKING UP   An indefinite term which is used in two very different ways. (i) In one sense it is used as being synonymous with "lifting", and means disturbing or softening a previous coating when applying a subsequent coat. (ii) In another sense it refers to keeping a wet edge in paintwork alive by joining it up with a new area and blending the two together so that no lap is visible.

PICKLE   A solution of caustic soda used to strip paint or polish from a surface or to clean painters' tools and utensils. See *Caustic Paint Remover* and *Caustic Pickle.*

PICKLED PINE   Common pinewood from which paint has been stripped. From the 18th century onwards pinewood has been used for panelling; its introduction for the purpose may have been due to its cheapness compared with oak or to the fact that the available oak was required for shipbuilding. Rooms panelled in pine were generally painted and it is only comparatively recently that the grain of pinewood itself has been appreciated; nowadays, however, the effect of pine from which paintwork has been stripped is esteemed by some people as providing a quiet background which shows off furnishing fabrics to advantage. There is also some call for the painted imitation of pickled pine; when this is required an off-white ground is used and the graining colour may be made up from raw and burnt umber and ultramarine.

PICKLING   (i) The traditional meaning of this term is the removal of paint, varnish or polish by means of an alkaline paint remover. (ii) In modern trade parlance, pickling refers to the process of removing rust and mill scale from structural steel before erection by means of immersing it in a bath containing both an acid solution and an inhibitor to prevent the metal from being unduly attacked by the acid. Pickling may be carried out with a cold solution of hydrochloric acid or a warm solution of sulphuric acid, followed in either case by a thorough rinsing with warm water. Until very recently a final rinse with a solution of slaked lime was given, but this practice has now been discontinued. A further method which is very much favoured by many authorities is one in which the metal is immersed in a solution of sulphuric acid, then washed with warm water and finally immersed in dilute phosphoric acid, no subsequent washing being required; this method leaves a slightly protective phosphate film on the steel.

PICTURE RAIL   A length of horizontal moulding separating the frieze from the wall filling, and from which pictures may be suspended.

PICTURE VARNISH   A protective coating composed of a spirit-soluble

P

resin dissolved in a volatile solvent which lends itself to easy removal and restoration.

PIER   A mass of masonry, as distinct from a column, supporting the arch or superstructure of a bridge. The term is also sometimes used rather loosely to mean a stone or metal pillar.

PIGMENTS   Insoluble substances in finely divided form which impart colour and opacity to a paint; they may also possess some other property, such as the power to inhibit rusting, resistance to some specific form of chemical attack, resistance to heat, etc., which enhances their value for some particular purpose.

PILASTER   A rectangular feature in the shape of a pillar, but projecting only about one sixth of its breadth from a wall.

PILING   A defect which occurs when a quick-drying paint is applied by brush and begins to set up during application, resulting in a thick uneven film.

PINE   The name given to a large and important group of coniferous trees providing softwoods for building and constructional purposes. It covers such woods as Scots pine (a tree native to Britain), Cembrian pine, Columbian pine, Weymouth pine (white or yellow pine), pitch pine (a very resinous tree and consequently providing a very durable wood), Corsican pine, etc.

PINHOLING   A defect in a painted or varnished surface in which the film is marred by the occurrence of minute craters which are slightly rough to the touch and which allow the passage of moisture. There are several possible causes. A frequent cause of pinholing in varnish is faulty application technique. If varnish is shaken up or poured carelessly it becomes frothy, the froth consisting largely of tiny air bubbles; similarly, the common practice of working a brush into a canful of varnish and wiping the brush on the lip of the can causes an accumulation of froth to form. If varnish is applied in this condition some of the air bubbles are conveyed to the work and tend to burst as the varnish is setting. The utmost care should be exercised to prevent the formation of air bubbles when dealing with varnish. Pinholing may also be due to the presence of grease on the surface, and frequently follows when cissing has occurred. It may also be due to the use of a cheap, poorly blended, varnish.

Pinholing is often seen in spray applied paint coatings and may often be traced to the presence of small quantities of grease or moisture in the air line. It may also occur in a paint coating when a quick-drying material is applied over a very porous surface such as previously distempered surface.

PINK PRIMER   The traditional primer for wood. It should be composed of white lead and red lead, possessing the easy brushing qualities of white lead and the ability to set firmly, even when locked within the pores of the timber and shut off from the air, conferred by the red lead. The proportions of red and white lead are not critical; the usual proportions are three of white lead to one of red lead, but this may produce too strong a colour if a very pale colour is to be superimposed, in which case there may be as many as nine parts of white to one of red lead used.

Cheap pink primers, composed of barytes or other extenders tinted with Venetian red, are very often bought by builders, but their use is to be strongly condemned; they have no protective power, and because the pigments used in their manufacture have a low degree of oil absorption, their binding agent is rapidly absorbed by the timber, leaving the pigment lying on the surface in a loose powdery film which provides a very poor basis for subsequent coats.

PITCH The most widely used type of pitch is the black residue left over from the distillation of coal-tar but the term also covers a great variety of dark brown or black resinous substances obtained from petroleum, pinewood, and oils and fats of various kinds.

PITCH (OF A ROOF) The inclination or angle of the roof surface to the horizontal.

PITCH PAPER A type of paper used in the treatment of damp walls, especially before the hanging of wallpaper. It consists of a stout brown lining paper coated on one side with pitch, and is supplied in rolls of the same size as normal wallpaper. It is hung with ordinary paperhanger's paste, preferably used fairly round, and it is the pitch coated side which is pasted and placed in contact with the wall.

PITCH PINE A wood with bright colour and bold contrasting grain. It is usually grained in oil colour working with raw sienna, burnt sienna and burnt umber graining colour ove: a warm cream ground; the figuring may very well be put in with a one-stroke writer.

PITTING The formation of holes, pits and craters in a metal surface due to corrosion or due, sometimes, to the injudicious use of pneumatic chisels and hammers for descaling.

P

PLANK The usual term for what is more correctly known as a scaffold board. Planks can be made from many kinds of timber, both softwood and hardwood, such as Canadian spruce, European spruce, Douglas fir, Western hemlock, East African camphor wood, etc., and should be free from defects such as spiral grain, splitting, shakes or decay. The slope of the grain should not exceed one in twenty on the edge or one in twelve on the face. The timber should as far as possible be free from knots. The thickness of a plank is related to its length; a plank 38mm thick should not exceed 2·74 metres, a 51mm plank should not exceed 3·35 metres and a 76mm plank should not exceed 3·96 metres in length. According to the Construction Regulations the width of a plank 51mm or more thick should not be less than 203mm, but in practice a width of 230mm to 280mm is more usual and more comfortable to work on. The ends of a plank may be treated to help to prevent splitting; they may be rounded or cut off at an angle of 45°, and in addition they may be bound with galvanized hoop iron or be finished off with strips of hardwood, the latter being less likely to cause injury to the hands or damage to polished floors. Planks should be tested at regular intervals.

PLANT A rather vague term meaning the tools, machinery and apparatus used by an industrial concern; in the case of the painter and decorator the term would be held to cover spray equipment, steam strippers, scaffolding, etc.

PLAQUE An ornamental or commemorative tablet fixed to a wall.

PLASTER A material applied in plastic state to provide a uniform finish to ceilings and walls; external plaster finishes are usually termed "renderings" For fuller details of the various types see *Gypsum Plasters* and *Lime Plaster*.

PLASTERBOARD A type of building board composed of a layer of gypsum on either side of which is a layer of very stout paper or fibre; the paper is tightly adhering because the gypsum contains a small quantity of glue. Plasterboard is quite inert and is perfectly safe to paint; the side which it is intended shall be exposed when the board is fixed in position is generally finished in ivory colour, and the surface is ready for immediate decoration. See also *Gypsum Plasterboard*.

PLASTER OF PARIS Hemihydrate gypsum plaster. Neat plaster of Paris is used for making good cracks and holes in plaster work; it is eminently suitable for the purpose because it hydrates and sets up very rapidly, because it expands slightly as it sets and therefore grips the existing plaster work very strongly, and because it is chemically inert and does not therefore exert any adverse effect upon superimposed paint, etc.

PLASTIC PAINT A decorative material which is applied to interior wall and ceiling areas and which while still wet can be manipulated in many ways to produce an extremely wide variety of textures; it can also be modelled to produce decorative motifs, can be applied through stencil plates to form decorative borders and can, when dry, be carved to produce sculptured effects. When dry it can be painted and glazed and wiped to produce an enormous range of broken colour effects. It is probably due to the very wide range of possibilities that it presents, and the fact that many decorators have used it with considerably more ingenuity than discretion, that it has become rather unpopular in recent years; when carefully applied to produce an evenly distributed and subdued texture, and coloured and finished with reasonable restraint, it is a useful decorative medium, especially for the decoration of public buildings. Plastic paint may be mixed with an oil medium and supplied in paste form but it is far more commonly supplied in powder form to be mixed to a paste with water on the site immediately prior to application. It is essential that the surface to which it is applied should be adequately sealed so as to be non-absorbent. Contrary to common belief, it is not effective in masking open joints in unplastered brickwork or cavities in plaster work; if an even texture is to be produced the surface must be reasonably smooth.

There is a growing tendency to describe paints and decorative materials based on synthetic resins as "plastic paints" or "plastic finishes". This usage should be avoided; otherwise, the time is not far distant when the use of the term will give rise to a great deal of confusion.

PLASTIC PAPER A wallpaper embossed and coloured in such a way that when it is hung it gives the appearance of a wall surface treated with plastic paint. The better qualities of plastic paper are of the duplex variety.

PLASTIC PRINTS Wallpapers upon which a pattern has been printed with a friable relief material similar to plastic paint. The back of the paper is usually smooth. Plastic prints need careful handling when they are being hung; any undue creasing or sharp bending will lead to the plastic material becoming dislodged, excessive soaking will lead to the softening and crumbling of the plastic matter, and careless use of the papering brush will damage the pattern.

PLASTICIZER A non-volatile substance which is incorporated into a paint, lacquer or varnish during manufacture in order to increase the flexibility of the dried film.

PLINTH The projecting moulded or stepped base of a building; also applied to the lowest square member of the base of a column.

PLUMB BOB or PLUMB LINE A weight suspended on a length of string, used to ensure accuracy in the setting out of any vertical work and to make sure that wallpapers and borders are truly vertical instead of being tilted at an angle when hung.

PLYWOOD Thin layers of wood, with the grain running in different directions, glued together under pressure. The introduction of synthetic resin bonded plywoods that do not soften under damp conditions has led to the increased use of plywood in situations where solid wood was formerly used.

P

PNEUMATIC TOOLS Tools and appliances operated by compressed air, e.g., pneumatic chisels and hammers for the descaling of steelwork, etc.

POCK MARKING A term used in many parts of the country to denote orange peeling, and sometimes used to refer to the pits and depressions which occur when a partially dry paint film is exposed to a shower of rain.

PODGER A tool used in the erection of tubular scaffolding for tightening up the couplers.

POLE LADDER Otherwise known as a builder's ladder. Pole ladders are those with half-round sides or stiles of softwood which are made from straight poles selected for their freedom from defects; the poles are sawn into halves down the centre and the two stiles of a single ladder consist either of the two halves of one pole or two sections from separate poles suitably matched. They are used for general building work and wherever a single ladder of considerable length is required. They usually range in length from 3 metres to about 20 metres, although longer ones are sometimes used.

POLISH See *French Polish*.

POLISHING VARNISH A quick-drying hard short-oil varnish made for use on furniture and other woodwork as an alternative to French polish; the resin used is hard enough to withstand polishing. It has the advantage of being more resistant to the effects of hot water, alcohol, etc., than French polish.

POLLARD OAK Wood displaying a large number of small knots and an irregular curly figure, due to the pollarding of the tree, i.e., the lopping off of the top part of the tree or of the main branches in order to encourage it to form a large number of side shoots. Willows and poplars are normally the only types of tree to be pollarded nowadays, but there is a constant demand for an imitation of pollard oak effects in graining; the effect is generally reserved for the panels of doors, etc., so as to contrast with the plainer rails and stiles; it is carried out in oil medium on a light buff ground, the graining colour being made up from burnt umber, raw sienna and burnt sienna, and should always be overgrained.

POLLUTION Pollution of the atmosphere with smoke, soot, sulphur fumes, etc., is an important factor in the premature breakdown of paint films in industrial areas. In certain factory premises the concentration of chemical gases in the atmosphere is considerably higher than the normal industrial pollution and the life of the paint film may be very severely reduced in consequence. The corrosion of steelwork is greatly accelerated by chemically polluted atmospheric conditions.

POLYCHROMATIC FINISHES Translucent shot-silk effects produced in cellulose and synthetic finishes and very popular in the fields of industrial finishing and motor car work. They are obtained by the suspension of small polished particles of beaten flakes of aluminium, bronze, copper or brass in the medium. They present a most attractive appearance when newly done, but they oxidize very rapidly and change tone; this makes it very difficult to touch up or refinish any local areas because of the impossibility of matching the paint exactly. Normally, when subjected to outdoor exposure polychromatic finishes need the application of a protective lacquer.

POLYCHROMATIC PAINTING Painting in several colours, as opposed to monochrome painting.

POLYCHROMES Wallpapers which are lightly embossed with an all-over miniature pebble-dash effect and which are printed in several colours, the colours being distributed in irregularly shaped patches and not forming any definite pattern.

POLYMER   See next paragraph on polymerization.

POLYMERIZATION   A term frequently met with in present-day technical literature, relating to the formulation of plastics; its particular relevance to the painter and decorator is its use in connection with the drying and setting of various substances employed in the formulation of surface coatings. The term, together with its associated terms such as "polymer", "copolymer", etc., causes some confusion to the decorator, who often complains that he is unable to understand the nature of modern paint materials and pleads that paint manufacturers should explain the composition of their products in a simpler manner. It is, however, impossible to understand the principles involved in the behaviour of modern materials without some preliminary knowledge of chemistry, and any attempt to simplify such terms as "polymerization" to the point where they are perfectly clear to the layman, as attempted in the following paragraphs, must inevitably lead to some dilution of what is, in fact, a very complex subject.

Polymerization may be described as a phenomenon in which a large number of similar molecules combine together to form a single multiple molecule, the compound thus formed being termed a "polymer" or "polymeride". In this connection a molecule can be defined as the smallest particle of a substance that is capable of independent existence while still retaining its characteristic chemical properties, a definition which would hold good except in the case of crystalline salts.

There are certain naturally occurring substances such as cellulose, starch, etc., which consist of relatively simple units repeated many times over in their structure, which are known as polymers. Within this century, however, chemists have discovered methods of linking together the molecules of various other substances to form synthetic polymers. These may be classified under two main headings.

Addition Polymers are formed by linking together the molecules of a substance end-to-end so as to form a long chain, many hundreds or even thousands of units in length. There is no change of substance involved, the resulting "long chain molecule" being composed of the same basic units as the initial compound. They are nearly always "thermoplastic", i.e., they can be repeatedly softened and resoftened by applying the appropriate heat and pressure treatment provided they are not decomposed or degraded. The properties of any given addition polymer can be altered or modified by increasing or decreasing the length of the polymeric chain, the chain length being controlled by varying such conditions as the temperature and pressure under which the polymerization takes place. Examples of addition polymers which are of interest to the painter and decorator are certain of the vinyl resins which at ordinary temperatures are hard plastics but which can be modified by the addition of plasticizers to form rubber-like materials for many purposes, e.g., polyvinyl acetate, which is the resin most frequently employed in this country in the formulation of emulsion paints, and polyvinyl chloride, which when dissolved in solvents and laid on a backing of cloth fabric forms a leathercloth material which is employed for wall decoration or upholstery.

P

Condensation polymers are formed by linking together a large number of basic units by means of a reaction between two different molecules during which water or some other simple compound is eliminated. It is important that a catalyst or accelerator should be present in the polymer-producing reaction; otherwise, polymerization would not take place at all or would proceed so slowly as to be uneconomical. These polymers are "thermosetting", i.e., they become permanently rigid under the action of heat. This is because the molecules instead of being linked in simple chains are converted into a mass of molecules cross linked in three dimensions. This process is not capable of repetition, a thermosetting polymer being destroyed by further heating. Examples of condensation polymers relevant to the painting and decorating trade are phenol formaldehyde resins, urea formaldehyde resins and alkyd resin.

Co-polymerization is a term used for a process of addition polymerization in which two or more distinct species of molecules are involved, each one of which species is capable of polymerizing by itself. The product is known as a "co-polymer".

The discussion so far has related to the more recent advances in the field of synthetic resins. The principles of polymerization have many other applications to painters' materials. For example, "stand oil" used in the manufacture of Dutch enamels, old oil gold size, etc., is produced by the polymerization of linseed oil by heating it to a temperature of 300°C (572°F), with all air excluded. Up to 250°C (428°F), no change in structure takes place but above this figure polymerization occurs and the oil increases in viscosity and density. Similarly, some oils such as tung oil, safflower oil, etc., so treated, are converted into a gelatinous material. An example of a natural thermoplastic polymer is shellac, a compound which under certain conditions shows marked qualities of elasticity. Polymerization also has some part in the process by which a straight oil paint of the traditional drying oil/pigment/drier/thinner type sets and hardens. It used to be stated dogmatically that such a paint dried by oxidation of the oil content; it is now believed that the oxidation of the oil is a phase followed by a gradual process of polymerization.

POLYPROPYLENE ROPES Strong low-stretch ropes which are acid- and alkali-resistant and are very suitable for use in scaffolding, particularly in situations exposed to destructive industrial conditions. See *Synthetic Ropes*.

POLYSTYRENE A resin produced by the polymerization of styrene, possessing important properties of resistance to light, heat and chemicals, and used in alkali resisting paints, fluorescent paints, metallic paints and insulating varnishes. Its use is limited to some extent by the difficulty of finding a completely satisfactory plasticizer. See also *Expanded Polystyrene*.

POLYTHENE The proprietary term used by one manufacturer for what is more strictly known as "polyethylene". A type of synthetic rubber produced by the polymerization of ethylene, which is tough, light and flexible and possesses high resistance to water and chemicals. It is not widely used as a surface coating material, but is of interest to the painter in a different connection. Dust sheets made from polythene are now being extensively employed, the special advantage that they offer being the fact that they are impermeable to moisture. This is obviously a great advantage when any operation involving the use of large quantities of water is being carried out; when washing down is in progress, or when wallpaper is being stripped, polythene sheets afford greater protection to floors and furniture than conventional fabric sheets. On occasions when it is impracticable to remove the carpets during redecoration, or when theatres or cinemas are being decorated, the use of waterproof dust sheets is clearly a great benefit, and should some mishap occur whereby a paint can is overturned the risk of severe damage is considerably lessened. Heavy grades of polythene are available for use as substitutes for tarpaulins and as temporary glazing on building sites, and have actually been used as an all-over protection for the side of a building enabling exterior painting to be carried out in wet weather.

POLYURETHANE LACQUERS These lacquers are of considerable interest and importance both in industrial finishing and in painting and decorating, and many formulations are in use to provide for a wide variety of purposes. They are available both as clear transparent lacquers and as pigmented coatings. Clear lacquers are available for wood finishing, panelling and timber cladding, boat finishing, etc., and pigmented types are obtainable to give a range of household paints of exceptional hardness and materials for ship painting, etc.

The name polyurethane covers a variety of materials based on similar types of resin but modified in various ways to meet some particular need or develop some special characteristic. In general, the properties for which polyurethane coatings are notable are film hardness, toughness and flexibility, extreme resistance to abrasion, water resistance, and durability under conditions of both indoor and outdoor exposure. As a rule their adhesion is excellent, but if they are applied on top of conventional paint coatings they tend to act as paint strippers due to the strength of the solvents employed in their formulation. After curing they develop high resistance to chemicals and solvents, and very little progressive change takes place in the coatings as compared with conventional paint systems. A critical feature in their formulation is the purity of the solvents used; if the urethane reacts with water or acid in the solvent, carbon dioxide may be formed which leads to the appearance of bubbles and blisters in the coating.

There are three main types in use. One type is a two-pack system consisting of a polyester or polyether resin blended with a polyisocyanate resin curing agent immediately before use. The two materials must be kept separate until required and it is important that the curing agent should be kept in a completely moisture proof container. The two packs must be mixed together in the precise proportions recommended by the manufacturer. The pot life varies from two to 24 hours according to the purpose for which the coating is made, the pot life depending on such factors as the type of resin employed, the temperature at the time of application, etc. These coatings can be applied by brush or spray, and on mass production work a catalyst spraying system may be employed. They are air

P

drying and are hard dry in four to six hours; full curing is complete after two or three days, after which time the coating will be impervious to the solvents from subsequent coats; it is therefore essential that when two or more coats are required they should be applied without undue delay, otherwise adhesion may suffer.

The second type is a one-pack system intended for stoving, and contains blocked adducts; these are resins in which the isocyanate groups are blocked by reaction with phenols or alcohols. When heated the phenols or alcohols split off allowing the isocyanates to react with the polyester. Their properties resemble those of the first type.

The third type is a one-pack system which is cured by moisture, the moisture from the atmosphere causing polymerization. They become touch dry in one to two hours and can be recoated after four or five hours. They can be applied by brush or spray. This type includes a range of pigmented coatings suitable for normal household painting, available in both eggshell and gloss finish; these paints possess exceptional properties of hardness and resistance to scratching and abrasion, and under certain circumstances can be applied over existing coatings of conventional paint provided, of course, that these are hard and in sound condition.

It should be noted that the Timber Research and Development Association does not recommend the use of polyurethane lacquers on exterior timbering. The association states that although they possess good durability there are also drawbacks to their use, the most serious of which is the virtual impossibility of satisfactorily maintaining a weathered coating because of the poor adhesion of subsequent coatings.

POLYURETHANE PAINT   A two-pack material composed of urethane resins mixed with a catalyst just before use, and used in situations demanding resistance to chemical attack. It is considered to be rather more weather resistant than the epoxy paints.

POLYVINYL ACETATE   Popularly known as PVA. A series of colourless resins obtained by the polymerization of vinyl acetate. They form the basis of the bulk of the emulsion paints produced in this country at present. They give a film with a good performance and require very little plasticization, but they tend to stimulate corrosion if used on steel. An important feature is their permeability to water vapour, which allows them to be used on damp porous surfaces.

POLYVINYL CHLORIDE   Popularly known as PVC. A synthetic resin produced by the polymerization of vinyl chloride under heat and pressure, which resembles rubber in its properties, is resistant to many chemicals, is non-inflammable and is a good electrical insulator. It is used more in the plastics industry than in paint, its application to the painter and decorator's work being in the field of coated fabrics. See also *Leathercloth* and *PVC coated fabrics*.

POPPING   An alternative term for the defect in plastering known as blowing. See *Blowing*.

POPPY OIL or POPPY SEED OIL   A drying oil obtained from the seeds of the opium poppy, produced mostly in India and the Levant. It is a very pale oil with a slow drying rate and, owing to its scarcity, it is too expensive to be used in ordinary commercial practice. It is, however, employed in artists' colours, its paleness and slow drying being an asset to the artist and mural painter. Fine tube colours are sometimes ground in it.

POROSITY   A term which is very often used loosely as an alternative to absorbency. To be precise, however, the porosity of a building material such as brick, stone, plaster, etc., is the ratio of pore space to the total volume of the material, and the pores do not usually absorb water to their full extent, their absorbency being governed by the capillary attraction they are able to exert.

POROUS   The condition of having pores or passages along which fluids may travel.

PORTABLE COMPRESSOR   A piece of spray equipment in which the complete outfit, comprising the compressor, the air receiver and the motor or engine, is mounted on a wheeled chassis and equipped with handles. The portable compressor is the only type suitable for normal painting and decorating work, since the work of a stationary compressor is obviously limited to factory or workshop production methods.

PORTER   A type of marble, also known as "Black and Gold", which is found in the Apennines. It has a black background clouded with grey, and is strongly veined with chain-like formations in yellow.

PORTICO   A porch or vestibule with columns.

PORTLAND CEMENT   The essential constituent in concrete, cement rendering and asbestos-cement sheeting, and also used in the backing material for gypsum plasters, Keene's cement and exterior renderings such as stucco. It is produced by burning limestone with clay or shale at a high temperature until it forms a clinkered mass, which is then cooled and ground to a fine powder. When the plasterer mixes Portland cement with water, part of the water combines chemically with the cement, causing it to set hard.

P

   Portland cement is highly alkaline, and until it has completely dried out it will rapidly attack and destroy any oil paint applied to the surface. Since the surface may remain active for a very considerable period it should always be tested with litmus before painting is undertaken. In the past a great deal of faith was placed in washing the surface of Portland cement with a zinc sulphate solution to "neutralize" the alkali; this practice is most undesirable not only because it is ineffective as a neutralizing agent but also because it defeats its own object by rewetting the cement and because it may lead to trouble due to the zinc sulphate crystallizing beneath the paint.

POSITIVE STENCIL   A stencil plate in which the ornament itself is cut out.

POT LIFE A term chiefly used in connection with two-pack materials to denote the length of time that they will remain in usable condition. Two-pack materials consist of two components, namely a base and an activator or catalyst, the two components being mixed immediately prior to application. Once the components are mixed, gellation may take place very rapidly, and the length of time which elapses before gelling occurs is termed the pot life. The pot life is dependent upon such factors as the type of material, the type of solvent, the solids content and the temperature at the time of mixing.

POUNCE A device for transferring the outline of a design on to a wall surface quickly and without causing damage to the surface. The design is drawn out on cartridge paper or detail paper, and holes are then pricked into the paper at close intervals along the outline. The paper is then held in contact with the wall while a "pounce bag" containing dry powder colour is lightly beaten against the lines; the dry colour passing through the pricked holes on to the wall leaves a mark sufficiently clear for the decorator to work to.

POUNCE BAG A small home-made bag, generally consisting merely of a piece of cloth secured at the neck with an elastic band, in which dry powdered pigment is placed for the purpose of pouncing a design.

POUNCING Applying a drawing by pounce.

POUND BRUSH Also known in some parts of the country as a "ground brush". The old-fashioned round brush made with hog hair bristle of up to 150mm in length, which has now been almost completely superseded by the 75mm flat paint brush. A pound brush needs bridling with string before being put into use, and needs careful breaking in during the early stages of its use. When these conditions are fulfilled it makes an excellent brush which distributes paint very evenly.

POWDER DISTEMPER A type of washable distemper prepared from Paris white and barytes, suitably pigmented and ground with a little linseed oil; it is then ground to a fine powder, and casein, lime and borax are added. The powder is prepared for use by mixing with hot water. The material is now largely obsolete.

POWDERED PUMICE An abrasive consiting of finely pulverized pumice stone which is used, with water as the lubricant, for felting down varnished or enamelled surfaces or for rubbing down paintwork between coats. It is an excellent material for the purpose, but has the disadvantage that any particles left behind after its use lead to very obvious bittiness occurring in the succeeding coats; it is particularly difficult to remove all traces of the powder from the quirks of mouldings.

PO-YOK OIL A very useful drying oil obtained from West Africa with characteristics midway between those of linseed oil and tung oil.

226

POZZOLANA See under *Fly Ash*.

PRECIPITATION Also called "colour striking". A method of preparing pigments by mixing together two soluble salts so that they react with one another to form one or more insoluble compounds; the pigments prepared in this manner include titanium white, Prussian blue, lithopone, lead chromates, etc.

PREPARATION The treatment given to a surface prior to the application of any paint or decorative material. It is a well-known fact that correct and thorough preparation is absolutely essential if the best results are to be obtained with any painting or decorating material; it is also well known that preparation is very often carried out badly and inadequately and is sometimes ignored altogether.

PRE-PASTED PAPERS Otherwise known as "ready-pasted papers".
Wallpapers which are supplied with the back surface already coated with an adhesive substance, the adhesive being activated by contact with water. A trough filled with cold water is placed against the skirting board directly beneath the area to be papered. The length of paper is rolled up from the bottom with the pattern side inwards and is immersed in the trough, feeding the top end under a guide wire which is fitted to the trough. The length is held by the top end and slowly withdrawn vertically with both sides wetted; it is drawn upwards to the cornice or picture rail and slid into position with the palms of the hands, and is smoothed to the wall with a wet sponge. The paper is supplied ready trimmed. The preparation of the wall surface is the same as for a normal paperhanging operation.
Prepasted wallpapers have enjoyed a steady sale in the U.S.A. for a number of years, and were introduced into this country in 1961, possibly with an eye to the amateur market but they made little impact. They were reintroduced in 1971 with more success.

PRESERVATIVE A substance which has the power of giving protection against injury or decay. In the broadest sense nearly all paints and decorative materials act as preservatives to the surface to which they are applied; in the narrower sense the term is usually reserved for the fluids such as creosote, etc., which are used to protect woodwork in situations where a paint treatment would not be appropriate, and it can also refer to substances which are added to various decorative materials to prevent them from putrefying, e.g., carbolic acid, which is sometimes added to glue size to prevent decomposition.

PRESSURE DROP A term used in spray painting to signify the lowering of air pressure between the source of air and the spray gun itself. Pressure drop is caused by friction between the flowing air and the walls of the hose through which it passes.

PRESSURE FEED BRUSH A paint brush, the hand-piece of which is connected by means of a flexible hose to a pressure feed paint container; when a button on the hand-piece of the brush is pressed the bristles are

P

automatically charged with paint. The brush is used in exactly the same way as a normal paint brush, and paint only flows when the button is pressed. The fact that constant dipping into a paint can is eliminated leads to a saving of time in application, and it is also claimed that there is less splashing than with an ordinary brush and less waste of paint.

The pressure feed brush was designed primarily for the industrial contractor engaged in heavy structural work and employing unskilled or semi-skilled labour. Its use is largely confined to industrial work, decorators having tended to adopt a conservative attitude towards it.

PRESSURE FEED CUP A type of fluid container attached directly to a spray gun, and designed for use with enamels, plastics and other materials too heavy for suction feed and in situations where only a comparatively small quantity of material is to be sprayed. There are two types of pressure feed cup; the regulator type is equipped with an air regulator which allows the pressure on the fluid to be varied, whereas in the non-regulator type the pressure on the fluid is the same as the atomizing air pressure.

PRESSURE FEED TANK A type of paint container used in spray painting. It consists of a robust steel cylindrical tank, heavily galvanized on both inside and outside, fitted with a clamp-on lid, inlet and outlet taps and valves, and a safety valve. The pattern commonly used by the decorator is also equipped with a pressure gauge or gauges, and is generally fitted with an agitator which may be either manually or mechanically operated. The capacity of the tank may vary between 4·5 and 270 litres, and obviously the higher the capacity the longer it will be possible to operate without interruption; in the type of work carried out by painting contractors the limiting factor is the size and weight of tank that can be conveniently handled, moved around the site, and hoisted when necessary on to a scaffold, and for general purposes the 9 litre size appears to be the most popular.

The pressure feed tank provides a constant flow of large quantities of paint at an accurately controlled pressure to the spray gun, and is an essential part of the outfit for all normal sized operations. It would be impracticable to engage in any spray work on a commercial scale without it, if only because of the frequent interruptions required for replenishing the supply of paint. In most cases the use of a double regulator type is an advantage as it permits fluid and atomizing pressures to be varied according to local operating conditions, e.g., for allowing adjustments to be made when the gun is operated at a considerably higher level than the tank, etc.

PRESSURE REDUCING VALVE See *Air Transformer.*

PRESSURE SWITCH A device included in a spray outfit to break the circuit when maximum pressure is reached in the air receiver, the circuit closing again when the pressure drops to the minimum setting.

PRETREATMENT A term covering such things as solvent wiping, grease removal, abrasive treatments, rust removal by various processes, and pickling processes, applied to metal surfaces prior to painting in order to improve the durability of the paint system by ensuring better adhesion, restricting corrosion, etc.

228

PRETREATMENT PRIMERS Also termed "wash primers", "wash coats" and "etch primers". Solutions used as a chemical pretreatment for metals. Their value as a treatment for non-ferrous metals such as zinc and aluminium, in order to improve the adhesion of paint, is well established and they are now being increasingly used in the surface preparation of steel. They normally consist of an etching agent such as phosphoric acid to which is added a film-forming synthetic resin called polyvinyl butyral, and a substantial proportion of chromate pigment. They are usually supplied in two parts to be mixed immediately before application in accordance with the manufacturer's instructions, the mixture remaining workable for about eight hours, but there are also some one-part primers available. Application is by brush or spray. There is a widespread belief that the use of a pretreatment primer is a substitute for a normal coat of paint, but in fact the film which is formed is very much thinner than a conventional paint film and it is therefore important that a normal priming coat should be applied without delay and should be followed by a full paint system. It is also important to note that thorough cleaning of the surface is essential before the pretreatment primer is applied.

A type of pretreatment primer has been developed which is based on the anti-corrosive properties of tannin, and is recommended by some authorities for use on steel. It is claimed that the film which it forms will last much longer than that of the normal etching primer, and that its use is therefore preferable in situations where an immediate follow up with priming paint is impracticable. Further advantages claimed are that it is not dangerous to the skin, that it gives off no fumes, and that it has a blackening effect upon the metal which clearly shows up any areas that have been missed. On the other hand, the tannin will not form a film on a greasy surface or on a surface that has been chemically cleaned.

Whatever type of pretreatment primer is used on steel it is necessary, if good results are to be obtained, that mill scale and heavy rust should be removed prior to application.

PRICKING WHEEL A device which facilitates the making of a pounce; it consists of a wheel of small diameter, from the outer edge of which a number of points protrude, mounted on a wooden handle in such a way that it can rotate easily.

PRIMARY COLOURS The fundamental basic hues which cannot themselves be formed by a mixture or combination of any other hues, and from mixtures and combinations of which all other colours can in theory be formed. The primary colours in pigments are red, yellow and blue; the primary colours of light are red, green and blue.

PRIMER The first coat of paint to be applied to any surface; the basis or foundation of the entire paint system, upon the stability of which the success of the whole system depends, and therefore a factor of the utmost importance in any paint system.

The functions of a primer may be listed as follows:
(i) To provide a durable and protective coating which acts as a bridge

between the underlying surface and the remainder of the paint system, enabling subsequent coats to fulfil their proper purpose.

(ii) To satisfy the absorption of porous materials such as timber, plaster, etc., while still leaving sufficient binding medium at the surface to bind the pigment adequately and hold up the subsequent coats.

(iii) To provide adhesion on non-porous materials such as zinc, aluminium or glass.

(iv) To form a barrier over chemically active materials such as new lime plaster, asbestos-cement sheeting, concrete, etc., which will prevent the alkaline content of these materials from attacking and destroying the paint film.

(v) To inhibit the corrosion of ferrous metal surfaces.

(vi) To form a coating upon radiators, heating pipes, etc., which will withstand the effects of heat and prevent it from softening, cracking or discolouring subsequent coats.

As a general rule it is most desirable that a primer should be applied by brush even if subsequent coats are to be applied by roller or spray.

PRIMING (a) The application of a primer, usually regarded as a task requiring little skill but actually an important one and essentially one calling for patience and care.

(b) The word "priming" is often used as a synonym for "primer".

PRIMING COAT First coat; primer.

PROCESS WHITE An opaque water-mixed white prepared from blanc fixé, used by designers and commercial artists.

PROPANE A flammable gas sometimes used as the fuel to operate a blow-torch. See *LPG Containers.*

PROTECTION The protection of a surface from decay or corrosion is one of the principal reasons for the application of paint.

PROTRACTOR An instrument taking the form of a graduated semicircle used to set out and measure angles.

PROUD Projecting above the level of the surrounding surface; on a higher plane. Thus we may speak of a nail which has not been properly driven home as "standing proud" of a surface, or of applying a filling composition in such a way that it "stands proud" of the surrounding area so that it can be rubbed down when dry to become level with the rest of the surface.

PRUSSIAN BLUE A blue pigment prepared by precipitating a ferric salt such as ferrous sulphate with a solution of potassium ferrocyanide. It varies in colour from a slightly greenish blue to a blue tinged with violet, and it has a characteristic bronze lustre, although non-bronzing blues are made for certain special purposes. The colour of Prussian blue is intense and it has very great staining strength, yet in spite of its strength it is notable for its great transparency. It is resistant to acid but is readily attacked by alkali and will discolour rapidly if used on new plaster, cement, concrete, etc., unless the surface has been adequately sealed with an alkali resisting primer. It is a very useful pigment when ground in oil, and because of its transparency it can be used as a glaze as well as for tinting purposes, but because of its vulnerability to alkaline attack it is not used in water paints or distempers.

Various qualities of Prussian blue are available, the better grades being known as Chinese blue or Milori blue and the cheaper grades as Brunswick blue. The cheaper qualities have a tendency to react with linseed oil and to develop the fault of livering.

PUGGING   A term used to describe the mixing of a pigment with medium in such a way that the pigment becomes "wetted" and forms a thick paste. The process is carred out, in the course of paint manufacture, in a pug mill.

PULLING   The term used to describe the drag or pull on the wrist which is felt when viscous materials such as varnishes or enamels are being app- lied by brush. It is due to the resistance to the free movement of the brush set up by the viscosity of the material.

PULLING OVER   The process of levelling a nitro-cellulose lacquer film, particularly on wood, by applying a pullover solution with a pad.

PULLING UP   The softening of a previously applied coat of paint when a further coat of paint or varnish is being applied. See *Lifting*.

PULLOVER SOLUTION   A levelling solution used to bring nitro-cellulose lacquers to a perfectly smooth finish resembling French polish; it is applied by means of a pad and smooths out irregularities by pulling the cellulose coating from one spot to another to produce a level film. The solution is composed of organic solvents which only partially dissolve the lacquer film.

P

PULPS   These are the cheapest variety of patterned wallpapers, in which the natural colour of the paper itself forms part of the finished surface. Pulps are usually thin papers. They must not be oversoaked,otherwise the colour printed on them tends to loosen; they should be hung immediately after pasting.

PULVERIZED FUEL ASH   See *Fly Ash*.

PUMICE BLOCKS   Regular rectangular shaped abrasive blocks made up from powdered pumice and very often containing a mild detergent for attacking the grease on a painted surface. They are useful for broad work but are inclined to be cumbersome on panelled surfaces. It is most im- portant that when pumice blocks are being used the surface should be thoroughly rinsed off with clean water immediately after rubbing, in order to remove all trace of detergent from the surface before any paint is applied.

PUMICE STONE A substance of volcanic origin; a light form of acid or silica-rich lava which became spongy and porous due to the escape of steam or gas while the lava was cooling. Pumice stone is used as an abrasive, with water as the lubricant, and is especially useful for the initial cleaning down and preparation of previously painted and enamelled surfaces prior to redecoration. Pumice stone is supplied in lumps of varying size and is prepared for use by cutting a lump across with an old hack saw blade so as to provide two pieces each presenting a flat face; the faces are then rubbed on a wet stone to make them smooth. The operative then takes a piece in each hand; after wetting the painted surface he uses one piece to rub the surface with a circular motion. The stone soon becomes clogged up; to prevent this, and to maintain the stone in useful condition, the two pieces are periodically rubbed together.

A good quality of pumice stone will float in water. A poor quality sinks, which indicates that it is not porous enough to abrade a painted surface properly.

PUNCHEON Any vertical tube, used in the erection of tubular scaffolding, which is not supported upon the ground or upon a base plate.

PURE STAINERS Pigments supplied in concentrated form, not reduced nor mixed with extenders.

PURITY The strength or intensity of a colour, denoted in the Munsell system by the word "chroma" and also sometimes referred to as "saturation"

PURLIN A horizontal beam or member in a roof construction, resting upon the principal rafters and supporting the common rafters and the roof covering.

PURPLE OF CASSIUS A purple dye, used in galss manufacture for the production of ruby glass, made by precipitating a solution of tin chloride with a solution of gold chloride; the precipitate forms a powder which contains colloidal gold and tin hydroxide. Gold was already familiar as a glass pigment in the early sixteenth century, but this particular material was developed by Andreas Cassius in Hamburg in the mid-seventeenth century and was rapidly accepted throughout the glassworks of Bohemia.

Its interest to painters and decorators lies in the fact that a fault has occasionally been known to occur on gilded work, especially in coastal districts, and when gold leaf has been applied to painted surfaces on yachts and boats; the defect takes the form of a purple stain which spreads into the surrounding paintwork. This fault has been attributed to a complex reaction between the gold, the paint pigments and media and salt spray which produces a compound similar to purple of Cassius.

PURPURE The heraldic term for the purple tincture.

PUTLOG A horizontal tube or other member in a tubular or pole scaffold, spanning from a ledger to the wall of the building. The putlog may be a tube specially made for the purpose with one end flattened to form a tongue about 75 mm in length, or it may be an ordinary tube to which a detachable end piece called a putlog end is added. In either case the whole of the flattened end should be bedded in the brickwork or stonework of the building.

PUTLOG COUPLER A non-load bearing coupler used in the erection of tubular scaffold for the purpose of fastening a transom or putlog to a ledger. It is perfectly adequate for this purpose but should never be used for coupling standards to ledgers where a full load-bearing coupler is necessary.

PUTLOG END or PUTLOG HEAD A flattened blade or tongue with a fitting which enables it to be attached to a normal plain-ended tube in order to convert the plain tube into a putlog.

PUTLOG SCAFFOLD A scaffold consisting of a single row of standards set some 1.3 metres from the wall and joined by ledgers. The putlogs are supported at one end by the ledgers and at the other end they are inserted in joints in the brickwork or stonework. Putlog scaffolds are used mainly in the erection of new buildings, and are therefore of less interest to the painter and decorator than independent scaffolds, but they cannot be completely overlooked because of the occasions when a painter engaged on a new building uses a builder's scaffold which is already in position.

PUTREFACTION The decomposition and decay of animal and vegetable matter due to a chemical change brought about by bacteria; it is generally accompanied by an unpleasant odour. Such materials as glue size are liable to putrefy fairly quickly, especially in hot weather, and a preservative in the form of carbolic acid or oil of cloves may be added to retard putrefaction. It is always wise, however, to insist on size, paste, etc., being mixed perfectly fresh for the work in hand. Exposure to persistently damp conditions can lead to the putrefaction of various decorative materials and may give rise to the occurrence of mould and fungoid growths.

P

PUTTY A stiff dough-like composition used for stopping holes and cracks in woodwork prior to painting and also for bedding the glass in window frames. A good quality putty is made from whiting ground in raw linseed oil. Cheap grades of putty are very often made with non-drying mineral oils and are unsatisfactory in every respect.

Ordinary linseed oil putty is not suitable for bedding glass in metal window frames, as it takes too long to harden; furthermore, if the window is exposed to the sun the frame becomes hot which causes the putty to sag and even, in extreme cases, to run, and this tendency to sag may continue for a very long time. Various proprietary putties are available for use on metal windows; if ordinary putty is used it should be stiffened by the addition of a hardening agent such as red lead or gold size.

PUTTY KNIFE A knife used for stopping holes and cracks with putty or hard stopping, and for bedding glass into window frames. Two patterns are available, one of which terminates in a pointed end, the other resembling a chisel knife except that its end is slanted; the choice is entirely one of individual preference. The blade of a well-made putty knife should be continued right through to form an integral part of the handle; the blade should be fairly stiff in order to press the putty well home.

PUTTYING UP The process of stopping holes and cracks with putty. It is important that this should be carried out *after* priming. If putty is applied to bare wood, or if the holes and cracks have not been satisfactorily sealed with paint, the bare wood absorbs the oil from the putty and leaves the putty in a powdery and crumbling condition.

PVA Polyvinyl acetate.

PVC Polyvinyl chloride.

PVC-COATED FABRICS Wall hanging materials consisting of finely woven fabrics such as linen, coated on the face with polyvinyl chloride which is attractively coloured, embossed and patterned to form a decorative finish. The range of patterns is no longer restricted to imitations of leather; there are, for instance, attractive self-coloured basket weaves and remarkably fine wood grain effects as well as colourful floral and abstract patterns. These materials can be obtained in runs of considerable length and in widths of up to 1320mm and in this form they are suitable for large scale work such as ship or hotel decoration, but it has been realized that narrower widths are less unwieldy for domestic work and various brands are available in smaller rolls; one popular brand, for example, is supplied in rolls 9 metres long by 635mm wide, while another is supplied in the size of a standard roll of wallpaper. Trimming has also been eliminated in many cases, and the material is designed to be hung without matching and with the edges butted. The rolls are individually wrapped and provided with cardboard end-cups to protect the edges. Special adhesives for hanging coated fabrics have been developed by various firms, and these adhesives contain the requisite fungicidal agent. Lining is seldom necessary prior to hanging the fabric, but where it is considered essential the same special adhesive should be used for attaching the lining paper. Distinctive properties of PVC fabrics include durability, washability, extreme resistance to abrasion and to chemicals such as detergents, etc.

PVC-COATED PAPERS These are a comparatively recent development in wallpaper manufacture. As their name implies they consist of a paper backing coated with polyvinyl chloride, and while they are obviously not as robust as PVC fabrics they do possess to a great extent the same feature of washability, resistance to abrasion, chemical attack and the action of detergents, and they are, of course, considerably cheaper. In their infancy they were produced as an offshoot of leathercloth manufacture but are now firmly established as part of the wallpaper industry, and designs are now being produced which are printed from the same rollers, and with the same colourings, as conventional wallpapers. They are supplied in ready trimmed form and are individually wrapped in cellophane. The surface of the paper is completely impervious to moisture and it is therefore important that whatever type of paste is used for hanging them should contain a fungicidal agent, as the paste tends to remain moist for a long time especially on non-absorbent surfaces. Some manufacturers advise the use of a heavy duty cellulose paste which contains a fungicidal additive. The quality of the work is improved if a lining paper is hung first, and in this case the same type of paste should also be used for the lining. After hanging, the edges of the paper should be wiped over with a moistened cloth to remove any paste which may have strayed on to the front surface. The edges must be accurately butted; PVC paper will not stick to itself, so overlapping joints will not stick down.

PYROXYLIN   An alternative term for nitro-cellulose, generally referring to the more soluble types.

Q

QUARTERING   Cutting a log of wood lengthwise along its radius, thus exposing the ray figure caused by the pith rays and showing the highly decorative "edge" grain or "silver" grain; hence quartered oak", etc.

Also a term used in heraldry to denote the sub-division of a shield into equal quarters in which are placed the various coats of arms its owner has inherited.

QUERCITRON   The North American black or dyer's oak, from the bark of which a yellow dye is prepared.

QUICKLIME   Calcium oxide; lime produced by heating limestone or chalk to drive off carbonic acid gas, and not yet slaked. See *Lime*.

QUICKSILVER   See *Mercury*.

QUILL   The hollow stem or barrel of a bird's feather. Signwriters' brushes are sometimes set in quills, which are fitted on to wooden handles by the purchaser. Many signwriters prefer this pattern of brush to the type which is set in a metal ferrule, maintaining that the quill, being flexible, has less tendency to cut the delicate sable hair when the brush is in use.

Whereas writers in metal ferrules are graded numerically for size, those set in quill are classified according to the bird from which the quill was obtained. They range in order of size from the lark, which is the smallest, to the swan, which is the largest, the full range being as follows: lark, crow, duck, extra duck, small goose, goose, extra goose, small swan, swan, large swan.

The fitting of a handle to a new quill brush is an operation requiring some care; otherwise, the quill will be split and the brush ruined. The handle should be very carefully shaped and pared to the size of the quill, being finally smoothed down with sandpaper until it is an exact fit. The quill should then be dipped in hot water for a few minutes, taking care that the sable hair does not become wet. When the quill has become flexible the handle is gently inserted; after a few minutes it will be found that the quill has hardened and has taken a firm grip on the handle.

Coachpainters' riggers and liners are often set in quill, but it is not usual to fit a handle to these brushes.

QUIRK   Strictly speaking, the sharp V-shaped recess in a moulding, between the moulding proper and the fillet or soffit; very often the word is loosely used to describe any deep cavity or incision.

R

RADIAL STIPPLER   A device used in the production of broken colour effects in glaze and paint, and also for texturing plastic paint. It consists of a circular aluminium plate to which rounded strips of rubber are attached, the strips radiating from the centre. The aluminium base is fitted with a wooden bridge handle. The stippler is used with a swirling motion.

RADIATION   The emission of rays of light or heat; the transfer of heat or light from one body to another without raising the temperature of the intervening medium. This is the principle of heat transfer upon which infrared drying is based.

RADIATOR BRUSH   Sometimes called a "flag". A small flat paint brush mounted on the end of a long strong wire handle, and designed for conveying paint to the less accessible parts of a heating radiator.

RAFTER   A sloping piece of timber supporting a roof or the framework upon which the roofing materials are laid.

RAG ROLLING   A method of producing a broken colour effect in tinted glaze medium. The general method adopted is to lay in a previously painted ground with glaze medium following up with the hair stippler; then, while the glaze medium is still wet, a chamois leather dipped in white spirit and well wrung out is tightly twisted up, taken between the fingers and thumb of both hands, and passed over the glaze with a rolling action from top to bottom. This has the effect of removing patches of glaze and revealing the ground colour. The leather should be rolled with an irregular twisting motion; if rolled in straight lines a somewhat mechanical effect is produced. Although the term specifically speaks of "rag" rolling, rag is not usually employed because of the lint which such material deposits on the surface. Provided the ground colour and glaze colour are well chosen, rag rolling can produce very charming effects.

RAILS   The horizontal members of a framed or panelled joinery construction.

RAKER A term used in connection with tubular scaffolding to signify an inclined tube having a bearing upon the ground or on an adjacent structure.

RAKING OUT A term used in reference to making good defective plaster work; the clearing of all loose and unsound material from a crack, usually with a knife or shavehook, before new stopping is inserted.

RAW LINSEED OIL The oil obtained by crushing the seeds of the flax plant, filtered and refined in order to clarify it for use; it is termed "raw" oil not, as might be supposed, because it is the crude oil fresh from the crushing but to distinguish it from heat-treated oils such as boiled oil, blown oil, stand oil, etc. When paints were normally mixed on the site by the decorator it was the principal binding agent used in paint. It is a thin liquid, brownish yellow in colour, and should become surface dry within four days when spread out in a thin film on some inert material such as glass.

RAW SIENNA A yellow-brown earth colour consisting chiefly of iron oxide and containing smaller amounts of silica, alumina, oxide of manganese and calcium carbonate, found principally in Sicily and Italy and taking its name from the Italian town of Sienna. It is a somewhat transparent pigment, and for this reason is very useful in the tinting of glazes, when it makes a rich golden colour, and in the mixing of graining colour. Due to its manganese content it is a better drier than ochre although otherwise similar in composition.

RAW UMBER An earth pigment similar in composition to ochre and sienna but containing a higher proportion of oxide of manganese and consequently a good drier. It is a good stainer and, like all the earth pigments, is fast to light, durable and inexpensive to produce. Mixed with white it produces a fine range of cool subtle colourings.

REACTION The chemical action of one substance on another.

R

READY BOUND A term used about spirit colours such as drop black, etc., to signify to the purchaser that they have been ground with a small quantity of gold size or varnish medium and merely need thinning with turps or white spirit to prepare them for use. In this way they are distinguished from colours ground in turps which, if not bound with a little gold size before use, would tend to lift when varnish was applied upon them.

REALWOOD A very thin veneer of actual wood, fastened to a backing of thin flexible card, which is supplied in large sheets. It is used in conjunction with stiles and rails to form panelling effects with panels of any desired dimensions; after hanging it is stained to the required colour and varnished, when it is practically indistinguishable from genuine wood panelling. Realwood is fixed to the wall with a latex solution, and great care is needed in hanging it because the fixative adheres immediately on contact so that a sheet wrongly placed cannot be slid back into position. A roller is used to press the material down. At all stages of the work, both when the Realwood is being hung and when the stiles and rails are being fastened, any glue or fixative solution which encroaches on to the face of the material must be removed immediately; otherwise, it will reject the stain and cause an unsightly blemish.

RECEDING COLOURS   Colours which have the effect of making the surfaces to which they are applied appear more distant than they actually are. It is generally stated that blues, greens and greys fall into this category. It should be noted, however, that this statement is only true if it is qualified and that blue, for example, may actually be an *advancing* colour in relation to its adjacent colours or surroundings. Decorators should beware of the increasing tendency to accept glib definitions and sweeping dogmatic statements about colour as being necessarily true under all circumstances.

RED   One of the primary colours, both of light and of pigment. Used in colour coding to signify danger and to call attention to the presence of fire appliances.

RED LEAD   A bright orange-red pigment which is of the utmost importance in priming paints both for wood and metal. It is prepared by oxidizing molten lead until a yellow crust called massicot is formed; the massicot is then ground, washed and levigated, and then roasted again to cause further oxidation until the desired colour is obtained.

Red lead is an oxide of lead which contains some free or uncombined monoxide of lead; when the pigment is mixed with an oil or varnish medium the free monoxide combines readily with the medium and causes it to oxidize. For this reason red lead possesses the property of drying and hardening even when it is not exposed to the air, and therefore when it is drawn into the pores of an absorbent surface such as wood or plaster it is able to set hard. The film which it provides is very tough and highly protective, due to the lead soap which forms from the interaction of the pigment and the medium. There are, however, certain objections to the use of straight red lead as a primer for woodwork; the feeding of the pigment with the medium, together with its tendency to settle in the can, leads to ropey brushwork which can mar the appearance of the finished painting. In consequence it is more usual to employ a pink primer composed of a mixture of red and white lead, combining the advantages of each.

The chief value of red lead, however, is in the field of anti-corrosive painting; it is a rust inhibitive pigment which actively discourages the formation of rust by electrolytic and chemical action. In spite of the considerable volume of research which has taken place into the problems of corrosion and the various treatments that have been evolved, no other pigment has yet been found to displace it for use on normal structural steelwork. It is particularly useful for steelwork which is to be left exposed for a long period during and after erection without any further paint treatment, especially if a straight red lead/linseed oil mixture is employed to give the requisite film thickness. In locations exposed to a heavy concentration of chlorine or sulphur, however, red lead may be an unsuitable primer.

Because it is affected, like all lead pigments, by sulphur contamination, red lead is not used in finishing coats. At one time red lead was supplied in a powder and was hand mixed with oil immediately prior to use. This practice is now forbidden by law, and red lead powder may only be used in stopping or filling compositions. The fact still remains that ordinary red lead reacts so quickly with the medium that it should be used very soon after mixing; otherwise, settling will occur and a good deal of waste will result. Non-setting red lead is now available, however, which overcomes the drawbacks attendant upon rapid setting and provides a paint which can be stored normally without loss; it must be understood that some slight loss in performance is bound to result.

RED LEAD/GRAPHITE PRIMER A primer in which up to twenty per cent of the total weight is composed of graphite and the remainder of red lead. This produces a paint which works and spreads much more easily than straight red lead and does not settle to the same extent. It produces a thinner film, which some authorities think is less suitable than a straight red lead/oil paint for steelwork to be left exposed for long periods.

RED LITHOPONE A pigment composed of a mixture of cadmium sulpho-selenide co-precipitated with barium sulphate.

RED OXIDE An iron oxide pigment prepared by calcining a yellow oxide of iron such as ochre at a high temperature. For a long while it was pop-ularly regarded as an ideal pigment for the priming of iron and steel; it is now generally realized that red oxide has no rust inhibitive properties and that in fact the cheaper grades actually stimulate corrosion.

REDUCER An American term for a paint thinner.

REDUCING POWER The strength of a white pigment; the extent to which a white pigment when mixed with a definite proportion of coloured pigment is able to produce a pale tint, the strongest white pigments pro-ducing the palest tints.

REDWOOD A coniferous tree which is native to the U.S.A., and closely related to the Wellingtonia; these trees, which are the largest and tallest in the world and which reach an immense age, provide wood for construc-tional purposes and for decorative turnery. After the first seasoning the wood tends to assume a violet tint, a discolouration which stains or bleeds into any superimposed paint. The wood should be primed with aluminium primer to prevent this, and in some cases it is even necessary to use a sealer coat of thin shellac.

R

REFLECTED COLOUR Colour which is reflected from one brightly coloured surface upon another.

RELIEF A moulded, carved or stamped design which stands out above a plane or curved surface, the extent to which it projects being more or less in proportion to the object depicted in the design.

RELIEF GOODS   Decorative materials consisting of pre-formed relief designs, either hollow backed or solid backed, to be applied by the painter and decorator. See *Anaglypta* and *Lincrusta*.

REMOTE CUP OUTFIT   A piece of spray equipment designed to combine the advantages of a full-scale pressure feed set-up with the portability of a suction or gravity cup attached directly to the gun. It consists of a pressure feed cup of 2.2 litre capacity fitted with controls to balance the flow of air and fluid, and is connected to the gun by short lengths of air and fluid hose (usually about 1200mm long).

REMOVABLE SPRAYHEAD   A spray gun assembly consisting of an air cap, fluid needle and sprayhead body, designed as a complete unit which may be detached from the main body of the gun in one section. Its use offers several advantages, such as making possible quick changes from one material to another and facilitating cleaning. In case of damage to the front portion of a gun, the sprayhead may be replaced without the expense of obtaining a complete new gun.

REPETITIVE PATTERN   A pattern or design which can be repeated or reproduced several times over by a process such as stencilling, silk screening, etc.

RESIN   A natural resin (as opposed to a synthetic resin, which is described under a separate heading) is an amorphous substance obtained chiefly as an exudation from certain plants or trees. *Recent* or *virgin* resin is derived from the living tree, generally as a result of a deliberate incision being made in the trunk, and exudes in the form of globules or tears which harden when exposed to the atmosphere. *Fossil* resin is obtained from trees which lived many centuries ago; it is dug up from the ground in the locations where it has rested since the trees in which it was formed decayed in past ages, and it may occur at any depth varying between about one and fourteen metres. Resin is generally glassy in appearance with a slightly yellow-brownish colour; it is soluble in oil when heated, and in certain solvents, but is insoluble in water; it has no tendency to crystallize and has no definite melting point. Its particular interest to the painter and decorator lies in its value as a constituent of varnish. For the manufacture of decorators' varnishes fossil resin is used, being much harder than recent resin; the main sources of supply are East, Central and West Africa, the East and West Indies, New Zealand and South America. Recent resin obtained from Malaya, North Africa and the Mediterranean countries is used in the manufacture of picture varnish, crystal paper varnish and map varnish.

Shellac is a form of resin which does not exude directly from a tree but is formed by insect parasites which collect in swarms and feed upon the sap of a tree, the twigs eventually becoming embedded in the sticky mass that they produce.

RESINOUS TIMBERS   Certain woods such as Columbian pine, pitch pine, etc., are extremely resinous, so much so that when they are used in construction the resin has a strong tendency to exude not only from the knots but all over the surface of the wood. This has the effect of forcing off any paint which is applied to the surface, causing it to develop a large crop of blisters. For these timbers an aluminium primer is better than a lead primer; it is non-penetrative, and clings to the surface by means of the adhesiveness of the medium, the leafing effect of the aluminium flakes forming a metallic barrier of sufficient mechanical strength to hold back the resin.

RESPIRATOR   Under the provisions of the Construction (Safety, Health and Welfare) Regulations, respirators are to be provided for the use of operatives whenever any cleaning down or spraying of paintwork or other materials produces injurious fumes or dust.

RETARDANT or RETARDER   An ingredient added to a substance or mixture with the object of delaying or slowing down a certain occurrence; for example, megilp added to graining colour to delay the setting, the agglutinant added to a hemihydrate gypsum plaster to slow down the set, the materials added to cellulose lacquers to retard the evaporation rate, etc.

RETIRING COLOURS   Synonymous with "receding colours".

REVEAL   The surface at right angles to the face of a wall, at the side of an aperture, doorway or window.

REVEAL PIN   A device embodying a screw-jack, used in erecting tubular scaffolding in order to secure a puncheon into a window opening for the purpose of tying-in the scaffold to the building.

REVERSIBLE   In painting and decorating this term is applied to any paint or surface coating which softens up under the action of a solvent, e.g., cellulose lacquer, soft distemper, etc.

REVERSING ALTERNATE LENGTHS   A method employed in the hanging of plain, semi-plain and mottled wallpapers in which no definite pattern is apparent, in order to avoid any shading effect being noticeable. Such papers are sometimes slightly darker on one side than the other; if hung in a straightforward manner this slight difference of colour or tone is seen along each edge. The reversing of the alternate lengths is carried out during the cutting up of the paper, so that when it is hung each dark edge is alongside another dark edge and each light edge alongside another light edge.

REXINE   A leathercloth used as a wall hanging and also for upholstery, in which the fabric is coated with nitro-cellulose material. See *Leathercloth.*

RIBBON GOLD   Transfer gold leaf made up in the form of rolls, to be applied by means of a gilding wheel. The rolls vary in width from 9·5mm to 76mm and are usually 20 metres long.

R

RIDGE The apex of a sloping roof, running from end to end.

RIGGER A colloquial term for a coachpainter's liner, set in quill.

RIGHT-ANGLED COUPLER Also known as a hinged coupler or a double coupler. The load-bearing coupler used in tubular scaffolding to connect standards and ledgers at the principal node points.

RINSING Washing or cleaning a surface by means of the application of liberal quantities of clean water.

RISER The vertical front of a step in a staircase.

RIVELLING Also called "shrivelling" and "wrinkling". A defect in a gloss film taking the form of wrinkles which appear during the drying period, usually caused by an unduly heavy or liberal application of varnish or enamel whereby the surface skins over while the material underneath is still soft.

ROAD PAINT or ROAD LINE PAINT A quick drying and bitumen-resistant material composed of Manila resin dissolved in industrial spirit with the addition of a plasticizer and a suitable pigment, used for painting lines and traffic indications upon road surfaces.

ROLLER (i) A revolving drum, mounted on a handle and covered with some fabric or other material which will pick up paint from a suitably shaped container and will transfer the paint to a wall or ceiling surface to form an even coating. Rollers have been enthusiastically adopted by amateur decorators but are still regarded with suspicion by many professional painters; this is unfortunate because if used under favourable conditions on work which is suited to the technique they can give very good results and produce a significant economy in labour costs. Over a given area roller application is more than twice as fast as brush application; even allowing for cutting in, cleaning of the tools, etc., it is some forty to fifty per cent quicker on suitable work. Generally speaking, a suitable site for roller application would be one with large plain areas with relatively few window or door openings or features involving cutting in; the advantage would be even greater if the surfaces were rough as in fair-faced brickwork or lightly textured, and if for any reason the use of the spray was precluded the roller could very well prove to be the most economical form of application. It must be remembered, too, that the roller often gives better covering than the brush. Rollers are generally either 355mm, 254mm, 178mm or 51mm wide and the drum is covered either with lambswool, mohair or sponge rubber. They may be charged from a paint tray, but this is usually an inconvenient method of working. On large-scale work it is better to charge them from a bucket in which a framed piece of perforated metal or wire mesh is placed to remove the suplus paint from the roller.
(ii) A tool used by paperhangers; it may take the form of an angle roller or seam roller for pressing down and helping to minimize the joints in

wallpaper, or it may be a felt-covered or rubber-covered broad roller to be used instead of a paperhanging brush for smoothing down delicate wallpapers such as satins or flocks.

(iii) A tool intended to transfer a repeating pattern in paint on to a wall surface. See *Pattern Roller*.

ROLLER COATING   A term used to describe an industrial painting process whereby paint is applied by rollers to flat metal articles; the process is extensively employed in the production of food containers and in the manufacture of metal signs.

ROMAN ALPHABET   The symbols devised by the Romans to represent the various sounds made by the human voice in speech. They were probably derived from the Etruscan alphabet, which in turn had been derived from the earlier Greek. Records written in the Roman alphabet have been found dating as far back as the seventh century B.C., but it was not until the first century B.C., that examples became common; in this century, however, they became so frequent as to be innumerable. By this time the Etruscan characters had been adapted and various additions from the Greek alphabet incorporated to form the classic Roman alphabet of twenty-three characters which is the basis of the English alphabets now in use.

To the painter and decorator the term "Roman alphabet" is generally taken to mean the series of symbols found in the monumental Roman inscriptions, the forms of which were directly evolved from the use of the chisel, and which reached their fullest stage of development towards the close of the first century B.C. The supreme example is generally held to be the inscription on the base of the Trajan column at Rome dating from the year 114 A.D. It is considered that lettering of this period reached a peak which for legibility and beauty has never been surpassed.

The characters or symbols in the Roman alphabet each have their own particular basic shape, varying in width from the O and the Q which are as broad as they are high, through the slightly narrower letters C, G and D to the narrowest letters of all, which are the E, F and L (except, of course, for the I). As a general rule, the vertical strokes of the characters are the "thick" strokes, their width being about one-eleventh of the height, and the horizontal strokes are the "thin" strokes and are about two-thirds as wide as the thick strokes; the exception to this rule is the N, in which the oblique stroke is thick and vertical strokes thinner. The strokes are terminated at top and bottom with serifs which develop naturally from the shaping of the stroke. The distinctive quality of Roman lettering is the subtlety of its formation, the strokes being shaped or curved gradually out to the serif, the curved forms of such letters as the R and the B being modified so as to form a strong angle with the adjacent forms, and so on. This subtlety is completely lost if any attempt is màde to reduce it to mechanical forms. Mechanical methods of production, whereby the proportions of the letters are based upon a system of numbers and the strokes of the letters formed with instruments such as rulers and compasses, should never be applied to Roman lettering.

R

ROOF LADDER A properly constructed roof ladder consists of a long wooden frame which is laid upon the sloping surface of the roof from the edge to the apex. Projecting battens are secured across the framework at regular intervals to provide footholds; a hook made of metal tubing, shaped so as to pass over the ridge and grip the other side of the roof, is bolted on the end of the framework, and small wheels are mounted on the upper part of the ridge hook to facilitate pushing the ladder up the roof.

ROOT OF OAK The wood obtained by cutting across the base of the tree where the growth of the root system is developed; the grain is very much twisted and curled and the wood is dark in tone. The graining is undertaken in much the same way as pollard oak.

ROPES In order to comply with the Construction Regulations, ropes used for scaffolding should be of good construction, sound material, adequate strength, suitable quality, and free from patent defects; if they are defective through contact with acid or other corrosive substance they are to be discarded. They should be inspected for possible damage at least every six months, and in fact it is good policy to inspect them after each occasion of use, and to facilitate this they should be marked (e.g., with a copper sleeve on which an identifying figure is stamped) and a record kept of the inspections.

Manila or sisal ropes treated with a water repellent are generally used for scaffold work, but synthetic fibre ropes offer considerable advantages over these, especially in situations where they are exposed to the risk of damage by corrosive liquids such as cleaning compounds which might affect their strength. See *Synthetic Ropes.*

ROPINESS Also known as "ribbiness" or "tram lines". A defect in paintwork, whereby the brushmarks fail to flow out and are extremely conspicuous. It is generally due to faulty workmanship; the following are some of the possible factors leading to its occurrence:
(i) Uneven or careless application of the paint.
(ii) Piling too much paint upon the surface.
(iii) Overbrushing the paint until it has begun to set.
(iv) Using paint of too round or thick a consistency.
(v) Failing to keep the edges of paintwork alive, so that newly applied paint disturbs that which is already setting.
(vi) The use of dirty or clogged up brushes.
(vii) Insufficient sealing of the porosity of preceding coats, leading to the too rapid absorption of the medium of the newly applied paint.
(viii) The use of paints of a heavily pigmented type that will not flow out.

ROSEWOOD A type of tree found in Brazil, Argentina, the West and East Indies and India. The wood, which is brown, red-brown or a dark brown which is almost black, has a striped grain suggestive of marble markings, and is used for veneering, furniture and cabinet making and shop fitting. The grained imitation of rosewood may be carried out in oil or water colour with a graining colour of Vandyke brown, mahogany lake and black on a ground of bright terra-cotta. Overgraining is carried out with mahogany lake and black.

244

ROSIN See *Colophony*, which is another term for rosin.

ROTATION DIP or ROTO-DIP A method of paint application which is a development or extension of normal paint dipping and which is employed in many branches of mass production industrial surface coating, especially in the motor car industry, where the process is used for the phosphating and priming of car bodies. The object to be treated is secured to a horizontal spit and is passed along a conveyor line to be rotated through tanks which contain the requisite fluids and paint.

ROTTENSTONE A mild abrasive in the form of a very finely powdered soft yellowstone which is used in the hand polishing of varnished work, linseed oil being used as the lubricant. The surface, after careful preparation and painting, is bodied up with three or four coats of polishing varnish. The varnish is felted down with powdered pumice stone and water or with waterproof sandpaper and water and is leathered off and allowed to dry. It is then systematically polished with an oiled cotton wool pad covered with a piece of cambric and charged with rottenstone. It is necessary that the rubbing, which is carried out with a circular motion, should proceed in short spells, since prolonged friction would lead to the softening up of the varnish. After rottenstone has been used the surface is generally hand polished with flour to pick up the oil.

ROUGE ROI A highly decorative fossiliferous marble quarried extensively in Belgium; its colour varies from deep fawn to rich red-brown, the surface being broken with irregular patches of grey and soft white interspersed with strong veins of opaque white. It is generally imitated on a ground of light grey or white.

ROUGHCAST Sometimes called pebble-dash or harling. A form of external plastering, normally consisting of two coats of mixed cement and sand, in which a coating of pebbles or gravel is thrown on to the second coat before it is set.

ROUGHING IN A term used in the making good of defective plaster work to apply to the backing or rendering coat which is used when extensive repairs are necessary. It generally consists of one part of a retarded hemihydrate plaster gauged with three parts of clean sand.

R

ROUND A term used by the painter to describe a paint or similar material of stiff consistency which, when applied, produces a fairly thick film giving a high degree of "build". A paint is said to be too round when it is too stiff to allow of easy brushing and requires thinning before it can be properly applied.

ROUND BRUSH An alternative name for a pound brush.

ROUND COAT A full coat of heavy bodied paint or varnish.

RUBBER (i) A material produced by the coagulation and drying of the latex which is contained in numerous species of trees, shrubs and plants; the chief source of natural rubber is the *hevea brasiliensis* tree grown in Malaya, Ceylon and Indonesia. Natural rubber, although tough and elastic at normal temperatures, becomes hard in winter and soft and sticky at summer temperatures; this thermal instability is overcome by a process of vulcanization whereby the rubber is mixed with sulphur and subjected to heat treatment.

(ii) The tool used in the application of French polish. It consists of a pad of cotton wool which is saturated with polish; the pad is covered with a piece of lintless cotton or linen cloth which has previously been well washed to remove all traces of dressing or lime.

RUBBER COMBS Tools made of rubber, used in graining for the purpose of imitating the straight grain of wood. They lift the graining colour from the ground more cleanly than steel combs. Rubber combs with teeth of varying widths can be purchased, a familiar pattern being the triangular shaped combs which present three separate sides each with a different tooth arrangement. Many grainers, however, prefer to make up their own combs by cutting notches in the edge of a piece of rubber flooring; with the home made article it is possible to devise teeth of varying widths and of a size and pattern suited to the individual piece of work in hand.

RUBBER-SET BRUSHES Brushes in which the bristles or hairs are locked into place in a cement made of vulcanized rubber.

RUBBER STIPPLER A tool used in producing broken colour effects and also very useful for texturing plastic paint. It consists of a flat wooden base upon which are set a number of thin flat pieces of rubber arranged in a variety of ways. The broken colour effect is obtained by squeezing the face of the stippler upon a surface laid in with wet tinted glaze; the rubber strips remove the glaze and expose the ground colour. It will generally be found that the glaze, instead of being removed cleanly, tends to form into thick ridges which stand proud of the surface and remain fairly soft for a long while; a further criticism is that rubber stippling often produces an unpleasant mechanical effect. Unless it is very carefully carried out and the colours chosen with great discretion, rubber stippling is notable for the ugliness of the effect it produces.

RUBBERSEED OIL An oil sometimes used in paint manufacture, derived from the seeds of the *hevea brasiliensis.*

RUBBING BLOCK A flat piece of wood or a pad of cork, felt or rubber of a size which can conveniently be held in the hand, and over the face of which a piece of sandpaper is stretched; the object of the rubbing block is to ensure that the pressure of the hand is distributed evenly over the whole face of the sandpaper during the process of rubbing down.

RUBBING COMPOUND A mildly abrasive paste used for burnishing nitro-cellulose finishes, either by manual or mechanical methods, in order to produce a high degree of gloss.

RUBBING DOWN   A term covering all the various processes of preparation in which an abrasive substance is passed over a surface prior to painting.

RUBBING IN   The application of a thin film of graining colour on to a painted ground prior to executing a piece of figure graining. The term probably derives from the fact that the graining colour has to be applied very sparingly and brushed very vigorously with a rubbing motion in order to spread it out evenly enough and thinly enough for the purpose.

RUBBING-IN BRUSH   A short well-worn brush, usually not exceeding 50mm in width, which is reserved for rubbing in graining colour and is kept perfectly clean for the purpose, being never dipped into an opaque paint.

RUBBING VARNISH   A hard short-oil varnish not intended as a finishing varnish but as a material which will withstand rubbing down with abrasives such as powdered pumice or waterproof sandpaper prior to the application of further varnish coatings. Rubbing varnish is made with specially selected resins which will not readily scratch and which can be rubbed down without exhibiting a tendency to soften up or "sweat"

RUMBLING   See *Tumbling.*

RUN LINES   Straight painted lines, produced by means of a lining fitch and straightedge, so called because if the lining fitch is used correctly the lines are produced by long rapid strokes.

RUNS   Runs are defects in a painted surface, occurring most commonly in gloss films but by no means restricted to these, which take the form of localized swellings where an excess of paint has flowed downwards and stands proud of the remainder of the surface. Runs are generally due to the material being unevenly distributed. They may also be caused by the accumulation of excess quantities of paint in various kinds of surface irregularities such as holes or cracks or in mouldings, the excess paint continuing to flow when the surrounding paint has set.

R

RUST   The product of the corrosion of iron or steel, due largely to electrolytic action. It consists mainly of hydrated ferric oxide with some basic ferrous or ferric carbonates also present.

RUST CREEP   A term used to describe the action which takes place when the paintwork protecting an area of iron or steel is broken or damaged, and the rust which forms on the exposed metal is not limited to the area of damage but tends to spread outwards beneath the surrounding paint work, leading eventually to the paint being pushed off and to widespread corrosion taking place. Rust creep is accelerated by the presence of salt due to electrolytic action (see the paragraph on *Salt* for further details). The presence of a phosphate coating under the paint stifles the electrolytic action and restricts the spread of rust.

RUST INHIBITIVE PIGMENTS Pigments which check the tendency of iron and steel to corrode, by precipitating a thin protective film on the surface of the metal. Since the pigment must pass into solution in order for this action to take place, it follows that an inhibitive pigment must possess some degree of water-solubility and that the medium which binds it must not completely prevent the access of water. Pigments known to possess rust inhibitive qualities include red lead, basic lead chromate, white lead, sublimed blue lead, zinc chromate and zinc dust.

RUTILE A mineral and commercial form of titanium dioxide with a characteristic crystalline structure.

S

SABLE (i) A type of animal hair obtained from an animal of the polecat family called the kolinski. It is a very slender and fine hair, yet is also very strong and resilient; for this reason it is an ideal material for signwriters' brushes, fine artists' brushes and water-colour brushes. The best quality is known as red sable.
(ii) The heraldic term for black.

SABLES The colloquial term used by signwriters to denote signwriting brushes made from sable hair.

SAFETY BELT A device intended to prevent an operative from falling when working in a precarious situation where an effective scaffold is impracticable. It generally consists of a leather belt, with or without harness, and a length of rope with a snap hook at the end. Nylon ropes may be used, and sometimes the belt itself is made from nylon or similar synthetic fibre.

SAFETY CHAIR A development from the normal type of bosun's chair, intended to give a greater measure of security to the occupant. Several patterns are available; the essential features of all of them are that the framework is of metal, that a back rest is provided, that the operative is compelled to sit with his legs astride the suspension unit or a portion of the metal framework, and that either a safety chain is provided or else the framework itself ensures that the operative is completely enclosed at waist level; the object of these features is to make it impossible for the operative to slip out of the chair even if for any reason he should become unconscious.

SAFETY FEET Devices consisting either of rubber suction pads or of adjustable metal units which are attached to the stiles at the base of a ladder to prevent it from slipping when in use on smooth floors. While ladders fitted with these devices are useful for factory work, the general experience seems to be that operatives tend to place too much reliance upon them and to pull out the foot of the ladder much too far for safety, defeating the purpose of the device.

SAFETY FOOTWEAR Boots or shoes fitted with internal steel toe caps, to give protection against falling objects and to prevent injury caused by striking the toes against hard objects. Modern safety footwear is available in a wide range of styles and sizes and is indistinguishable from normal footwear. It is not much used in the painting and decorating trade, but is a wise safety precaution for those engaged in factory work or work on building sites.

SAFETY HELMET Another device rarely used in painting and decorating but of great value on large building sites, since a large number of accidents are caused by falling objects. Modern safety helmets are often made from resin bonded fibreglass, with a head harness of polythene.

SAFETY SHEETS, SAFETY NETS Also called "protection sheets", "man-catching protection sheets" and "safety nets". Canvas sheets available in various sizes, the usual sizes being 6 metres by 4·5 metres, 6 metres square, and 9 metres by 4·5 metres, which are strong enough to support the weight of a person falling into them and which are very often the only safeguard for operatives engaged in roof work. The canvas should be rot proofed and provided with diagonal webbing reinforcements.

SAFFLOWER OIL A drying or semi-drying oil derived from the seeds of a plant grown in India, Egypt, Asia Minor, U.S.A. and Australia. It oxidizes at a slower rate than linseed oil, but is a useful material for the modification of alkyd resins and is also used in artists' colours. A yellow dye is derived from the flower of the safflower plant; this is often confused with saffron but is actually quite distinct from it.

SAFFRON A water stain derived from a bulbous plant of the crocus family grown in Asia Minor; it is used in staining satin and birch wood.

SAGGING Another term for curtaining. See *Curtains* and *Curtaining*.

SALT The name given to a class of compounds which can be regarded as acids the hydrogen of which is wholly or partially replaced by a metal. A typical example is sodium chloride, otherwise known as common salt, which is a compound of the metal sodium with the gas chlorine and which is found in large deposits in many parts of the world and is present in dissolved condition in sea water.

S

Common salt sets up a strong corrosive action upon iron and steel, a factor which is of great importance when considering the protective treatment of these metals where they are to be exposed to marine atmospheres, and which also affects the treatment of motor car bodies because of the practice in large towns and cities of distributing salt on the roads to clear ice and snow in the winter. Should the paint film protecting the metal be broken or scratched, the exposed metal begins to corrode and rust is formed. The salt which is present acts as an electrolyte; the rust assumes anodic polarity, and is surrounded by a cathodic area where caustic soda is formed. The caustic soda, being alkaline, saponifies the priming paint and loosens the whole paint system on either side of the damaged part. When the loosened paint peels off, the newly exposed metal rapidly corrodes and the electrolytic action proceeds at an accelerated rate.

Common salt is a hygroscopic material, i.e., it readily imbibes moisture from the atmosphere. This is a factor which sometimes assumes great importance to the painter and decorator. If sea sand has for any reason been incorporated into building materials there is a strong tendency for the affected areas either to remain permanently damp or persistently to become damp in periods of humid weather; in the same way, property which is subjected to damage by flooding from sea water is likely to be badly affected by persistent damp. See *Deliquescent Salts.*

SALT SPRAY TEST   A test applied by paint manufacturers to metal finishes in order to assess their anti-corrosive properties. It involves spraying a painted panel with salt solution at frequent intervals.

SALUBRA   The proprietary name given to a range of imported wallpapers with a washable smooth surface.

SAND BLASTING   A method of removing rust and scale from steelwork prior to painting, leaving a roughened surface to which paint adheres readily. The method is particularly useful in the preparation of cast iron where the use of wet treatments based on acids or alkalis might lead to chemicals being trapped in the porous casting, giving rise to blistering in the paint film.

SAND DRY   The point at which a paint film is dry enough for dry silver sand sprinkled on the surface to be removed by means of a soft hair brush without suffering damage.

SANDARIC RESIN   A natural resin produced in North Africa, used in the preparation of map varnishes and paper varnishes.

SANDING   An abrasive process used to level a surface before the application of a decorative or protective coating; sanding may be applied to a variety of surfaces but the term is chiefly used in connection with the preparation of wood. In woodworking factories and in workshops devoted to the manufacture of furniture, large power feed drum sanders and belt sanders are employed; to the painter and decorator, the sanding machines in most common use are portable tools, which may be powered either by electricity or compressed air and which may take the form of belt sanders, rotary discs, straight line machines or orbital sanders. For most types of work orbital sanders are the most suitable but for wood which is to be stained or clear finished the final sanding should be carried out with the straight line type; otherwise, scratches across the grain will mar the appearance of the work.

The most usual abrasive is a garnet paper, but for the harder types of wood an aluminium oxide paper is more suitable, being tougher. In the interests of economy on labour costs it is best to use the coarsest grade of grit that will produce a sufficiently smooth finish.

SANDING SEALER   A hard sealer coat applied to wood, in order to fill the grain without obscuring it, prior to sanding.

SANDPAPER   The most commonly used of all the abrasive materials; it consists of stout cartridge paper coated with glue and strewn with powdered glass, sand or flint. It should be stored in a dry place; otherwise, the glue becomes soft and the grit is loosened.

SANITARY WALLPAPER   A type of wallpaper printed in oil colours, which is used in the decoration of kitchens, bathrooms, canteens, etc., where a steamy atmosphere prevails and where the more customary distemper printed wallpaper would rapidly suffer damage. Sanitary papers are very often varnished after hanging. They are now, however, practically obsolete.

SANS SERIF   Literally, "without serif". A type of plain block alphabet devoid of serifs.

SAPONIFICATION   The process by which an oil or fat is decomposed by reaction with an alkali and converted into a soap. It affects the work of the painter and decorator when oil paint is to be applied to an alkaline surface in the presence of moisture, the free alkali attacking the oil and decomposing it, causing free glycerine to be released. This results in the paintwork blistering, discolouring, losing its gloss and becoming soft and sticky. The affected areas often develop drops or runs of a sticky brown liquid; in really severe cases the whole of the paintwork becomes sticky and liquefied. Surfaces which affect paint in this manner include new plaster, concrete, cement, asbestos-cement sheeting, etc. Portland cement products are very highly alkaline. Pure lime plaster alone is not particularly destructive to oil paints but if contaminated by soluble alkali from the backing material it becomes highly destructive; gypsum plasters are not in themselves harmful to oil paint but lime is sometimes added to them by the plasterer in order to make them work more easily, and they may be contaminated by alkaline material brought forward from the backing. When an oil paint system is to be applied to such surfaces they should be given ample time to dry out, and should then be sealed with alkali resisting primer.

S

   Saponification can also be produced by failure to remove the detergents used in preparing a surface for repainting, or when paint has been removed from a porous surface by means of a caustic paint stripper if sufficient care is not taken to neutralize or remove all trace of the stripper. The binding medium in oil-bound water paints is not usually affected by alkaline action but saponification may occur if the surface is very strongly active and if the work is carried out while the surface is still very damp.

   It should be noted that although alkaline attack only takes place when moisture is present, so that if the surface is completely dry it should in theory be safe to apply oil paint directly upon it, any penetration of water into the surface at a subsequent date may re-activate the alkali and cause saponification.

It has been indicated that saponification is generally due to the alkaline nature of the surface to which the paint is applied. It is also possible, however, for paint applied to a completely inert surface such as wood or metal to be saponified by external attack, if alkaline materials or solutions are allowed to splash it or encroach upon it.

SAPWOOD The younger, outer zone of wood in a tree trunk, lying nearest to the bark, generally softer and often paler than the remainder of the timber. The word is very often used wrongly by the painter and decorator, who confuses sapwood with heartwood, and speaks of a piece of heartwood graining as "a sap".

SASH TOOL A round brush, bound either with string or metal, of a size suitable for cutting in window putties. Now generally superseded by the 25mm paint brush.

SASH WINDOW A window formed with sashes, i.e. with sliding, glazed frames running in vertical grooves.

SATIN FINISHES A name often applied to wall paints which dry with an eggshell sheen.

SATIN PAPER Wallpaper grounded with distemper which is then polished and glazed to produce a satin-like sheen before printing. Satin papers need careful handling so that the glazed surface does not become cracked during pasting and folding or scratched during hanging. Some paperhangers use a felt covered roller in preference to a papering brush to reduce the risk of scratching the surface.

SATINWOOD A very light coloured wood used in furniture and cabinet making; a somewhat darker wood also known as satinwood is used for constructional purposes. The light wood can be imitated by a similar process to that used in mahogany graining; the graining colour is made up from raw sienna, burnt sienna and raw umber, on a ground of yellowish white, and the work is overgrained with a very thin glaze of blue-black or ivory-black.

SCAFFOLD BOARD The correct term for what is more commonly known as a plank. See *Plank*.

SCAFFOLD BOARD CLIP A device for anchoring scaffold boards to tubular scaffold either in a vertical position (for toe boards) or in a horizontal position.

SCAFFOLDING A temporary framework consisting of poles or metal tubes and planks, etc., on or from which work may be performed during constructional or maintenance operations on a building, or by means of which access may be obtained to the working area.

SCAGLIOLA An imitation stonework effect. Scagliola itself is generally confined to indoor work and consists of fine plaster of Paris mixed with glue, which is polished after application, and into which pieces of gypsum and marble may be embedded. This term is sometimes used to refer to plastic paint treatments giving similar effects.

SCALDING An operation carried out in the process of glass gilding, in which very hot water (*not* boiling, because of the danger of cracking the glass) is lightly swabbed across the face of the gold leaf with a squirrel hair mop in order to improve the lustre; it has the effect of dissolving and clearing any traces of gelatine that remain between the gold and the glass to mar the appearance of the gold. The operation needs to be carried out extremely carefully, especially in frosty weather.

SCALING Another term for flaking.

SCARLET A bright red colour tending towards orange.

SCARLET CHROME A lead chromate pigment obtained by replacing part of the chromium radical with molybdenum.

SCORCHING Scorching is liable to occur when a surface is being burned off if the lamp or torch flame is allowed to linger in one spot. It is permissible and indeed desirable to scorch any large knots in order to extract as much of the resin as possible, but scorching of any other part of the wood is to be avoided as it destroys the cellular properties of the timber and has an adverse effect upon the adhesion of the paint.

SCOTCH GLUE The best quality cake glue.

SCOTS PINE A general purpose softwood, the one most widely used in the building trade for constructional purposes, formerly known as fir but now almost universally called Scots pine.

SCRIM A thin strong type of muslin, sold in long rolls of varying widths, and used by the decorator for the preparation of bad surfaces prior to paperhanging. It is particularly useful when papers or fabrics have to be hung on woodwork; unless scrim is hung first the movement of the wood soon causes the paper to split.

S

There are two methods of applying scrim; one method is to paste the surface of the wood, hang the scrim dry, and then apply paste all over the face of the scrim; the other method is to dip the scrim in paste, wring it out, apply it to the wood and secure it with tacks, the tacks being removed when the work is dry. As the scrim dries out it shrinks and the wrinkles disappear.

Narrow rolls of scrim are available for covering the joints in building boards.

SCUMBLE A semi-transparent stain or glaze which is applied over a hard dry ground of a different colour; while the scumble is wet it is manipulated in such a way as to expose portions of the ground colour. If differs from a glaze in that it is used to produce a broken colour effect by means of a sharp distinction between the scumble colour and the ground colour, whereas a glaze is used solely to modify the ground colour and is similar in colour to the ground.

The essential features of a scumble are that it should remain open long enough to be manipulated but should retain the markings made in it without flowing out. A scumble may be made of oil colour or water colour; oil scumbles include proprietary scumble stains and mixtures, made up on the site, of transparent glaze medium tinted with various stainers, and water scumbles are made with powdered pigments bound with fuller's earth or stale beer with a little glycerine added where necessary to retard the drying.

SCUMBLE STAIN A semi-transparent oil stain, often of a rather pronounced colour, used for graining (especially brush graining) and other broken colour effects. Some excellent proprietary brands of scumble stains are available which work far more smoothly than home mixed varieties and which have the capacity to remain open longer for manipulation without the drawback of flowing out and losing their clarity; proprietary scumbles are usually ready for immediate use, merely requiring thinning with white spirit and sometimes easing out with oil. Scumble stain may also be used as a stain applied directly to bare wood.

SCUMBLING The production of broken colour effects by means of scumbles applied over appropriately tinted grounds, and suitably manipulated. The methods by which the effects are achieved include graining, brush graining, combing with steel or rubber combs, rag rolling, rubber stippling, rolling with crinkled paper, and, in the case of plastic painted or other textured surfaces, wiping with soft cloth to reveal the highlights.

Dark brown scumbles are often applied over metallic paints and then wiped to produce antique leather or oxidized effects. When water scumble is used for this purpose it may be applied directly on to the metallic paint, but if oil scumble is being used the metallic paint should be given a buffer coat of clear lacquer before scumbling is commenced.

SEALERS Liquids, which may be either clear or pigmented, and which are used to reduce the suction of absorbent surfaces, to bind down previous coatings or loose material, or to prevent any soluble matter on or in the surface from damaging the new paint system. The term includes such materials as quick-drying varnishes for checking porosity, thin oily solutions for penetrating oil coatings and binding down loose matter, shellac solutions for treating the knots in timber or for preventing bleeding in its various forms, and aluminium powder, which may be used in conjunction with other sealer materials such as shellac and which is also used for preventing bleeding.

SEALING COAT Sealer.

SEAM ROLLER A narrow roller used by paperhangers in order to press down the joints in paper and render them less conspicuous.

SEASONED TIMBER Wood which has been treated in such a way as to reduce drastically its moisture content in order that it may become stable and may be used without serious risk of distortion. Timber which is freshly felled very often has a moisture content of 100 per cent of its oven-dry weight, i.e., its moisture content accounts for half the total weight of the log. Wood which has been seasoned naturally in the open air has a moisture content of about 15 per cent of the oven-dry weight. Natural seasoning is a lengthy process, and for this reason much timber nowadays is artifically seasoned or "kiln dried"; the moisture content of artificially seasoned wood is often as low as 10 per cent of the oven-dry weight. From the painter's point of view, the low moisture content of kiln dried timber presents certain disadvantages, as it means that the wood tends to take up moisture from outside sources, and considerable fluctuation may take place.

SECOND COATING Applying the second coat of paint on top of a previous coat.

SECONDARY COLOURS Colours produced by the combination of two primary colours, e.g., orange composed of red and yellow, green composed of blue and yellow, and purple composed of red and blue.

SEEDINESS Also called "pepperiness". A defect in a gloss paint film, taking the form of evenly distributed minute specks. It is generally due to the use of a coarse or insufficiently ground pigment but it may also develop in a paint which has been stored for a long period.

SELECTIVE TREATMENT The treatment of one or more walls in a room, or of some particular feature of the interior or exterior of a building, in such a way as to make it markedly different from the remaining areas, e.g., the painting of one wall in a different colour from the remainder, or the use of some special pattern or texture on one particular wall or feature. Selective treatments are justified when there is some legitimate reason for emphasizing a feature, when used to add interest to what would otherwise be a dull and pedestrian scheme, or when used to compensate for the difference between a heavily shaded wall and a wall receiving strong sunlight. When used just for the sake of producing novel effects they tend to become irritating.

S

SELENIUM RED Cadmium red.

SELF-ADHESIVE Capable of being attached to a surface without the application of some additional adhesive, e.g., self-adhesive masking tape, which is supplied ready for use and which sticks to a surface on contact, or the ready pasted wallpapers which have been in use in the U.S.A. for some time and which are now on sale in this country.

SELF-CHALKING LINE A snap line which, when withdrawn from its container, is automatically charged with chalk or powdered colour.

SEMI-GLOSS The term applied to a material which is designed to present a higher degree of gloss than a flat or eggshell sheen product but which has not the mirror-like appearance of a full gloss paint.

SEMI-TRIMMED PAPERS Wallpapers or ceiling papers which are perforated along each side so that the selvedge can be removed without the use of trimmers. There are two methods by which the perforated strip can be removed; one method is to cut the paper to length, paste it and then pull the strip away; the other method is to take the complete roll of dry paper and strike each edge in turn sharply against a rigid surface, when the perforated strip will be cleanly removed in one piece. The second method is quicker and probably more effective, but care is needed to make sure that only the extreme tip of the roll is struck against the rigid surface; otherwise the paper may be damaged.

SEPARATION See *Floating*.

SEQUENCE OF COATS The principle underlying the formation of a sound paint system, whereby each separate coat is mixed in such a way that it contributes some definite characteristic to the system as a whole. Opinion has always been sharply divided as to the most satisfactory sequence of coats, some authorities maintaining that flat coats and oily coats should alternate throughout the system while others contend that each coat should be made progressively more oily and elastic than the previous one. The matter is no longer of major importance; the drying mechanism of modern finishes is not subject to the limitations of old-time products, and the undercoatings supplied by the manufacturers are designed to build up a carefully balanced system which would only be disturbed by the ill-considered addition of random quantities of linseed oil.

SETTING OUT The preliminary marking out of a piece of work as a guide to the actual execution.

SETTLING Separation of a pigment from the medium whereby it no longer remains in suspension but sinks to the bottom of the container where it forms a hard solid cake. Certain pigments such as red lead, ultramarine blue, vermilion, etc., are notoriously prone to settling. Flat oil paints and other heavily pigmented materials tend to settle if kept in storage for long periods; this tendency can be checked to some extent by inverting the tins on the shelves at regular intervals.

SGRAFFITO or GRAFFITO A method of producing an ornamental device by scratching through a layer of plaster to reveal a differently coloured ground. The technique is a very old one, and examples are to be seen in the ancient town of Pompeii. The process has been adapted in many ways for painted decoration; sgraffito effects are frequently used in plastic paint, for example. It is occasionally employed as a purely painted treatment; on a dry and hard painted ground a flat oil paint (usually with glaze medium added to retard the set) is laid in, and the ornament is then boldly drawn in the wet paint. Very often an indiarubber is used to remove the paint cleanly. Sgraffito is essentially a freehand technique and needs to be carried out confidently without any niggling.

SHADE Strictly speaking, a colour darkened by the addition of black. The word is very often used loosely and incorrectly; people frequently speak of a shade when they mean a colour, or speak of a "pale shade" when they mean a tint.

SHADE CARD A card upon which several small samples of colours are mounted in order to exhibit the colour range of a manufacturer's product or to describe or correlate certain groupings of colours.

SHADING (i) The process of comparing several rolls of wallpaper with one another to ascertain that the colour in each case is exactly the same. In spite of the great care that is taken at the wallpaper mills it occasionally happens that slight variations of colour occur between one batch and another, and it is important that the paperhanger should "shade" the papers in good light before trimming them or cutting them up.
(ii) A term used in signwriting to denote painting an inscription in such a way as to make it appear that each individual letter is a solid three-dimensional object projecting outwards from the surface. It is carried out by painting what purports to be a shadow to each letter, in the position where a shadow would be cast upon the background surface if the letters were solid and a bright light were coming from one single point. Sometimes the shading is in black, but very often all attempt at realism is discarded and shading becomes a means of providing a pleasing multi-colour effect. The purist despises shading, and indeed shading would be out of place on work demanding a dignified piece of lettering; nevertheless, there are occasions when shading is a legitimate method of enriching a signboard.
    For shading to be successful, certain points should be observed:
(a) The shading colour should be markedly deeper in tone than the colour of the letters; otherwise, the shape of the letters becomes confused.
(b) A narrow gap should be left between the edge of the letters and the edge of the "shadow".
(c) The perspective of the shadows should be exaggerated.
    It is generally considered that shading to the right of the letters gives a more effective appearance than shading to the left, but that shading to the right takes longer to execute.

S

SHARP COAT A thin coating of paint, generally white lead paint, which has been well thinned down with turps or white spirit and which contains a minimum of oil, e.g., the type of paint mixture used in "following the trowel".

SHARP COLOUR or SHARP PAINT A colloquial term for any rapid drying paint yielding a flat film.

SHAVEHOOK A tool used in burning off, especially designed for removing paint from mouldings. It is used with a pulling motion and is therefore less liable than a knife to cause damage to the contours of the moulding. Three patterns are available, namely those with triangular heads, those with pear-shaped heads and those with combination heads offering a variety of different shapes suitable for various contours.

SHEARINESS A defect in a paint film similar to flashing. The term can be applied to any film which exhibits an uneven degree of gloss, but is chiefly used to refer to flat or semi-gloss films in which localized glossy streaks are seen or in which small areas are pulled up. It may be due to overbrushing, or to failure to keep the edges alive so that a partially set area of paint is disturbed. It may also be due to applying the material on an excessively porous surface or a surface which has been inadequately sealed and undercoated.

SHEEN The slight degree of gloss or lustre seen on an eggshell finish or semi-gloss finish.

SHELF LIFE The length of time that a paint or other decorative material will remain in usable condition when placed in storage.

SHELLAC A spirit soluble resin formed from the secretion of insect parasites which attach themselves to the branches of trees, the twigs eventually becoming encrusted with the substance. The chief source of supply is India. The best quality is known as orange shellac, cheaper grades being called button shellac or garnet shellac. White shellac is made by bleaching the resin with alkali.

Shellac forms the basis of French polish and of many kinds of spirit varnish. When dissolved in methylated spirits it is used by the painter as knotting, to prevent the resin from the knots in timber from bleeding into a paint film; it is also used as a sealer to prevent various other substances from bleeding.

SHELLING Another term for flaking.

SHERARDIZING A method of treating iron and steel in order to obtain a rust-proof surface; it consists of heating the iron or steel in the presence of zinc dust in such a way that an amalgamation of the two metals takes place, an iron-zinc alloy being formed. Provided the bare metal is thoroughly prepared and cleaned, a high degree of protection is afforded. Since sherardizing is a heat treatment carried out in enclosed containers of limited size, there are certain obvious limitations to its use. It is, however, employed in the manufacture of steel window frames, iron railings, gates and door furniture of various kinds as well as in many other fields which are not of direct concern to the painter. It is also used for the treatment of steel scaffold couplers and of the metal fittings on other types of scaffolding equipment such as steps, etc.

When sherardized surfaces are to be painted it is generally found that they are roughened enough to give good paint adhesion and no further pre-treatment is necessary.

SHIP'S BOTTOM PAINT Anti-fouling paint containing poisonous ingredients to deter the formation of marine growths.

SHOP PRIMING Priming paint applied to wooden or metal articles while they are still in the workshop prior to delivery on the building site. In theory this is the ideal treatment, since the articles are given a good measure of protection under ideal conditions before they are subjected to outdoor exposure; in practice the quality of the priming paint very often leaves much to be desired, and the shop priming proves a most unsatisfactory foundation for a painting system.

It should be remembered that even when the shop priming is of excellent quality there is always the possibility of the film being damaged in course of transit to the site, and that the primed articles should be inspected and any damage rectified immediately they arrive on the site.

SHORT OIL A term applied to a varnish or varnish medium indicating that it contains a low proportion of oil in relation to its resin content. The British Standards Institution defines a short oil varnish as one containing not more than 1¼ parts of oil by weight to 1 part by weight of resin. Short oil varnishes are more lustrous but less elastic than long oil varnishes; they are used for interior work where a high gloss is of more importance than durability, and for gold sizes; if used on exterior work they would tend soon to craze and perish. A short oil alkyd is an alkyd resin containing not more than 40 per cent of oil as a modifying agent.

SHOT BLASTING A very effective method of removing rust and mill scale from steelwork prior to painting, which leaves the surface slightly roughened and therefore more receptive to paint than a smooth surface; it consists of directing at the surface a blast of air laden with small particles of metal, generally small steel shot. There are obvious limitations to the use of this process on erected steelwork because of the danger to other operatives and also because of the waste of shot involved. There is, however, a proprietary type of shotblasting plant which incorporates a vacuum device to reclaim the shot, clean it and pass it back into circulation, and which also includes a device to prevent the shot from straying beyond the steelwork; this equipment is perfectly safe for site use.

The size of shot, the blasting pressure and the distance of the nozzle from the work all need to be carefully controlled; otherwise, instead of producing a slight roughness which improves the adhesion of the paint the process may roughen the steel to the extent of producing pits and peaks of steel which project through the paint film. Some authorities maintain that although shot blasting is excellent for removing scale it is less successful in cleaning a badly rusted surface on the grounds that the particles of shot merely bridge the pits in the corroded metal and tend to hammer the rust in instead or removing it.

SHOT SILK EFFECTS Effects whereby a painted object appears to change its colour according to the position of the viewer. Such effects may be achieved on a textured surface, such as a wall textured in plastic paint,

S

by careful manipulation of a spray gun. A typical method is as follows:

The whole surface is coated with aluminium or bronze and allowed to dry; the surface is next sprayed lightly with one colour with the spray gun held at an angle to the work so that only one side of the depressions and cavities in the surface is struck; the surface is then sprayed again with a different colour with the gun held at a different angle, and so on. By this means three or four colours may be superimposed on the metallic ground.

For industrial finishing, a polychromatic metallic cellulose is produced which, with a special technique of spray gun application, gives a two-tone translucent shot silk effect.

SHRIVELLING See *Rivelling.*

SI UNITS During the development of science and industry over the centuries two main systems of measurement evolved: the Imperial system, e.g., inch, foot, yard, pound; and the metric system; e.g., millimetre, centimetre, metre, kilogramme. Both these systems grew at random, i.e. they were not worked out in detail from the beginning, and consequently they both contain many inconsistencies, which are now becoming a serious handicap in our modern complex world. In the early 1960s, therefore, a move was made to look to the future and *plan,* once and for all, a logical system of units that would be suitable for use throughout the world. That system is known as SI (Système International) and is a rationalized, simplified metric system which has been internationally agreed as the system of the future. It is simpler than either of the systems it replaces.

From the painter and decorators's point of view the effect is that:
Length is measured in millimetres (mm), metres (m), kilometres (km)
Weight is measured in grammes (g), kilogrammes (kg)
Volume is measured in millilitres (ml), litres (l)
Force is measured in newtons (N)
Pressure is measured in bars (b)*
Energy is measured in joules (J)
Horsepower is measured in kilowatts (kW)

SICCATIVE An alternative term for *driers.*

SIENNA A type of marble distinguished by its warmth and richness of colour, with groups of stone-like shapes of various sizes linked by fine veining. It is imitated on a white ground with a palette of raw sienna, burnt sienna, chrome yellow, Indian red, ultramarine blue and white; the effect should be of soft masses of pale cream, rosy red, grey and deep yellow, with veins of purple, reddish grey and brown.

SIERRA LEONE COPAL A fossil resin used in varnish manufacture, derived from West Africa. The supply is practically exhausted, but recent resin from the same type of tree is obtained from the same region.

SIGN KIT A small toolbox containing tubes of fine colours, tins of gold

---

* 1 bar = 10^5 N/m² = 10^5 pascals = 1·02 kg/cm² = $14\frac{1}{2}$lb/in²

size of various drying times, a screw-top jar for turps, a number of dippers, a chalk line and folding rule, an expanding mahlstick and, of course, a set of signwriting brushes.

SILICA   The oxide of the metal silicon obtained from quartz, flint and similar materials. It is used in the manufacture of Japan fillers, and also as an extender and suspending agent in certain types of paint.

SILICATE WATER PAINTS   Water paints based on sodium silicate or potassium silicate. Their main feature is their non-inflammability, which places them in group 1 of the available fire-retarding paints, but they are not greatly used by the painter and decorator because of their alkaline nature which restricts the number of pigments that can be used with them and because they cannot be followed up with normal oil paints unless sealed with alkali resisting primer. They tend to cause efflorescence to develop if they are used on plaster, concrete or brickwork.

SILICONE RESINS   A group of resins containing a substantial amount of silicon which have recently attained considerable importance in various fields affecting painting and decorating.
(i) Paints based on silicone resins have outstanding properties of resistance to heat, and are largely unaffected by acids, alkalis, salt solutions or oils, particularly at ordinary temperatures. The type of most interest to the industrial painting contractor is that which is pigmented with aluminium powder, with silicone resin as the sole medium; this type of paint is capable of withstanding temperatures which exceed 540°C (1000°F) and is used for the surface coating of steel smoke stacks and factory chimneys, boilers, heaters, mufflers, etc., and is also being increasingly used in the aircraft industry. Its adhesion to steel surfaces is not so positive as that of conventional oil modified coatings; it is therefore essential that the surface should be thoroughly cleaned and all organic paints, scale and rust removed. The full heat and corrosion resistance of the paint is not developed until it has been stoved at a temperature of between 200 and 250°C (392 and 482°F) in order to polymerize the resin; this presents no obstacle, however, as although it would obviously be impossible to apply normal stoving technique to such huge articles as boilers or smoke stacks, these temperatures are reached when the articles are put into use. The resistance of silicone resin paints to organic solvents is poor until the paint has been cured.

Although they are of less interest to the painter and decorator it is worth mentioning that a wide range of coloured silicone resin paints is available for the coating of numerous items of industrial and household equipment such as cookers, heaters, etc., where vitreous enamel is normally employed. An important feature is that white silicone paints retain their colour without yellowing when exposed to heat. The pigments used have a marked effect upon the properties of the paint; rutile and anatase pigments are used for white paints, while for coloured paints Monastral blue, Monastral green, cadmium sulphide, red iron oxide, carbon black and aluminium are used. Lead pigments are not employed as they promote rapid gellation of the silicone varnishes. Corrosion resistance has been improved by the use

S

zinc primers based upon silicone resins. All these paints need stoving in order to develop their full heat resistance.

Recent developments have led to the combination of silicone resins with organic resins such as phenolic, epoxy and alkyd resins to yield heat resisting paints which also possess the properties of the organic resins employed, and to the introduction of air-drying paints based on a chemical combination of silicone and alkyd resins.

(ii) A recent extension in the use of silicone resins which is of importance to painters and decorators is their introduction into waterproofing or water-repellent fluids for building surfaces such a brickwork, stonework, reconstituted stone, cement, concrete, cinder block, stucco, etc., for which purpose they are very effective. The fluid is applied by brush or spray, preferably during a good spell of dry weather. It operates not by filling the surface pores but by lining them with a water-repellent film which inhibits capillary absorption, with the result that water falling on the treated surface does not form a continuous film but remains in the form of droplets which run off. Until recently, water-repellent fluids were based upon waxes, oils, fats or metallic soaps and although advertised as colourless they did cause a slight but noticeable alteration in the tone or texture of some types of surfaces. Fluids based on silicone resins are completely colourless, and in fact it is the practice of some manufacturers to incorporate a proportion of fugitive dye so that the operative can be sure of not missing any parts, the dye disappearing after a few days. Another point is that products based upon wax or fat may encourage dirt retention which eventually darkens the surface; silicone based products have no such effect. The fluid penetrates to a distance of between 1·5 and 6mm according to porosity. It should be noted that while the use of the fluid allows the masonry to breathe and does not therefore hinder the drying out of the structure, the presence of soluble salts in the structure may give rise to trouble; the salts are prevented from rising to the surface in solution, and may therefore be deposited within the pores at the depth to which the fluid has penetrated, causing spalling of the treated face. Water-repellent fluids, therefore, should not be used till efflorescence has ceased to form.

(iii) Silicone resins are now being widely used in the manufacture of furniture polishes and car polishes. It is very important that any surface known to have been maintained with periodic applications of furniture polish should be most carefully cleaned down before repainting. This remark applies with even greater force when any motor vehicle is being repainted or resprayed; it should be assumed that silicone polishes have at some time been applied and great care taken to remove all traces of polish during the preparation.

SILK   The fabric made from the fine soft glossy fibre spun by the larvae of certain moths, especially the silkworm, and sometimes hung by the decorator as a wall fabric.

SILK SCREENING   A method of reproducing an unlimited number of repeats of a motif or pattern; it has been used for many years by commercial artists, is now the principal method employed in the production of hand printed wallpapers, and has been adopted by some decorators as a useful technique in place of conventional stencilling in paint. The process offers several advantages; it produces a design in solid colour and is excellent for patterns in which intricate detail is involved.

Certain manufacturers produce ready made silk screen designs, but some decorators prefer to design and cut their own. The technique briefly consists of using a wooden frame with a silk screen stretched across it; the design is cut into a masking material, very often a shellac coated paper, which is then pressed into contact with the silk so that the mesh is blanked off except where the design occurs. Printing is carried out by placing the frame in the required position and drawing colour across the screen with a rubber squeegee, the colour passing through those parts where the mesh is exposed.

SILKING A defect in a varnish or gloss film taking the form of very fine wrinkled lines which give the film a silky sheen. The wrinkles usually follow the lines made by the brush; on dipped or flow coated articles they appear in the direction of the flow. The defect is usually due to a fault in the varnish manufacture or to immaturity of the varnish.

SILVER GRAIN The grain markings exposed when a log is cut quarterwise.

SILVER LEAF The metal silver prepared in the form of thin leaves for use in a similar manner to gold leaf. It is supplied in books of 50 leaves, each leaf measuring 115mm by 115mm. Silver leaf tarnishes very rapidly when exposed to the air, and in fact the edges of each leaf tend to tarnish while it is still in the book; the leaf needs a protective coating of clear lacquer immediately after application.

SILVERING The silvering of glass to make mirrors is carried out with an ammoniacal silver solution mixed either with Rochelle salt (sodium potassium tartrate) or with a nitric acid—cane sugar—alcohol mixture; the solution is poured on to chemically clean glass where it deposits a film of silver. This is washed clean, given a protective coating of varnish, and then coated with a protective film of paint.

SINGLE SECTION LADDERS Ladders which are constructed as a single unit, as opposed to extension ladders in two or three units.

S

SINKING Any local loss of gloss or sheen in a paint film, due to absorption of the medium by the undercoats or to the porosity of the surface to which the paint is applied.

SIZE See *Glue Size*.

SIZE BOUND DISTEMPER A composition of common whiting and glue size. See *Distemper*.

SIZE BRUSH The name loosely given to the flat squirrel hair brush used for applying the isinglass in glass gilding.

SKEWINGS The unavoidable waste entailed by gilding operations. In loose leaf gilding some surplus is bound to occur through overlapping of edges, etc., just as in any glass sign work it is impossible to work precisely to the shapes of the letters; in transfer gold operation it is impossible to clear all the leaves completely, especially if very small lettering is being gilded; any waste of this kind, known as the "skewings", is carefully collected and retained until there is a sufficient quantity to be returned to the gold beaters, who will make a cash allowance for it.

SKIMMING The thin top film of a plastered ceiling or wall surface.

SKIN GLUE SIZE The best quality of glue size; because it is practically colourless it is used for sizing wallpaper which is subsequently to be varnished acting as a buffer coat to prevent the varnish from striking into the paper.

SKINNING The formation of a surface skin on a film of paint or on a quantity of paint in a container, due to contact with the air.

SKIP A rather primitive form of suspended scaffold which used to be extremely popular and is still used to some extent in the woollen and cotton towns of the North. It consists of a wicker basket fitted with wheels which enable it to run down a wall surface. It is suspended by block, pulley and rope, and accommodates one man who is able to lower himself as desired. In the Construction Regulations a skip comes under the same provisions as a bosun's chair, and is only to be used in situations where a more elaborate scaffold or a full cradle is impracticable or unreasonable. It must be at least 762mm deep and must be carried by two strong bands of metal.

SKIRTING BOARD The board running round the base of the wall of a room.

SLAKED LIME Calcium hydroxide, or quicklime which has been slaked by the addition of water.

SLATE FILLER A Japan filler composition made up of slate powder and Japan gold size; it is an extremely good and strong filler, but needs to be rubbed down smooth within a reasonable length of time after application, otherwise it sets extremely hard and difficulty is experienced in getting it really smooth.

SLATE POWDER A very finely ground powder consisting of aluminium silicate, obtained from slate, which is used to make up slate filler.

SLEEPINESS or SLEEPY GLOSS The condition of a gloss film in which the natural glossiness is reduced as the material dries, but not by any process allied to blooming. It may be due to the application of the gloss over an unsuitable undercoat, an undercoat which is unduly absorbent, or an undercoat which is not completely hard and within which some solvent is trapped which subsequently escapes through the gloss. It may also be due to some defect in the formulation of the gloss material itself.

SLEEVE COUPLER　A coupler used in tubular scaffolding to join two tubes end to end; the term refers specifically to the type of coupler which grips the outside face of the tubes, as opposed to a joint pin which grips the internal surfaces.

SLIP or SLIDE　(i) The condition of a surface whereby a material applied to it can be moved around with some freedom. Slip is an important characteristic in a surface upon which wallpaper is being hung. One of the objects of applying glue size to a surface is to impart some measure of slip, so that the paper can be moved around until it is in the correct position rather than that it should stick immediately upon contact.
(ii) The term is sometimes used to describe a paint with low surface tackiness, such as graphite paint, etc., which can be brushed out very thinly.

SLUNG SCAFFOLD　A scaffold suspended from wire bonds from the underside of the roof or ceiling of a building where a scaffold built from the ground would be impracticable, e.g., in a theatre or cinema where normal performances are not to be interrupted, in railway stations, etc. The ledgers are usually about 3 metres apart and the transoms about 1·2 metres apart. The scaffold is close boarded to provide a broad working platform.

SLUSHING　A term used to describe a method of applying paint to inaccessible surfaces, by which paint is flooded on freely and the surplus allowed to drain off.

SMOKE STAINS　A frequent source of trouble on plaster work in the vicinity of chimney breasts due to smoke continually eddying around the surface or seeping through to the surface from the chimney by means of hair cracks. Such stains, unless cleaned off and sealed, will bleed into new paintwork.

SMUDGE　A paint mixture made up with the residue of paint left over in tins or returned from jobs; traditionally, the material used for painting the inside of gutterings, etc.

SNAP LINE　A length of string or twine which is rubbed with a piece of chalk, held firmly at each end, and plucked in the centre to give a clean straight line when setting out a piece of decorative work.

S

SOAKING　Causing a material to absorb as much moisture as possible, e.g., repeatedly wetting wallpaper in order to soften it prior to stripping, rendering powdered pigments into the condition whereby they can be mixed with distempers, etc. Sometimes the term is used to indicate that some measure of control is exercised in the application of moisture such as, for example, when speaking of a wallpaper being allowed to soak for, say, ten minutes, meaning that when it is pasted and folded it should be laid aside for a period of ten minutes before it is hung; in the same way one can speak of "oversoaking" a wallpaper, i.e., allowing it to remain pasted and folded for too long a time before hanging it, which leads to excessive stretching.

SOAP A substance composed of the salt of an alkali and fatty acid, which possesses detergent and cleansing properties.

SOFT DISTEMPER Another term for size distemper. See *Distemper*.

SOFT SOAP A blend of vegetable and animal oils saponified with caustic alkali often used by the painter in washing down prior to decoration.

SOFTENER A brush used in graining for the purpose of softening the markings, for relieving any harshness or crudity from the work, and for blending. Hog hair softeners are used for oil colour; badger softeners are reserved for water colour.

SOFTWOOD Coniferous timbers such as fir, spruce, pine, etc., used for constructional purposes. Although the wood is sometimes quite hard, they are all known by the general term of softwood.

SOIRETTE PAPERS Self-coloured satinette wallpapers with a low-relief pattern.

SOLE PLATE A strong plank of wood to which the base plates are screwed or spiked when a tubular scaffold is being erected on soft or uneven surfaces; it forms the basis of the scaffold and distributes the weight evenly over a wide area. Sole plates should also be used with an internal scaffold in situations where it is necessary to protect the floor from damage, such as, for example, when erecting a scaffold on a wood block floor.

SOLUBLE Capable of being dissolved—hence "water soluble" is a term applied to a substance which will dissolve in water, "spirit soluble" to a substance which will dissolve in alcohol, etc.

SOLUTION A liquid with some substance or substances dissolved in it.

SOLVENT A liquid used in the manufacture of a paint or decorative coating in order to dissolve or disperse the film-forming constituents with the object of making the mixture thin enough and fluid enough for easy application; the solvent evaporates from the film after application and therefore does not become part of the dried film.
  The traditional solvent for oil paints and varnishes is turpentine, distilled from the resinous exudation of the pine tree. This has largely given place to solvents derived from petroleum such as white spirit, or from coal-tar distillation such as benzole, naphtha, xylol, etc. The solvents for cellulose include toluol, obtained from coal-tar distillation, and esters formed by a chemical reaction between alcohols and acids. Methylated spirit is the solvent used for spirit stains and varnishes.

SOYA BEAN OIL A semi-drying oil obtained from the seeds of a legum-inous plant found in China, Japan and Manchuria; extensive cultivation now takes place in the U.S.A. The oil is used in non-yellowing stoving finishes, especially of the alkyd type, and the seeds can be processed by solvent extraction to yield an oil with drying properties similar to linseed oil.

SPACING The arrangement of individual letters in a word or an inscription, and of the separate words in an inscription, in such a way as to produce an even and regular effect which makes for good legibility. The object is to make the area of the space between each of the letters appear to be the same, allowing for the differences in contour and shape of each individual letter. Good spacing is one of the most important aspects of lettering and demands a keen eye and a sense of proportion which can only be cultivated with conscious effort and constant practice; there is no means of employing mechanical aids.

SPANISH RED OXIDE A brightly coloured oxide of iron pigment with good staining properties, found in Spain.

SPANISH WHITE Another term for Paris white.

SPAR VARNISH A boat varnish formulated in such a way as to give exceptional water resistance.

SPATTER or SPLATTER A spraying technique whereby paint is ejected from the spray gun in such a manner as to fall on the surface in thick blobs which remain separated and which do not flow together to form a continuous film. This is achieved by using an air pressure too low to atomize the paint and sufficient merely to eject it. Spatter is very often carried out with water paint to produce a low-relief treatment known as spray plastic; the surface is coated up by spray or brush with oilbound water paint to produce a solid coating, and when this is dry it is followed up by spattering in one, two, three or more colours differing from the ground, the darkest colour being spattered first and the lightest colour last; the spray gun is used with a circular motion with the trigger continuously pressed.

SPECIFICATION A detailed statement of particulars of the materials to be used and the extent of the work to be undertaken by a painting contractor.

SPIGOT An alternative term for a joint pin used in tubular scaffolding.

SPIRIT COLOUR A very thin fluid consisting of a coloured pigment alone with no admixture of white, the fluid being well thinned down with turps and containing just sufficient gold size to bind the particles when dry. It is purely and simply a decorative coating, having no protective properties at all. It is applied over a suitably prepared, painted and undercoated surface, and after application, when dry, it is varnished. At one time it was commonly used as the best practical method of achieving a high class varnish finish; it has now very largely fallen into disuse except for drop black, many people maintaining that a drop black and varnish finish is superior to a black gloss paint.

S

SPIRIT PAINT REMOVER A paint remover consisting of a powerful solvent with the addition of a thickening agent to enable it to cling to the surface to be stripped and also to retard evaporation of the solvent. It is used in circumstances where burning off would be unsuitable (see Paint Remover) and operates by dissolving the old film.

Correctly used, a spirit paint remover is extremely effective, cases having been recorded of paint films composed of as many as eighty separate coatings being stripped by one application. A great many people regard it as ineffective, due to the fact that its correct use is rarely understood. A very common fault, due to impatience, is to apply the paint remover and then begin to scrape the surface after an interval of only a few minutes; this is quite useless as well as being very wasteful of material. The proper technique is to apply the paint remover and allow it to stand for some twenty minutes until it begins to etch the surface of the old paint film. At this point a second application is given, and for this purpose the remover is piled on very liberally. No attempt is made to use a scraper until the entire film is softened, a process that may take several hours, but when this stage is reached stripping is thorough, clean and simple.

Spirit paint remover is more expensive than caustic paint stripper but is much more effective and leaves no harmful residue to damage the new paint system. If any residue at all remains it consists of the wax that is sometimes used as the stiffening agent, and this may retard the drying of the new paint coating; after stripping, therefore, the surface should be cleaned down with white spirit to remove any residual wax.

Some paint removers are inflammable, and should not be used in situations where the vapour given off from them can come into contact with a naked flame. Whatever type of spirit paint remover is in use, the room should be well ventilated; otherwise, the vapour given off may give rise to unpleasant symptoms of nausea.

SPIRIT STAIN A solution of spirit soluble dye such as nigrosine, turmeric, gamboge, etc., in industrial alcohol, very often with the addition of a resin such as shellac as binder. It is a very penetrative stain and evaporates rapidly, for which reason it is a difficult material to apply evenly.

SPIRIT VARNISHES Varnishes made by dissolving resins in industrial spirit, sometimes with the addition of a plasticizer of either castor oil or balsam. Shellac is the principal resin used, but manila, mastic, damar and sandaric are sometimes employed.

SPIRITING OFF or SPIRITING OUT The last stage in French polishing, in which the last traces of oil are removed from the work and a brilliant finish produced by burnishing the surface. It is performed by drawing a rubber moistened with methylated spirit repeatedly across the surface, or by applying a dilute acid solution with the palm of the hand over the work (which also has the effect of hardening the film of shellac) or by the use of grinding rubbers.

SPLICING OF LADDERS Increasing the effective height of a ladder by means of lashing another ladder securely to its face by means of ropes passed round the rungs and stiles. It is generally carried out with the ladders standing upright.

SPLICING ROPES Ropes used for lashing ladders together. They should be at least 6 metres in length in order to give the requisite number of turns round rungs and stiles.

SPLIT COMPLEMENTARY A variation or extension of the method of using two contrasting colours to form a complementary colour scheme, made by taking one hue and contrasting it with the hues immediately to the right and left of the hue directly opposite to it on the colour circle. For example, on the Munsell system the complementary colour to red is blue-green; a split complementary based on red as the main hue would have blue and green as the other two hues, since blue and green lie on either side of blue-green on the circle.

A split complementary combination gives three hues to work with instead of only two as in a complementary pair; this gives more hue variety, when building up a scheme, without the risk of discord which would result from picking three hues at random.

SPLIT SPRAY A defective spray pattern resulting in bands of paint of uneven thickness being applied, due to the atomizing pressure, fluid pressure and spray width being wrongly adjusted.

SPLITHEADS Also known as "splits" and "bandstands". Adjustable supports with which a working platform can be quickly and safely erected. They consist of a tripod base, which nowadays is generally made to fold up for ease of transport, and a centre prop surmounted by a swivelling fork head into which one or two planks can be fitted on edge, the planks acting as ledgers to support the platform. They generally extend to a maximum height of almost 3 metres.

SPONGE An essential part of a painter's kit. Natural sponges are a primitive form of animal life, those sold commercially being found in the Eastern Mediterranean. Synthetic (cellulose) sponges are now becoming popular both for house painting and industrial work; it is claimed that they hold a greater quantity of water and the flat face covers a greater area at one sweep.

S

SPONGE STIPPLING A decorative effect readily produced in flat oil paint or water paint. The technique consists of painting the wall surface with a suitable colour in the normal manner and allowing it to dry; the colours to be stippled on are then mixed and a little of the darkest of these colours is placed on a flat palette board. A dry natural sponge, cut across the centre to present a flat face, is used to pick up the colour from the board and transfer it to the wall; the stippling is carried out with a light dabbing motion, the wrist being continually turned to and fro so as to avoid any regularity in the pattern. This is followed by stippling in each of the other colours in turn, the lightest colour being applied last of all.

SPONTANEOUS COMBUSTION Ignition of a substance without the direct application of a flame, which is particularly liable to occur with substances susceptible to oxidation. Rags and cloths, which have been used for graining, for wiping out scumble, and for glazing effects should never be left crumpled up at the close of a day's work but should be opened up and spread out to dry, preferably in the open air, because of the danger of spontaneous combustion.

SPOT PRICE An estimate of price arrived at purely by a visual examination of the work, without the aid of any measurements, and based upon the estimator's fund of experience which enables him to compare the extent of the work mentally with previous jobs he has handled.

The trained estimator uses spot pricing as a check on the accuracy of his work. He compares his spot price with the price he arrives at by carefully working out all his figures and measurements; should there by any startling discrepancy between the two it may very well indicate that some significant figure has been omitted from or multiplied wrongly in his calculations, and he is warned of the advisibility of rechecking his figures.

SPOT PRIMING A term used, especially in the painting of structural steelwork, to mean stripping off the paint from small local areas and touching in these areas with priming paint prior to applying a coat of paint over the entire surface. It is generally carried out when the condition of the surface does not demand complete paint removal but when small local patches have been subjected to abrasion or damage.

SPOUT BRUSH or STRIKER A long handled brush used for bridge work, for roof work, for painting the mouths of spoutings, etc. The brush head is set at an angle to the handle.

SPRAY BOOTH A compartment or enclosure designed to confine spray painting operations and to extract the overspray and the fumes resulting from these operations. Many types are available, most of them fireproof. Spray booths have no application to the normal work of the painter and decorator but are of interest to those undertaking any form of industrial finishing.

SPRAY GUN The essential tool in spray painting, using compressed air to break up paint into a fine mist and to convey it to the surface which is to be treated.

SPRAY GUN EXTENSION A rigid extension, 1200mm in length, which is fitted to the air and fluid inlets of a spray gun and which includes a device enabling the trigger of the gun to be operated from the other end of the extension. Its purpose is to enable the operative to spray high walls, ceilings and other features which are out of reach without the use of scaffolding.

SPRAYHEAD Part of a spray gun; an assembly consisting of air cap, fluid tip and fluid needle.

SPRAY PAINTING A method of paint application whereby a controlled stream of paint is broken up or atomized and directed on to a surface in the form of a fine mist, the chief advantage of the method being speed of application and the ease by which a relatively smooth film can be produced.

SPRAY PATTERN The pattern produced by the paint which is ejected on to a flat surface from a spray gun, when the trigger is pressed once and released and the gun kept stationary. The pattern is adjusted, by means of various controls on the gun, to suit the particular job in hand. The pattern becomes distorted if the settings or pressures are wrongly adjusted, if the horn holes are clogged or the fluid tip clogged up with dirt or dried paint, or if the gun has been damaged by careless handling or cleaning.

SPRAY PLASTIC See *Spatter*.

SPRAY SILVERING The application of silvering to glass by means of spray equipment. For this purpose on mass production work a twin-headed spray gun is used.

SPREADING CAPACITY or SPREADING POWER The area covered by a given quantity of paint, varnish or other decorative fluid when applied in a normal manner over a suitable surface. It is generally expressed in terms of square metres per litre (or per 5 litres) of material, although paste materials are reckoned in square metres per kilogramme. It is influenced by many factors, such as the porosity, and texture of the surface, the method of application and the skill of the operative. It should be remembered that the figures quoted by a manufacturer for his products are often based upon application under ideal conditions, such as on a nonporous surface at a carefully controlled temperature, with no waste involved.

SPRING WOOD That part of the annual ring of a tree's growth which forms in the spring, which is relatively soft and spongy compared with the denser summerwood, and which therefore tends to absorb stain and paint more freely.

STABILIZER Another term for emulsifying agent.

S

STABLE Unchanging: a product is said to be stable if under normal conditions of use it retains its characteristics.

STACK PROCESS See *Dutch Process*.

STAGGERED JOINTS A term used in tubular scaffolding, to refer to the practice of arranging that the end to end joints in standards should be at varying heights and that the joints in ledgers should be at varying lengths along the scaffold, a practice which is very necessary to prevent the occurrence of lines of weakness along which the scaffold might break apart.

STAGING A working platform of any kind. See also *Lightweight Staging.*

STAIN (i) A discolouration or blemish.

(ii) A fluid which is used to colour a surface by penetrating without obscuring it; in most cases the surface to which stain is applied is woodwork. Woods of good quality are stained in order to enhance the beauty of the grain markings and generally improve their appearance; inferior timbers may be stained in order to hide defects and to give the semblance of better quality; sometimes wood is stained in order to bring it to a colour matching or harmonizing with other parts of a decorative scheme; in many cases staining is used for reasons of economy because it is one of the cheapest methods of colouring the woodwork.

The term "stain" includes a number of different types of material. Water stain usually consists of vegetable dyes such as logwood, saffron, etc., in solution, but it can also be made up of semi-transparent pigments such as Vandyke brown or sienna bound with gum arabic. This type of stain tends to emphasize the grain markings, especially those of a softwood, because it penetrates freely into the springwood but is rejected by the hard resinous summerwood. It has the drawback of raising the grain of the wood.

Spirit stain consists of spirit soluble dyes such as nigrosine, turmeric, etc., in solution with shellac. It evaporates quickly and needs careful handling to produce an even effect. It tends slightly to subdue the grain markings, and if used too strongly gives a "bronze" semi-opaque effect.

Oil stain consists of semi-transparent pigments such as sienna, crimson lake, etc., ground in linseed oil and thinned with turps or white spirit. It is less penetrative than water or spirit stain and can therefore be more evenly applied, especially on softwood. Because the colouring matter is pigmentary it has the effect of subduing the grain markings.

Varnish stain is a pigmented hard varnish which leaves a top coating on the surface. It is generally used by amateurs rather than professional painters. Chemical stains are sometimes used by the French polisher; they may consist of an aqueous solution applied direct (e.g., permanganate of potash) or of a fume process (e.g., ammonia).

It should be noted that a true stain is a solution containing soluble dye. Pigmentary materials do not give the same measure of purity and transparency.

STAINERS Coloured pigments ground in a paint medium, which can be added to a paint in order to change or modify its colour.

STAINING STRENGTH or STAINING POWER The degree to which a coloured pigment imparts colour to a white pigment, assessed by grinding a definite weight of coloured pigment with a specified weight of opaque white pigment and comparing it with the tint produced with a known standard.

STAND OIL A drying oil, generally best quality linseed oil, which has been polymerized by heat treatment without the additon of driers. It is very pale in colour, and has outstanding qualities of flow.

STANDARD A term used in pole or tubular scaffolding to mean a vertical tube, column or support which transmits the load to the ground or to a base plate.

STANDING LADDER A ladder with rectangular sides or stiles. This type of ladder is neither so heavy nor so robust as a pole ladder, and is used where lightness is required. Standing ladders are not usually made more than 8 metres in length.

STANDING PART That portion of the suspension rope on a cradle or bosun's chair which stands between the top pulley block and the point of suspension.

STARCH A carbohydrate which is found in rice and all kinds of grain.

STARCH PASTE A fixative made by beating up starch with a little cold water to form a creamy batter which is then scalded with boiling water until it thickens. It forms a fine colourless paste which is extremely useful for delicate wallpapers such as satins, etc.

STARVED A term applied to a surface the porosity of which has not been satisfied by the coats of paint applied to it, resulting in a patchy film.

STEAM CLEANING A method sometimes used for cleaning the stone fabric of a building; provided steam alone is used the fabric suffers no ill effects. The work is usually carried out by specialists in this field.

STEAM JENNY A large water tank of 255 litre capacity, a solution tank in which detergent compound is placed, and a fuel tank, all mounted on a wheeled chassis, together with a length of flexible hose leading to the nozzle. Within a few seconds of lighting the machine delivers steam at a pressure of 80 lb/in^2 [5·6 kg/cm^2 (metric) 5·5 bars (SI)]. Different nozzles can be used for a variety of purposes such as the steam cleaning of stonework and the degreasing of industrial plant; there are two methods by which the appliance can be used for paint stripping, one of which involves brushing a paint removing fluid on the the surface and then clearing the softened paint with the steam jet, while the other involves adding a detergent to the water tank so that the steam which emerges under pressure is charged with detergent. The equipment is generally used by transport undertakings and big contractors, since the initial cost and the running costs are high and could hardly be justified on normal decorating operations.

S

STEAM SPRAYING A system of spray application developed in the U.S.A. which uses superheated steam as the propellant instead of air in order to reduce spray rebound; it is claimed that it produces a material saving of between ten and twenty per cent.

---

1 bar = 10^5 N/m^2 = 10^5 pascals = 1·02 kg/cm^2 = $14\frac{1}{2}$lb/in^2

STEAM STRIPPER This piece of equipment, originally designed for the stripping of wallpaper, is very useful for the removal of plastic paint, water paints, emulsions and distempers which do not yield readily to other forms of stripping, and it can also be supplied with an attachment for the removal of paint and varnish. It consists of a water tank and burner by which steam is generated at low pressure and conveyed by means of a flexible hose to a perforated metal plate called a concentrator; this is placed in contact with the papered or painted surface so that the steam can penetrate and soften the material, which is then removed by scraping.

STEARIC ACID A hard wax-like saturated fatty acid derived from animal and vegetable fats and oils. It is the basis of metallic stearates used as flatting and gelling agents, and some of its esters are used as plasticizers.

STEEL Steel, which is made by a variety of processes, consists of iron combined with carbon in various proportions. When assembled for the load-bearing framework of buildings and other engineering structures it is known as structural steelwork. It corrodes rapidly in the presence of air and moisture, and corrosion is accelerated by a smoke or chemically polluted atmosphere, by sea air and so on. The arrest of corrosion and the protective treatment of steel are among the most important aspects of the painter's work.

STEEL COMBS Tools used in graining for the portrayal of coarse grain. They are rectangular in shape, one edge being divided to form a number of narrowly separated teeth. A wide choice is available, the combs themselves ranging from narrow to broad, and the teeth also ranging from fine to coarse. When combs are purchased the teeth are set at regular intervals, but the grainer very often breaks out several teeth in order to form an irregular pattern. Useful effects are gained by using broad combs wrapped round with cloth followed by fine combs taken across at a slight angle. Combs should be wiped clean after every stroke.

STEEL STRAIGHTEDGES These are available in several lengths and are used for various purposes such as, for example, in conjunction with a sharp knife for the trimming of high class papers.

STEEL WOOL An abrasive material which is available in several grades varying from very fine wool to coarse steel shavings; it has several applications to painting and decorating. The finest grades may be used for rubbing down both old and new paintwork; the medium grades provide an excellent material for stripping paint and polish from intricately carved or modelled work when used in conjunction with paint remover, and are also useful for the preparation of non-ferrous metals, in order to roughen their surface and provide a key for paint; the coarse grades are used for rough scouring. According to the needs of the particular surface, steel wool may either be used dry or lubricated with water; when used for removing rust from steel, it is lubricated with paraffin or white spirit. It is important that all traces of the steel wool are removed before paint is applied; there is a tendency for fine specks of the metal to be left embedded in the surface or to become bound to the surface by the paint coating, and these can cause trouble through subsequently rusting and staining the paint film. Gloves should be worn to protect the hands while steel wool is being used.

STENCIL A thin plate from which a pattern or design is cut out; the plate is laid upon the surface which is to be decorated, and colour is applied through the voids or cut out portions so as to reproduce the design on the surface and, of course, by moving the position of the stencil plate the design can be reproduced many times over. The stencil plates used by the decorator generally consists of paper, but for certain purposes they may also be made from thin cardboard, sheet zinc or lead foil. It is essential that the stencil plate should be strong and robust enough to hold together as a complete unit, and for this reason the pierced sections of the plate are held together with "ties"; the art of designing a stencil is to arrange that the ties form an integral part of the pattern.

STENCIL BRUSH A round brush with the bristles set in a metal ferrule, mounted on a short stubby handle; the brush is so shaped as to present a circular flat working face. The method of using a stencil brush is to pour a little colour on to a flat palette board, moisten the tips of the brush with the colour and then stipple the colour gently and sparingly with a backwards and forwards dabbing motion on to the surface which is to be decorated; under no circumstances should the brush be dipped into a can of paint, otherwise it will pick up far too much colour and produce a smudgy, untidy piece of work with paint straying under the plate beyond the bounds of the design.

Stencil brushes are made in several sizes. After use the tips should be moistened in solvent and the brush then washed out with soap and water; after the brush has been washed and rinsed it should be wrapped around with a piece of stout paper, secured with an elastic band to bring it back tightly into shape and to prevent the tendency for it to splay outwards. When a stencil brush is being purchased it is important to see that the handle fits the hand comfortably; otherwise, prolonged use will lead to chafing and blistering of the skin.

STENCIL CUTTING The process of preparing a stencil plate. One of the most effective methods for practical purposes is as follows:

S

(a) The design is drawn out accurately on a sheet of stout cartridge paper. Accurate setting out is essential, especially with a multi-plate, all-over pattern, in which any error, however slight, is magnified by each repetition.
(b) The portions to be cut out are painted in with strong poster colour, and the paper then pinned up and examined from a distance. This enables the decorator to judge the probable effect of the completed work and to decide whether the pattern is well balanced; the effect cannot be properly judged when only a pencil outline has been drawn in.
(c) The paper is oiled with a cloth soaked in raw linseed oil; this makes the paper easier to cut.
(d) The paper is placed on a piece of heavy plate glass, and the pattern cut out with a suitable knife which is kept well sharpened.
(e) The completed plate is coated on both sides with shellac knotting to stiffen it up, and to make it possible to clean the plate by wiping paint off.

STENCIL KNIFE A short knife with a wooden handle, made especially for stencil cutting and supplied by a decorators' merchant. The knife should be sharpened periodically while in use; otherwise, it will tend to produce ragged edges.

STENCIL PAPER A dark brown oiled paper sold specially for stencil cutting. Many decorators, however, prefer to work on white cartridge paper, as described under the heading *Stencil Cutting*.

STENCIL PIN A stout pin set in a fairly large plastic or composition head, which is used for pinning a stencil plate into position.

STENCILLING Producing a decoration with stencil plates; the paint may be applied in many ways, such as by stencil brush, spray or sponge stipple. The work must be carried out carefully to avoid any paint creeping under the plate and blurring the work.

STEPLADDER A single section ladder, with rectangular stiles, and with rectangular treads which should, as far as possible, be horizontal while the ladder is in use.

STEPS Stepladders with a hinged frame which swings back to make them self supporting. They are made of softwood and need to be of sturdy construction, since they are constantly subjected to hard use. Steps should be fully extended while in use; otherwise they are liable to kick. If used on uneven ground the feet should be packed so as to stand firmly and solidly. The ropes should be long enough to prevent any possibility of the steps closing while in use. Bricks should not be placed on the treads in order to raise a plank to extra height. The practice of standing on the lower rails at the back of the steps is a dangerous one. Care should be taken to maintain steps in good condition; they should not be painted because of obscuring defects and adding to the weight, and the ropes should be inspected periodically and checked for fraying and the hinges checked for corrosion.

STIBNITE The ore from which the pigment antimony is obtained.

STICKINESS Stickiness which persists in a paint film, which has been applied long enough to have become hard and dry under normal conditions may be due to inadequate preparation and the presence of grease; stickiness which occurs in a film which has previously dried is generally due to saponification.
   A stickiness occurring in the bristles of a distemper brush which is being washed out after use in water paint is now becoming a common complaint; it is very often caused by the oil-in-water emulsion binder of the water paint breaking down due to the heat of the washing water or the friction entailed in the washing, which results in the release of the varnish or oil used in preparing the binder. When this occurs, continued washing in soap and water is useless, as the brush will not come any cleaner; should the brush be stored away in this condition, however, the sticky varnish medium dries and the bristles become firmly matted together. When it is

observed that the brush is becoming sticky, ordinary washing methods should be suspended and the brush should be well rinsed out in white spirit or paraffin; this removes the offending medium, and washing in soap and water can then be resumed.

STIPPLE   A term with several meanings. As a general rule, to stipple a surface means to strike a wet newly-painted surface repeatedly and systematically with a brush specially designed for the purpose with the object of levelling out the coat of paint and eliminating brushmarks. It can also mean the use of a fitch, stencil brush or sash tool to add a little paint of a different colour to a previously painted surface, or the production of a broken colour effect or a textured finish by partially lifting the wet paint or wet glaze with a rubber stippler. When paint is applied to a sheet of glass or a glass sign in order to obscure it, the coating may be levelled out more satisfactorily by stippling with a soft cloth than by using a stippling brush.

STIPPLER   A type of brush specially designed for some form of stippling. Unless it is qualified by some distinctive description, the word is usually understood to refer to a hair stippler, which consists of a large number of wire-drawn tufts of soft hog hair arranged on a flat base plate, and made so as to present a flat rectangle of hair; this type of stippler is used for levelling out a coat of paint and eliminating the brushmarks, or for blending colours in order to produce a gradation of colour on a large area, or for levelling up an area of tinted glaze prior to rag rolling, rubber stippling, scumbling or other broken colour effects. See also *Hair Stippler*. A modification of the hair stippler is the "two-row stippler, which is used to perform similar operations in a confined space.

Special kinds of stipplers are available for specific purposes. Rubber stipplers of various patterns and shapes are made for the production of broken colour effects and textured plastic paint effects. A radial stippler may also be used for broken colour work and plastic paint effects. A type of stippler was produced at one time by a well-known firm of paint manufacturers and was made on the same principle as a hair stippler except that the face was divided into four separate rectangular areas; this tool was used in conjunction with a metal tray also divided into four sections, a different colour of paint being placed in each section, and was designed to produce a broken colour effect by adding the four different colours simultaneously to a previously painted ground.

S

STIPPLING   The process of striking a painted surface with a stippler or similar tool for any of the purposes described in the previous paragraphs.

STOCKHOLM TAR   The material from which crude tar is obtained.

STOP   To stop a surface is to fill up the holes and cracks in it with a suitable stopping. It should not be confused with the application of filler; stopping is applied to a definite hole or cavity, whereas filling is used for the treatment of shallow indentations in the surface.

STOP TAR KNOTTING A material usually consisting of a compound of shellac and manila in industrial spirit, with the addition of a plasticizer to render it more elastic. It is used to prevent such materials as tar, creosote, bituminous paint, bronze paint or oil soluble dyes from bleeding into a superimposed paint film.

STOPPING A stiff paste used to fill up holes, cracks and similar defects in a surface; in the case of woodwork it may consist of putty, or better still of a hard stopping, applied after the priming coat is dry, while in the case of plastered surfaces it may consist of plaster of Paris, Keene's cement or a proprietary brand of filler.

STOVING The process of drying and hardening a paint coating by means of the application of heat, either by convection in a stoving oven, or by radiation in which infra-red equipment is used. The term is taken to mean drying at a temperature of above $65°C$ ($150°F$), as opposed to forced drying in which only moderate temperatures are employed.

STOVING MATERIALS Known variously as stoving enamels, stoving finishes, stoving paints, etc., these are materials which are dried by heating, irrespective of the type or source of heat applied, as opposed to air-drying materials.

STOVING OVEN A thermostatically controlled oven into which a painted article is placed and in which heat is transferred to the article by convection in order to dry the paint.

STRAIGHTEDGE The type of straightedge used by the decorator is generally a length of bevelled wood, and is employed in conjunction with a lining fitch for the production of straight painted lines. For some purposes, however, such as in mitring Lincrusta strapping or the knife trimming of wallpaper, a steel straightedge is used.

STRAINER A sieve which allows fluid to pass through but which prevents the passage of lumpy matter, skins or other foreign bodies. Normally it consists of a truncated cone of light sheet metal, in the base of which a circular rimmed piece of gauze is fitted; the gauze, popularly known as the "strainer bottom", is replaced when worn or clogged up. The strainer is placed on top of a paint can and the fluid strained through, its passage being often assisted by strokes of a fitch or 25mm tool. The usual size of strainer is some 200 or 225mm at the top and 88 to 112mm at the base, with gauzes to fit; the gauze is available in varying degrees of mesh. Until recently, miniature strainers could be purchased and these were very useful for dealing with small quantities of enamel, etc., for high class work; unfortunately, these seem to be no longer obtainable. On the other hand, it is now possible to buy disposable strainers which are cheap enough to be discarded immediately after use and which, because no cleaning out is necessary, represent a saving in labour that more than compensates for their purchase price.

STRAINING   The sieving of paint in order to trap out skins and foreign bodies; most essential if paintwork is to be free from nibs and especially necessary when paint is to be applied by spray if gun blockages are to be avoided.

STRAINING CLOTH   Fine-mesh lintless cloth, which is secured to the top of a paint can by means of an elastic band and through which varnish or enamel is allowed to strain by gravity.

STRIKER   Alternative term for a spout brush.

STRIKING   (i) To the painter this term means the harmful penetration of a material by some liquid substance; for example, when varnishing a wallpaper, if any part of the paper has not been effectively sealed with glue size the varnish penetrates and stains the paper at this point, and this is referred to as "the varnish striking into the paper".
(ii) To the paint manufacturer, striking is synonymous with precipitation.

STRIPPING   The removal of some previous coating from a surface, e.g., the removal of old wallpaper or old paint.

STRIPPING KNIFE   A broad knife used for paint or wallpaper removal.

STUCCO   Also known as "Roman cement". A hydraulic cement obtained by burning a naturally occurring cement rock consisting of clay and limestone; the material was widely used in the 18th and 19th centuries as an external rendering for buildings. The word is an Italian one which has passed into the common speech of several languages and is often used rather loosely to describe any type of plaster rendering.

STYPTIC KNOTTING   Styptic is a general term covering certain types of medical preparation which arrest bleeding; styptic knotting is a term derived from this, and is usually applied to a white or colourless knotting which is used in place of the more usual orange shellac knotting to arrest the bleeding of knots of woodwork which is to be finished in white or light coloured enamel. When enamels were notorious for their lack of opacity it was most desirable to exclude from the paint system anything which added to the difficulties of covering, and the use of a dark coloured knotting could very well mean that an extra coat of paint was needed to obliterate it. With modern gloss finishes of high opacity, the need for styptic knotting has declined.

STYRENE   Also called "vinyl benzene"; a liquid produced from benzene and ethylene (i.e., from coal and petroleum) which polymerizes on heating to form a solid resinous substance. This can be reacted with the oil component of an alkyd resin to produce a wide range of air-drying paints and stoving finishes; polystyrene resin is also used in the production of emulsion paints, but has been less widely used in this country than in the U.S.A. In general it may be said that the incorporation of styrene into a material gives increased water resistance, better flow and quicker drying.

S

SUBLIMATION The process of converting a solid substance, first to a vapour by heating and then back again to a solid by cooling.

SUBLIMED BLUE LEAD A grey pigment consisting of basic lead sulphate; it is a rust inhibitive pigment and is used as a primer for iron and steel, especially in locations exposed to a polluted atmosphere, e.g., on gas producing plant, etc.

SUBLIMED WHITE LEAD A basic sulphate of lead produced by the sublimation of lead sulphide; it is similar to white lead in many ways, having good spreading power and good opacity, but does not combine so readily with linseed oil and has a greater tendency to chalk.

SUCTION Strictly speaking, the act or process of sucking, i.e., the production of a vacuum in a confined space causing a fluid to enter under atmospheric pressure. In the painting trade the term is used rather loosely as an alternative term for absorbency.

SUCTION CUP A small paint container (usually slightly more than one litre in capacity) which is attached to the under part of a spray gun and which allows atmospheric pressure to enter and force the paint up to the fluid tip when a current of air is flowing and creating a vacuum at the orifice of the gun.

SUCTION FEED GUN A spray gun, used in conjunction with a suction cup, in which a stream of compressed air creates a vacuum which causes the atmospheric pressure to force paint up from the cup. It is used in spraying small quantities of thin material such as cellulose, synthetic enamel, bronze, etc., and where frequent changes of colour are involved.

SUEDE FINISHES Industrial finishes owing their effect to the presence of fine wrinkles, produced by inducing the paint film to skin over under controlled conditions. These materials may be air drying but as a general rule they are made as stoving finishes.

SUGAR SOAP A soluble alkaline soap preparation used by the painter and decorator for washing down paintwork, for preparing old paintwork for repainting or for stripping old paintwork, the sugar soap being added to water in varying quantities to produce a solution of the strength suitable for the particular purpose required. Its chief constituent is washing soda, which is mixed with yellow bar soap and to which is added a small quantity of crude palm oil and a small amount of Russian or Swedish turpentine.

When sugar soap is used for washing down, work should commence at the lowest parts of the walls or woodwork and should proceed upwards; this is to prevent any soap solution from running down a dry surface and causing streaks to appear. The soap solution must not be allowed to dry on the surface, nor must it be allowed to remain on the surface long enough to soften the paintwork; as soon as possible the whole of the area that has been wetted and washed should be swilled off with clean water, rinsed well with several changes of clean water and then sponged and leathered off. If any of the soap is left behind it is liable to attack the new paint film and lead to local saponification.

SULPHURIZED OIL See *Valcanized Oil.*

SUMMERWOOD The harder, denser portions of the annual rings of a tree's growth, less absorbent to stain and paint than the spongier springwood.

SUNFLOWER OIL A semi-drying, non-yellowing oil.

SURFACE DRY The term used to describe a paint film which is dry on the surface but still soft and tacky underneath.

SURFACE TENSION The force which acts at the surface of a liquid, tending to make it behave as though it were enclosed in an elastic membrane. Surface tension has an important bearing upon the capillarity of liquids.

SURFACER A pigmented filler composition applied to a slightly uneven surface and which, when sanded down, presents a smooth level surface upon which the paint system is applied.

SUSPENDED SCAFFOLD A suspended scaffold is defined in the Construction (Safety, Health and Welfare) Regulations as being a scaffold suspended by means of ropes or chains and capable of being lowered or raised by such means.

SUSPENDING AGENT A substance incorporated in a paint formulation in order to keep the pigments in suspension and prevent or delay settlement, e.g. asbestine, mica, silica, etc.

SUSPENSION A liquid in which particles of solid matter are held up or suspended, either because the particles are very small or because the liquid is highly viscous.

SUSPENSION POINT The point of connection between a bosun's chair or one side of a cradle and the suspension rope or bottom pulley block used for suspension.

S

SUSPENSION ROPE The rope passing through the pulley block or blocks for suspending a cradle or bosun's chair, commonly referred to as the "fall".

SWEAT OUT A defect in plaster work whereby the plaster fails to achieve its proper strength and hardness due to the fact that the surface was sealed too early, and while still containing moisture, by an impervious paint system.

SWEATING A defect in a paint or varnish film whereby oily matter from the undercoats exudes through the surface causing it to become permanently tacky; the defect is often due to the application of a quick-drying coating over an insufficiently hard undercoat. The term is also very often loosely and incorrectly used in the trade to refer to the condensation of moisture upon structural surfaces.

SWEATING BACK   A defect in which a dry paint or varnish film develops tackiness when ageing, due to the hydrolysis of the glycerides present.

SWEET CHESTNUT   A wood which is very similar in appearance and properties to oak, but with very narrow pith rays as a result of which it lacks ray figuring.

SWIVEL COUPLER   A coupler used in tubular scaffolding for joining tubes at any angle other than a right angle, and intended for use in forming diagonal bracings.

SWORD LINER   A brush set in a quill, used by coach painters for the freehand production of painted lines, and so called because the shape of the working surface resembles the shape of a scimitar.

SYCAMORE   A highly decorative whitish or honey coloured wood with most pleasing and subtle mottled markings, although when exposed to light and air it tends to develop a somewhat unpleasant yellowish colour. The imitation of sycamore is sometimes called for in modern decorative schemes and may be carried out with a graining colour of raw sienna, Vandyke brown and ultramarine blue on a white or cream ground; for the best results water-colour graining should be used.

SYNTHETIC PAINT   A term used very loosely in the trade to describe any type of paint containing some proportion of synthetic resin medium. The term is derived from the word "synthesis" which means the composition or building up of a complex whole by the union of two or more substances; many painters are under the mistaken impression that the word means that a synthetic material is an inferior substitute.

SYNTHETIC RESIN   Originally the term was meant to apply to a chemically produced substance which resembled a natural resin in appearance and properties, but it now has a much broader application and is used to describe materials which bear little or no resemblance to natural resins, which offer qualities that are not to be found in any natural product, and which are made under perfectly controlled conditions so that they are uniform and consistent in character. Synthetic resins include polymerized condensates, in which two substances are heated together in the presence of a catalyst and the product subsequently polymerized (e.g., phenolic resins, alkyd resins, etc.) and direct polymerization products in which a substance is polymerized in the presence of a catalyst (e.g., vinyl resins, coumarone resins, etc.) each having their own special properties; the formulation can be controlled to produce a material suited to meet a particular set of conditions such as a peculiarly corrosive environment or a distinctive type of atmospheric pollution. In general it may be said that synthetic resins impart to a paint film a greater measure of flexibility, a higher degree of chemical resistance, better flow and more rapid setting than is obtained with natural products.

SYNTHETIC ROPES Ropes produced from man-made fibres, which offer distinct advantages over those produced from natural fibres because of their greater strength, low moisture absorption, and resistance to alkalis, soap solutions, oils and petroleum. They are especially useful for scaffolding purposes and for the suspension of cradles in situations where a high concentration of chemical substances is encountered or where the ropes are liable to be fouled by alkaline solutions in the course of operations involving the cleaning of buildings. Many forms of synthetic rope are available, including *Nylon* which is a strong alkali-resistant rope with a high degree of stretch which enables it to absorb shock loads but which makes it unsuitable for some purposes, *Terylene* which is a very strong and flexible acid-resistant rope and which, because of its low even stretch, is preferable to nylon for suspended scaffolds, *Polypropylene* which is a low-stretch rope highly resistant to acid and alkali and therefore suitable for destructive industrial conditions, and which is available in a variety of textures, and *Polythene* which is a fairly stiff rope resistant to acid and alkali. The manufacturers of synthetic ropes should be consulted for advice and information about the most appropriate type of rope for any specific purpose.

T

TACK RAG A device for removing dust and grit from a surface prior to painting. It consists of a length of cotton fabric impregnated with a non-drying tacky or adhesive substance and folded so as to form a pad of convenient size for handling. When passed across a piece of work it picks up any dust which is present, the dust clinging to the pad, in contrast to a duster brush, which flicks the dust away but sends it swirling into the surrounding air from whence it gradually settles back again on to the work. A tack rag is designed in such a way that when one face has become clogged up and too dirty for further use it can be folded over to present a fresh clean face, a process which can be repeated several times over so that one pad provides thirty-two clean faces.

T

Tack rags are widely used in industrial and coach painting, but are not yet used to a great extent in painting and decorating and certainly not used as much as they should be. In the initial stages of a job, at the burning off, rubbing down and priming stages, it is probable that the conventional duster brush is more effective than a tack rag in clearing away the debris, but in the later stages of the work when undercoats are being applied, and particularly in the finishing stages when gloss materials are being used, the tack rag is undoubtedly the most efficient form of dust removal and ensures a much cleaner piece of work than can be achieved with a duster.

TACKINESS Stickiness; a paint or varnish which has begun to set, has lost its initial wetness and fluidity and has become sticky is said to be tacky. An essential feature of gilding with oil gold size or Japan gold size is that the gold size must have reached the right degree of tack before the gold leaf is applied.

TALC A magnesium silicate used as an extender in paints; French chalk is a well-known variety of talc.

TALL OIL A by-product of the paper pulp industry, sometimes used as a substitute for linseed oil.

TALLOW A substance composed of the harder and less fusible fats of animals, especially beef or mutton fat, which is sometimes incorporated into limewash (see *Limewash*) and is also used in glass embossing for the purpose of building up a wall round a piece of glass to form a reservoir which will hold the acid while the etching is in progress.

TANNIN An astringent substance found in various types of wood, notably in oak (See under *Pretreatment Primers* for its use as an anti-corrosive for steel). Whenever iron wedges or nails are in contact with newly cut oak a blue-black stain similar in composition to writing ink is formed, due to the action of the tannin in the wood upon the metal.

TAR BLACK A cheap coal-tar product used for such purposes as treating wooden posts which are to be in contact with the soil, etc.

TARNISHING The formation of a film of discolouration on the exposed face of a metal, destroying the lustre. Some metals are very susceptible to tarnishing, silver being notorious in this respect. See *Silver Leaf*.

TEAK An Asiatic tree the wood of which is used for various constructional purposes, such as dock and waterside work, woodwork for the chemical industry, coach and waggon construction and for doors, windows and gates, and also for furniture and cabinet work, especially for such items as laboratory benches, etc.; it is, of course, widely used in the shipbuilding industry. Its colour ranges from deep yellow to dark brown and indeed almost to black. Its value is enhanced by the fact that it exists in abundant quantities, and it is superior to all other woods in its freedom from movement. It contains a natural oil and feels oily to the touch; the natural secretions of some woods have a corrosive effect upon any metal which is in contact with them, but the oil contained in teak actually has a preservative effect upon metal fittings, bolts, etc., which are adjacent to it. When teak is to be painted the oil content presents a difficulty by preventing the paint from drying; it is necessary to wash the work down either with acetone or white spirit, and some firms supply a special teak sealer which acts as a primer and is followed by normal undercoats.

TEKKO The name given to a range of beautiful metallic silk-faced wallpapers with the appearance of damask. They are imported from the

Continent and were originally produced in Holland. They are wider than English papers, being 762mm wide. Unless supplied ready for immediate use, they need careful trimming with knife and straightedge. It is most important that the wall surface be perfectly smooth and completely free from nibs, as the metallic sheen of the paper shows up every defect, however slight. A lengthy period of soaking is usually needed after pasting.

TELESCOPIC SCAFFOLD Scaffolding equipment which is designed to be adjustable in length or height, e.g., telescopic scaffold boards used by house decorators, telescopic mobile towers used by highways departments for the maintenance and painting of lamp standards, etc.

TEMPERA One of the earliest painting techniques ever practised, and still occasionally used for decorative or mural work. The pigments are ground in water and bound with egg yolk, mixed white and yolk of egg, milk, or glue.

TEMPLATE A pattern or mould, usually made of thin card, thin wood or metal, used as a guide in the shaping or setting out of a piece of decoration.

TEREBENE A solvent obtained by treating turpentine with sulphuric acid, the product being steam distilled. The material is seldom seen nowadays.

TEREBINE A very strong liquid drier made by dissolving drying agents such as lead or manganese salts in linseed oil at a high temperature, usually with the addition of rosin, and thinning down the mixture with white spirit. It is rather dark in colour, which restricts its use in paints of pale colour, and it produces a somewhat brittle film. Unless used very sparingly it can readily lead to cracking. It is very often wrongly spelt as "terebene", which is a totally different substance (see above).

TERRA ALBA Alternative term for gypsum or calcium sulphate.

TERRE VERTE See *Green Earth.*

TERTIARY COLOUR A colour produced by mixing two secondary colours, e.g., olive green produced by mixing purple and green.

TERYLENE ROPES Very supple, strong and hard-wearing acid-resistant ropes, with a low and even degree of stretch, eminently suitable for use with suspended cradles. See *Synthetic Ropes.*

TEXTURE Originally applied to the distinctive feel and appearance of a woven fabric, imparted by the arrangement of its threads; and more generally applied to the sensation produced by any material which by the disposition of its structure or components offers a distinctive tactile and/ or visual experience.

T

TEXTURE PAINTS Paints deliberately made to produce a rough finish; for example, plastic paints, made to remain pliable long enough to be manipulated to a low relief pattern, or paints to which sand, powdered pumice or similar materials are added for various purposes.

THICK EDGES See *Fat Edges.*

THICKENING A decrease in the fluidity of a paint material, due generally to the loss of some of the solvents by evaporation, but also sometimes allied to "fattening".

THINNERS Volatile liquids added to paints in order to make them more fluid and bring them to a workable consistency. The essential features of a thinner are that it should be colourless so as not to affect the colour of the paint to which it is added, that it should be completely miscible with the paint at a normal working temperature, that it should completely evaporate and form no part of the dried paint film but should not evaporate so quickly as to make application difficult, and that it should act only upon the medium and not react with the pigment to cause precipitation. In the case of house painters' materials it is also necessary that the thinners should not be powerful enough to disturb or soften up the previous coatings. The thinner most widely used by the painter and decorator is white spirit; water paints, emulsion paints and distempers are, of course, thinned with water. The thinner for cellulose is generally a material which does not dissolve the nitro-cellulose but merely dilutes the solvent; petroleum and coal-tar distillates are used for the purpose, and it is important that the selected thinner should evaporate at the same rate as the solvent. For this reason it is essential that the correct thinner specified by the paint manufacturer for use with any particular cellulose product should always be used.

THINNING Adding a thinner to a paint or allied substance in order to render it more fluid and bring it to a suitable consistency for the intended method of application, whether it be spray, brush, etc. The thinning of paint for this purpose is perfectly legitimate, and in fact if the paint were applied in too ropey a condition several serious defects might develop in the film; nevertheless, in some quarters the idea is prevalent that thinning is a form of adulteration which should not be allowed to occur, and in some cases the paint manufacturers foster this idea by offering to "guarantee" their products provided they are used exactly as supplied. It should be noted that a reasonable degree of thinning improves the adhesion of the paint to certain types of surfaces by helping it to penetrate; on hardwoods, for example, the addition of a greater quantity of thinners than usual is to be recommended in order to secure this penetration. On the other hand, of course, over thinning should most certainly be avoided; the effect of adding too much white spirit to a paint or water to a water paint is that a given quantity of the medium is forced to cover too great an area and the proper cohesion of the particles is affected. This may result in the material lying on the surface in an underbound or powdery condition.

THINNING RATIO The proportion of thinners to paint recommended by the manufacturers of a product in order to give the most satisfactory results.

THIXOTROPIC PAINTS Paints which have a jelly-like structure which is broken down when the paint is stirred, shaken or heated or when it is subjected to the shearing action of a brush or a roller, and which return to their jelly-like state a short time after the shearing action ceases. The advantages claimed for them are that they do not require stirring before use, that no settlement takes place while the material is in storage, that they are easy to apply, that they can be used with large brushes without any dripping or splashing (thus leading to economy in time and material) and that runs and sags are not likely to occur because the material reverts to its high viscosity before such defects can form. Thixotropic paints should not be confused with materials possessing false body; glaze medium, for instance, possesses high viscosity which breaks down under the shearing action of a brush but its viscosity is resumed immediately the brushing ceases and before the brushmarks have time to flow out; with thixotropic paints, however, an interval occurs between shearing and the resumption of high viscosity during which the brushmarks do flow out.

Thixotropy can be imparted to certain normal paint formulations by means of modifications and additions made during manufacture; for instance, a thixotropic alkyd can be made by adding a polyamide resin into the alkyd resin cook, yielding a paint with all the normal properties of an alkyd resin as well as thixotropic qualities.

Two drawbacks are met with in thixotropic paints. One is that such paints do not possess the property of filling any surface depressions or indentations in the way that a conventional paint does; instead of this the thixotropic materials closely follow the contours of any defects in the surface. The other drawback is that they tend to sweat when stored and this tendency is increased with any rise in temperature such as that, for instance, caused by exposure to sunlight; the defect may often be overcome by shaking or stirring the paint vigorously and then allowing it to resume its high viscosity.

THIXOTROPIC RED LEAD PRIMER A primer for iron and steel similar to conventional red lead but with a slight modification to produce a jelly structure. Its advantages over the traditional material are that it does not settle in the can and that it flows out to a film reasonably free from bush marks. When used on clean steel, its performance does not seem to be inferior to that of the conventional red lead primer.

THIXOTROPY From a Greek work meaning "changing by touch"; the condition whereby a material possesses a high viscosity while allowed to rest undisturbed, undergoes a reduction in viscosity when shaken or stirred, and resumes its high viscosity when the disturbance ceases.

TIE-IN or TYING IN A necessary measure in order to give a tubular scaffold stability. An independent scaffold needs to be tied in to the building, throughout its length. The best method is to extend certain of the transoms to pass through window openings and to couple them to tubes placed inside the building and wedged against the inner wall. Where this is not feasible, some of the transoms are coupled to puncheons wedged into the window openings and tightened by means of reveal pins; when this method is employed a greater number of ties should be provided to compensate for the lesser strength of each individual tie. Ties normally should be provided at the level of the second vertical lift from the ground, and thereafter at every second lift.

TIES (i) Those parts of a stencil pattern, which are included in order to hold the plate together and impart strength to it.
(ii) Tubes used to couple a scaffold to some rigid construction in order to form a tie-in to the building.

TINT That which is produced when a colour is lightened or reduced by the addition of white.

TINTERS Alternative term for stainers.

TINTING Adjusting the colour of a paint to the precise colour that is required, by means of adding small quantities of stainers.

TINTING STRENGTH The staining power of a coloured pigment.

TITANIUM DIOXIDE Also known as titanium white. The strongest known white pigment, prepared from the mineral ilmenite. It is a brilliantly pure white, non-poisonous, with enormous staining strength; it is chemically inert and does not react with oil or varnish media of high acid value, hence there is no danger of livering in paints pigmented with it; it is resistant to chemical concentration in the atmosphere and is not therefore discoloured by sulphur fumes. It is an expensive pigment, but because of its great opacity a high degree of pigmentation is not necessary to produce a paint of good hiding power, and it also can be added to paints formulated with other pigments in order to increase their opacity. Two varieties of crystalline titanium oxide are available commercially; these are the anatase and the rutile varieties, each possessing its own particular properties. Titanium white has a marked tendency to chalk on exposure when used as the sole pigment in a paint; this tendency is corrected in various ways, such as by using a chalk-resistant rutile type of oxide, or by admixture with other pigments or with certain heat treated oils.

TOE BOARDS Scaffold boards or lengths of wood turned on edge, and running along the boundary of a working platform; together with the guard rails they form a protection to prevent the fall of persons, materials or tools from the platform. Under the Construction Regulations it is required that toe boards or some other suitable form of barrier be provided on any platform from which it might be possible to fall a distance exceeding two metres (6ft 6in). The height of the toe board or barrier is to be at least 150mm (6in) and the distance between the toe board and guard rail must not exceed 762mm (30in).

N.B. At the time of this edition going to press the Construction Regulations have not been converted to metric measurements. Until such time as they are converted it should be noted that the figures given in feet and inches in brackets are still legally binding.

TONE A word which is frequently misused. It refers to the amount of light reflected from the surface of a colour irrespective of all other characteristics. From this it will be seen that in a colour circle the colour of lightest tone is yellow and that of deepest tone is violet; when white is added to a colour a lighter tone is produced while the addition of black deepens the tone; the tone is also modified by the amount of light falling upon it and hence the amount of light that can be reflected.

TOOTH A characteristic of a dried paint film into which has been mixed a quantity of coarse or abrasive pigment. Tooth improves the rubbing properties and the adhesion of a paint; paints which are to be applied to a smooth non-absorbent surface may have tooth imparted to them by the addition of a crystalline pigment such as silica. Pigments such as graphite are liable to scale due to their greasy nature; this tendency can be checked by adding silica to them to give tooth.

TOSHER A slang term used to describe an operative, generally an unskilled workman, employed on rough industrial painting work.

TOUCHING IN Applying colour to a very small area.

TOUCHING UP Repairing and restoring small defects and small localized damaged areas in decorative work which is otherwise in sound condition.

TOXIC Poisonous; hence "toxicity", the state of being poisonous, or possessing poisonous properties.

TRACING Reproducing a drawing or pattern by drawing over its outlines, usually on a superimposed transparent sheet. There is a method of tracing which the decorator very often uses as an alternative to pouncing when transferring a motif from a paper to a wall surface; this consists of rubbing the reverse side of the paper with chalk, laying it with the chalked side on the wall in the required position, and then tracing the outlines through by drawing over them with a sharp pointed hard blacklead pencil, which produces the outlines in chalk on the wall.

T

TRACING PAPER Paper which has been made transparent by treatment with oil of turpentine; tracing paper can be laid over a drawing or pattern and the outline of the drawing traced upon it.

TRAMLINES Colloquial term for ropiness.

TRANSFER GOLD LEAF Gold leaf which is attached to a sheet of waxed tissue. See *Gold Leaf.*

TRANSFERS   Designs for decorative devices, trade marks, etc., which are prepared and printed on thin backing sheets in such a form that they can be affixed to a suitable surface and the backing sheet peeled off; they are available as individual items or in strips or sheets that can be cut into separate items or torn off along perforated lines. There are various types of transfers sold, including the water type in which water-soluble adhesive is the fixative, the spirit type in which a spirit soluble gum is used, and the heat fixing type in which a thermoplastic resin or gum coating is used with the application of heat; in all these types the adhesive is present on the backing sheet as a thin coat applied after the device has been printed. In addition there is a varnish type, which does not carry an adhesive but to which a varnish coating is applied by the painter, and also a slip-off type which is an extension of the water type. The actual process of application varies according to the particular type of transfer which is being used, but provided the manufacturers' instructions are followed the operation presents no difficulty; the main considerations are to see that the surface to which the transfer is to be applied is perfectly clean, to ensure that no air bubbles are formed and to see that the backing is peeled off without pulling up any part of the transfer design with it.

TRANSLUCENT   A term applied to a substance or material which although not transparent allows light to pass through it.

TRANSOM   A term used in scaffolding to denote a short tube spanning between two ledgers and at right angles to them; transoms are spaced at suitable intervals in order to support scaffold boards or a working platform. In an independent scaffold the transom performs the same function as a putlog in a putlog scaffold. Also (in building) a horizontal bar across a window.

TRAVELLING CRADLE   A type of scaffold in which a steel or aluminium alloy track slung from outriggers carries the jockeys from which the cradle is suspended; this permits the cradle to be moved not only up and down but also from side to side in either direction as required.

TREAD   The horizontal upper part of a step on a staircase, between the vertical risers.

TRESTLE   A trestle consists of two frames or sections hinged together in such a way that when they are closed they lie flat and when open they form a firm support, resting on four feet, for one end of a working platform. The frames consists of rectangular softwood stiles into which cross bars or bearers, also rectangular and capable of supporting the working platform, are morticed and tenoned. Trestles are generally available in lengths varying between 2 and 4·5 metres when closed. A single trestle is generally referred to in the trade as a pair of trestles.

TRESTLE SCAFFOLD   A scaffold in which two or more pairs of trestles are used to provide the supports for a working platform. The Construction Regulations have widened the term to include any scaffold in which the supports for the platform are split heads, folding step-ladders, tripods or similar movable contrivances. The Regulations further lay down that trestle scaffolds (a) shall not be so situated that a person working on the platform might fall a distance of more than 4·5 metres (15 ft); (b) shall not consist of more than one tier if folding supports are used, and (c) shall not be erected on a scaffold platform unless the trestles or supports are firmly attached to the platform and are adequately braced and unless sufficient space is left for the transit of materials along the platform. These requirements are in addition to the usual provisions that the trestle, etc., shall be of sound material, adequate strength and properly maintained.

TRICHLORETHYLENE A powerful chlorinated solvent, used as a degreasing agent for metal prior to painting.

TRIMMER A device for removing the selvedge from a roll of wallpaper.

TRIMMING The process of removing the selvedge from wallpapers and other wallcoverings. Until recently this was a matter of prime importance, but within the last few years the situation has completely changed, due to the fact that so many wall hangings are now supplied ready for immediate use, without the necessity for trimming.

Trimming, where still required, may be carried out by various methods as follows:

(a) *By scissors.* The paper is trimmed dry, a roll at a time, with the paperhanger sitting down trimming with one hand and re-rolling the paper with the other. This is a somewhat laborious process and is now rarely used. The scissors may also be used for wet trimming, the paper being already cut to length, and then pasted and accurately folded before trimming.

(b) *By knife and straightedge.* This again may be applied to either dry or wet trimming. For this process the pasteboard must be very rigid and must be fitted with a three-inch wide strip of zinc. The edge of the paper is laid on this, the straightedge placed on the register of the pattern, and a sharp knife used to run along the straightedge and cut off the selvedge. Knife and straightedge trimming is used for high quality work and is considered the best method for this purpose. Dry trimming by this method is advocated by the wallpaper manufacturers for many high-class modern papers; it is particularly useful for those with a strongly coloured ground, since the paper can be undercut to prevent the trimmed edge from showing up as a white line when hung. Wet trimming by this method is useful for heavy relief patterns to produce a clean edge with no paste on the face.

(c) *By wheel trimmer and straightedge.* The straightedge is specially shaped with a track running along one edge, and the trimmer has a brass guide which fits in the track. The selvedge is removed by a large circular cutting blade. The result is similar to that produced by knife and straightedge; this method can be applied to dry or wet trimming and to trimming several lengths simultaneously.

(d) *By pocket trimmer.* This is the most popular method in commercial use today; it is essentially a dry trimming process. Various patented patterns are on sale and they generally consist of an adjustable guide plate and self sharpening circular cutters through which the paper is drawn, the selvedge being trimmed off one side along the entire length of the roll.

T

(e) *By mechanically operated trimmers.* Wallpaper can be very quickly trimmed in the workshop by means of power-operated or electrically driven machines which cut the selvedge off both edges of a complete roll simultaneously. The great drawback from the trade point of view is that the edges of the paper may easily be damaged while in transit to the site, and the whole object of having a selvedge in the first place is defeated.

TRITIUM A radioactive material which is now being used in the U.S.A. to replace radium as the common base for the luminous paints employed in the preparation of dials for watches and instruments. The use of radium is known to be dangerous, particularly at the stage when the luminous paint is actually being applied, and in fact the damage caused to the bone tissues of operatives engaged in the luminizing industry has become a classic source of information about the hazards of radioactivity. The completed luminous dials have themselves been quoted as a possible source of danger to those using such instruments. Tritium is considered to be much safer because the atomic particles given off during its radioactive decay are of a type whose energy cannot penetrate even the simplest shield, not even the thin layer of watch glass that encases the dial, and are unable to penetrate the outer layer of skin on human tissues.

TROWEL A tool used by the painter primarily for making good defective plaster work prior to decoration. Plastic paint is sometimes applied with a floating trowel when heavy relief effects are required.

TRUE CONTRAST The contrast obtained by placing side by side two colours which are exactly complementary; in light, by any pair of colours which when added together will produce white light (e.g., yellow and blue, red and blue-green, purple and green); in pigmentary colours, by any pair of colours which when mixed together will produce neutral grey.

TUBULAR SCAFFOLD A form of scaffolding composed of a series of hollow metal tubes, suitably coupled. The tubes may consist of either steel or aluminium alloy; steel tubes may be welded, seamless or close jointed and should be galvanized to make them resistant to corrosion or should be painted or varnished throughout their length; aluminium tubes are seamless and are not usually given any form of surface treatment to protect them from atmospheric attack. Aluminium is, however, softened by alkaline materials and therefore if the scaffold is to be in contact with wet cement, concrete, etc., for any length of time the tubes should be painted. Aluminium alloy tubes are sometimes preferred to steel because of their lightness, but they are not as strong as steel and therefore the deflection of alloy tubes used as horizontal beams is higher than that of steel tubes subjected to the same load; for this reason the standards need to be set more closely together to reduce the deflection of the ledgers.

The selection of tubes and couplers and the whole process of the erection, maintenance and dismantling of tubular scaffold is covered by numerous provisions of the Construction (Safety, Health and Welfare) Regulations, which should be carefully studied by anyone concerned with the use of such scaffolds.

TUMBLING or RUMBLING A method of paint application used in industrial finishing for the treatment of small articles which cannot be satisfactorily coated by other methods. It consists of placing the articles in a drum together with a small quantity of paint, the drum being rotated until the surface of the articles is completely covered. The articles are then placed on a wire mesh to be dried, usually by stoving.

TUNG OIL See *China Wood Oil.*

TURKEY RED An artificial red oxide with high opacity, produced by calcining yellow iron oxide at a relatively low temperature.

TURKEY UMBER A type of umber obtained from Cyprus, and owing its name to the fact that it was originally exported through Turkey.

TURK'S HEAD A large coarse-haired round brush, with the hairs set in pitch, mounted on a wooden stock which is attached to a long wooden handle; it is used for limewashing and for rough work generally.

TURMERIC A plant with long leaves and cream flowers, grown in Ceylon, from the rhizomes of which a fine yellow dye is produced that is used in spirit stains.

TURPENTINE A valuable solvent obtained by distillation from the oleoresin of the pine tree, the main sources of supply being America, France, India, Portugal, Spain and Russia. When the trees are eventually felled, having reached the point where they fail to yield any further, a stronger solvent with a pungent smell is obtained by steam distillation from the pine wood stumps and this is known as wood turpentine.

Turpentine is practically the ideal paint solvent. It is clear, limpid and colourless, it evaporates almost completely, leaving no visible residue when exposed in a thin film, and while it readily dissolves all vegetable and mineral oils it does not dissolve the linoxyn formed by the drying of a paint film, for which reason it does not disturb previously applied coatings. Its use, however, has now considerably declined and given place to the cheaper white spirit.

TURPENTINE SUBSTITUTE White spirit. Also termed turps. substitute and known colloquially as sub-turps.

T

TWIN-HEADED SPRAY GUN A type of spray gun designed to spray a protective coating and a catalyst simultaneously so that the two materials mix in the spray pattern after they have left the gun and before they reach the surface. The instantaneous mixing in atomized form eliminates the problem of spraying formulations which have too short a pot life to be mixed before use. The gun is used for spraying various types of two-pack material, including polyurethane lacquers, and can also be used for spray silvering.

TWO-KNOT DISTEMPER BRUSH See *Distemper Brush.*

TWO-PACK MATERIALS   A term used to describe certain modern materials, such as, for example, the amine-cured epoxy resin coatings, which are supplied in two packs one of which consists of an activator or catalyst which is to be added to the paint immediately before use. When the two materials have been mixed together the pot-life of the product is short, gellation taking place within a few hours.

TWO-ROW STIPPLER   A very narrow hair stippler consisting, as the name implies, of only two rows of tufts of hair instead of the usual 175mm by 125mm or 150mm by 100mm flat surface of the full sized stippler. It is intended for use in locations too narrow to be reached by a normal stippler, and to enable stippling to be carried right into the angles of sharp corners or into the corners of panels and mouldings.

U

ULSTRON ROPES   Multi-filament polypropylene ropes of soft texture. See *Synthetic Ropes*.

ULTRAMARINE BLUE   A fine rich blue pigment which has been known from ancient times; for a very long time it was prepared by grinding a semi-precious stone, lapis lazuli; it is now produced artificially from a mixture of silica, china clay, sulphur and soda ash, subjected to prolonged calcination. Ultramarine is attacked by acids but has good resistance to alkalis; it has good staining strength and opacity in water, but poor opacity and only moderate staining strength in oil. When ground in oil paint it has a strong tendency to settle and cake in the container, the colour of the paint becoming progressively lighter, and particles of the separated pigment tend to work up under the brush and produce an unfortunate streakiness. It should not be mixed with pigments composed of lead or copper because, being a sulphur pigment, it reacts with them to cause discolouration. It possesses excellent qualities of fastness to light.

Because of the drawbacks attendant upon its use as an oil colour, its use in this medium is largely restricted to mural and decorative work; it is, however, an excellent pigment for use in water paints and distempers. It is also ground in turpentine for coachpainting purposes. Low grade ultramarine reduced with terra alba is sold as "lime blue" for correcting the colour of limewash and distemper.

ULTRAMARINE GREEN   A pigment produced in the process of making ultramarine blue; it is reduced and sold as "lime green".

ULTRAMARINE VIOLET   Similar in properties to ultramarine blue, but with slight differences of composition and processing.

ULTRA VIOLET RAYS   Non-visible light rays of short wave length, occurring just beyond the violet end of the spectrum, which are very destructive to paint and varnish films. Known also as actinic rays.

UMBER A natural brown earth pigment derived from coloured clays composed of hydrated silicate, the colouring being due to the presence of iron oxides and a high proportion of manganese oxide. The best quality comes from Cyprus and is known as Turkey umber, but umber is also found in Italy, France, the U.S.A. and Great Britain. Like all the earth pigments, it is permanent, stable and cheap to produce; it is a much better drier than ochre or sienna because of its manganese content, manganese being a powerful drying agent. It possesses good staining strength; the natural product, raw umber, has a peculiar greenish cast and when mixed with white it produces a fine range of cool subtle colours. Raw umber can be calcined to produce burnt umber, which is a rich dark brown colour and when mixed with white gives a much warmer range of colours. Burnt umber has only moderate staining strength, but is very useful in the production of stains and graining colour because of its partial transparency.

UNDERCOATS The coatings applied to a surface after priming and filling or, in the case of previously painted work, after the preparation. The main functions of undercoats are to provide "build" or film thickness, opacity, and the most suitable ground for the reception of the finishing coat, while filling small local depressions in the surface.

UNSEASONED TIMBER Timber which still contains an excessive quantity of moisture; when a tree is freshly felled its moisture content is equal to a hundred per cent of the net weight of the timber, and thorough seasoning is required to allow the bulk of this moisture to dry out before the wood is fit for use in joinery. The painting of unseasoned wood is always most unsatisfactory. The contraction of the wood as further drying out takes place loosens the adhesion of the paint film and forces it off, and the pressure of the contained moisture seeking to escape causes blistering, peeling and flaking to occur. If the wood is painted on both sides so that the moisture is completely trapped inside, the wood itself may become rotten.

UREA RESINS These are practically colourless resins made by combining urea, which is a white crystalline solid, with formaldehyde; they are thermosetting resins and are used in the manufacture of stoving enamels, particularly those of pale tints. A blend of urea formaldehyde resin and alkyd resin produces a stoving enamel of great hardness and with good resistance to alkalis and solvents, and is widely used as the basis of white stoving enamels for domestic goods such as refrigerators, etc.

URETHANE PAINT A one-pack material composed of urethane-modified oils or alkyds, producing a chemically resistant high gloss paint which is easier to use than chlorinated rubber or epoxy-ester paint.

UV

URETHANE/PITCH A chemically resistant paint composed of urethane resins combined with coal tar pitch, with properties similar to coal tar/epoxy paints. It has the capacity to cure even at low temperatures and in areas of high humidity. It is usually spray-applied.

V

VANDYKE BROWN A deep brown richer in colour than burnt umber, which used to be derived from a natural peaty earth found in Germany but is now prepared by the partial decomposition of beechwood bark or cork. It is a semi-transparent pigment and besides being sold as an artist's colour it is used by the decorator in making up graining colour and glazes for graining. Although it is esteemed for its rich colour it is a very unsatisfactory material to use. It is a very poor drier and has a retarding effect upon oil, and it is very prone to fading; it is used chiefly in water medium, but even in this form it has a bad effect upon the drying of a superimposed varnish film. It is also strongly inclined to cracking.

The material which is sold to the decorator nowadays is not usually true Vandyke brown but an imitation made up from ochre, oxide of iron and lampblack; this is a more durable material but lacks the richness of colour of genuine Vandyke.

VARNISH A transparent liquid which, when applied to a surface in a thin film, usually produces a hard protective lustrous coating which enhances the appearance, but may in certain cases be used to give a matt coating of little protective value. The term covers three main types of material, namely (i) oil varnish, which is composed of a hard resin combined with a drying oil, with the addition of driers and a volatile solvent, (ii) spirit varnish, composed of semi-hard or soft resin dissolved in a volatile solvent, and (iii) water varnish composed of a solution or emulsion of a resin in an acqueous medium. The term does not cover the clear compositions based upon cellulose; these are described as lacquers. Of the above three types, water varnish is of little or no interest to the painter and decorator, and of the other two, oil varnish is by far the more important; unless the word is qualified in some way, "varnish" is generally understood by the decorator to refer to an oil varnish.

Oil varnishes can be divided broadly into two main types, long oil in which the oil predominates, which are tough and elastic and which are used chiefly for outdoor exposure, and short oil in which the resin predominates, which are harder, more lustrous and generally quicker drying and are used chiefly for indoor work. These two headings cover a large number of varnishes formulated for some particular type of work, including coach varnish, boat and spar varnish, church oak varnish, floor varnish, flatting or rubbing varnish, polishing varnish, mixing varnish, etc.

VARNISH BRUSH An oval brush with a filling of fine pure bristle in a stout metal ferrule. An oval brush is the best type for the application of varnish because its shape lends itself to the production of a good, evenly spread film.

VARNISHING The application of varnish, the main object of the operation being to produce an even level film free from runs, sags and pinholing and not marred by dust or bittiness. It is essential that varnish should be applied firmly and confidently; if the coating is rubbed out too bare it is practically impossible to obtain an evenly distributed film and the usual result is the formation of runs and the production of a finish with a starved appearance.

VEGETABLE FIBRE   Coarse material used as the filling for cheap brushes for the application of alkaline materials and for washing down. See *Fibre Brushes.*

VEHICLE   The liquid components of a paint consisting of the binding medium and the thinner; so called because it "carries" the pigment, or holds it in suspension. See *Medium.*

VEILING   The formation of a cobweb pattern during spraying.

VEINING HORN   Another term for graining horn.

VENETIAN RED   Originally a natural red iron oxide pigment found in Italy, now generally produced by calcining yellow oxide of iron at a high temperature. It has a strong yellowish or brick red colour and has good staining strength. It very often contains a large proportion of gypsum which is soluble in water; for this reason it is unsuitable for use on iron work.

VENICE TURPENTINE   The oleo-resin of the Tyrolean larch.

VERD ANTIQUE   Also called Verde Antico or Vert Antique. A beautiful serpentine marble showing irregularly shaped and variable sized patches of white, dark green and black interspersed with a fine network of streaks in various tints and shades of green. There are various methods of imitating the marble, and it may be worked on a ground of white, black or grey.

VERDIGRIS   A green crystalline substance, copper acetate, which forms on the surface of copper which is exposed to the atmosphere. Metallic paints based on copper bronze, if not protected by lacquer, are liable to discolour due to the formation of verdigris.

VERMICULITE   A micaceous mineral which occurs very freely and which is produced commercially in the U.S.A. and the Transvaal. The ore is heated to a temperature of $1093°C$ ($2000°F$), producing a flaky porous substance which is extremely light in weight and which readily absorbs and retains air and moisture. It is now used extensively in the building industry, giving nearly ten times as much thermal insulation as the equivalent quantity of sand-gravel concrete. It is used to produce vermiculite plasters with excellent acoustic properties and heat insulating and anti-condensation qualities. It is also used to some extent in finely ground form as a paint filler.

V

VERMILION   A very expensive red pigment consisting of sulphide of mercury which has been used from ancient times; originally it was obtained from a mineral called cinnabar, but it is now produced artificially. It is a fine bright red colour with good opacity, but because of its cost is rarely used except as an artist's colour and for high-class decorative work. Being a sulphide pigment, it should not be mixed with lead, copper or antimony pigments.

VERT The heraldic term for green.

VERT DE MER A marble with a greenish black ground with pronounced veining in white and varying tints and shades of green.

VINEGAR A weak solution of acetic acid obtained by the acetous fermentation of wine, beer and other dilute alcoholic fluids. It is used by the painter for such purposes as neutralizing the effects of caustic paint removers, etc.

VINYL DISTEMPERS AND VINYL WATER PAINTS Water-thinned materials, usually consisting of PVA copolymer emulsion, and cheaper than normal emulsion paints. They are intended for interior use on walls and ceilings in situations where the conditions are relatively undemanding. Their performance is roughly equivalent to that of oil-bound water paints.

VINYL RESINS A large group of resins derived from polymerized vinyl acetate or vinyl chloride or the acetate and chloride polymerized together. They are used in the plastics industry, and in the paint industry they form the basis of most of the emulsion paints used today and are also used in the production of etch primers, in lacquers for roller coating, and in protective coatings to give resistance to splash or fumes from water solutions of acids, salts and alkalis. They are now very widely used in the production of vinyl wallpapers and other wall hangings.

VIRIDIAN See *Guignet's Green.*

VISCOSITY The internal resistance to motion or flow possessed by a liquid, which is measured in terms of the force required to overcome it. For practical purposes it can be understood as the "stickiness" of a fluid.
   The more viscous a liquid is the more slowly it flows. The viscosity of a paint medium is therefore clearly of the utmost importance, having a direct bearing upon the ease or lack of ease of its application, and its suitability for application by various methods such as by brushing, spraying, dipping, etc.

VOLATILE A word meaning "readily evaporating", derived from the Latin word *volare,* to fly. Hence we speak of a "volatile solvent", meaning a paint solvent which evaporates freely when exposed to the air, leaving no part behind in the dried paint film.

VOLATILIZATiON A process used in the preparation of certain pigments including antimony white, carbon black, zinc oxide and basic lead sulphate, in which the raw materials are heated and converted to gases from which the pigment is deposited on cooling. Pigments produced by this process are characterized by their fineness and smoothness of working.

298

VOUSSOIRS   Wedge-shaped blocks of stone, shaped for constructing an arch.

VULCANIZED OIL   Also called sulphurized oil. A vegetable drying oil, e.g. linseed oil, perilla oil, etc., which has been reacted with sulphur or sulphur chloride. Such an oil possesses a higher degree of chemical resistance than the untreated oil, but the outstanding feature of a vulcanized oil is its ability to set very rapidly even while the paint film of which it is a part is still quite wet; because of this property it is possible to include it in a paint formulation which permits a second coat to be applied before the first coat is dry, without picking up, such formulations being the basis of the wet-on-wet process.

VULCANIZED RUBBER   An insoluble cement made of a compound of rubber and sulphur subjected to heat treatment, which is used to lock the bristles of a brush firmly into place.

W

WAINSCOT OAK   Another term for quartered oak.

WALLBOARDS   Building boards and sheetings used to form a rigid lining construction for walls and ceilings; the term includes hardboards, plasterboards, fibre boards, insulating boards, etc., details of which are given under the appropriate headings.

WALL BRUSH or FLAT WALL BRUSH   A rather vague term which refers to a flat paint brush of a sufficiently large size to be used to apply flat and semi-gloss oil paint economically to broad surfaces. In various parts of the country it is known by colloquial terms such as wallboard, wallband, weatherband, etc. The term "wall brush" can be used to refer to brushes of various widths such as 75mm, 100mm, 125mm, 150mm and 175mm.

WALLPAPER   The term covers an enormous range of patterned and coloured papers supplied in rolls to be cut up, pasted and applied to ceiling and wall surfaces by the decorator. Wallpapers may broadly be classified under two main headings, namely machine printed and hand printed. Machine-printed papers are printed from cylindrical rollers, a separate roller for each colour. The paper is fed in as a continuous roll and passes under each roller in turn, the printing of all the colours being finished in one operation. Hand-printed papers are printed from blocks or silk screens, each colour being printed separately and each roll of wallpaper being treated individually. Machine-printed papers can be mass produced far more cheaply than hand prints; hand prints are used where a comparatively small quantity of some particular design is required, where a special colour scheme is needed, or to produce a pattern with a very large repeat. By far the greatest number of wallpapers used is produced by machine printing.

W

299

WALLPAPER, STANDARD DIMENSIONS From 1963 onwards the size of a roll of machine-printed wallpaper of British manufacture has been standardized at 10·05 metres long (11 yards) by 533mm wide when trimmed. Prior to this the length was 11½ yards. The reduction was made so that British paper would conform to the dimensions used by Continental manufacturers. The British Standard Specification was amended accordingly in August 1963.

WALNUT A highly decorative wood obtained from a tree of the *Juglandaceae* family which is native to Asia Minor but which is now widely distributed in many parts of the world. It is used to a considerable extent in furniture manufacture and cabinet making, being a wood that works easily and takes a good polish. The grain is rather obscure, but the colouring gives a strong impression of grain markings. Walnut shows very great variations of colour ranging through grey-brown, grey-green, greyish yellow and grey-red, the curly bands of the contrasting tones flowing over the surface regardless of the boundaries of the annual rings. Burred wood, obtained from the Mediterranean countries, is in very great demand by cabinet makers. Walnut is a favourite wood with grainers and the methods of imitating the wood are legion. It may be grained in either oil or water medium.

WASH COAT See *Pre-treatment Primers*.

WASH DOWN BRUSH A coarse fibre brush which can be used for washing down with alkaline detergents without sustaining damage.

WASH PRIMER See *Pre-treatment Primers*.

WASHABILITY The extent to which dirt can be removed from a decorated surface without damaging the face of the decoration.

WASHABLE DISTEMPER A distemper consisting of whiting or other mineral white and borax and lime, bound with casein (see *Distemper*). When the material is applied in a thin coating and is completely hardened it may to some extent be sponged down to remove loose dirt. The term is sometimes used very loosely to refer to oil-bound water paints; this usage is not correct.

WASHING DOWN Removing grime from a painted surface, or washing a painted surface preparatory to repainting, very often with the aid of sugar soap. See *Sugar Soap* for further details.

WATER COLOURS Artists' colours made by grinding suitable pigments into aqueous gums or shellac solutions.

WATER PAINT The term is not used indiscriminately for any water thinned material but is applied specifically to an oil-bound water paint.

WATERPROOF SANDPAPER An abrasive made for the wet rubbing down of paintwork, which is a cleaner and more effective process than dry rubbing down and which is compulsory by law for any painted surface containing lead. The type used by the decorator is similar in appearance to dry sandpaper, and the abrasive consists of flint or garnet; the type used by the coachpainter is dark grey in colour and the abrasive is emery or corundum. Both varieties are available in a wide range of cutting strengths varying from very fine to coarse.

WATER-REPELLENT FLUIDS Colourless, or relatively colourless, liquids intended to increase the resistance to rain penetration of porous and absorbent walls that are substantially free from cracks. They consist of solutions or emulsions of water-repellent substances such as waxes, oils, resins or fats or metallic soaps such as aluminium stearate; in recent years great use has been made of silicone resins for the purpose. The liquids are applied by brush or spray, preferably during a spell of dry weather. Before they are applied the surface should be carefully examined and all defects made good. For further details, see paragraph (ii) under *Silicone Resins.*

WATER RESISTANCE The ability of a surface coating to resist the passage of water in liquid form.

WATER STAIN A stain consisting either of vegetable dyes in solution or of semi-transparent pigments bound with gum arabic. See *Stain.*

WATER-THINNED PAINTS Considerable progress has been made in recent years in the production of water-thinned materials both for structural painting and decorating and for industrial finishing systems. Paint chemists for a long time have been attracted by the obvious advantages that such materials would offer, and have carried out a great deal of research into the subject. In the field of industrial finishing the advantages take the form of reduced fire hazards and the elimination of the heavy wastage caused by the evaporation of volatile solvents; in the painting of structures the value of these coatings lies chiefly in the saving of time resulting from the possibility of applying primers, undercoats and finishing materials in quick succession, in speed of application and the elimination of residual paint odour. In the industrial finishing world several plants have already been modified to permit the use of water-thinned primers and primer-surfacers, especially in the motor car industry, and there are indications that water-thinned finishing paints are reaching a critical stage of development. In painting and decorating various formulations are already on the market, but it is reasonable to suppose that the final stage of development has not yet been reached, and it may be that the future trend of paint technology will be principally along these lines.

Since 1950 a well-known firm of paint manufacturers has been offering to the trade a glossy water paint for indoor use, i.e., a material similar in its ease and manner of application to a conventional oil-bound water paint but which dries with a high gloss finish and when dry possesses all the properties of wear, washability, etc., associated with an orthodox enamel paint. The basis of the material is a polymerized ester gum varnish emulsified in water, the emulsifying agent containing ammonia. The same

W

301

firm in 1958 introduced a water-thinned undercoating for use with the material. In 1964 another firm introduced a complete range of water-thinned materials for indoor work, consisting of an acrylic primer/undercoat, a latex flat wall paint and a latex gloss finish. Since then several brands of similar materials have appeared on the market, and it would seem that the present trend is towards the development of this type of material.

Water-thinned primers of this type consist of a good quality pigment such as a non-chalking titanium dioxide bound with a 100% acrylic resin; they dry by the evaporation of the water content to form a continuous film with properties similar to that of perspex. Drying is rapid, since there is no oil to be oxidized, and the surface can be recoated within $\frac{3}{4}$-hour. The primer is easy to apply and is capable of sealing knots satisfactorily without the prior use of shellac knotting. It is claimed that it gives excellent protection to timber, both soft and hard woods, and prevents the ingress of moisture. It is non-toxic, and can be applied by brush, roller or spray. Sufficient data is not yet available to enable a comparison to be made between the durability of this material and that of conventional lead-based primers which have stood the test of time, nor is there any indication at present as to whether water-thinned primers will supersede conventional materials. In their present stage of development a great drawback to the use of acrylic primers lies in the difficulty of eliminating brush marks so that the dried film of the primer presents a ropey surface which is not conducive to a smooth finish or a good standard of appearance.

The water-thinned latex wall paints possess the same general properties as a PVA emulsion paint—east of application, freedom from odour, rapid drying (more rapid than PVA), washability, tolerance of damp, resistance to alkali, etc. The water-thinned gloss paints, based on latex, contain no oil and are therefore presumably free from the progressive embrittlement that affects gloss paints based on drying oil media. They are said to be non-yellowing and to be unaffected by chemical atmospheres even when ammonia or other nitrogenous substances are present in large quantities. They are resistant to steamy atmospheres. It is not yet possible to assess the durability of these coatings in comparison with that of the conventional synthetic resin enamel paints.

WAX The name given to various animal, vegetable or mineral substances which possess a certain lustre and resemble fats in that they are lighter than water and melt upon heating. Beeswax, which is secreted by bees and is obtained by heating the honeycombs in water, is used in the preparation of wax polishes and wax stains. Paraffin wax, the most important of the mineral waxes, is used in the manufacture of flat varnishes and also as a stiffening agent in spirit paint removers.

WAX STAINS Preparations composed of semi-transparent pigments mixed with beeswax and thinned with turpentine, used for the treatment of hardwoods. They are brushed on and allowed to dry, and then polished with a short soft-haired polishing brush or a piece of coarse fabric.

WEATHER BOARDING See *Clapboard*.

WEATHERING Undergoing the effects of exposure to the atmosphere, e.g., the weathering of a paint film when subjected to outdoor exposure, the weathering of new steelwork in order to loosen the mill scale, etc.

WEBBING A fault which sometimes develops in a paint or varnish film during drying, and which takes the form of a fine network of wrinkles extending over the surface. It is similar to frosting, and is caused by the swelling of the partially dried surface skin; the condition can be aggravated by exposure to impure gas fumes in a gas fired stoving oven, when it is known as "gas checking", and is especially liable to occur in films containing a tung oil medium since one of the defects of tung oil is its tendency to web if not properly heat-treated.

WET-ON-WET A system of paint application in which several coats of paint are applied by spray at short intervals, each coat being applied while the preceding coat is still wet. This is made possible by the use of vulcanized oil, which possesses the curious property of setting rapidly while the paint of which it is a part is still quite wet. As each coat sets up a further coat is applied, and in this way a thick composite coating is built up which hardens throughout its thickness and forms a good durable film. The process is of considerable interest and value in the field of industrial coating and finishing, being used on a large scale, for instance, in car factories on the mass production of automobiles. The obvious advantages of the system are the great saving in production time and the economy in space, since drying time between coats is drastically reduced and several banks of stoving plant at intervals along the line are not necessary. It is usual for the priming coat to be allowed to dry normally before the wet-on-wet system is adopted; careful control of the viscosity of the paint in relation to the spraying pressure is called for, and if for any reason one of the coats becomes surface dry it should be allowed to dry completely before being recoated, otherwise there is some danger of the film lifting.

WET RUBBING DOWN Any system of rubbing down paintwork that involves the use of a liquid lubricant, usually water; for example, rubbing down with pumice stone, powdered pumice, cuttle fish bone or waterproof sandpaper, each of which is used in conjucntion with water. Occasionally the use of some other lubricant may be necessary, such as, for instance, during humid weather when waiting for water to evaporate would lead to considerable delay, in which case pumice stone may be used in conjunction with a mixture of white spirit and raw linseed oil, or when steel wool is being used to remove rust from steelwork, when the lubricant is white spirit. The use of rottenstone and oil, however, is not regarded as coming under this definition. Under the terms of the Lead Paint Regulations it is required that all painted surfaces be rubbed down wet unless it can be proved that they are lead free within the meaning of the Act.

WETTING The ability of a paint medium to spread uniformly and rapidly over the surface of the pigment particles. This is a matter of great importance in paint formulation; if the pigment is merely dispersed in the medium and not thoroughly wetted, the particles tend to fall through the medium and settle in a hard cake at the bottom of the container. Surrounding the pigment particles, and very often firmly attached to them, is a layer of moist air and sometimes a layer of gas, and it is necessary that the medium should be able to expel these substances and take the place that they occupied; the wetting power of the medium is the extent of its ability to do this.

WHIRLING A system of speeding the drying of small painted items by means of centrifugal action.

WHITE JAPAN A very loose and inaccurate term sometimes applied by the painter to an ordinary air drying white enamel.

WHITE LAC Shellac which has been bleached with alkali.

WHITE LEAD A basic carbonate of lead which is a very valuable white pigment and one which has been of the utmost importance in the painting and decorating trade for a very long time. The traditional method of preparation is the Dutch or Stack process, in which metallic lead is corroded by the action of moist acetic acid vapours in the presence of carbon dioxide, but this method is not much used now; the Chamber process, which like the Stack process is rather slow, is still used and so is the electrolytic process; but the precipitation method of preparation, in which the reactions can be more accurately controlled, seems likely to replace them.

White lead possesses several very useful qualities. It is a valuable protective material with the ability to combine with a drying oil and produce a lead soap which forms a tough leathery elastic film capable of expanding and contracting in harmony with the surface to which it is applied. It also possesses good opacity, and is characterized by its smooth brushing qualities, which make for ease of application, and it is a good drier. Another advantage of white lead is that after long exposure to the weather it tends to break down by a gentle chalking action but rarely exhibits any tendency to crack, and for this reason it is more easily and less expensively prepared for repainting than harder and more brittle materials. On the other hand, it is not a pure white in colour compared with certain other pigments, and it has a tendency to "feed" or thicken when mixed with varnish media of high acid value. A great drawback to its use is its susceptibility to the presence of sulphur, which leads to its discolouration if it is exposed to urban and industrial atmospheres contaminated with sulphide gases. Another drawback is its poisonous nature, which is so pronounced as to have led to the introduction of special legislation to control its use (the Lead Paint Regulations).

WHITE SPIRIT A solvent produced by the distillation of crude petroleum which has now almost completely replaced turpentine as the paint solvent in normal use in the trade, being considerably cheaper and for all practical purposes just as effective. It is sometimes known as turps substitute and in some quarters the term is still used disparagingly, but a good quality of white spirit is colourless and evaporates without leaving any residue.

Cheap grades of white spirit should be avoided, as any residue which fails to evaporate does not oxidize and take its place as part of the film as residual turpentine does, but remains greasy and may retard the hardening of the paint film. White spirit should not be used for reducing gold size or varnish as it tends to precipitate the resins from solution.

WHITEWASH Any cheap form of distemper based on whiting loosely bound with glue, glue size, casein or similar binder.

WHITING A material prepared by grinding and pulverizing natural chalk. The main source of the chalk is the North European countries such as Great Britain, France, Belgium, Denmark, etc.; there are extensive deposits in America but the chalk is not sufficiently pure to give a good quality of whiting. Whiting loses its opacity when mixed with water, but regains it when the water evaporates, and when spread out in the form of a thin film it has good hiding power; for this reason, and because it is unaffected by the alkaline properties of new plaster, etc., it is used in the preparation of distempers and some varieties of water paint. When mixed with oil it has little opacity, and its use in oil paint is limited to employment as an extender. Whiting is, however, the chief constituent of putty, in the manufacture of which it is mixed with raw linseed oil.

WIPING OUT The production of decorative effects by means of lifting part of a coating while it is still wet in order to reveal the ground, e.g., in glazed and scumbled effects, in figure graining, etc.

WIRE BRUSH An abrasive tool with a rubbing surface formed with clumps or tufts of stiff steel wire, used for the removal of rust and mill scale from iron and steel surfaces, and for general harsh scouring purposes.

WIRE DRAWN BRUSH A brush in which the bristle is drawn through holes in the base of the brush in separate tufts and secured on the reverse side by wire. Brushes set in this way are usually those which are to be used dry, such as dusters, paperhangers' brushes, etc.

WOOD ALCOHOL A crude alcohol known also as wood naphtha or wood spirit, which has good solvent properties but is not generally used because of its toxic qualities; it is sometimes used in paint removers.

WOOD OIL See *China Wood Oil*.

W

WOOD PRESERVATIVES Fluids made for the protection of timber in situations where a paint treatment would be impracticable. They generally consist of either coal-tar derivatives, creosote, spirit soluble metallic compounds such as copper or zinc naphthanates, or water-soluble metallic salts such as zinc chloride, mercuric chloride, copper sulphate, etc.

WOOD TURPENTINE   See *Turpentine*.

WOOL GREASE   Lanoline obtained as a by-product from the cleaning of sheep's fleeces, the crude grease being treated with caustic soda. It can be readily emulsified in water, and wool grease emulsions have been used in the manufacture of water paints, especially during wartime as a substitute for more conventional binders; water paints made in this way are durable and withstand a reasonable measure of outdoor exposure, but they tend to remain rather soft and plastic and for this reason are easily damaged by abrasion when used on interior surfaces.

WRINKLING   See *Rivelling*.

WRITER   A sable signwriting brush terminating in a chisel edge, as opposed to a "pencil", which is pointed.

WRITER'S GOLD SIZE   See *Japan Gold Size*.

X

XYLOL   A solvent obtained by the distillation of coal-tar. It is less inflammable and evaporates more slowly than toluol, but evaporates far more quickly than white spirit. Because of its evaporation rate it is not greatly used in brushing paints but is widely used in spraying finishes, especially those based on synthetic resins such as alkyds and urea and melamine formaldehyde resins.

Y

YELLOWING   The discolouration of a paint on ageing whereby it develops a progressively deepening yellowish tinge. It is most noticeable on light grey, white and clear varnish finishes.

YORKSHIRE PATTERN DISTEMPER BRUSH   See *Distemper Brush*.

Z

ZINC   A bluish-white brittle metal found in many parts of the world, including the U.S.A., Queensland, New South Wales, Mexico, Canada, Russia, Germany, France, Sweden, etc. It is malleable at temperatures of between 100 and 150°C (212 and 302°F). It is permanent in dry air at ordinary temperatures, but like lead it is liable to corrode in both alkaline and acidic conditions. A number of alloys are formed by combining zinc with other metals. Probably the most significant use of zinc in building is as a protective coating for steel; for this purpose it is applied by various methods such as hot dipping, hot spraying, electro-galvanizing, etc.

Zinc surfaces, whether in the form of sheet zinc or galvanized iron, were until recently regarded as difficult surfaces to paint. When ordinary paints are applied to new zinc or zinc coated surfaces they tend very quickly to develop extensive flaking and peeling, especially when exposed to the weather. This may be due to the smooth greasy nature of the metal, which offers very little adhesion to paint; a contributing factor may be that a chemical reaction takes place between the metal and the oil medium which causes loosely adhering zinc soaps to form at the surface. Many painters still pin their faith on the use of vinegar or copper sulphate solutions to etch the surface of the metal, but it should be noted that while such treatments give some initial advantage they do not produce permanently lasting results, and in fact the use of copper salts causes a thin loose film of metallic copper to form on the surface which actually encourages flaking and also stimulates corrosion of the metal.

Weathering for a period of some six months produces an inactive surface to which paint will adhere fairly well. When an immediate paint treatment is required some form of chemical pre-treatment is necessary; zinc reacts quickly with phosphating solutions, and these may be used either at the works or on the site; various proprietary brands of phosphating solution designed for brush application are available for site use. Sherardized surfaces are usually rough enough and sufficiently oxidized to be painted without any pre-treatment. Surfaces which have been hot sprayed with zinc are slightly rough and are usually in ideal condition for the reception of paint but a pre-treatment primer may well be used on them especially if they are to be exposed to marine atmospheres. Priming paints composed of graphite or lead are liable to react with the zinc, and are not therefore suitable for use on zinc coated surfaces; priming should be carried out with a zinc chromate primer, zinc-rich primer, red oxide, or calcium plumbate.

To the painter and decorator the main interest of zinc, apart from consideration of the painting of zinc coated surfaces, lies in the use made of the metal as a constituent of paint. Zinc pigments offer a number of attractive qualities for various purposes, including fineness of particle size, good colour retention and strong anti-corrosive properties.

ZINC CHLORIDE A white deliquescent substance made by dissolving zinc in hydrochloric acid, which is used in certain kinds of wood preservative fluid to discourage fungoid growths.

ZINC CHROMATE PRIMER A priming paint with very useful rust inhibitive properties. It is not affected by exposure to sulphuretted hydrogen, and is particularly useful for the shop priming of steel because it can be safely left for several months before the succeeding coats are applied. It is also useful where obliteration with a minimum number of coats is required and where red lead would be too strong in colour to be

XY Z

covered easily. Zinc chromate can be incorporated in several different types of medium and can therefore be adapted to brushing, spraying or dipped application and to either air drying or stoving paints. As it is non-poisonous there is no restriction upon spraying it. Zinc chromate primer is generally acknowledged to be the most suitable primer for use on the metal aluminium.

ZINC CHROME A pale lemon pigment which though less opaque than the lead chrome is more permanent. It is mixed with various other pigments such as Guignet's green, Monastral blue, Prussian blue and ultramarine to produce a very wide range of greens. It is unaffected by alkali and is therefore a very useful pigment for the tinting of water paints, distempers, etc.

ZINC DUST A material of pronounced rust-inhibitive properties made by the vaporization of metallic zinc.

ZINC OXIDE A brilliant permanent white pigment, produced by the volatilization of metallic zinc, which because of the fineness of its texture is an excellent pigment for use in enamels, nitro-cellulose lacquers, etc. It is also used in combination with various other pigments such as white lead, titanium white, antimony oxide, etc., to produce a range of paints especially suitable for outdoor exposure.

ZINC PHOSPHATE PRIMER A recently developed primer for use on steel, and composed of zinc phosphate in oil or oleoresinous medium. It is quick-drying and non-toxic, and is probably superior to zinc chromate as a steel primer although it has not been in use long enough to have been completely evaluated.

ZINC-RICH PAINTS or ZINC-RICH PRIMERS Paints made entirely with zinc dust and medium, the zinc dust content amounting to between ninety-two and ninety-five per cent of the dried film; materials such as plasticized polystyrene, chlorinated rubber, etc., are used as the medium. They possess very powerful rust inhibitive properties and are of great value in the priming of steel, which they protect by means of an electro-chemical action due to the fact that the metal particles are in contact with each other and with the steel; the paint film behaves in the same way as a film of metallic zinc in the presence of an electrolyte. It is claimed that the rust inhibitive action of zinc-rich paints is so strong that they will protect steelwork from further corrosion even if it is rusty when they are applied, but obviously the cleaner the metal surface at the time of application the more effective they will be, and all scale and rust should be removed as far as possible before they are applied. Some difficulty may be experienced in choosing a suitable undercoating and finishing system to apply on top of a zinc-rich primer due to the reaction between the metallic zinc and the medium in the superimposed paint.